Communications Policy and Information Technology

Published in association with the Telecommunications Policy
Research Conference

*The Internet Upheaval: Raising Questions, Seeking Answers in
Communications Policy*
edited by Ingo Vogelsang and Benjamin M. Compaine, 2000

Communications Policy in Transition: The Internet and Beyond
edited by Benjamin M. Compaine and Shane Greenstein, 2001

*Communications Policy and Information Technology: Promises,
Problems, Prospects*
edited by Lorrie Faith Cranor and Shane Greenstein, 2002

Communications Policy and Information Technology: Promises, Problems, Prospects

Edited by
Lorrie Faith Cranor and Shane Greenstein

The MIT Press
Cambridge, Massachusetts
London, England

This book was set in Sabon by The MIT Press.

Printed and bound in the United States of America.

Library of Congress Cataloging-in-Publication Data

Research Conference on Information, Communications, and Internet Policy (29th : 2001)
  Communications policy and information technology : promises, problems, prospects / edited by Lorrie Faith Cranor and Shane Greenstein.
    p. cm.
  Includes bibliographical references and index.
  ISBN 0-262-03300-3 (hc: alk. paper)
    1. Telecommunication policy—Congresses. 2. Information technology—Congresses. I. Cranor, Lorrie Faith. II. Greenstein, Shane. III. Title.

HE7645 .R47 2001
384—dc21   2002026347

Contents

Preface

In the fall of 2001, about 300 people gathered near Washington, D.C., for the 29th Research Conference on Information, Communication, and Internet Policy. Originally called the Telecommunications Policy Research Conference, or TPRC, the conference was renamed in 2000 to reflect the emergence of the Internet as a central issue in telecommunications policy debates. However, the conference is still known as TPRC for short. TPRC 2001 is the latest installment of an annual dialogue among policy makers, researchers, advocates, and industry participants. One of the longest-running communications policy conferences in the United States, TPRC acquaints policy makers with the best recent research and familiarizes researchers with the needs of policy makers. This book includes 15 of the papers presented at TPRC 2001.

For the past several years, the number of TPRC submissions has increased dramatically each year. In 2001, TPRC once again set a new record, receiving over 240 abstract submissions. The program committee selected 100 of these submissions to be presented as TPRC 2001 papers. These papers were arranged into twenty-five 100-minute sessions, distributed across four parallel tracks: Local and International, Internet Use, Legal and Institutional Design, and Network Economics and Architecture. For this volume we selected 15 of these papers from across the four tracks. These papers are representative of the wide array of topics discussed at TPRC. (All of the TPRC 2001 papers are available from the TPRC web site at <http://www.tprc.org/>.) We hope that this book will help to continue the TPRC dialogue, inspire new research, and lead to to more informed policy decisions.

I write this preface as chair of the TPRC 2001 Program Committee. The other members of the program committee were Andrew Blau,

Flanerie Works; Jean Camp, Harvard University; Robert Cannon, Federal Communications Commission; Rob Frieden, Pennsylvania State University; Neil Gandal, Tel Aviv University; Hudson Janisch, University of Toronto; Mark Lemley, University of California-Berkeley; Lee McKnight, Tufts University; Michael Niebel, European Commission; Sharon Strover, University of Texas; and Theresa Swinehart, WorldCom. The members of the program committee did an outstanding job of assembling the program. Jean Camp and Robert Cannon deserve special thanks for developing and running the first-ever TPRC Sunday night trivia game, which proved to be an educational and fun experience for all who participated.

TPRC Inc. is a nonprofit organization governed by a board of directors. In 2001 the board was chaired by Jorge Schement of Pennsylvania State University and included Walter Baer, RAND; Michael Nelson, IBM; Robert Blau, BellSouth; Marjory Blumenthal, Computer Science and Telecommunications Board; Benjamin Compaine, MIT; Lloyd Morrisett, Children's Television Workshop; Larry Strickling, Federal Communications Commission; and Richard Taylor, Pennsylvania State University. The TPRC board deserves thanks for keeping the conference well funded and providing the continuity needed to keep TPRC going.

A few other people deserve thanks for helping TPRC 2001 come together. Ruth Doyal and her staff at Danya International took care of the conference logistical arrangements. Anne Hoag of Pennsylvania State University chaired the student paper awards committee, and did an excellent job of recruiting judges, overseeing the judging process, and recommending finalist papers to the Program Committee within a tight time schedule. Jeff Mackie-Mason and his students at the University of Michigan maintained the TPRC web site and kept up with my many requests for additions and changes. Chuck Cranor of AT&T Labs-Research (and also my husband) developed the electronic abstract submission and review system, which was essential to processing the record number of TPRC submissions. Chuck's support and assistance with babysitting also made it possible for me to get the TPRC program finalized within weeks after giving birth and to attend TPRC 2001 with a six-month-old baby.

This year the TPRC Program Committee was particularly interested in increasing the interaction between researchers, policy-makers, and advocates. To that end, we organized a tutorial on the first day of the conference for scholars interested in learning more about how to connect their research to the telecommunications policy process. Our keynote speakers—Gerry Faulhaber of the University of Pennsylvania and Matt Blaze of AT&T Labs-Research—both talked about their personal experiences as researchers who ventured into the policy-making process. We hope that this volume will serve to further the ongoing dialogue between researchers and policy-makers.

Finally, I would like to thank the TPRC board for giving me this opportunity to organize TPRC 2001 and to edit this book with Shane Greenstein. Shane and I hope that this book will have a positive impact and that you, the reader, will be able to put the book's contents to good use.

Lorrie Faith Cranor
AT&T Labs-Research

Introduction

As Langston Winner writes, it is not until "after the bulldozer has rolled over us" that we "pick ourselves up and carefully measure the tread marks."[1] That is, a technologist's forecast may not be scrutinized until well after a new technology has been deployed. To be sure, new technology is often developed in an air of optimism, as an attempt to solve problems. But, more often than not, new technologies actually create many new problems, fall far short of their predicted abilities, or bring with them a myriad of unintended consequences. When all effects are considered together, technology has an arguably positive impact on the quality of life. Yet, the emphasis should be on "arguable."

In the communications policy arena, the optimistic technologist perennially forecasts that new communications technologies have the ability to directly or indirectly address the most intractable problems. Communications technology promotes the dissemination of ideas, the free flow of information, and more direct political participation. Internet connections give remote communities access to medical information, libraries, or even university courses. In the most Utopian views, universal access to advanced communications technologies have a role to play in feeding the hungry, curing the sick, educating the illiterate, improving the overall standard of living around the world, and ultimately bringing about world peace.

Policy analysis often involves tempering this enthusiasm with a dose of sobering reality. While communications technologies probably have a role to play in making the world a better place, the impact of any specific technical advance is likely to be modest. Technologies often turn out to have limitations that are not immediately apparent—they don't hold up to everyday use in the real world, they don't scale, or they have side effects. In addition, there are limitations in their benefits. The limits may not be inherent in the technological capability, but rather due to the regulatory institutions or the economic constraints that govern the deployment of a commercial implementation. While the technology may exist to deliver any information anywhere in the world, many people lack the money to pay for it, the equipment to access it, the skills to use it, or even the knowledge that any of this might be useful to them in the first place. Indeed, there may not be a viable business model for delivering basic services associated with a new technology at all.

Many of the papers presented at TPRC 2001 examine the impacts of new communications technologies and their associated institutions. Despite the novelty of the technologies and the optimism which first surrounded their deployment, these examinations echo recurring themes. Technologies and institutions are often slow to deliver on their promises, many kinks remain to be worked out, and many questions remain to be answered. The tension between promising prospects and vexing conundrums arises in every paper in this volume.

Regulatory Conundrums and the Internet

As the Internet gained popularity in the 1990s, it was predicted to be a tool that could be used to break down national borders and their associated troublesome institutions. The Internet was heralded as both an enabler of direct digital democracy, and the incubator of a utopian society that had no need for government. But it has not worked out that way. As discussed in this book, Internet governance has emerged, but not smoothly. The vision of digital democracy has yet to materialize and papers in this book suggest that many obstacles still remain.

"Governments of the Industrial World. . . . You have no sovereignty where we gather," wrote Electronic Frontier Foundation cofounder John Perry Barlow in his 1996 Declaration of the Independence of Cyberspace.[2] "We have no elected government, nor are we likely to have one. . . . You have no moral right to rule us nor do you possess any methods of enforcement we have true reason to fear." Five years later, governments throughout the world are attempting—and in many cases succeeding—to enforce their laws in cyberspace, and an elected government for the Internet has emerged in the form of ICANN. But the imposition of government and governance on cyberspace has not gone smoothly. While Barlow and others have maintained that "legal concepts of property, expression, identity, movement, and context do not apply" to the Internet, courts around the world have found that they do apply, although not always in consistent or predictable ways. And while Barlow foresaw that "from ethics, enlightened self-interest, and the common weal, our governance will emerge," the governance that has emerged has been widely criticized for its lack of commonweal or enlightenment, and for frequently acting only in its self-interest and not for the benefit of the larger Internet community. Experience has shown that the Internet can be regulated, but that doing so is not easy. In this book we present three chapters that offer insights into some of the difficulties associated with Internet regulation: a case study in ICANN decision making, an analysis of the policy issues associated with attempts to establish a universal addressing system, and a discussion of how legal jurisdiction should be determined in Internet-related cases.

In chapter 1, Jonathan Weinberg tells the story leading to ICANN's selection of seven new Internet top level domains in November 2000. ICANN staff, in setting the ground rules for considering new TLDs, emphasized that only a few applicants would be allowed in, and imposed strict threshold requirements. Staff determined that the board should pick TLDs by looking at all relevant aspects of every proposal, and deciding which ones presented the best overall combination of a variety of incommensurable factors. As Weinberg explains, aspects of the resulting process were predictable: Anyone familiar with the FCC comparative hearing process for broadcast licenses can attest that this sort of ad hoc comparison is necessarily subjective, lending itself to arbitrariness and biased application. Yet the process had advantages that appealed to ICANN decision-makers. The board members would be free to take their best shots, in a situationally sensitive manner, at advancing the policies they thought important. The approach allowed ICANN to maintain the greatest degree of control. The end result, though, was a process that Weinberg describes as "stunning in its arbitrariness, a bad parody of fact-bound, situationally sensitive (rather than rules-based) decision-making."

As Robert Cannon explains in chapter 2, ENUM marks either the convergence or collision of the public telephone network with the Internet.

ENUM is an innovation in the domain name system (DNS). It starts with numerical domain names that are used to query DNS name servers. The servers respond with address information found in DNS records. This can be telephone numbers, email addresses, or other information. The concept is to use a single number in order to obtain a plethora of contact information. By convention, the Internet Engineering Task Force (IETF) ENUM Working Group determined that an ENUM number would be the same numerical string as a telephone number. In addition, the assignee of an ENUM number would be the assignee of that telephone number. But ENUM could work with any numerical string or, in fact, any domain name. ENUM creates multiple policy problems. What impact does ENUM have upon the public telephone network and the telephone numbering resource? For example, does this create a solution or a problem for number portability? If ENUM truly is a DNS innovation, how does it square with the classic difficulties experienced with DNS and ICANN? Is ENUM, while presenting a convergence solution, also encumbered with the policy problems of both the DNS and telephony worlds?

A unique challenge presented by the Internet is that compliance with local laws is rarely sufficient to assure a business that it has limited its exposure to legal risk. In chapter 3, Michael Geist identifies why the challenge of adequately accounting for the legal risk arising from Internet jurisdiction has been aggravated in recent years by the adoption of the Zippo legal framework, commonly referred to as the passive versus active test. The test provides parties with only limited guidance and often results in detrimental judicial decisions from a policy perspective. Given the inadequacies of the Zippo passive versus active test, Geist argues that it is now fitting to identify a more effective standard for determining when it is appropriate to assert jurisdiction in cases involving predominantly Internet-based contacts. The solution Geist suggests is to move toward a targeting-based analysis. Unlike the Zippo approach, a targeting analysis would seek to identify the intentions of the parties and to assess the steps taken to either enter or avoid a particular jurisdiction. Targeting would also lessen the reliance on effects-based analysis, the source of considerable uncertainty since Internet-based activity can ordinarily be said to create some effects in most jurisdictions. To identify the appropriate criteria for a targeting test, Geist recommends returning to the core jurisdictional principle—foreseeability. Foreseeability in the targeting context depends on three factors—contracts, technology, and actual or implied knowledge.

Digital Democracy: Prospects and Possibilities

As the popularity of the Internet has increased, so too has enthusiasm for "digital democracy." Many are excited about the prospects of citizens participating in virtual town halls, voting from home in their pajamas, and using the Internet to better inform themselves about candidates and ballot issues. Indeed, since the Reform Party held the first (partially) online election to nominate a candidate for U.S. President in 1996, there have been a flurry of electronic voting experiments, online government initiatives, and other forays into digital democracy. The 2000 Arizona Democratic primary, which allowed voters the option of casting their ballots over the Internet, was either a great success or a dismal failure, depending on whom you ask. While digital democracy enthusiasts have applauded each step forward, critics have raised concerns about digital divide issues and security considerations, and even questioned whether digital democracy can deliver on its promise of increasing political participation. In this book we address three areas where the Internet may play a role in political participation in the United States and elsewhere: voting, petition signing, and dissemination of political information.

In the aftermath of the 2000 U.S. presidential election, many states are considering changes to their voting systems in the hopes of avoiding the kinds of problems that occurred in Florida. Electronic voting machines and Internet voting are often cited as possible solutions. In chapter 4, Avi Rubin examines the security issues associated with running national governmental elections remotely over the Internet. He focuses on the limitations of the current deployed infrastructure in terms of the security of the personal computers people would use as voting machines, and the security and reliability of the Internet itself. He concludes that at present, our infrastructure is inadequate for remote Internet voting.

In many states people must collect thousands of signatures in order to qualify candidates or initiatives to appear on a ballot. Collecting these signatures can be very expensive. A recent California initiative would authorize use of encrypted digital signatures over the Internet to qualify candidates, initiatives, and other ballot measures. Proponents of Internet signature gathering say it will significantly lower the cost of qualifying initiatives and thereby reduce the influence of organized, well-financed interest groups. They also believe it will increase both public participation in the political process and public understanding about specific measures. However, opponents question whether Internet security is adequate to prevent widespread abuse and argue that the measure would create disadvantages for those who lack access to the Internet. Beyond issues of security, cost, and access lie larger questions about the effects of Internet signature gathering on direct democracy. Would it encourage greater and more informed public participation in the political process? Or would it flood voters with ballot measures and generally worsen current problems with the initiative process itself? In chapter 5, Walter Baer explores these and other issues related to Internet petition signing.

It has been suggested that increased access to the Internet and other new media should lead to a greater availability of political information and a more informed electorate. However, studies have shown that while the availability of political information has increased, citizens' levels of political knowledge have, at best, remained stagnant. In chapter 6, Markus Prior explains why this increased availability of information has not led to a more informed electorate. He hypothesizes that because the availability of entertainment content has increased with the availability of political information, people who prefer entertainment to news may in fact be exposed to less political information than they used to be. Prior analyzes existing NES and Pew survey data to build a measure of Relative Entertainment Preference that describes the degree of preference individuals have for entertainment versus news content. He finds that people who prefer entertainment to news and have access to cable television and the Internet are less politically knowledgeable and less likely to vote than people who prefer news or have less media access.

Monopoly and Competition in Communications Markets

The decade of the 1990s was full of optimism for new communications services. New technologies were supposed to give users choices among a variety of alternatives where one had previously existed. Competitive pressures were supposed to lead slumbering monopolists to innovate, cut prices and offer new services. The passage of the 1996 Telecom Act heralded in this new era, the impending end of monopoly provision of communication services and the obsolescence of old regulatory institutions. Actual events have tempered these optimistic forecasts or recast them in new light. Competitive markets have emerged only haltingly or in pockets, but also in some places where it was not expected.

One major goal of the Telecommunications Act of 1996 was to promote competition in both the local exchange and long distance wireline markets. In section 271 Congress permitted the Bell Operating Companies (BOCs) to enter the long distance market only if they demonstrate to the FCC that they have complied with the market-opening requirements of section 251. Many have questioned the logic behind section 271. Was it a reasonable means of achieving increased competition in both the local and long distance markets? What type of regulatory structure suits the technical characteristics of the industry and the legal and informational constraints on regulators who must ensure compliance?

In chapter 7 Daniel Shiman and Jessica Rosenworcel examine a variety of schemes for ensuring BOC compliance that Congress could have used. Given the characteristics of the industry and the limitations on regulators' ability to observe BOC's efforts, they determine that the use of a prize such as BOC entry into long distance is a superior incentive mechanism. They further argue that conditioning a BOC's long distance entry on its demonstrating compliance with section 251 was a logical method of protecting the long distance market against a BOC discriminating against long distance competitors once it has gained entry. They also provide an update on the extent of competitive entry in the local exchange market five years after enactment of the act. They argue that statistical evidence—primarily ILEC lines sold to CLECs for basic telephone services—appears to confirm that section 271 has thus far been effective in ensuring compliance.

Sean Ennis takes an original approach to understanding the links between competitive structure and conduct in chapter 8. He examines the relationship between changes in telecommunications provider concentration on international long distance routes and changes in prices on those routes. Overall, he finds that decreased concentration is associated with significantly lower prices to consumers of long distance services. However, the relationship between concentration and price varies according to the type of long distance plan considered. For the international flagship plans frequently selected by more price-conscious consumers of international long distance, increased competition on a route is associated with lower prices. In contrast, for the basic international plans that are the default selection for consumers, increased competition on a route is actually associated with higher prices. Thus, somewhat surprisingly, price dispersion appears to increase as competition increases.

This section finishes with chapter 9. It takes a close look at the newspaper market, where local concentration exists in many cities. Student paper award winner Lisa George examines the effect of ownership concentration on product position, product variety and readership in markets for daily newspapers. Most analysts presume that mergers reduce the amount and diversity of content available to consumers. However, the effects of consolidation in differentiated product markets cannot be determined solely from theory. Because multi-product firms internalize business stealing, mergers may encourage firms to reposition products, leading to more, not less, variety. Using data on reporter assignments from 1993–1999, George tests how Newspaper variety varies with city newspaper concentration. The results show that variety increases with the decline in the availability of newspapers. Moreover, there is evidence that additional variety increases readership, suggesting that concentration benefits consumers.

The Future of Wireless Communications

New wireless markets have begun developing, but also await co-development of a variety of institutional features. By all accounts there are opportunities to create enormous value, but the regulatory issues are quite challenging.

Lee McKnight, William Lehr, and Raymond Linsenmayer compare two models for delivering broadband wireless services: best effort and Quality-of-Service (QoS) guaranteed services. The "best effort" services are more commonly known as unlicensed wireless services, while the "Quality of Service guaranteed" services are more commonly referred to as traditional landline telephony, as well as cellular telephone services of either the second or third generation. This chapter highlights the differing "market" versus "engineering" philosophies implicit in alternative wireless service architectures.

In chapter 11 Doublas Webbink examines a problem of interest to many consumers. Increasingly wireline and wireless services, including those provided by terrestrial and satellite systems, are considered to be substitutes and sometimes complements, regardless of the laws and regulations applicable to them. At the same time, many writers and even government agencies (such as the FCC) have suggested that users of the spectrum should be given more property-like rights in the use of the spectrum and at a minimum should be given much more flexibility in how they may use the spectrum. Two recent developments have important implications with respect to spectrum property rights and flexible use of the spectrum. The first development involves several proposals to provide terrestrial wireless services within spectrum in use. Such service may also interfere with spectrum used to provide satellite services. The second development is the passage of the 2000 ORBIT Act, an Act that specifically forbids the use of license auctions to select among mutually exclusive applicants to provide international or global satellite communications service. This paper discusses some of the questions raised by these two events, but does not necessarily provide definitive answers or solutions.

Expanding the Understanding of Universal Service

New technologies also have not eliminated concerns about equitable availability and use of communications technologies. Communications infrastructure remains expensive and there are no easy quick-fix solutions to the lack of available infrastructure or the lack of adoption of Internet technology. It is also quite unclear whether American definitions for universal service are portable to other countries.

In chapter 12 Kyle Nicholas focuses on how state-level policy and access patterns work to structure Internet access within rural communities. Combining both quantitative and qualitative data, he examines the role of geo-policy barriers in Texas, one of the largest and most rural states in the nation. Expanded Area Service policies are state policies wherein phone customers can expand their local calling area. Because useful Internet access requires a flat-price connection, EAS policies can play a crucial role in connecting citizens to one another. EAS policies (including Texas') tend to vary along five dimensions (community of interest, customer scope, directionality, pricing mechanism and policy scope). He shows that EAS policies that rely on regulated market boundaries for definition can generate gross inequities in rural Internet access. Interviews with Internet Service Providers in a case study of 25 rural communities reveals that LATA and exchange boundaries, along with geographically restricted infrastructure investments, curtail service provision in remote areas. A statistical analysis of 1300 telephone exchanges, including 208 rural telephone exchanges in Texas reveals that the farther a community lies from a metropolitan area the less likely they are to have reliable Internet access.

In the same spirit, Sharon Strover, Michael Oden, Nobuya Inagaki, and Jeremy Gustafson investigate the relationship between telecommunications infrastructure, economic conditions, and federal and state policies and initiatives. In chapter 13 they present a detailed look at the telecommunications environment of the Appalachian region, particularly focusing on broadband technologies. A strong, positive association exists between telecommunications infrastructure and economic status. They examine the effects of federal and state universal service policies, as well as some of the ways states have leveraged their own infrastructure to improve telecommunications capabilities in their region.

Student paper award winner Martha Fuentes-Bautista surveys the universal service policies in Argentina, Brazil, Chile, Mexico, Peru, and Venezuela in chapter 14. This study explores the evolution of the concept of "Universal Service" during the rollout of the telecommunication reform in the last decade in these six Latin American countries. Country profiles and a set of universal service indicators provide a frame for discussing issues of accessibility and affordability of telephone service in the region. She finds that the reconfiguration of national networks fostered by liberalization policies offered risks and opportunities to achieve universal service goals. The diversification of access points and services enhanced users' choices, but price rebalancing and lack of Universal Service Obligations (USO) to target groups with special needs depressed the demand and threatened to exclude significant parts of the population. The situation requires the reformulation of USO incorporating all technological solutions existing in the market, factors from the consumer-demand accounting for the urban–rural continuum, and different social and economic strata. This study identifies the emergence of a second generation of USO targeting some of these needs. However, Fuestes-Bautista recommends that more competition and special tariff plans for the poor be incorporated to the options available in the market.

Finally, in chapter 15 Michelle Kosimidis examines a key dimension in which the Internet is changing the way people around the world communicate, learn, and work. As has been noted, one way to address the "digital divide" is to ensure Internet access to all schools from an early age. While both the United States and European Union have embraced the promotion of Internet access to schools, the two have decided to finance it differently. This paper presents a variety of data on how different countries are promoting Internet access to schools. Kosımıdıs argues that the main costs of Internet access to schools are not communications-related (telecommunications and Internet services) but rather noncommunications-related (hardware, educational training, software). This paper goes on to discuss whether and how the identified costs should be financed. Should it be funded by the telecommunications industry and its users or by a general governmental budget (educational budget).

Epilogue

Communications policy analysis often looks like a refereed contest between naïve hope and jaded experience. Optimistic entrepreneurs embark on commercial ventures founded on near-utopian technology forecasts, casting aside the doubts of more chastened observers. Regulatory institutions slow these commercial processes down, spending enormous energy preventing monopoly bottlenecks from interfering, trying to ensure equitable provision of services, or injecting public interest politics into every facet of decision making. Both sides complain about the lack of closure.

And, yet, it never ends. While regulatory institutions complicate matters to no end, prophets for new communications technology keep arriving. The prophets declare a business revolution in communications activities—such as broadcasting, entertainment, retail marketing, or wireless communications. These same prophets proclaim that this year's technology novelties dilute standard lessons from the past. Because this technology contains so many unique features, it is ushering in a new commercial era which operates according to new rules. Jaded observers look on skeptically, labeling such prophesizing as self-serving or misguided. Many voices stand in opposition, representing users, political interests, or commercial adversaries. It is a wonder that anything gets done at all.

More recently this contest takes place against a backdrop of institutional change. We are entering a millennium where technical developments, market events, and unceasing regulatory restructuring will place considerable tension on long-standing legal foundations and slow policy discussions. Legacy regulatory decisions had previously specified how commercial firms transact with the regulated public switch network. Until recently, the pace of technical change in most communications services was presumed to be slow and easily monitored from centralized administrative agencies at the state and federal level. It is well known that such a presumption is dated, but it is unclear what conceptual paradigm should replace it.

The scope of the problems are vexing. Do these legacy institutions act in society's interest or foster experimentation in technically intensive activities? To put it simply, do the existing set of regulations enhance the variety of approaches to new commercial opportunities or retard such developments? Going forward it is unclear whether these legacy institutions are still appropriate for other basic staples of communications policies

In this spirit, this book presents a series of policy papers. To be sure, there is probably a grain of truth to the declarations coming from all parties. Every new technology holds the promise of a better future if it addresses an actual problem. Every new technology holds the prospect of unforeseen dangers if it contains no protection from unintended consequences.

Yet, the momentary euphoria affiliated with commercializing new technology does not, nor should it, justify too simplistic a view of what actually happens, nor what issues policy makers face. With that in mind, we ask the reader to read the analyses contained herein and consider whether hope or experience will triumph in the future.

Notes

1. L. Winner (1986) The Whale and the Reactor: A Search for Limits in an Age of High Technology (Chicago: University of Chicago Press), p. 10.

2. J. Barlow (February 1996) A Declaration of the Independence of Cyberspace. <http://www.eff.org/~barlow/Declaration-Final.html>.

I

Regulatory Conundrums and the Internet

1

ICANN, "Internet Stability," and New Top Level Domains

Jonathan Weinberg*

Since 1998, an entity known as the Internet Corporation for Assigned Names and Numbers (ICANN) has administered the Internet domain name system. Last November, the ICANN board of directors agreed to add seven new top level domains to the name space. ICANN staff then embarked upon extensive negotiations with representatives of the registries that would operate the new domains, with the goal of signing agreements describing nearly every aspect of the registries' operations. ICANN's role vis-à-vis these new top level domains is historically without precedent. It is dramatically different from the role played by Jon Postel, who was largely responsible for the governance of the domain name system until his death in 1998. Yet while ICANN's activities are unlike Postel's, they are unexpectedly familiar to the United States communications lawyer: ICANN's actions strikingly parallel the Federal Communications Commission's historic course in licensing broadcasters.[1]

ICANN has selected top level domain registries through processes that, if they were vastly improved, would look like the FCC's historic "public interest"–based comparative licensing. Like the FCC, ICANN has used this licensing process to regulate registry conduct, although ICANN's regulation goes far beyond anything the FCC ever attempted. And as with the FCC, ICANN's regulatory imperative has flowed largely from scarcity—in this case, the scarcity of generic top level domains in the ICANN root. The scarcity of top level domains is not a technological artifact, though, as with broadcast licensing; rather, ICANN is maintaining it as a policy matter.

This paper provides a history: It tells the story leading to ICANN's selection of seven new top-level domains in November of 2000. In telling that story, and selecting from the universe of facts to include, I will focus on facts illuminating two basic themes. The first of those themes relates to the method that ICANN chose to select the new TLD registries. ICANN's selection process was badly dysfunctional; it was described by one media observer as "torturous," "channeling the spirit of [Walt] Disney," "a bad parody of Florida's election process," and "bizarre."[1] ICANN's incoming chairman compared the selection process to that of a venture capital firm, and urged that ICANN find a way to "extract" itself. How did ICANN reach that point, and what alternatives did it have? What alternatives, indeed, does it have now?

The second theme relates to the degree of ICANN's control over the day-to-day operations of the new registries. After ICANN's selection of the seven new registries, the registries and ICANN staff sat down to negotiate contracts. ICANN staff had originally contemplated that negotiating all the contracts would take no more than six weeks. Instead, as of this writing (ten months after the registries were selected), ICANN has completed agreements with only three, and negotiations with the other four are still ongoing. The most important reason for this delay is the extraordinarily detailed and comprehensive nature of the new contracts; a single one is about two inches thick in hard copy. The contracts incorporate an extensive set of commitments by the registries to ICANN, with ICANN specifying many aspects of their operations; their negotiation amounts to extensive regulation on ICANN's part of registry activities. What led ICANN to seek to impose that regulation, and is it necessary?

I will not resolve these questions in this paper; I will address the first to a limited extent, and the second not at all. I will leave the answers to a later, longer, article. What I am presenting in this paper, rather, is simply a history. But it may be useful to the reader, in reading that history, to keep these questions in mind.

I Background

A Technical Basis of the DNS
The domain name system matches Internet protocol (IP) addresses, which identify individual host computers on the Internet, with domain names. An IP address is a unique 32-bit number, usually printed in dotted decimal form, such as 128.127.50.224;[3] a domain name is a set of

text labels set off by dots, such as threecats.net or law.wayne.edu. A system matching names to numbers, so that a user can locate an Internet resource knowing only its domain name, has two advantages. First, domain names are relatively easy to remember and to type. IP addresses, by contrast, are opaque and harder to remember. Second, the use of domain names provides a "level of indirection" making it possible for network operators to change the IP addresses associated with various machines while leaving their names—which outsiders use to find them—untouched.

The current domain name system, developed by Postel and Paul Mockapetris (both of the University of Southern California's Information Sciences Institute), is hierarchical. The overall name space is divided into top level domains, or TLDs; each top-level domain is divided into second level domains. At each level, the pyramidal structure of the name space replicates itself. The owner of each second level domain is at the apex of a pyramid consisting of the third level domains (if any) within that second-level domain, and so on. Thus, the .edu TLD is divided into about 4000 second level domains such as wayne.edu; wayne.edu is divided into third level domains including law.wayne.edu, gradschool.wayne.edu, and socialwork.wayne.edu.

This hierarchy makes it easy for the job of name-to-number translation to be shared by a large number of servers. At the apex of the DNS pyramid is a set of thirteen root servers, each of which lists the IP addresses of the computers containing the zone files for each of the top-level domains. At the next level are the computers holding those top-level domain zone files, each of which lists the IP addresses of the name servers for each second-level domain it controls, and so on. When a user looking for a particular Internet resource types in a domain name, her computer begins at the bottom of the pyramid: it queries a set of local DNS servers, specified in its software, to find the IP address corresponding to that domain name. If those local servers do not know the answer, they move the request up the line.

This structure has far-reaching implications. On the one hand, it lends itself to decentralization, since the person controlling any given host can adopt policies governing registration below it (but not elsewhere) in the pyramid. The owners of wayne.edu, for example, have complete control over whom they will allow to register third-level domains such as law.wayne.edu; there is no snorlax.wayne.edu, because that label does not fit within the naming scheme that the proprietors of wayne.edu established.

On the other hand, control over the root zone—at the very top of the pyramid—carries with it considerable power. If a user types in a domain name incorporating a top level domain that is unknown to the root servers, then the DNS will be unable to find the corresponding computer. The power to control the root servers, thus, is the power to decide (1) which top-level domains are visible in the name space; and (2) which name servers are authoritative for those top-level domains—that is, which registries get to allocate names within each of those top-level domains. Historically, the Internet root zone was overseen by Postel and others at USC's Information Sciences Institute; beginning in the late 1980s, their activities coordinating the root zone and IP address allocation came to be referred to as the Internet Assigned Numbers Authority (IANA).

There is no technical or legal requirement that a person use the root servers established by IANA to resolve DNS queries. Users can point their computers at entirely different DNS servers that in turn point to different root servers, referencing a different set of top-level domains. Such alternative root servers do exist, so that if one points one's computer at the right DNS server, one can send email to addresses that the rest of the Internet does not recognize, such as <richard@vrx.zoo>. Very few Internet users, though, look to alternative root servers. The vast majority rely on the single set of authoritative root servers, historically supervised by Postel and IANA, that have achieved canonical status.

B Building the Domain Name Space
The first top level domains set up in the current domain name system, beginning in January 1985, were .arpa (which during an initial transitional period contained all then-existing Internet hosts, and now is limited to certain infrastructural functions); .com (initially intended for businesses); .edu (for universities); .gov (for U.S. government agencies), .mil (for the U.S. military); .net (for Internet "network-type organizations," such as network service centers and consortia or network information and operations centers); and .org (for entities "that do not clearly fall within the other top-level domains").[4] Only one other of these so-called generic domains was created during Postel's lifetime—the .int domain, for international treaty organizations, in 1988.

Beginning in February 1985, though, Internet engineers began adding "country-code" top level domains (ccTLDs) to the root zone. The first ones added were .us, for the United States; .gb and .uk, for Great Britain; .il, for Israel, and .au, for Australia. Early in 1994, Postel memorialized the criteria for adding new top-level domains in a document known as *RFC 1591 (Domain Name System Structure and Delegation).* At the time, he was adding new country-code TLDs at a rate of about one every sixteen days; he had created more than one hundred since 1985.

Before Postel would add a new country-code top-level domain, the following requirements had to be met. First, "significantly interested parties" within the country in question had to agree on a manager to supervise the domain. Postel emphasized that the burden was on contending parties within a country to reach agreement among themselves; he would not change a delegation once made, absent substantial misbehavior by the manager, unless all of the contending parties agreed on the change. Second, the proposed ccTLD manager had to understand its responsibilities. A ccTLD manager, RFC 1591 emphasized, is a trustee for the people of the nation in question, with a duty to serve the local community, and a trustee for the global Internet community as well. It must operate the domain in a technically competent manner, maintaining adequate Internet connectivity. It must treat all users equally, processing requests in a nondiscriminatory fashion, and treating academic and commercial users on an equal basis.

Apart from these general considerations, though, RFC 1591 conspicuously avoided any instructions about how a new country-code domain should be run. RFC 1591 said nothing further about a registry's business model. It did not speak to whether a registry should charge for domain name services, or whether it should limit registration to residents of the country in question. It said nothing about how the registry should structure the name space within the ccTLD. Indeed, it said very little about the registry's technical operations. These decisions were up to the manager of the domain; they were no business of IANA's.

In RFC 1591, Postel stated that it was "extremely unlikely" that any new generic TLDs would be created. In the mid-1990s, though, dissatisfaction with the domain name system began to mount. Registration services in .com, .net, .org and .edu were then performed by a company known as Network Solutions, Inc (NSI), pursuant to a cooperative agreement with the U.S. National Science Foundation (NSF). Initially, NSF paid for all registrations, which were free to users; as the number of registrations began to rise, though, NSF and NSI agreed to take the U.S. government out of the funding loop. Rather, NSI would charge a $50 annual fee to each domain name registrant.

The NSI fee crystallized growing unhappiness with the structure of the domain name system. Registrants wondered why, in seeking to register names in the generic top level domains, they were stuck with the service provided, and the fees charged, by the NSI monopoly. NSI also generated animosity with its domain name dispute policies, under which it would suspend a domain name upon receiving a complaint from a trademark owner, without regard to whether the trademark owner had a superior legal claim to the name. Many saw the dominance of the .com domain in the name space as unhealthy. Finally, there was growing consensus in the technical community that the architecture would support many more top-level domains than had been authorized so far.

Accordingly, in 1996, Postel suggested that IANA authorize up to 150 new generic top-level domains, to be operated by new registries.[5] The qualifications he deemed necessary for a person or organization seeking to operate one of the new domains were lightweight. First, the applicant would have to show that it could provide a minimum set of registration services: maintenance of up-to-date registration data in escrowable form, capability to search the second level domain database via the whois protocol, live customer support during business hours, etc. Second, it would need adequate Internet connectivity, and at least two nameservers in geographically diverse locations running an up-to-date version of the BIND software. Finally, it would need to present some documentation lending credibility to the conclusion that it was proposing a viable business, "likely to operate successfully for at least five years."

Postel was emphatic, though, that a person applying to operate a new gTLD would not have to submit a business plan, and that "[i]nternal database and operational issues . . . including pricing to customers of the registry" were no business of IANA's. These were "free-market issues," to be decided by each registry for itself.

Postel's proposal met with a guardedly favorable reaction from the Internet Society (a nonprofit membership organization that is home to key Internet technical bodies). Other groups, however, soon came forward to object. Postel's plan only began a long and contentious process in which participants debated the nature of new TLDs and the future of Internet governance. That story has been told elsewhere;[6] let it suffice that two years later the U.S. government determined that "the challenge of deciding policy for new domains" should be put in the hands of a new nonprofit corporation that would step into IANA's shoes.[7]

Historically, all of the major actors involved with the name space had fulfilled their responsibilities pursuant to agreements with the U.S. government. USC's Information Sciences Institute, which housed Postel, had long had contracts with the U.S. Defense Department covering the IANA work; NSI, which operated the registry for the .com, .net., .org and .edu domains, did so pursuant to a cooperative agreement with the National Science Foundation. As part of its solution to the controversies raging over the domain name space, the U.S. government determined that it should "withdraw from its existing management role" in favor of a new, not-for-profit corporation formed and run by "private sector Internet stakeholders." The new corporation, which would manage domain names, the IP address allocation system, and the root server network, would be run by a board of directors broadly reflecting the Internet private sector. The U.S. government would recognize it by entering into agreements with it that would give it effective policy authority over the root zone.

In late 1998, after an extended series of negotiations between IANA and NSI—and consultations with the U.S. government, a variety of foreign governments, large corporations, and others—Postel took a crucial step to implement these directions by transmitting to the U.S. Department of Commerce documents creating the new corporation. These documents included the articles of incorporation of the new Internet Corporation for Assigned Names and Numbers; biographies of a proposed initial board of directors; and a set of proposed bylaws. The new directors were drawn, for the most part, from the worlds of telecommunications and information technology; few of them had specialized knowledge of the Internet or of domain name issues. The plan was that the board members would be guided by the wisdom of Postel as the new corporation's chief technical officer and could lend their influence and neutrality to bolster his decisions.

Two weeks later, Jon Postel died of complications following open heart surgery. This was a tremendous blow to the new organization; on what basis, now, were industry members and the public to have faith in ICANN's decision-making? The U.S. government, though, had issued its policy statement and committed itself to the new organization. It pushed forward. It solicited public comment on ICANN's proposal, and began negotiating with ICANN's lawyer (Joe Sims of the Jones, Day law firm) over failings in the proposed bylaws. Ultimately, the government entered into a memorandum of understanding with ICANN, recognizing it and authorizing it to exercise DNS management functions subject to the government's continuing oversight.

ICANN came into existence under a cloud. Its board members, who had been chosen in a closed process, were many of them unknown to the Internet community. While ICANN had the U.S. government's seal of approval, the government's own authority over the DNS was murky and contested. There were some who contended that ICANN was simply illegitimate. On the other hand, ICANN had control of several of the levers of power. Most importantly, with the U.S. government's support, it had policy control of the root zone, because NSI operated the primary root server subject to U.S. government instructions. The U.S. government, moreover, was able to use its negotiating leverage to cause NSI to recognize ICANN's policy authority (while NSI simultaneously secured favorable terms for itself relating to its ability to exploit the lucrative .com, .net, and .org top level domains). Finally, ICANN was tasked by the Department of Commerce with supervising a process under which multiple new competitive "registrars" would sell domain names in the NSI-operated TLDs. Any company wishing accreditation as a registrar, therefore, had to recognize ICANN's authority and agree to its terms.

The new organization's internal structure was complex. In theory, the job of developing policy was lodged in three "Supporting Organizations"—one to address policy relating to domain names, one for policy relating to IP address allocation, and one for policy relating to "the assignment of parameters for Internet protocols." The organization charged with developing policy relating to domain name issues was the Domain Name Supporting Organization (DNSO); within that body, policy authority was exercised by a Names Council, whose membership was selected by seven industry groupings (known in ICANN lingo as "constituencies").

According to ICANN's bylaws, the Names Council has "primary responsibility for developing" domain name policy within the ICANN structure. It is supposed to do this by managing a "consensus building process" within the DNSO; it has the power to designate committees and working groups to carry out its substantive work. If the Names Council determines that the DNSO has produced a "community consensus" on some matter of domain name policy, it is to forward that consensus to the board. The bylaws state that as a general matter, ICANN may not enact domain-name policy without the approval of a Names Council majority.

These formal rules, though, grossly misdescribe the actual ICANN process. The Names Council has turned out to be incapable of generating detailed policy recommendations, and the DNSO has not proved to be an important locus for policy development. Rather, that role has been taken over by ICANN staff.[8]

II   Adding New Top Level Domains

When ICANN was formed, the most important substantive policy question facing the new organization was whether, and under what circumstances, it would add new generic top level domains to the name space. On May 27, 1999, ICANN's board of directors instructed the DNSO to formulate recommendations on the question of adding new generic top level domains. The DNSO in turn passed the matter to a working group.

By now, it had become clear that Postel's proposal to add hundreds of new top level domains, although technically straightforward, was politically infeasible. Trademark lawyers had organized early to oppose any expansion of the name space. They feared that increasing the number of TLDs would force trademark owners, seeking to prevent the registration of domain names similar or identical to their trademarks, to incur higher policing costs. At the very least, the trademark bar argued, before there could be any expansion of the name space there had to be a well-established, thoroughly tested mechanism built into the DNS architecture that would allow trademark owners to gain control of offending domains without going to court. The trademark lawyers convinced leaders of the technical community that they had the political clout to stop any expansion of the name space to which they had not agreed.

In the DNSO's working group, the battles raged anew. Some participants repeated that ICANN should immediately add hundreds of new top-level domains. Such a step would maximize consumer choice, making many new appealing names available. It would ensure meaningful competition among top level domain registries, eliminating market-power problems that were unavoidable with a smaller number. It would minimize trademark problems, because consumers, understanding that a given SLD string could belong to different registrants in different TLDs, would not be confused into thinking that any given domain name was associated with a given company.

Trademark lawyers, by contrast, urged that no new TLDs should be added until a set of new trademark protections had been built into the system and it was "clear that the proposed safeguards are working"; only then, the opponents indicated, would they entertain the possibility of introducing one or more new gTLDs "on an as needed basis." Nor were trademark lawyers the only group expressing skepticism about expanding the name space. Business players that had prospered under the existing system worried about disruptive change. Internet service providers worried that name space expansion would encourage their users to acquire their own domain names, weakening the link between user and ISP and increasing the ISP's costs. Existing commercial domain name registries (NSI and a few of the ccTLDs) saw new top level domain registries as competition.

After extensive debate, the working group reached what it termed "rough consensus" (defined as a two-thirds vote of its members) in support of a compromise position, put forward by the group's co-chair, under which ICANN would begin by adding six to ten new gTLDs, followed by an evaluation period.[9] It agreed as well that the initial rollout should include a wide range of top level domains, including both "open" TLDs, in which anyone could register, and restricted TLDs for the benefit of particular groups.

But the working group failed to reach consensus on other issues. Some within the working group had urged that ICANN should require all registries in the initial rollout to be operated on a not-for-profit, cost-recovery basis; others argued, just as strongly, for a mix of for-profit and not-for-profit registries. The working group was able to come to no resolution on this point. More importantly, the working group failed to resolve *how* ICANN should select the new top-level domains.

The Names Council, upon receiving the working group report, declined to fill in the gaps. It agreed on a general statement supporting the introduction of new gTLDs but recommending that their introduction be "measured and responsible," giving due regard to the goals of generating an "orderly" process for initial registration in the new domains; protecting intellectual property rights; and safeguarding user confidence in the technical operation of the domain name space. The Names Council statement said little about the number of new gTLDs, the nature of the new registries, or how they should be selected.

This left ICANN staff, tasked by the board with bringing new gTLDs online, with freedom of action. After the Names Council pronouncement, ICANN staff released a report, styled a "discussion document," stating that the addition of new top level domains should be well-controlled and small-scale, with the goal of establishing a "proof of concept" for possible future introductions—that is, that the point of the initial rollout would simply be to establish (or disprove) the proposition that new top-level domains could be added to the name space successfully.[10]

The report requested public comment on seventy-four policy and technical questions. There were a variety of questions, though, that the document did *not* ask. The document elaborately justified, and treated as settled, its conclusion that any introduction of gTLDs should be small-scale, intended only to serve as "proof of concept." The "proof of concept" notion was not intuitively obvious, since it was not entirely clear what concept was to be proved: It was already abundantly clear that adding new gTLDs was *technically* feasible, and would not threaten successful name resolution. After all, IANA had added ccTLDs to the root zone quite frequently over the years, and adding a gTLD was no different from adding a ccTLD from the standpoint of whether domain name servers would return accurate responses to DNS queries. But staff was on relatively firm ground in calling for a small-scale rollout: The Names Council had requested "measured and responsible" introduction, and had noted its concern that the introduction of a large new gTLD would be marred by lack of "orderly" process and developments unfavorable to trademark owners. The DNSO's working group, along similar lines, had suggested that the initial rollout of six to ten be followed by "evaluation" before ICANN proceeded further.

Also implicit in the staff document was its rejection of any suggestion that new top level domain registries had to be not-for-profit. The discussion document assumed that the new TLDs would be run by multiple new entities that had applied to ICANN for the right to do so, and it explicitly contemplated that at least some of those registries would be profit-oriented firms. The report contained no discussion recognizing that these were, in fact, decisions.

Most important were choices about how the new registries would be chosen. When ICANN inserts a new TLD into the root, the new zone file entry reflects a series of choices. The zone file must identify the string of letters that will sit at the right of all domain names in the new TLD, such as ".edu" or ".info". It must also identify the particular organization that will administer the master registry database for that TLD, and enter the IP addresses of name servers controlled by that organization into the root zone. In considering how ICANN should go about selecting new TLDs, the DNSO's working group had confronted a range of options. Should ICANN first identify the TLD strings that would be desirable additions to the name space, identify how it wanted those TLDs to be run, and only then solicit applications for registries to operate the TLDs according to its specifications? If so, should it establish a master plan (such as a Yellow Pages-style taxonomy), or should it identify the desirable new TLD strings on an ad hoc basis? Or should ICANN take an alternative approach, picking a set of registries according to objective criteria, and afterwards allowing the selected registries to choose their own strings? Or should each would-be registry apply to ICANN, explaining which string or strings it wished to run a registry for, so that ICANN could select registry and string together?

The staff report answered all of these questions: It charted a path in which ICANN would request an application from each organization seeking to operate a new gTLD. Each of these organizations would set out its business, financial and technical qualifications, together with the mechanisms it proposed for the benefit of trademark owners, its proposed TLD string, and the characteristics of the proposed top level domain. It would address such issues as the market targeted by the proposed TLD, and the TLD's criteria for registration. The staff document thus eliminated at the outset such possibilities as first identifying the TLD strings that would be desirable additions to the name space and only then soliciting applications for registries to operate the TLDs in question, or picking a set of registries according to hard-edged, objective criteria, without regard to the nature of the TLDs they wished to run. Rather, the document—essentially without discussion of alternatives— assumed a process in which ICANN, picking a small number of TLDs to allow into the initial rollout, would look at all relevant aspects of every proposal and decide which ones presented the best overall combination of TLD string, TLD charter, business plan, robust capitalization, and other (incommensurable) factors.

When staff made this choice, some aspects of the resulting process were predictable. One of the lessons learned from the Federal Communications Commission (FCC) comparative hearing process for broadcast licenses is that this sort of ad hoc comparison is necessarily subjective.[11] Before the fact, it is difficult to predict what results such a process will generate; afterwards, it is hard to justify why one proposal was chosen and not another. Because decisions are unconstrained by clear-cut rules, the process lends itself to arbitrariness and biased application. Yet the process had advantages that appealed to ICANN decision-makers. The board members, in comparing the applications, would be free to take their best shots, in a situationally sensitive manner, at advancing the policies they thought important. They would not have to worry about being bound by hard-and-fast rules yielding unfortunate results in the particular case. More importantly, given business and trademark lobbyists' fear of new gTLDs and their potential for disruptive change, this approach allowed ICANN to maintain the greatest degree of control over the selection process. It gave assurance that any new gTLDs emerging from the process would be not only few, but also safe.

ICANN's board of directors formally authorized submission of applications to operate the new TLDs, and staff published a remarkably detailed application form. ICANN instructed prospective registry operators that they had to complete and return the forms in six weeks. Each application was to be accompanied by a nonrefundable $50,000 fee, to cover the costs of what staff described as a "very intensive review and analysis of applications on many levels (including technical, financial, legal, etc.)." Staff emphasized that each applicant "must submit a detailed, multi-part proposal accompanied by extensive supporting documentation. The effort and cost of preparing a sufficient proposal should not be underestimated. . . . Those who are planning to apply are strongly urged to secure now the professional assistance of technical experts, financial and management consultants, and lawyers to assist in formulation of their proposals and preparation of their applications."

Indeed, staff continued, "your own cost of formulating a proposal and preparing an adequate application will likely be much more" than the $50,000 application fee. Together with the application form, ICANN released a document describing nine broad values staff would look to in assessing the proposals.

Forty-seven firms filed applications; of those, ICANN returned two for failure to include the $50,000 fee. Staff's evaluation of the remaining applications was compressed. The ICANN meeting at which the selections were to be made would begin in just six weeks, on November 13. The opportunity for public comment was even more compressed: Members of the public could not comment until the application materials were made available on the Web for the public to see, and that process was significantly delayed. Staff announced that they had posted "most of" the materials by October 23; they reported on November 1 that they had posted all of the "basic" materials, with "a few partial omissions."

On November 10, just one working day before the four-day ICANN meeting was to begin, staff made available its crucial "Report on New TLD Applications." The document incorporated contributions from three outside technical advisors, together with advice from the Arthur Andersen accounting firm and Jones, Day Reavis & Pogue (ICANN's outside counsel). It included a brief summary of each application, consisting of a thirteen-item template for each and a brief summary of any public comments received. This was the first moment that any applicant learned of the staff's assessment of its proposal; staff had declined to meet with applicant representatives at any point during the process.

The body of the report divided the applications into eight categories. Within each category, the report first identified applications that "did not merit further review" because they were deemed unsound for technical or business reasons. That disposed of sixteen applications. The report discussed the remaining applications in more detail, attempting to compare applications in each category. In the final analysis, the report described fifteen applications as plausible candidates for going forward; it cautioned, though, that the board "could responsibly select" only a limited number of them.

The staff report kicked off frenzied activity on the part of many of the applicants, as they attempted in the meager time remaining to generate and file comments refuting staff's characterizations of their applications. On November 15, in a spectacle reminiscent of nothing so much as television's "The Gong Show," each of the forty-four applicants was given exactly three minutes to appear before the board, respond to questions, and make its case. The board, after all, had allocated only an afternoon to hear the applicants and take public comment; even giving each applicant three minutes (plus enough time to walk to and from the microphone) ate up nearly two hours of that time. Most of the applicants played along gamely, trying to make the best of their three minutes. When one applicant used its time to criticize ICANN's "highly flawed process," departing chair Esther Dyson was tart: "I'm really sorry," she said, "we gave you the chance to speak and you did not take very good advantage of it."

Four of the board members had recused themselves (although they remained on the dais), and three others chose not to participate. The following day, when the board met to make its decisions, discussion among the twelve members remaining was lively. While ICANN critics had on other occasions worried that the board's open meetings simply ratified decisions already reached elsewhere, it seemed plain in this case that the board members had not discussed the applications with each other before. They had a single day's session to make their decisions (along with conducting other, unrelated business), and they were making those decisions from scratch.

The board's discussion was halting at the outset; the board members had varying views on what they should be doing and how. They settled on an approach in which they would consider the applications one by one, putting the plausible ones into a metaphorical "basket," and returning to the basket when the list was done. Their procedure was anything but well-organized, though; after their initial identification of plausible applications, the board went back through the applications in their basket multiple times, changing their minds as they went. One director maintained a "parallel basket," containing applications that had not succeeded on the first pass, but which stayed in the running nonetheless.

Oddnesses seemed to abound. A commercial aviation trade association had applied for the .air TLD, proposing to mirror its content under .aer and .aero. One director questioned whether ICANN could really allocate ".air"; the air, after all, was a public resource. The board gave the applicant .aero instead.

Another application, from Sarnoff, proposed the .iii TLD string for a personal domain name space (that is, the TLD would issue domain names such as jonweinberg.professor.iii). Well after the Sarnoff application was placed in the basket, and reconfirmed on a second pass, Mike Roberts, ICANN's CEO, objected that the string was unacceptable because it was "unpronounceable" and without semantic meaning. (While one of ICANN's announced selection criteria had suggested a preference for strings with semantic meaning across a wide range of languages, none had indicated that the *sound* of the label when pronounced should be a factor.) Roberts urged that the application be deleted. After discussion, there seemed to be a broad consensus in favor of granting the application either in its original form, or contingent on staff's negotiating with the applicant over an alternate string.

Joe Sims, ICANN's outside counsel, then suggested that the application be denied because Sarnoff had at the last minute agreed to enter into a joint venture with another strong applicant; this created "uncertainties" that cut against granting the application. Louis Touton, ICANN's general counsel, suggested that negotiating with Sarnoff over a new string could be seen by other applicants as unfair. The board took three additional votes on the application in quick succession; ultimately it was not selected. Watching the process unfold, it was hard to avoid the conclusion that a solid proposal had faded, notwithstanding strong board support, as a result of concerted opposition from staff.

To a great extent, the board was handicapped by its self-imposed obligation to make all decisions in a single afternoon and on the fly, without further research or consultation. Faced with the question whether the proposed sponsor of a .travel TLD fully represented the travel industry, Board Chair Esther Dyson urged that the possibility that the sponsor was unrepresentative, whether it was so or not, was enough to doom the application. She explained, according to the scribe's notes, "We're not here to do everything that might make sense if we fully investigate it; we're choosing proof-of-concept domains that don't have these problems."

Perhaps the most confused moments came in connection with the decision of what character string to award in connection with the successful application from Afilias. Afilias wanted .web, but that string had long been used by another applicant, which operated a registry accessible via an alternate root. Vint Cerf, ICANN's incoming chair, was sympathetic to that other .web application; finding insufficient support for granting the other application, he urged that .web should instead be "reserved," and that Afilias should receive another string. Cerf then sparred with Touton and Sims over the questions to be voted on, Touton and Sims seeming to formulate those questions so as to favor giving Afilias .web, with Cerf doing the opposite. Several (confusing) votes followed, and Cerf prevailed; Afilias was assigned the .info TLD.

When the day was through, the ICANN board had approved the opening of negotiations with seven prospective TLD registries. It had not covered itself in glory; the new TLDs were a lackluster lot. It was hard to characterize the afternoon's decision-making process as anything but arbitrary.

Eleven of the disappointed applicants filed petitions for reconsideration. Petitioners urged, among other things, that the staff report contained gross inaccuracies; that ICANN had given applicants no meaningful opportunity to respond to the report or to make their cases; that the selection criteria were vague and subjective; that the board sandbagged applicants by rejecting applications on the basis of unannounced criteria; and that the board's consideration was arbitrary, treating similarly situated applicants differently.

ICANN rejected all of the petitions, issuing a remarkable statement that in important extent conceded the failings that petitioners complained of. That the selection criteria and the ultimate judgments were subjective, ICANN explained, was not a flaw to task it with; that subjectivity was "inherent" in the process.[12] It was "clearly articulated from the beginning of the process" that similar proposals could be treated differently.[13] Moreover, it was not a sufficient basis for reconsideration that "there were factual errors made, or there was confusion about various elements of a proposal, or each member of the board did not fully understand all the details of some of the proposals." After all, given the subjective and fact-intensive nature of the evaluation, *any* process—even one unmarred by confusion and error—would yield results on which reasonable people could differ. That reasonable people could conclude that other selections would have better advanced ICANN's goals was simply "inevitable."[14]

Moreover, ICANN continued, the board could not be faulted for departing from the announced selection criteria. Those criteria were never "intended to be a rigid formula for assessing the merits of TLD proposals"—they were simply drafting guides for the applicants. Finally, because ICANN's goal was proof of concept, it had never intended to treat "the absolute or relative merit of any application [as] the single factor determining the outcome."[15] To the extent that the board had passed over more meritorious applications in favor of less meritorious ones, that was simply irrelevant.[16]

It is hard to know what to do with such an extraordinary explanation. ICANN tells us here that the selection process it chose was so inherently subjective, so much in the nature of a crap-shoot, that there is simply no point in identifying errors in its consideration of the applications; any such errors are simply irrelevant. This statement is not accompanied by any abashedness, by any suggestion that such a process might be inherently flawed. The ad hoc, subjective nature of the process, rather, is presented as a feature and not a bug. It is presented as the only possible path available to ICANN to initiate the proof of concept. Indeed, a later ICANN statement suggested, ICANN's public trust *demands* that it add TLDs to the root only through processes like these, in which the board, with the applications before it, endeavors to make those selections that best achieve the larger public interest as the board perceives it.[17]

III   Conclusion

A number of things are notable about the history I have just told. The story begins with Jon Postel's proposal to expand the name space. That proposal contemplated hundreds of new top level domains, and an administrative process that was lightweight in two respects. First, applicants for new TLDs could get them without jumping through complicated procedural hoops. Second, the applicants would not have to satisfy onerous substantive standards. Precisely because Postel proposed to make many new TLDs available, he did not need to limit the universe of those who applied.

Postel's proposal ran into immediate opposition from business groups. They feared the consequences of quick domain name expansion for trademark owners. More broadly, players sympathetic to business concerns raised questions under the banner of "Internet stability"—if many new registries were easily formed, might not some fail? Would that dampen the consumer's enthusiasm for e-commerce? Might not some consumers be confused by the multiplicity of new domains, again making the Internet less hospitable to buying and selling?

At the same time (and largely in response to the fears stirred up by Postel's proposal and the events that followed), the United States government was restructuring the mechanisms of Internet governance. ICANN was striking, in comparison with IANA, in the increased representation it gave business interests. IANA was controlled by the technical elite; one of its functions was to serve as editor for a key series of documents generated by the Internet Engineering Task Force. By contrast, ICANN empowered business users: Its Names Council was nothing but representatives of various industry groupings. Operating in a world in which business and governments had woken up to the importance of the domain name space, and "working within the system to balance competing interests, many of which possess economic power," ICANN showed great sensitivity to business concerns.

In putting forward proposals to expand the name space, therefore, ICANN's approach was far different from Postel's. It emphasized that only a few lucky applicants would be allowed in, and only as a "proof of concept." It imposed extensive threshold requirements for even considering the application, in an attempt to ensure (in part) that no new TLD registry would fail or suffer difficulties, thus threatening "Internet stability." And it selected the lucky winners through a process designed to give it the greatest degree of control over the ultimate outcome, notwithstanding the dangers of subjectivity and arbitrariness inherent in that approach.

This paper is part of an ongoing examination of ICANN and its relationship with the top level domain registries. In a later paper, I will examine the striking parallels between ICANN's comparative process in this case and the FCC's now-abandoned comparative hearing process for broadcast licenses. Both processes are usefully examined as examples of ad hoc, situationally sensitive rather than rule-based decision making. A variety of other issues ICANN has confronted in this process are similarly familiar to lawyers familiar with FCC processes.

ICANN's selection of seven registries, further, was not the end of the story. I will examine the command-and-control regulation ICANN has imposed through its negotiation of contracts with the new registries it has chosen. The new contracts give ICANN closely detailed control over the new registries and their business models. Here, too, I will draw parallels—and note contrasts—with the FCC's experience. In many ways, I will argue, ICANN is picking the worst of the FCC history to adopt. Critics has ruthlessly criticized the FCC processes, most of which that agency has now abandoned; ICANN has effortlessly managed to surpass the worst that the FCC ever approached.

Most of ICANN's regulatory imperative derives from its decision to maintain scarcity of top level domains, rolling them out only slowly. (Once again, the parallel with the FCC is instructive.) I will assess this decision. To what extent were—and are—alternatives feasible?

Acknowledgments

I owe thanks, as always, to Jessica Litman; without her, this narrative would be even more turgid, and would have rather less to say. I was the co-chair of a working group established as part of the ICANN process to formulate recommendations regarding the deployment of new generic top-level domains. The views expressed in this article, however, are solely my own. This is a shorter version of the paper I presented at the TPRC, with nearly all of the footnotes deleted for reasons of space. The reader can find the most recent version of the longer paper, complete with footnotes, at <http://www.arxiv.org/pdf/cs.CY/0109099>.

Notes

1. In the words of Harold Feld: "ICANN recapitulates the FCC, and does it badly."

2. Brock Meeks, ICANN and the seven dwarves (Nov. 22, 2000), <http://www.msnbc.com/news/493721.asp>.

3. My reference to an IP address as "unique" is oversimplified. Techniques such as network address translation can allow a computer to function using an IP address that is unique only within that computer's local network. Most residential Internet users get their IP addresses pursuant to a dynamic allocation system under which the user may get a different address each time she logs on to her Internet service provider.

4. See Mary Stahl, RFC 1032, Domain Administrators Guide, <ftp://ftp. isi.edu/in-notes/rfc1032.txt> (1987).

5. Jon Postel, New Registries and the Delegation of International Top-level Domains, draft-postel-iana-itld-admin-02.txt (Aug. 1996), <http://sunsite.org.uk/rfc/draft-postel-iana-itld-admin-02.txt>, at secs. 5.6, 6.1.

6. See, e.g., A. Michael Froomkin, Wrong Turn in Cyberspace: Using ICANN to Route Around the APA and the Constitution, 50 Duke L.J. 17 (2000); Milton Mueller, ICANN and Internet Governance: Sorting Through the Debris of 'Self-Regulation," 1 Info 497 (1999); Craig Simon, The Technical Construction of Globalism: Internet Governance and the DNS Crisis, <http://www.rkey.com/dns/dnsdraft.html> (Oct. 1998); Jonathan Weinberg, ICANN and the Problem of Legitimacy, 50 Duke L.J. 187 (2000).

7. Management of Internet Names and Addresses, 63 Fed. Reg. 31,741, 31,746 (1988).

8. During the time period covered by this paper, key ICANN staff personnel were CEO Mike Roberts, Chief Policy Officer Andrew McLaughlin, and Vice President and General Counsel Louis Touton. Because the documents they issued on behalf of the corporation were usually unsigned, so that their individual roles could not be discerned, I will refer to them collectively here as "staff."

9. Full disclosure: I was the working group's cochair, and the author of the compromise proposal.

10. ICANN Yokohama Meeting Topic: Introduction of New Top-Level Domains (June 13, 2000), <http://www.icann.org/yokohama/new-tld-topic. htm>.

11. See Jonathan Weinberg, Broadcasting and Speech, 81 Calif. L. Rev. 1101, 1168–69 (1993).

12. Reconsideration Request 00-8 (Abacus America): Recommendation of the Committee (Mar. 5, 2001), <http://www.icann.org/committees/reconsideration/ rc00-8.htm>. The reconsideration committee incorporated its statement in Reconsideration Request 00-8 (Abacus America), by reference, into all of the reconsideration decisions it rendered in connection with the new TLD process.

13. Reconsideration Request 00-13 (Image Online Design): Recommendation of the Committee (Mar. 16, 2001), <http://www.icann.org/committees/reconsideration/rc00-13.htm>. This seems extravagant. ICANN staff did make clear at the outset that they intended the process to generate only a small number of TLDs, so that worthwhile TLD applications might not be granted. They did not, however, state that they anticipated the process to be arbitrary. The statement in ICANN's New TLD Application Instructions that "only a limited number of TLDs will be established in this round of applications, and it is likely that only applications with very high qualifications will be accepted" better exemplifies staff's initial description of the process.

14. Reconsideration Request 00-8 (Abacus America): Recommendation of the Committee, supra n. 12.

15. Reconsideration Request 00-14 (SRI International): Recommendation of the Committee (Mar. 16, 2001), <http://www.icann.org/committees/reconsideration/rc00-14.htm>.

16. Turning to more concrete process concerns, ICANN stated that the weekend and three working days between the staff report's release and the board's decision provided applicants with sufficient opportunity to respond to any errors— and all applicants, after all, were subject to the same hurried schedule. (Though ICANN repeatedly states that the process was fair, this answer does suggest that ICANN deemed it less important that the process be accurate and reliable, than that it be equally inaccurate and unreliable for all.) The three minute dog-and-pony-show, ICANN stated, was appropriate because "the opportunity to make a presentation at the public forum was simply the final step in an extensive process, available so that any last-minute questions could be asked or points made." Indeed, it "re-emphasized ICANN's commitment to maximum transparency," by making clear (if only after the fact) that all input to the process from applicants needed to have been in writing, "so that the entire Internet community would have the opportunity to read it, consider it, and respond to it."

17. In ICP-3: A Unique, Authoritative Root for the DNS (July 9, 2001), <http://www.icann.org/icp/icp-3.htm>, ICANN urges that it would be inappropriate to include any gTLD in the root where the particular gTLD has not been subjected to "tests of community support and conformance with consensus processes—coordinated by ICANN." The policy statement states that ICANN would betray the public trust were it, in introducing new TLDs, to place positive value on the fact that a particular applicant was already operating in an alternate root, for that would derogate ICANN's own selection process. ICANN may introduce a particular new gTLD only once the gTLD has been confirmed through "the community's processes," and only where doing so serves the public interest.

2

ENUM: The Collision of Telephony and DNS Policy

Robert Cannon

Introduction

ENUM marks either the convergence or collision of the public telephone network with the Internet. ENUM is an innovation in the domain name system (DNS). It starts with numerical domain names that are used to query DNS name servers. The servers respond with address information found in DNS records. This can be telephone numbers, email addresses, fax numbers, SIP addresses, or other information. The concept is to use a single number in order to obtain a plethora of contact information.

By convention, the Internet Engineering Task Force (IETF) ENUM Working Group determined that an ENUM number would be the same numerical string as a telephone number. In addition, the assignee of an ENUM number would be the assignee of that telephone number. But ENUM could work with any numerical string or, in fact, any domain name. The IETF is already working on using E.212 numbers with ENUM.

ENUM creates multiple policy problems. What impact does ENUM have upon the public telephone network and the telephone numbering resource? For example, does this create a solution or a problem for number portability? If ENUM truly is a DNS innovation, how does it square with the classic difficulties experienced with DNS and ICANN? Is ENUM, while presenting a convergence solution, also encumbered with the policy problems of both the DNS and telephony worlds?

IETF ENUM proponents suggest that ENUM needs a single unified database administered through national and international government sanctioned monopolies. The IETF took the unusual step of requesting that the International Telecommunications Union (ITU) regulate an aspect of the Internet, that is, participate and have authority over the international ENUM service provider. But this notion of establishing a new communications monopoly collides with the deregulatory efforts of the Telecommunications Act of 1996, the attempts to privatize DNS through ICANN, and U.S. policy that the Internet should be left unregulated. ENUM is an unproven innovation with no evidence of commercial viability. It faces a strongly competitive market of other directory assistance innovations and services. Proponents are asking governments to sanction one competitor over others.

ENUM offers two lessons. First, involving the government in a standards process is fraught with problems and delays. It starts with the cliché of having too many cooks in the kitchen, producing a mediocre cake at best. And it ends with a cumbersome bureaucratic process resulting in fatal delay and ultimately collapsing in upon itself. Similar efforts in the past rose to grandiose levels and failed. These include X.500 and OSI.

Second, a number by any other name remains a number. A significant portion of the DNS wars has been focused on resolving who has the right to a name. Is it first come, first serve, a trademark holder, someone using the domain name pursuant to free speech rights, or perhaps some other right? With ENUM, the question presented is who has the right to a numerical string. ENUM attempts to resolve this question by convention, concluding that the assignee of a telephone number has rights to an ENUM number. But an ENUM number is not a telephone number. A telephone number is an address used on a telephone network to reach a telephone. An ENUM number is a token used to access a database. Transferring a numerical string from one context to another does not likewise transfer the rules and regulations of the original context. Rules and regulations created for telephone numbers assume a particular purpose in a particular context; they do not apply to numerical strings in a foreign context with a different purpose. It is illogical and dangerous to transfer the policy concerning one type of number to a different type of number. This means, among other things, that the regulatory authority over telephone numbers has no more jurisdiction over ENUM numbers then when telephone numbers are used to rent videos or access savings clubs at the grocery store.

U.S. policy has been to keep information technology unregulated to permit it to innovate at the speed of the market and not at the pace of bureaucracy. Yet ENUM proponents beg for government entanglement.

It would be unprecedented for the government to sanction a monopoly for something as unproven as ENUM where the appropriateness of a government monopoly has not been demonstrated. Were such government involvement in fact approved, the delay experienced would likely be fatal to the innovation.

There are those who are strong advocates of an ENUM unified data base. An ENUM unified database can likely be achieved by private industry through some level of a joint venture devoid of government entanglement. This is the best hope for ENUM achieving the goal of a swift implementation.

ENUM

ENUM is an IETF proposed standard[1] (RFC 2916[2]) created by the IETF ENUM Working Group.[3] It is an Internet domain name system (DNS) innovation.[4] Personal contact information within DNS records can be retrieved using an ENUM number. When an ENUM number is entered, it queries a DNS name server which then responds with telephone numbers, IP telephony numbers, fax numbers, e-mail addresses, and telephone number after 5:00 p. m. on weekends.[5] It can also provide information about the priority pursuant to which the record owner wishes to be contacted. Thus, having only a single identifier, a user could acquire all of the contact information for an individual.[6]

ENUM numbers are converted by ENUM devices into domain names, and then used to query the domain name system. If an ENUM record exists, then the database produces the contact information. The ENUM device is on the Internet, the query is over the Internet, and the ENUM database is on the Internet. It can be used in conjunction with a multitude of applications on or off the Internet including telephony, email, fax, and others.[7]

Sample ENUM DNS Record:

```
$ ORIGIN 2.1.2.1.5.5.5.2.0.2.1.1.E164.foo⁸
    IN NAPTR 102 10 "u" "tel+E2U" "!^.*$!tel:+112025551212!".
    IN NAPTR 10 10 "u" "sip+E2U""!+(.*)!sip:
    johndoe@company.com!"
    IN NAPTR 100 10 "u" "mailto+E2U" "!^$!mailto:
    johndoe@company.com!".
```

The IETF ENUM WG determined that ENUM numbers would have the same value as a person's telephone number. The assignee of a telephone number would be the assignee of an ENUM number.[9] This achieves several goals. It creates a global standard form for ENUM numbers—they could be anything. It creates a standard for how ENUM numbers shall be assigned. It also means that ENUM numbers, which are domain names, are numeric (unlike most domain names, which utilize letters and words), can be entered into telephone number pads, are linguistically neutral, and can take advantage of the familiarity of the public with telephone numbers.[10]

ENUM would function as follows: A user in Washington, D.C. may wish to reach Joe.

• The user inputs into an ENUM enabled device the ENUM number 555-1212.

• The ENUM device expands the ENUM number into the same numerical string as the full E.164 number: 1-1-202-555-1212.[11]

• The ENUM device reverses the number, removes non-number symbols, and converts the number into a domain name. The device would create the ENUM number domain name <2.1.2.1.5.5.5.2.0.2.1.1.foo>.

• This domain name would then be sent to a designated ENUM name server on the Internet. A DNS query would be conducted for each zone of the domain name.[12]

• If a record exists, the database would produce the result that could, for example, direct the user first to call Joe's IP telephony number, second to contact Joe's e-mail address, or finally to call Joe's number.[13] The result would also reflect the preference of the person on how that person prefers to be contacted.[14] If no record exists, the user will receive an error message similar to receiving an error message when requesting a webpage that does not exist.[15]

• Based on the user, the person the user desires to contact, and the ENUM information provided, the communication would then be set up by other applications (not by ENUM). If the information used is a URI, an additional DNS lookup must be conducted to get the IP address.

In order for ENUM to work, there must be an ENUM enabled device. All a device would need is a bit of software, meaning any device capable of running the software that has Internet access could be enabled. The device would receive the ENUM number, convert it into a domain name, and then conduct the query. It is edge technology at either the originator's or the terminator's edge. ENUM devices would be programmed to point to a designated Internet name server where it would have access to an ENUM database. Either the vendor or the user could program the device.[16]

ENUM Administration

One of the central ENUM issues is how will the database be administered. This issue marks an area of significant contention within the ENUM community. There is strong consensus in favor of the technical aspects of the protocol, however, consensus with regard to ENUM administration does not appear to exist.

Pursuant to RFC 2916[17] and the ITU ENUM Liaison,[18] the database is to be administered in a hierarchical model with a single international database pointing to single national databases for each telephone country code, that in turn point to authorized service providers. This model is broken down into tiers, with Tier 0 being the international level, tier 1 being the national level, and tier 2 being the competitive service provider levels. The hierarchical model is being actively discussed by the ENUM industry and the ITU, and is evolving.

Tier 0: The administrative contact for the international database is the Internet Architecture Board[19] and the technical contact is RIPE NCC.[20] The international database administered by RIPE NCC will be located in the *E164.arpa* domain.[21] The ITU will supply information on the E.164 database, encourage member states to participate, indicate to RIPE-NCC who the authorized provider of a member state is (recognize the credentials of national service providers), and have a vague level of authority.[22] RIPE NCC, having been informed by the ITU what the E.164 numbers are and who should be recognized at the national level, will populate the database only as instructed and authorized by the nation (lacking authorization from a nation, the database will not be populated[23]). The RIPE-NCC database will point to the national database (a.k.a., Tier 1); it would appear that this is the limit of the scope of RIPE-NCC's role and that its database will not contain additional information.[24] Tier 0 would not know about service-specific information associated with individual ENUM numbers.[25]

Tier 1: National ENUM Service Provider are to be set up by a national regulatory authority, possibly through a procurement process.[26] It would be a government sanctioned monopoly, designated to the ITU as the Tier 1 provider.[27] The Tier 1's role is to point to the Tier 2 providers where the actual Naming Authority Pointer (NAPTR[28]) records are retained and authentication of data occurs. Tier 1 does not interact directly with end users.[29]

Tier 2–3: The lower tiers would be comprised of competitive registries who interact with customers and users. They would create, authenticate, and hold the NAPTR records.[30]

End User: Implicitly at the bottom of this model is the end-user. The end-user is the ENUM number assignee and telephone number assignee who is able to create an ENUM DNS record and enter information into the NAPTR records. As the Internet Corporation of Assigned Names and Numbers (ICANN) regulates by contract,[31] requiring all domain name registrants to agree to certain terms, ENUM registrants may be bound by certain terms and conditions of the Tier-1 ENUM service provider including dispute resolution.[32] Registrants could update their records to reflect changes, but if the information is held in the DNS NAPTR records, the information could not be updated in real time. It could only be updated at the speed of DNS refresh.[33]

This hierarchical model[34] creates an open platform where any service provider who receives authorization may participate. The full extent of what it means to be authorized and who issues the authorization is undefined and could impact on how open a system this model is. The database here would be unified and validated at Tier 1.

The rationale for this model is that it is based on the DNS and the DNS requires a single authoritative root for each node in the DNS tree.[35] If multiple roots existed, the question arises concerning how an ENUM device would know which database to look into and how an ENUM device could resolve inconsistent results from inconsistent databases. It is argued that a single root is required to ensure the integrity of ENUM.[36]

Alternative ENUM models suggest that ENUM can be provisioned as a wholly competitive service without need for a government sanctioned unified database. Detailed examination of the rational in favor of this argument will be visited in the Issues section below. In short, this contingent argues that ENUM is standardized data in an open database. Multiple ENUM services located in different domains therefore presents no significant challenge. On the occasion where the user does not know the full ENUM number, including its domain, the ENUM device can conduct a look up in all known ENUM services or the user could take advantage of a search engine. Once acquired, the information could be essentially "bookmarked" and search would not need to be repeated. Removing government regulation from this version of ENUM would make implementation faster, more flexible, and more responsive to consumers.

Directory Services Market

ENUM provides a directory service by providing a means of finding an individual through aggregated address information. The market for directory services or address services is highly competitive. Competition comes from different services, different strategies, and different protocols.

There are numerous ENUM projects. Some are essentially IETF ENUM implementations (marked by usage of a golden tree using a single top domain) and other alternative implementations.[37] All ENUM projects enter data in a standardized format into the open database DNS. These ENUM projects include an ENUM trial at *enum.org*[38] administered by Neustar,[39] the Internet-Telephony Addressing Board (I-TAB),[40] Verisign's ENUMWorld[41] and WebNum,[42] and NetNumbers.[43] Similar projects that do not use the ENUM standard include Dialnow[44] and DotPHone (.ph).[45]

There are multiple Internet directory assistance projects. Essentially, online white pages or 411, these companies acquire subscriber list information pursuant to Sec. 222 of the Telecommunications Act[46] and upload the information as a searchable database. This highly competitive market includes Switchboard, Anywho, Worldpages, 555-1212.com, MSN Reverse Look Up, Netscape White Pages Reverse Look Up, The Ultimate White Pages, Yahoo People Search, and Whowhere.

Other competitive alternatives that provide solutions to the same problem include Unified Messaging,[47] Microsofts .Net initiative,[48] and Palm Pilots and other personal information management software.[49]

There are also services that use a single address and build multiple communications applications on top of that address. If the user knows the single address, the user can use fax, telephony, messaging, or other applications to contact the desired individual at that address. This strategy is followed by SIP[50] and Instant Messaging.

What ENUM Is Not

ENUM is not an application. ENUM is a database. It is queried with an ENUM number and responds with contact data. Consequently, ENUM is not telephony. ENUM can be used is association with a multitude of applications including telephony, email,[51] fax, and others.[52]

ENUM does not do call set up.[53] The ENUM database provides data that the communication device may use to set up a call, but ENUM itself is more analogous to directory assistance.

ENUM is not a part of the public telephone network. ENUM does not interact with the SS7 network. An ENUM device is on the Internet, the ENUM query is over the Internet, and the ENUM database is a part of the Internet DNS database. Once the user obtains address information, the user may set up a call on the SS7 network, but that is separate and after the use of the ENUM protocol.

Issues

ENUM is described as a convergence technology between the PSTN and the Internet world. This can make things messy. It may mean that policy considerations must consider the implications for both the regulated PSTN world and the unregulated Internet world. In this way, ENUM could be described more as a collision than convergence, bring both the best and the worst of both worlds together.

A Number by Any Other Name . . .

Essential to ENUM is the connection of telephone numbers to ENUM numbers. This connection determines who has the right to assignment of an ENUM number and what government authority has jurisdiction over ENUM administration. If the connection is, however, broken, ENUM will be confronted with multiple challenging problems.

An ENUM number is a domain name. It could be anything that a domain name could be. The IETF ENUM Working Group was attempting to solve the problem of how to find devices on the Internet with two parameters. First, the IETF ENUM WG wanted to be able to do this using a numeric keypad. This limits an ENUM number to a numerical string. But it could still be any numerical string. Next, the IETF ENUM WG wanted to take advantage of phone numbers.[54] But the IETF ENUM WG could have selected other types of numbers, as is demonstrated by current ENUM work considering the use of E.212 numbers with ENUM.[55] The IETF ENUM WG determined, by convention, an assignee of an ENUM number would use the same numerical string as the assignee's public telephone number.

An ENUM number, however, is not itself a telephone number. A telephone number is an address used on the telephone network to reach a telephone.[56] An ENUM number is not an address. There is no communications device that is assigned and can be reached by using an ENUM number. You cannot set up a communications with an ENUM number itself. An ENUM number is a "token" used to query a database. This is the only function of an ENUM number. The database contains the addresses that can then be used in communications.

A numerical string standing by itself is a numerical string and is nothing more out of context. It becomes a type of number in a particular context. 5550100 is a numerical string. Use this number to reach a telephone on the telephone network and it is a telephone number. Use this number to access money in a bank account and it is a bank account number. Use this number to access an ATM and it is a PIN. What type of number a numerical string is, depends upon the context in which it is used. Outside of that context, it is no longer that type of number. Simply because two numerical strings have the same value does not make them the same type of number.

Good examples are other databases tied to telephone numbers such as grocery store savings plans and video rental membership. If you forget your card you can give the cashier your phone number and you have access to the relevant the database. The mere use of a phone number in a database does not give the FCC jurisdiction over grocery store savings plans or video clubs.[57] The reason why is, in that given context, the numerical string has the same value as a telephone number but is, in fact, a savings plan number. The use of the telephone number serves as a pneumonic device but has no further connection to the telephone network. There is a difference between something *being* a telephone number and *having the same value as* (same numerical string) a telephone number.

Members of the ENUM industry implicitly recognize this point. Documents that describe ENUM discuss it as transferring one number into another number. The industry repeatedly uses such works as mapping,[58] tied,[59] translating,[60] transforming,[61] and converting[62] to describe this process. ENUM is also described as a "telephone number-based Internet directory service."[63] All of this recognizes the process of taking one numerical string out of its original context and using it in a new context.

The argument that ENUM numbers and telephone numbers are distinct is supported by the fact that the two types of numbers are operationally distinct. Telephone numbers can operate without ENUM; telephone numbers can cease to operate regardless of ENUM. ENUM numbers, which can be anything, can technically be created without a corresponding telephone number. An ENUM number can be deleted from the DNS without an affect on the telephone number. Telephone numbers are used on the telephone network; ENUM numbers are used on the Internet.

This is highlighted by one of the primary issues for ENUM: what happens when a telephone number is disconnected? The ENUM industry is working hard on developing relationships so that ENUM service providers can be informed when a telephone number is terminated.[64] If the numbers were the same, then when a telephone number ceased to exist, the ENUM number could no longer function. The fact that the ENUM number can technically live on when no corresponding telephone number is in existence demonstrates that they are distinct. The connection between telephone numbers and ENUM numbers has to be established by convention because it is not established by law or technical requirement.

The reasons why the distinction is important are jurisdiction, authority, and rights to a number. If ENUM numbers are telephone numbers, then they possibly fall under the jurisdiction of telephone authorities. If, however, ENUM numbers are not telephone numbers, then they do not necessarily fall under the jurisdiction of telephone authorities. In addition, there would be no right to an ENUM number based on being the assignee of a telephone number. This could complicate conflicts over ENUM number assignments and who has authority to set up Tier 1 ENUM providers.

This is an intriguing issue of rights to numbers. Rights to one type of number do not transfer to another type of number simply because the numerical strings are the same. Otherwise, rules and regulations concerning one type of number in one context developed with a particular history and concerns, would be applied to foreign numerical strings and in alien contexts. The rules and regulations of one situation would be expanded to reach contexts never anticipated or intended. Well founded restrictions on one type of number could be irrational in another context. An individual with one type of number could control the use of that numerical string in other contexts, extracting fees or concessions for its use. This could create a dangerous precedent and have far reaching ramifications.

DNS Issues

The core issues raised by ENUM are issues of administration of the DNS database. The core issue for a national government to resolve is whether to sanction a national Tier 1 service provider and related administrative issues.[65]

Unified Database

The first issue raised is whether ENUM requires a unified global database, also known as a "global tree." Proponents of a unified database argue that if there are multiple databases, an ENUM device would not know which to query. Furthermore, there is a risk of incompatible records in different databases.[66]

Even if it is assumed that a unified database is needed, one already exists. ENUM is a DNS innovation and the DNS is a unified database. Any user anywhere in the world can query a DNS name server for www.cybertelecom.org and they will get the appropriate result. The DNS is both unified and global. Thus, the question presented by ENUM is whether there needs to be a unified database *inside* the unified database of DNS.

Pursuant to the ENUM protocol, data would be entered into the open DNS in a standardized format. Since the data exists in a standard format across open, interconnected, distributed databases, searches of that data are relatively easy. If there were multiple ENUM databases, and if a user did not know which one to search, an opportunity would be created for metasearch engines to be created, creating an ability to find the data in any known database. Alternatively, an ENUM resolver could query known ENUM databases to determine if records exist.[67] NetNumbers indicates that it already has such a publicly available resolver.[68]

As consumers could access the information in the open DNS at multiple ENUM service providers as easily as a single provider, there is nothing that would drive the consumers to use only a single provider. Network effect is a factor for ENUM as a whole (for ENUM to work there has to be overall network effect), but not for individual competitors. In other words, if ACME ENUM has only a few thousand records, but is reachable through metasearch engines, a resolver, or the use of extensions, then ACME could have as competitive a place in the market as large service providers.

In addition, if the issue with multiple databases is knowing which database to search, the answer would seem obvious: tell the ENUM device which database to search. One possible way in which this could be achieved is by adding extensions to numbers. 5551212#36 could mean NetNumbers where 5551212#46 could mean NeuStar. Since the device now knows which database to look in, this is no longer an issue.[69]

Furthermore, ENUM databases, due to network effect, have an incentive to cooperate. ENUM has more value if it has more data; a means of getting more data is to cooperate with other ventures and create open data platforms.[70]

While it is not clear that a Golden Tree approach is necessary,[71] such an approach could have advantages. A centralized database could arguably facilitate data verification, authentication, and integrity. Through a central database, only data that met specifications would be entered. Unverified data would be rejected and only one record for a given number would be created. Competitive service providers would be interconnected through the unified database.

Additionally, a joint partnership could have the advantage of branding and joint marketing. A joint effort can be marketed to the public as the service endorsed widely by industry participants.

A disadvantage of a global unified database is the tremendous amount of global coordination required in order to succeed. There could be 150+ Tier-1 service providers that need to be established and coordinated. The effort involved in order to achieve coordination may result in delay in ENUM implementation and administration.[72] An additional disadvantage is possible restraints on creativity and innovation. As ENUM is administered is highly centralized through a global system, innovations could only be achieved through that centralized structure. This reduces the ability of a competitive process to create new solutions that users might desire.[73]

Whether the Golden Tree approach is adopted may not immediately rise to a public policy concern if further questions are not reached. In other words, if a Golden Tree does not require government sanction, then numerous concerns are alleviated. However, if industry continues to press for a government sanctioned Tier 1 provider, it must be recognized that the election of the Golden Tree approach is one of preference and not necessity. In other words, selecting a unified approach which requires regulatory intervention and the creation of a government sanctioned monopoly is a path of choice and it could be avoided.

E164.arpa?

If it is concluded that there should be a unified database, where should that database be located?[74] RFC 2916 indicates that IANA should delegate the domain name *e164.arpa* pursuant to the recommendation of Internet Architecture Board (IAB).[75] Pursuant to IAB recommendation, *e164.arpa* is to be technically administered by RIPE NCC.[76] The IETF selected *e164.arpa* as the location of the ENUM database because *.arpa* is dedicated to infrastructure issues and is well managed, stable and secure.[77]

France has objected to this arrangement and argued that the administration should be done under *e164.int* under ITU authority. France argued that management of ENUM must be subordinate to E.164 management, and that E164 management is under the authority of the ITU. Thus, the French argue that "the most coherent approach is obviously to use a suffix managed by the ITU."[78]

Robert Shaw of the ITU has argued that the ENUM DNS name servers need to be "dispersed around the world." He then points out that 8 of the 9 *.arpa* name servers are deployed in the United States and are not dispersed around the world.[79]

Originally *.arpa* was the domain of the U.S. Defense Advanced Research Projects Agency (DARPA). On April 14, 2000, DARPA disassociated itself with the *.arpa* domain with the understanding that *.arpa* would be dedicated to infrastructure (along with *.int*) under the authority of the Internet Assigned Number Authority (IANA),[80] which is currently a part of ICANN.[81] There was an effort to rename ARPA domain as the *Address and Routing Parameter Area* in an attempt to distinguish it from U.S. DARPA.[82] IANA administers *.arpa* in compliance with IETF protocols.[83] *.arpa* has been traditionally used for reverse-DNS lookup.[84] U.S. industry notes that *.arpa,* unlike *.int,* meets the security, performance, and reliability requirements of an infrastructure domain as set forth in IETF RFC 2870.[85]

.int was originally an infrastructure domain along with *.arpa.*[86] Currently it is dedicated to international treaty organizations.[87] .int is not under the control of the ITU.[88] Placing ENUM under *.int* does not necessarily place it under the control of the ITU or anyone else.

The selection of TLD itself may not be significant. The most compelling argument in favor of *.arpa* is that the infrastructure related to it is superior. But the infrastructure related to *.int* could be upgraded if necessary (assuming someone bore the cost). Perhaps the most compelling difference is one of appearance. If ENUM is under *.int*, there is an appearance that it is under greater ITU control. If it is under *.arpa*, there is an appearance that it is under greater IETF control. But under ENUM as currently envisioned, the user will be aware of the ENUM number, not the TLD. In the final analysis, this issue may be one of sound and fury, signifying very little.

Government Sanctioned Monopoly?

If there is to be a unified database, how will it be administered and does it require a government sanctioned monopoly? The IETF ENUM model calls for ITU involvement at Tier 0 and national governments setting up Tier 1 providers. Even if it is assumed that Tier 0 and Tier 1 providers are necessary, government sanctioning of these providers would be inappropriate.

The possible benefits of creating a government sanctioned monopoly must be weighted against the costs. Such monopolies impact competition in their market; normally they eliminate competition in their market. This, in turn, has an impact on innovation and responding to consumer needs. The monopoly service becomes encumbered with government entanglement, dramatically reducing the speed of deployment and innovation. Centralized decision making in compliance with federal administrative law is slow and less responsive to needs. In addition, there is the cost of the bureaucracy and the lawyers and lobbyists employed to interact with that bureaucracy.[89]

Particularly problematic is the potential delay resulting from government involvement.[90] In order to implement a U.S. government sanctioned ENUM service, there must be (1) legislative authority, (2) regulation, and (3) a government procurement process. This could result in multiple years of delay in which alternatives could make the government sanctioned ENUM implementation obsolete. In addition, further evolution in ENUM policy would likewise be encumbered by government process.

At the international level, NetNumbers points out that "it is simply time consuming and difficult to coordinate the selection of Tier-1 ENUM service providers access 200+ ITU Member States."[91] The resources dedicated to "achieving consistent policies regarding registration procedures, conflict resolution, disclosure of registrant information, etc."[92] may significantly impede progress of ENUM in the International arena.

The issue of the delay caused by the need for government involvement may be one of the most insurmountable problems for ENUM.

Technological Viability

ENUM is not a final IETF standard; it is a proposed standard.[93] A proposed standard is a standard on paper that has not been tested or tried. Although it is a stable standard, it is subject to change based on further experience. An RFC becomes a final "Internet Standard" when it has a significant implementation, is operationally successful, and has a "high degree of technical maturity."[94] ENUM, as of yet, has not demonstrated that it is a mature technology. Government sanctioning of a standard that is not final would be unusual.

Commercial Viability

Whether ENUM is likely to be commercially viable is less then certain. There are no known consumer studies concerning whether ENUM is a service that consumers desire. There has been limited trial market deployments.[95] Even if ENUM were to be viable, there has been no study on what the market penetration might be (would it be widely deployed or useful only to a limited niche market) or whether the viability might be short lived.

Conversely, there are several indicators that suggest that ENUM may have difficulty being commercially viable. The primary concern is privacy; people may not want all of their contact information aggregated in a single open space. Similarly, ENUM is mono dimensional; an ENUM number goes in and all of the contact information comes out, without flexibility or further alternatives. Alternatives, such as the proposed Microsoft Hailstorm offers greater consumer empowerment, offering greater control over what information will be released to different queries of the system. Based on privacy concerns, alternatives could be more compelling then ENUM's rigid option.

The second factor is network effect; ENUM will not be valuable unless a large number of individuals register ENUM numbers. But until there is a large number of registrations, there were be a low incentive to register with ENUM (a catch-22). Likewise, the numerous competitors to ENUM challenge its possibility for success. Even if ENUM enjoys a degree of success, it is unclear whether it will continue to enjoy such success. Telephones are becoming increasingly intelligent; ENUM's restraints, such as the limitation to the numeric keypad, may make it antiquated.[96] There is a possibility that ENUM seeks to solve yesterday's problem.

Further difficulty could be experienced internationally, where several countries have expressed concern over IP telephony bypass of the public telephone network and sought to bar such bypass. As ENUM could be perceived as facilitating bypass, it could be expected that several countries might bar ENUM, limiting its network effect and thus commercial viability.

The commercial viability of ENUM is not established and may even be doubtful. It would therefore be imprudent for a government to sanction a monopoly for a service where its viability is in question.

Directory Assistance Competition

ENUM is a directory assistance service. It provides a solution to the problem of how to find a means of communicating with an individual. As noted above, the directory assistance market is highly competitive.

ENUM faces competition from such powerful market players as Microsoft, AOL, VeriSign, and Palm Pilot.[97] A golden tree approach to ENUM would likely have to compete with private implementations of ENUM[98] (NetNumbers has been commercially launched since November of 2000 and has acquired 14 partners without any need of government sanctioning[99]). ENUM also faces competition from SIP, Instant Messaging, and TRIP. This competitive market gives users the ability to sort out which services are the most useful and compelling. Endorsement by the government of one competitor over all others would distort the market, be inappropriate, and determine market winners through regulation instead of competition.

ITU Involvement

IETF presentations have indicated that all countries must address the same issues for ENUM.[100] There is no further explanation of why this is so. Given the wide diversity of regulatory and market environments, it would seem that any requirement that national tier 1 providers address ENUM issues in exactly the same way would be unnecessary, inaccurate, and cause significant delay while coordination is resolved.

The IETF is cooperating with the ITU partly because the ITU is the authority for the E.164 numbering system. Originally, as stated in the ENUM RFC, the role of the ITU was limited:

Names within this zone are to be delegated to parties according to the ITU recommendation E.164. The names allocated should be hierarchic in accordance with ITU Recommendation E.164, and the codes should assigned in accordance with that Recommendation.[101]

The role was limited to the fact that country codes in *e164.arpa* are to comport with the ITU E.164 Recommendation. The ITU had no authority pursuant to this text; it was not asked to do anything.

In October 2000, the ITU released the *Liaison to IETF/ISOC on ENUM*.[102] This Liaison requires national governments to designate to the ITU their Tier 1 service provider. Thus the ITU would act as an international ENUM gate keeper and credential recognizer. The Liaison also appears to attempt to obligate any ENUM effort, whether part of the golden tree or not, to comply with ITU direction.[103]

In June of 2001, Robert Shaw recommended an even further role for the ITU, suggesting that the ITU should be responsible for outsourcing the responsibilities of administering the Tier 0 service provider and "define and implement administrative procedures that coordinate delegations of E.164 numbering resources into these name servers."[104]

One explanation for ITU involvement is the concern on the part of the IETF and RIPE that it does not want to be put into the position of determining who is the appropriate authority for an E164 code. If the ITU recognizes the credentials of an entity as the proper authority for that code, that relieves the IETF and RIPE of the risk of getting involved in skirmishes over who the proper authorities are.

The *ITU Liaison* design does not appear necessary. As articulated in RFC 2916, ENUM requires receiving the data of what E.164 country codes map to what countries. Other than this public available information that does not require ITU action or authority, there appears to be no need for ITU authority or involvement.

Much of the ITU's involvement is based on the premise that ENUM are telephone numbers, and the ITU is the authority over the E.164 standard. As demonstrated above, ENUM numbers are not telephone numbers.

The benefit of the RIPE NCC acquiring a gatekeeper must be weighed against the costs. There are other means by which this can be achieved. RIPE NCC could set forth the criteria for the representatives it will recognize. For example, RIPE NCC could indicate that the head of a nation's ITU delegation must specify the Tier 1 ENUM provider to RIPE NCC. The nation would interact directly with RIPE NCC without the ITU intermediary.

The relationship between the IETF and ITU is one of mutual recognition. The ITU Liaison recognizes the IETF effort and the IETF in turn recognizes ITU authority. By such recognition, the IETF ENUM effort is set apart from other private ENUM projects. Indeed, the ITU has opposed ENUM efforts that do not recognize the need for the ITU.[105] Mutual recognition is an insufficient justification for ITU authority and has a negative impact on competition.

Joint Venture

If governments do not sanction ENUM service providers, the ENUM industry itself could cooperate and set up a unified tree ENUM project without the government. This could, for example, be a joint venture.[106] However, one concern with such cooperation would be antitrust concerns.

NeuStar has cursorily concluded that there is no anti trust concern.[107] An antitrust analysis is beyond the scope of this paper. However, it is worth noting that the issue exists.

Conclusion

The question of whether ENUM should have government sanctioned monopoly providers is in the historical context of the deregulatory environment of the Telecommunications Act of 1996, the efforts to privatize the DNS through the work of ICANN, and the U.S.'s policy position that Internet issues are outside the jurisdiction of ICANN. The ENUM question runs directly into U.S. policy in the area of IP Telephony and ICAIS where the U.S. has been defending the notion countries will experience the greatest benefit from high tech innovation if they leave these markets unregulated. In an age where the government is embarked in a tireless battle to tear down monopoly positions in the market, ENUM asks that it be blessed with monopoly status.

Historically, the government sets up two types of monopolies: production monopolies or standards monopolies. Production monopolies are typified by AT&T in the 1930s where, in the opinion of the government, there was an efficiency in only have one company produce the service.[108] Standards require government sanction where there is something about the standard that compels sanctioning. The North American Numbering Plan (NANP) is a standard that requires unique assignment of telephone numbers. There can be only one.

ENUM fits within neither of these situations. The directory assistance market is competitive. The barrier to entry is low as is the risk of monopolization. Conversely, sanctioning one competitor over others could thwart innovation and service to the consumer. Likewise, ENUM is not a standard that requires government sanction.

The ENUM industry has already made contingency plans, in the event that the U.S. government fails to act, to implement ENUM domestically through an ENUM forum. They have conceded that government sanctioning is not necessary to make this succeed. The cost of having the government involved will like be multiple years of delay, giving alternatives first mover advantage and making that delay fatal to ENUM. Not only is government sanctioning of ENUM inappropriate, it would also probably assure that ENUM would never be a commercial success.

International Administration
If there is to be a government sanctioned unified database, then policy considerations about how that will be implemented will need to be considered. Internationally, the administrative contact for the Tier 0 provider at *e164.arpa* domain is the IAB and the technical contact is RIPE NCC. But the authority of the IAB and RIPE NCC is not clear. At the national levels, the Tier 1 service provider would have authority derived from the national government. RIPE NCC and the IAB, however, have no international or national authority. This raises questions such as From where is their authority derived; To whom are they accountable; How will their ENUM work be funded; How would disputes be resolved; How would they behave in the event of war or national disaster; How would they be protected from litigation or local process (i.e., search warrants or wiretaps); How would they be open and transparent; How would they be responsive to member states; How would they resolve new policy questions; Who would have the authority to resolve those questions; and How will reliability be assured.[109]

Unless the authority for the Tier 0 provider is properly established, it could make ENUM vulnerable to continuous challenges and problems. It may be appropriate to consider whether the documentation behind *.arpa* and the delegation of *E164.arpa* to IAB and RIPE NCC is sufficient to be legally stable. If ENUM becomes essential to communications, it would be in the public interest to ensure its full stability and reliability.

DNS Conflict Resolution
How will potential conflicts between ENUM numbers be resolved? In the DNS, ICANN regulates by contract, requiring domain name registrants to agree to be bound by the Uniform Dispute Resolution Process before WIPO. Indeed, NeuStar has suggested that ENUM registrants comply with ICANN's Uniform Dispute Resolution Process.[110] As ENUM numbers are domain names, it is possible that this would be required. A NetNumber's IETF Internet Draft suggests that ENUM number assignees should be bound by terms and conditions of Tier 1 service providers, including dispute resolution.[111] Like ICANN, this would be top down regulation through contract.

Hijacking, Cybersquatting, and Data Authentication

There are several identified naming and fraud problems. These include hijacking, cybersquatting, eavesdropping, and denial of service attacks.[112]

Hijacking or redirection of communication: ENUM numbers query the DNS database for contact information. If access to the NAPTR records is compromised, a third party could alter the contact information. This could result in redirection of traffic away from the desired end point.[113] An example of this would be an ENUM number for a popular call center for the ACME company. The BETA company fraudulently causes the ENUM record to be revised, changing the SIP addresses from ACME to BETA. Now communications go to the BETA call center and BETA attempts to steal ACME's customers.

Eavesdropping: Similar to redirection of traffic, eavesdropping permits the traffic to go through to the desired end point, but only after going through a third party.[114] In this way, the third party can monitor all communications using the ENUM number. For example, communications from CHARLIE to ACME would go through BETA first.

Denial of service: If a company becomes dependent upon traffic directed to it through its ENUM number, and if the security of the ENUM record is compromised, a third party could alter the ENUM record data and effectively block all traffic to the company. This could essentially result in a denial of service attack.

A number of these problems, although not necessarily all, are covered by existing law. For example, if someone hijacked ENUM records, the individual could be in violation of *The Identity Theft and Assumption Deterrence Act*.[115]

In order to respond to these concerns, ENUM services will need to authenticate users and the data submitted. The IETF ENUM convention, again, is that the assignee of a telephone number should be the assignee of an ENUM number. This means that a user's telephone information would need to be authenticated. This could be achieved in a number of ways.

• Directory assistance information for telephone numbers.[116]

• Open Network Architecture, under Computer III, where the Bell Operating Companies are arguably under an obligation to provide this information to enhanced service providers.[117]

• Line Information Database (LIDB).[118]

• Automatic Number Identification where the signaling in the network itself will confirm the callers identity.[119]
• The phone number itself can be called.
• The registrant could be required to show a phone bill.[120]
• Independent authentication or verification through commercial verification services.[121]

There is no indication that currently existing means of authenticating telephone number information is insufficient. In other words, there is no indication that new regulations facilitating assignment are necessary.

Telephone Number Issues
ENUM is a DNS innovation. ENUM numbers are not telephone numbers even though they have the same numerical string as telephone numbers. ENUM presents no telephone number administration issue and will not change the numbering plan.[122]

Numbering Assignment
ENUM does not affect telephone number assignment. Assignment of public telephone numbers is conducted through the appropriate public telephone authorities. Nothing about ENUM changes this. For all practical purposes, the public telephone network authority does not even have to know that ENUM exists.

Telephone numbers are assigned to telephone network devices so that people can reach them on the telephone network. Assignment of a telephone number for use off of the telephone network makes no sense. If the numerical string is not used on the telephone network, then it is no longer a telephone number. One could no more meaningfully assign a telephone number solely for ENUM purposes than one could assign a telephone number to identify an elephant.

By convention, ENUM numbers are to be assigned according to correlating telephone number assignment. Only assigned telephone numbers would be eligible for ENUM registration. Unassigned telephone numbers would not be assigned.[123] However, if ENUM numbers were assigned that correlate to unassigned telephone numbers, nothing about the assignment would bind the NANP. The assignment of the ENUM number 5551212 to ACME does not give ACME rights to that numerical sting in other contexts; it does not give ACME rights to 5551212 as a telephone number. If the telephone authority assigned 5551212 to BETA, ACME would have no legal rights to challenge this assignment. This is, in effect, the flip side of the argument that ENUM numbers are not telephone numbers. Not only do telephone number regulations not apply to ENUM, but ENUM number assignments do not apply to and do not bind telephone number assignment.

As noted, ENUM numbers and telephone numbers are operationally distinct. If an ENUM number is assigned that correlates to an unassigned telephone number, the ENUM number will still work. The ENUM records would have whatever contact information belongs to the registrant. The fact that the registrant does not have the correlating telephone number does not affect this. Furthermore, as the ENUM query is done entirely over the Internet and not in the telephone signaling network, it would not affect the telephone network.

Slamming and Cramming

Fraudulent alternations of ENUM records are a concern. However, slamming and cramming, as defined by the FCC, are not. Slamming is the changing of a user's service provider without authorization (i.e., change of long distance service). Cramming is the adding of services without authorization. Neither involves altering the telephone number (the address information) of the user. A person can be slammed (change long distance from AT&T to MCI) and crammed (adding service of call waiting) and no information in ENUM will be changed. Conversely, all of the information in ENUM can be changed without slamming or cramming. ENUM records contain addresses and not information about the services provided for those addresses. The related issues are hijacking, cybersquatting, and DOS attacks, discussed above.[124]

Number Portability

The IETF has stated that ENUM does not create number portability nor does it create a number portability problem.[125] The assignment of an ENUM number is based on assignment of a telephone number. ENUM therefore needs to authenticate the assignee of a telephone number. Some ENUM supporters assume that authentication will be done by the LEC that serves the telephone customer.[126] If the customer ports the number to another LEC, the source for authentication changes. When a number is ported from Carrier A to Carrier B, Carrier B becomes the holder of the customer information and can verify assignment.[127] AT&T argues that this makes number portability an ENUM issues.

This is incorrect. First, the AT&T scenario describes how number portability affects ENUM, not how ENUM affects number portability. The act of porting a number would change the information source for ENUM, but nothing about telephone number portability has changed.

In addition, as noted above,[128] there are multiple means of verifying number information. The assumption that the LEC serving the customer will be the ENUM source of authentication is not necessarily true.

The ITU is studying the implications of ENUM for number portability; it is believed that the ITU's work will not impact the IETF's ENUM work.[129]

Non-E164 Numbers (i.e., 911, 711, 411)

How will ENUM handle non-E164 numbers, such as a 911 call? By design, non E.164 numbers would be handled by the device prior to calling the ENUM protocol. If, for example, 911 is dialed, the CPE would set up the call without dipping into the ENUM database.[130] A modern phone is a collection of multiple protocols and programs; not every program is used with each use of the phone. In the case of a 911 call, the ENUM protocol would never be used.

NANP Number Shortage and New Area Codes

ENUM has no direct impact on the numbering resource;[131] numbering resources are not assigned to ENUM service providers. However, there could be some anticipated indirect impacts.

An indirect pressure could be if ENUM were successful. If ENUM is successful, if many people want ENUM records, and if the one way to have an ENUM record is to have a telephone number, this could create a demand for telephone numbers. Currently a house may have one number but 4 occupants. If each occupant wants an ENUM record, would this mean that the house would now want 4 phone numbers? This could create a drain on the numbering resource.

In addition, ENUM records are frequently referred to as permanent. The assignment of telephone numbers is not. If an individual is known by that individual's ENUM record, that individual may not want to give up the phone number associated with that record. Thus, if the individual sets up a record based on a Virginia phone number, but then moves to California, there is an incentive to keep the subscription Virginia phone number and not recycle it into the numbering pool. This too could create a new demand upon the resource.

Carrier Selection

ENUM is not about carrier selection.[132] The ENUM database would be populated with address data of various types. Information about the carrier is not included and not relevant. In other words, if the ENUM record reflects that Joe should be reached long distance on a regular telephone at 703-555-1212, it makes no difference in the context of ENUM whether that call is carried by AT&T, MCI or Sprint.

Telecom Bypass

IETF presentations indicate that ENUM is not about telecom bypass.[133] This is uncertain and indeed contradicted by other IETF presentations.[134] Enabling ENUM seems like an excellent way to provide the originating party options on how to set up the communications; the originating party now has a selection of networks to select from and can now bypass networks the originating party does not desire to use.

Privacy

ENUM has the potential to aggregate a tremendous amount of contact information behind a single identifier. This is likely to raise significant concerns.[135] ENUM has been described as an opt-in system.[136] However, there is nothing in the protocol that indicates that ENUM should be an opt-in. Nor is there any known technical reason why it would be limited to an opt in system. Much would depend upon individual business plans. Three business plans can be imagined. ENUM may be implemented at the corporate level so that everyone on a corporate network will have access to contact information and an enhanced ability to contact other people on the network—employees would have no *option* on whether to participate. Second, ENUM may be implemented by a major network as individuals subscribe. One can imagine AOL creating ENUM records as individuals subscribe, utilizing ENUM as a means for members to contact each other. This could be an *opt-out* scenario. Finally, owners of

ENUM enabled wireless telephones could, on an individual basis, set up ENUM records. This could be an *opt-in* situation.

There is no limit to the scope of personal information that could be included in the ENUM database. It is conceivable that it could include such things as social security numbers, drivers license numbers, or credit card numbers. No known analysis has been conducted concerning how ENUM complies with the EC Policy on Privacy and Data Protection.[137] Nor has an analysis of privacy implications been provided by privacy public interest organizations or the U.S. Federal Trade Commission.

Conclusion

ENUM has the potential to be a tremendous innovation. Then again, so do many other innovations such as Instant Messaging, SIP, PalmPilots, and the multiple other directory assistance services. The key policy consideration that ENUM presents is whether it should have government entanglement. The answer is no. Not only would it be contrary to pro-competitive policy, not only is there no justification for a government sanctioned monopoly, but government involvement would likely be fatal to the ENUM effort itself, injecting delay and encumbering the project with bureaucracy. The U.S. Government has long held the policy that it should stay out of the way of the innovation in the highly competitive information technology market; this policy should be maintained.

Disclaimer: Views expressed are probably those of Robert Cannon and certainly are not necessarily those of anyone else, including, but not limited to, Robert Cannon's employer.

Notes

1. *See* S. Bradner, IETF RFC 2026, The Internet Standards Process—Revision 3 (October 1996) (hereinafter RFC 2026) (explaining IETF process and difference between proposed, draft, and Internet standards), *at* <http://www.ietf.org/ rfc/rfc2026.txt>.

2. P. Faltstrom, IETF RFC 2916, E.164 number and DNS (September 2000) (hereinafter RFC 2916), *at* http://www.ietf.org/rfc/rfc2916.txt. *See also* Report of the Department of State ITAC-T Advisory Committee Study Group A Ad Hoc on ENUM (Jul. 6, 2001) (hereinafter Ad Hoc ENUM Report) (presenting US industry views to US State Department concerning implementation of ENUM), *at* <http://www.cybertelecom.org/library/enumreport.htm>.

3. *See* IETF ENUM Working Group Charter (last visited August 14, 2001), *at* <http://www.ietf.org/html.charters/enum-charter.html>.

4. *See* Ad Hoc ENUM Report, *supra* note 2, Sec. 2 (stating ENUM is a protocol whereby "'Domain Name System (DNS) can be used for identifying available services connected to one E.164 number.'"), *at* <http://www.cybertelecom.org/ library/enumreport.htm>; Contribution of NeuStar, Inc., US Study Group A Ad Hoc, ENUM Questions, p. 5 (March 23, 2001) (hereinafter NeuStar, Inc., US Study Group A Ad-Hoc,) (stating "ENUM is a DNS-based service"); NeuStar, ENUM Frequently Asked Questions, FAQ–7 (n.d.) (hereinafter NeuStar FAQ) (stating "This is a DNS-based system. . ."), *at* <http://www.enum.org/information/files/enum_faq.pdf>; S. Lind, IETF Informational Internet Draft, ENUM Call Flows for VoIP Interworking, para 2 (Nov. 2000) (hereinafter Lind, Callflows) (stating "ENUM provides the capability to translate an E.164 Telephone Number into an IP address or URI using the Domain Name System (DNS)"), *at* <http://www.ietf.org/internet-drafts/draft-lind-enum-callflows-01.txt>; Penn Pfautz, James Yu, IETF Informational Draft, ENUM Administrative Process, Sec. 1 (March 2001) (hereinafter Pfautz, ENUM Administrative Process) (stating "after all it is a domain name that is being registered"), *at* <http://www.ietf.org/drafts/draft-pfautz-yu-enum-adm-01.txt>. *See also* Richard Shockey, IETF-ENUM ITU-T Workshop for International Regulators, slide 7 (January 17, 2001) (hereinafter Shockey, ITU-T) (explaining reason for placing ENUM in DNS is "It's there. . . It works. . . It's global. . . It scales . . . It's fast . . . It's open."); A. Brown, G. Vaudreuil, IETF Internet Draft, ENUM Service Reference Model, Sec. 5.1 (Feb. 23, 2001) (hereinafter, Brown, ENUM Service Reference Model) (stating "The Internet Domain Name System provides an ideal technology for the first-tier directory due to its hierarchical structure, fast connectionless queries, and distributed administrative model."), *at* <http://www.ietf.org/internet-drafts/draft-ietf-enum-operation-02.txt>.

5. Ad Hoc ENUM Report, *supra* note 2, Sec. 6.1, *at* <http://www.cybertelecom. org/library/enumreport.htm>.

6. *See* Lind, Callflows, *supra* note 4, para 2 (noting ability to change contact information without changing ENUM number).

7. In addition, it has been discussed that instead of having addressing information in the NATPR record, the NAPTR would point to a third-party database such as the LDAP database.

8. The use of "foo" as a TLD is an informal IETF convention indicating that the TLD is unspecified. *See* D. Eastlake, C. Manros, E. Rayond, IETF Information RFC 3092, Etymology of "Foo" (April 1, 2001) (explaining origins and use of term "foo" in IETF documents; "foo" is used "as a sample name for absolutely anything, esp. programs and files."), *at* <http://www.ietf.org/rfc/rfc3092.txt>.

9. Several presentations describe the purpose of ENUM as being a means of finding a device on the Internet using a telephone number. *See* Shockey, ITU-T, *supra* note 4, Slide 5; ENUM.ORG > Welcome Page (visited March 27, 2001) ("ENUM was developed as a solution to the question of how to find services on

the Internet using only a telephone number, and how telephones, which have an input mechanism limited to twelve keys on a keypad, can be used to access Internet services.") *at* <http://www.enum.org>; Patrik Faltstrom, ENUM Technical Issues, ITU ENUM Work Shop, slide 12 (Jan 17, 2001) (hereinafter Faltstrom, ENUM Technical Issues). However, the ENUM database can contacted personal and contact information for all types of devices and locations, not just Internet devices.

10. *See* NeuStar FAQs, *supra* 4, FAQ-1 (stating ENUM was designed to permit access to Internet services using a telephone keypad), *at* <http://www.enum.org/ information/files/enum_faq.pdf>; Richard Shockey, IETF-ENUM SGA-Workshop on ENUM, slide 9 (n.d.) (hereinafter Shockey, SGA).

11. E.164 is the international telephone numbering plan administered by the ITU. *See* Recommendation E.164/I.331 (05/97)—The International Public Tele-communications Numbering Plan, *at* <http://www.itu.int/itudoc/itu-t/rec/ e/e164.html>; Robert Shaw, ITU, Global ENUM Implementation, DTI ENUM Workshop, Slide 3 (June 5, 2001) (hereinafter Shaw, DTI ENUM Workshop), *at* <http://www.itu.int/infocom/ enum/dtijune501/dti-june–5–2001–1.PPT>; Robert Shaw, ITU, ENUM Imple-mentation, ICANN Governmental Advisory Committee, Slide 3 (1–2 June 2001) (hereinafter Shaw, ICANN), *at* <http://www.itu.int/infocom/enum/ GACjune1201/gac-june–2–2001–1.PPT>.

12. *See* Brown, ENUM Service Reference Model, *supra* note 4, Sec. 6.1, *at* <http://www.ietf.org/internet-drafts/draft-ietf-enum-operation-02.txt>.

13. *See* NeuStar FAQ, *supra* note 4, FAQ–1 (stating that "once the authoritative name server is found, ENUM retrieves relevant NAPTR Resource records . . ."), *at* <http://www.enum.org/information/files/enum_faq.pdf>. NAPTR stands for "Naming Authority Pointer."

14. *See Id.,* FAQ-1 (stating user can specify preferences for receiving communications).

15. *See Id.,* FAQ-5.

16. For a description of potential call flows, *see* Lind, Callflows, *supra* note 4, *at* <http://www.ietf.org/internet-drafts/draft-lind-enum-callflows-01.txt>; Ad Hoc ENUM Report, *supra* note 2, Sec. 6.2, *at* <http://www.cybertelecom. org/library/enumreport.htm>.

17. RFC 2916, *supra* note 2, *at* <http://www.ietf.org/rfc/rfc2916.txt>.

18. ITU, Liaison to IETF/ISOC on ENUM (October 2000) (hereinafter Liaison), *at* <http://www.itu.int/infocom/enum/wp1-39_rev1.htm>. *See also* IETF Inform-ational RFC 3026, Liaison to IETF/ISOC on ENUM (January 2001) (hereinafter RFC 3026), *at* <ftp. rfc-editor.org/in-notes/rfc3026.txt>. Note that an informa-tional RFC is an informational vehicle only and does not indicate the recom-mendation or endorsement of the IETF. RFC 2026, *supra* note 1, *at* <http://www.ietf.org/rfc/rfc2026.txt>.

19. The IAB is a technical advisory group, under the corporate structure of the

Internet Society, that provides leadership for the IETF. The IAB selects the IETF's Internet Engineering Steering Group which in turn selects the leadership of the different IETF working groups. The IAB also provides oversight of the standards process and a forum for appeals concerning the process. *See* Internet Architecture Board Home Page (last modified Dec. 4, 2000), *at* <http://www.iab.org/iab/>.

20. E164.ARPA InterNic WHOIS Record (last modified June 22, 2001); E164.ARPA Network Solutions WHOIS Record (last modified Mar. 13, 2001). RIPE NCC is one of three high level Internet numbering authorities. It receives number blocks from the Internet Assigned Number Authority (IANA) which is under the authority of the Internet Corporation for Assigned Names and Numbers (ICANN). It distributes numbers to networks in Europe and Africa. RIPE NCC is located in the Netherlands. About RIPE (n.d.), *at* <http://www.ripe.net/ripe/about/index.html>.

21. *See* Shockey, ITU-T, *supra* note 4, slide 11 (explaining that IAB selected *.arpa* because *.arpa* is dedicated to infrastructure issues and is well managed, state and secure).

22. *See* note 101, and accompanying text (discussing expanding role of ITU in ENUM).

23. Liaison, *supra* note 18, *at* <http://www.itu.int/infocom/enum/wp1-39_ rev1.htm>. The Liaison indicates that the decision to participate in this particular technology is one of national sovereignty on the grounds that nations control the use of their e164 codes. RFC 3026, *supra* note 18, para 1, *at* <ftp://ftp. rfc-editor.org/in-notes/rfc3026.txt>. Ad Hoc ENUM Report, *supra* note 2, Sec. 4.1 (describing ENUM as an opt-in system for nations), *at* <http://www.cybertelecom.org/library/enumreport.htm>.

24. *See* NeuStar FAQ, *supra* note 4, FAQ-8 (stating "Optimally, the root should contain a small listing of all of the national ENUM top-level country code name servers."), *at* <http://www.enum.org/information/files/enum_faq.pdf>.

25. Brown, ENUM Service Reference Model, *supra* note 4, Sec. 4, *at* <http://www.ietf.org/internet-drafts/draft-ietf-enum-operation-02.txt>.

26. *See* Contribution of NeuStar, US Study Group A Ad-Hoc, *supra* note 4, p. 4.

27. *See* Pfautz, ENUM Administrative Process, *supra* note 4, Sec. 1, *at* <http://www.ietf.org/drafts/draft-pfautz-yu-enum-adm-01.txt>.

28. M. Mealling, R. Daniel, IETF RFC 2915, The Naming Authority Pointer (NAPTR) DNS Resource Record (Sept. 2000), *at* <http://www.ietf.org/ rfc/rfc2915.txt>. *See* Ad Hoc ENUM Report, *supra* note 2, Sec. 2 (detailing use of NAPTR records), *at* <http://www.cybertelecom.org/library/enumreport.htm>.

29. Jordyn A. Buchanan, Register.com, SGA Ad Hoc—ENUM, slide 5 (Feb. 12, 2001) (hereinafter Register.com, SGA Ad Hoc).

30. *Id.,* slide 6-10.

31. *See* ICANN | Home Page (n.d.) *at* <http://www.icann.org>.

32. D. Ranalli, D. Peek, R. Walter, IETF Informational Internet Draft, Tier-1 ENUM System Roles and Responsibilities, Sec. 4.4 (Feb. 2001) (hereinafter Ranalli, Tier–1 ENUM), *at* <http://www.ietf.org/internet-drafts/draft-ranalli-peek-walter-enum-t1roles-01.txt>.

33. Brown, ENUM Service Reference Model, *supra* note 4, Sec. 4.1 (stating that "Information changes infrequently"), *at* <http://www.ietf.org/internet-drafts/draft-ietf-enum-operation-02.txt>.

34. The tiered model is detailed is multiple documents. *See* Ad Hoc ENUM Re-port, *supra* note 2, Sec. 5, *at* <http://www.cybertelecom.org/library/enumreport. htm>; Ranalli, Tier–1 ENUM, *supra* note 32, *at* <http://www.ietf.org/internet-drafts/draft-ranalli-peek-walter-enum-t1roles-01.txt>; Brown, ENUM Service Reference Model, *supra* note 4, Sec. 5, *at* <http://www.ietf.org/internet-drafts/draft-ietf-enum-operation-02.txt>; Pfautz, ENUM Administrative Process, *supra* note 4, Sec. 1, *at* <http://www.ietf.org/drafts/draft-pfautz-yu-enum-adm-01.txt>; Contribution of NeuStar, US Study Group A Ad-Hoc, *supra* note 4, p. 5; Register.com, SG-A Ad Hoc, *supra* note 29.

35. *See* Contribution of NeuStar, Inc., US Study Group A Ad-Hoc, *supra* note 4, p. 3.

36. *Id.*, p. 6.

37. US industry ENUM supporters acknowledge that there will be alternative ENUM implementations and recommend that such alternatives not be precluded. Ad Hoc ENUM Report, *supra* note 2, Secs. 1 & 4.1, *at* <http://www.cybertelecom.org/library/enumreport.htm>.

38. ENUM.ORG > Welcome Page (n.d.), *at* <http://www.enum.org>.

39. NeuStar is the current administrator of the North American Numbering Plan. NeuStar, in a joint venture doing business as NeuLevel, was also recently awarded the new Top Level Domain (TLD) ".biz". NeuStar Press Release, NeuLevel Awarded Dot BIZ Top Level Domain by ICANN Board (Nov. 17, 2000), *at* <http://www.neustar.com/pressroom/announcements/press_release.cfm?press_id =28>.

40. The Internet-Telephony Addressing Board was created as a part of Pulver's and NetNumber's *.tel* application to ICANN. Internet Telephony Addressing Board, I-TAB (n.d.) *at* <http://www.i-tab.org>.

41. *See* ENUM World Home (n.d.), *at* <http://www.enumworld.com>.

42. VeriSign, Inc.—WEBNum (n.d.), *at* <http://www.webnum.com>.

43. NetNumber Global ENUM Service (n.d.) *at* http://www.netnumber.com/.

44. DailNow.Com—The Internet Phone Company (n.d.), *at* <http://www.dialnow.com/Investor_Information.asp>.

45. DotPHone, Both dotCOM domains and dotPH domains are functionally identical (n.d.), *at* <http://www.domains.ph/answer.html>.

46. 47 U.S.C. § 222.

47. *See*, e.g., Unified Messaging, E-mail, Fax, Voicemail, SMS, Phone all in one In-Box (n.d.), *at* <http://www.unified-messaging.com>.

48. Microsoft, Building User-Centric Experiences: An Introduction to Microsoft Hailstorm (Mar. 2001), *at* <http://www.microsoft.com/net/hailstorm.asp>.

49. *See* Sprint PCS Press Release: Sprint PCS Phone QCP–6035 by Kyocera and Mobile Connectivity Kits for Palm Handhelds Are First in a Series of Palm Powered Solutions Offered By Sprint PCS (Apr. 11, 2001), *at* <http://www.prnewswire.com/cgi-bin/micro_stories.pl?ACCT=153400&TICK= PALM&STORY=/www/story/04–19–2001/0001473179&EDATE=Apr+11,+200>

50. Tony Rutkowski, ENUM Directory Services in the Marketplace, DTI Workshop on ENUM, Slide 6 (Jun. 5, 2001) (noting "Email or SIP addresses may be more attractive.")

51. *See* Lind, CallFlows, *supra* note 4, para 2 (noting use of ENUM with email), *at* <http://www.ietf.org/internet-drafts/draft-lind-enum-callflows-01.txt>.

52. *See supra* note 5 and accompanying text (noting different uses of ENUM).

53. Brown, ENUM Service Reference Model, *supra* note 4, Sec. 4, *at* <http://www.ietf.org/internet-drafts/draft-ietf-enum-operation-02.txt> (stating "It is up to the client initiating the service request to sort through the set of NAPTR records to determine which services are appropriate for the intended action.")

54. *See* note 10, and accompanying text.

55. Gopal Dommety, Paddy Nallur, Viren Malaviya, Niranjan Segal, IETF Internet Draft, E.212 number and DNS (June 2001) (stating "This draft is adaptation of RFC 2916 to E.212 numbers."), *at* <http://www.ietf.org/internet-drafts/draft-dommety-e212-dns-00.txt>.

56. Federal Standard 1037C, Definition: telephone number (Aug. 23, 1996) (stating "telephone number: The unique network address that is assigned to a telephone user, i.e., subscriber, for routing telephone calls."), *at* <http://glossary.its/bldrdoc.gov/fs–1037/dir-036/_5369.htm>.

57. While it is true that the ENUM database is unlike the others cited in that the ENUM database contains communications data, it is also true that a great deal of that communications data is data that the FCC lacks jurisdiction over, including e-mail addresses, web addresses, IP telephony addresses, physical addresses, and other personal identifying information. To suggest that the FCC has jurisdiction just because a phone number is in the database would also be to suggest that the US Post Office would have jurisdiction over ENUM because the database would likely contain physical addresses as well.

58. Brown, ENUM Service Reference Model, *supra* note 4, Sec. 5.1, *at* <http://www.ietf.org/internet-drafts/draft-ietf-enum-operation-02.txt>; *SS8 Links Multiple PSTN and IP Devices to Single Phone Number,* COMMUNICATIONS DAILY, p. 7, Jun. 25, 2001.

59. Pfautz, ENUM Administrative Process, *supra* note 4, Sec. 1, *at* <http://www.ietf.org/drafts/draft-pfautz-yu-enum-adm-01.txt>; Penn Pfautz, ENUM Administration, Slide 2 (Feb. 12, 2001), *at* <http://www.itu.int/infocom/enum/workshopusafeb12–13/pfautz.htm>.

60. Shockey, SGA, *supra* note 10, slide 2; Marc Robins, *ENUM's Got Your Number,* INTERNET TELEPHONY, Jun. 2001, *at* <httpı//www.tmcnet.com/it/0601/0601mo.htm> .

61. Ad Hoc ENUM Report, *supra* note 2, Sec. 2, *at* <http://www.cybertelecom.org/library/enumreport.htm>.

62. *SS8 Links Multiple PSTN and IP Devices to Single Phone Number,* COMMUNICATIONS DAILY, p. 7, Jun. 25, 2001.

63. Brown, ENUM Service Reference Model, *supra* note 4, Secs. 3, 4 (emphasis added), *at* <http://www.ietf.org/internet-drafts/draft-ietf-enum-operation-02.txt>.

64. Ranalli, Tier–1 ENUM, *supra* note 32, Secs. 4.2, 6.3.

65. Pfautz, ENUM Administrative Process, *supra* note 4, Sec. 1, *at* <http://www.ietf.org/drafts/draft-pfautz-yu-enum-adm-01.txt>.

66. Ad Hoc ENUM Report, *supra* note 2, Sec. 4.1, *at* <http://www.cybertelecom.org/library/enumreport.htm>.

67. Ad Hoc ENUM Report, *supra* note 2, Sec. 4.1 (noting alternatives to golden tree approach), *at* <http://www.cybertelecom.org/library/enumreport.htm>.

68. Douglas Ranalli, Is E164.arpa The Only Answer for Tier–1 ENUM Registry Services? (n.d.) (also noting that "there is no evidence of the market deployment of hundreds or thousands of ENUM services," meaning that querying those ENUM services that exist would be manageable), *at* <http://www.netnumber.com/news/e164arpaComp.pdf>.

69. ENUM also *seeks* to solve the problem of telephone restrained by merely having numeric keypads with which to enter addresses. New wireless phones have touch screens that can be configured in any way for any type of data input, increasing the opportunity for address design and ability to designate the appropriate database. *See* Kyocera—Kyocera SmartPhone Series (n.d.) (showing wireless phone with touch screen in place of keypad), *at* <http://www.kyocera-wireless.com/kysmart/kysmart_series.htm>.

70. Ad Hoc ENUM Report, *supra* note 2, Sec. 4.1 (noting possible interconnection alternative to golden tree approach), *at* <http://www.cybertelecom.org/library/enumreport.htm>.

71. *See also* Ad Hoc ENUM Report, *supra* note 2, Sec. 8.1 (Minority View of Report, indicating alternative to golden tree implementation), *at* <http://www.cybertelecom.org/library/enumreport.htm>

72. *See* Doug Ranalli, Is E164.ARPA the Only Answer tor Tier-1 ENUM Registry Services? (n.d.) (noting delay resulting from global coordination), *at* <http://www.netnumber.com/news/e164arpaComp.pdf>

73. *See Id.* (noting impact on creative process).

74. If it is concluded that a unified database is not needed, then there is no reason to reach the question of whether it should be located at *e164.arpa* or elsewhere.

75. RFC 2916, *supra* note 2, Sec. 4 (stating "This memo requests that the IANA delegate the E164.ARPA domain following instructions to be provided by the IAB."), *at* <http://www.ietf.org/rfc/rfc2916.txt>.

76. E164.ARPA WHOIS Record, Network Solutions (May 17, 2001). While IAB Meeting minutes reference *E164.arpa*, no record of IAB instruction to IANA for delegate to RIPE NCC has been found.

77. Ad Hoc ENUM Report, *supra* note 2, Sec. 8.1, *at* <http://www.cybertelecom.org/library/enumreport.htm>; Shockey, ITU-T, *supra* note 4, slide 11; Shockey, SGA, *supra* note 10, slide 13.

78. France, Conditions for Implementation of ENUM, ITU SG2 Delayed Contribution on D.15-E (Jan. 23, 2001), *at* <http://www.ngi.org/enum/pub/15_ww9.htm>.

79. Shaw, DTI ENUM Workshop, *supra* note 11, slides 13–15, *at* <http://www.itu.int/infocom/enum/dtijune501/dti-june-5-2001-1.PPT>. *Compare* Shaw, ICANN (where this argument appears to have been omitted), *at* <http://www.itu.int/infocom/enum/GACjune1201/gac-june-2-2001-1.PPT>.

80. *.arpa* and *.int* are designated as Internet infrastructure domains to be managed by IANA. *See* Jon Postel, IETF Draft, New Registries and the Delegation of International Top Level Domains, para 1.3 (May 1996) (stating that *.arpa* and *.int* were "created for technical needs internal to the operation of the Internet *at* the discretion of the IANA in consultation with the IETF."); IAB Statement on Infrastructure Domain and Subdomains (May 10, 2000), *at* <http://www.iab.org/iab/DOCUMENTS/statement-on-infrastructure-domains.txt>; Annex 8: Responsibilities for e164.arpa, Sec. (2) (n.d.) ("IAB requested on May 17 2000 that assignment of subdomains of arpa should be a task of IANA."), *at* <http://www.itu.int/infocom/enum/workshopjan01/annex8-responsibilities-fore164.arpa.htm>; IANA | Contact Information (modified November 3, 2000), *at* <http://www.iana.org/contact.htm; Letter from Karen Rose, NTIA Purchase Order Technical Representative, to Mr. Louis Touton, Vice-President, Secretary, and General Counsel, ICANN (Apr. 28, 2000) (hereinafter Rose Letter) ("The Department of Commerce considers this an Internet Assigned Numbers Authority (IANA) function and has requested that the WHOIS entry for the ARPA domain reflect IANA as the registrant."), *at* <http://www.ngi.org/enum/pub/DOC_28Apr2000.htm>.

81. *See* Contract Between ICANN and the United States Government for Performance of the IANA Function (Feb. 9, 2000), *at* <http://www.icann.org/general/iana-contract-09feb00.htm>; IETF Informational RFC 2860, Memorandum of Understanding Concerning the Technical Work of the Internet Assigned Numbers Authority (Jun. 2000), *at* <ftp://ftp. ietf.org/rfc/rfc2860.txt>; Rose Letter, *supra* note 80 (stating "Purchase Order no. 40SBNT067020 provides that '[ICANN] will perform other IANA

functions as needed upon request of DOC.'"), *at*
<http://www.ngi.org/enum/pub/DOC_28Apr2000.htm>.

82. Rose Letter, *supra* note 80, *at*
<http://www.ngi.org/enum/pub/DOC_28Apr2000.htm>.

83. B. Carpentar, F. Baker, M. Roberts, IETF Informational RFC 2860, Memorandum of Understanding Concerning the Technical Work of the Internet Assigned Numbers Authority, Sec. 4 (June 2000) (indicating that disputes between IANA and IETF are resolved by IAB), *at* <http://www.ietf.org/rfc/rfc2860.txt>.

84. *See* IETF Best Current Practice RFC 2317 Classless IN-ADDR.ARPA delegation (March 1998), *at* <http://www.ietf.org/rfc/rfc2317.txt>. in-addr.arpa domain "is used to convert 32-bit numeric IP addresses back into domain names. This is used, for example, by Internet web servers, which receive connections from IP addresses and wish to obtain domain names to record in log files." Connected: An Internet Encyclopedia: The in-addr.arpa Domain (n.d.), *at* <http://www.freesoft.org/CIE/Course/Section2/15.htm>.

85. Ad Hoc ENUM Report, *supra* note 2, *at* <http://www.cybertelecom.org/library/enumreport.htm>.

86. *See* discussion, note 80.

87. J. Postel, IETF RFC 1591, Domain Name System Structure and Delegation, Sec. 2 (Mar. 1994), *at* <http://www.isi.edu/in-notes/rfc1591.txt>.

88. However, there are some indications that the ITU is attempting to gain control of *.int*. *See* Joakim Stralmark, ENUM- functions that maps telephone numbers to Internet based addresses, Post & Telestyrelsen, 3 (Mar. 23 2001), *at* <http://www.enum.org/information/files/enum_summary.pdf> (stating "ITU has ambition of becoming the registrar for the top-level domain .int."); ITU, INT Top Level Domain Name Registration Services (January 15, 1999), *at* <http://www.itu.int/net/int/>.

89. *See* Douglas Ranalli, *Is "E164.arpa" The Only Answer for Tier–1 ENUM Registry Services?* (n.d.) (stating that coordination *at* international level would be time consumer, difficult, and artificially limit creative process).

90. *See* Anthony Ruthkowski, the *ENUM golden tree*, INFO (Apr. 2001) (recounting failed experience of standard X.500).

91. Douglas Ranalli, *Is "E164.arpa" The Only Answer for Tier–1 ENUM Registry Services?* (n.d.).

92. *Id.*

93. *See* RFC 2026, *supra* note 1, (explaining IETF process and difference between proposed, draft, and Internet standards), *at* <http://www.ietf.org/rfc/rfc2026.txt> .

94. *Id.,* Sec. 4.1.3.

95. *See* Tony Rutkowski, ENUM Policy Briefing to US Dept of State, FCC, and NTIA, slide 9 (n.d.) *at* <http://www.enumworld.com/resources/NTIA_policy_brief.ppt>.

96. *See* note 69 (noting that modern phones offer greater flexibility for address input and need not be limited to numeric strings).

97. *See, supra* p. 33 (listing competitive alternatives to ENUM).

98. Two documents so far have suggested that alternative implementations of ENUM should be restricted or prohibited. *See* France Conditions, *supra* note 78, *at* <http://www.ngi.org/enum/pub/15_ww9.htm>; Stralmark, *supra* note 88, *at* <http://www.enum.org/information/files/enum_summary.pdf>.

99. *See* note 43, and accompanying text.

100. *See* Steve Lind, AT&T, Tony Holmes, BT, ENUM Administration Issues, slide 5 (Jan. 17, 2001) (hereinafter Lind, ENUM Administrative Issues); Chairman's Report of the ITU ENUM Workshop, ITU, Geneva (Jan. 17, 2001), Annex 7: ENUM Issues: Issue 3, *at* <http://www.itu.int/infocom/enum/workshopjan01/report-jan17–2001.htm>

101. RFC 2916, *supra* note 2, para 4, *at* <http://www.ietf.org/rfc/rfc2916.txt>

102. Liaison, *supra* note 18, *at* <http://www.itu.int/infocom/enum/wp1–39_rev1.htm>. This was subsequently released as an informational RFC. RFC 3026, *supra* note 18, *at* <ftp://ftp. rfc-editor.org/in-notes/rfc3026.txt>. "An 'Informational' specification is published for the general information of the Internet community, and does not represent an Internet community consensus or recommendation." RFC 2026, *supra* note 1, para 4.2.2, *at* <http://www.ietf.org/rfc/rfc2026.txt>.

103. According to the Liaison, "All administrative entities, including DNS administrators, will adhere to all the applicable tenets of all pertinent ITU Recommendations, e.g., E.164, E.164.1, E.190, and E.195, with regard to the inclusion of the E.164 resource information in the DNS." Liaison, *supra* note 18, *at* <http://www.itu.int/infocom/enum/wp1–39_rev1.htm>. The ITU's role is further described as follows: "For all E.164 Country Code Zone resources (Country Codes and Identification Codes), the ITU has the responsibility to provide assignment information to DNS administrators, for performing the administrative function. The ITU will ensure that each Member State has authorized the inclusion of their Country Code information for input to the DNS. For resources that are spare or designated as test codes there will normally be no entry in the DNS. However, the ITU will provide spare code lists to DNS administrators for purposes of clarification. The entity to which E.164 test codes have been assigned will be responsible for providing any appropriate assignment information to DNS administrators." *Id.* And again, "The ITU may request the consultation of the WP1/2 experts as necessary and as prescribed in Resolution 20." *Id. See also* Shockey, SGA, *supra* note 10, slide 18 (stating "ITU will insure that Member States have authorized inclusion of their Country Code in e164.arpa" and "ITU to coordinate with RIPE NCC as the Root Administrator."), *at* <http://www.itu.int/infocom/enum/workshopusafeb12–13/shockey.htm>.

104. Shaw, DTI ENUM Workshop, *supra* note 11, slide 16 *at* <http://www.itu.int/infocom/enum/dtijune501/dti-june-5-2001-1.PPT>; Shaw, ICANN, *supra* note 11, slide 14, *at* <http://www.itu.int/infocom/enum/GACjune1201/gac-june-2-2001-1.PPT>.

105. The ITU sent a letter to ICANN opposing Pulver's application to create a new TLD *.tel*. ITU Letter, *supra* note *at* <http://www.icann.org/tlds/correspondence/itu-response-01nov00.htm>.

106. The ENUM industry *seems* to have implicitly recognized that it can set up a domestic ENUM golden tree without government involvement. During the summer of 2001 AT&T and WorldCom had competing proposals concerning how industry could cooperatively and without government involvement, launch ENUM domestically. Steven D. Lind, AT&T, U.S. ENUM Frame Document Implementation Framework (n.d.) (distributed *at* June 18, 2001 State Department ENUM Ad Hoc Meeting); Peter Guggina, WorldCom Contribution for Independent ENUM Forum (Jun. 12, 2001). *See* also Ad Hoc ENUM Report, *supra* note 2, Sec. 8.1 (discussing industry forum), *at* <http://www.cybertelecom.org/library/enumreport.htm>.

107. Contribution of NeuStar, US Study Group A Ad-Hoc, *supra* note 4, p. 2 (stating in one sentence and without supporting analysis that there is no antitrust concern).

108. Milton Mueller, *Universal Service in Telephone History: a reconstruction*, TELECOMMUNICATIONS POLICY 17, 5 (July 1993) 352–69.

109. *See also* Shaw, DTI ENUM Workshop, *supra* note 11, slide 14, *at* <http://www.itu.int/infocom/enum/dtijune501/dti-june-5-2001-1.PPT>; Shaw, ICANN, *supra* note 11, slide 13 (recommending that ENUM infrastructure be "country-neutral" and that transparency is needed "as to clear legal and policy framework, roles, responsibilities, and relationships."), *at* <http://www.itu.int/infocom/enum/GACjune1201/gac-june-2-2001-1.PPT>.

110. Contribution of NeuStar, Inc., US Study Group A Ad-Hoc, *supra* note 4, p. 14.

111. Ranalli, Tier–1 ENUM, *supra* note 32, Secs. 4.4, 6.2, *at* <http://www.ietf.org/internet-drafts/draft-ranalli-peek-walter-enum-t1roles-01.txt>.

112. Ad Hoc ENUM Report, *supra* note 2, Sec. 7.1, *at* <http://www.cybertelecom.org/library/enumreport.htm>; Ranalli, Tier–1 ENUM, *supra* note 32, Sec. 7, *at* <http://www.ietf.org/internet-drafts/draft-ranalli-peek-walter-enum-t1roles-01.txt>.

113. *See* Brown, ENUM Service Reference Model, *supra* note 4, Sec. 8, *at* <http://www.ietf.org/internet-drafts/draft-ietf-enum-operation-02.txt>. Records could be altered either intentionally and fraudulently or unintentionally or negligently.

114. Pfautz, ENUM Administrative Process, *supra* note 4, Sec. 5.2, *at* <http://www.ietf.org/drafts/draft-pfautz-yu-enum-adm-01.txt>.

115. FTC, *ID Theft: When Bad Things Happen to Your Good Name* (August 2000). *See also* Identity Theft and Assumption Deterrence Act of 1998, Public Law 105–318, 112 STAT. 3007 (Oct 30, 1998); USDOJ, Identity Theft and Identity Fraud (last modified 6/5/2000), *at*

<http://www.usdoj.gov/criminal/fraud/idtheft.html>. Such actions could also be construed as Computer Fraud, 18 U.S.C. §§ 1030.

116. *See* 47 USC § 222 (giving directory assistance providers rights to list information held by telephone carriers); In re *Provision of Directory Listing Information under the Telecommunications Act of 1934 (sic), as amended,* CC Docket 99–273, First Report and Order, 2001 WL 69358 (Jan. 23, 2001) (clarifying that online databases are directory assistance providers under Sec. 222 and have rights to list information).

117. *See* Robert Cannon, *Where Internet Service Providers and Telephone Companies Compete: A Guide to the Computer Inquiries, Enhanced Service Providers and Information Service Providers,* 9 Comm. Conspectus 49 (2001).

118. *See* Kevin McCandless, Illuminent, Number to Name Authentication, SGA Ad Hoc Meeting (March 28, 2001) (advocating LIDB services of Illuminent as solution to data authentication).

119. *See* Ad Hoc ENUM Report, *supra* note 2, Sec. 7.1, *at* <http://www.cybertelecom.org/library/enumreport.htm>; Tony Rutkowski, Bryan Mordecai, Approaches to ENUM Implementation in the USA, Dept of State ITAC-T Advisory Committee, SG-A AdHoc Meeting in ENUM, slide 13 (Feb. 12, 2001) (hereinafter Rutkowski, SGA).

120. Pfautz, ENUM Administrative Process, *supra* note 4, Sec. 5.1, *at* <http://www.ietf.org/drafts/draft-pfautz-yu-enum-adm-01.txt>.

121. *See* Ad Hoc ENUM Report, *supra* note 2, Sec. 7.1, *at* <http://www.cybertelecom.org/library/enumreport.htm>; Rutkowski, SGA, *supra* note 119, slide 13 (noting possible use of digital certificate like services); Pfautz, ENUM Administrative Process, *supra* note 4, Sec. 5.1, *at* <http://www.ietf.org/drafts/draft-pfautz-yu-enum-adm-01.txt>.

122. *See* NeuStar FAQ, *supra* note 4, p. 1 ("ENUM does not change the Numbering Plan and does not change telephony numbering or its administration in any way. ENUM will not drain already scarce numbering resources because it uses existing numbers.") *at* <http://www.enum.org/information/files/enum_faq.pdf>; Id., p. 4 ("ENUM will not change the existing right-to-use rules and principles for telephone numbers. ENUM is not intended to change how telephone numbers are administered, but instead facilitate a wide range of applications using phone numbers as subscriber names. ENUM also will not interfere with existing PSTN functions and technology, such as circuit switching, SS7 (ISUP or TCAP), or Intelligent Networking, where similar resource discovery activities are performed through the PSTN legacy technologies."); Shockey, SGA, *supra* note 4, slide 15 (stating "ENUM does not change the Numbering Plan"), *at* <http://www.itu.int/infocom/enum/workshopusafeb12–13/shockey.htm>.

123. Contribution of NeuStar, Inc., US Study Group A Ad-Hoc, *supra* note 4, p. 13.

124. *See* discussion on page 33.

125. Richard Shockey, IETF ENUM Working Group, FAQs About ENUM (Jul. 26, 2000), *at*

<http://www.ngi.org/enum/pub/DRAFT-SHOCKEY-enum-faq-01.TXT>. The statement that ENUM does not affect numbering portability has been noticeably absent from subsequent presentations. *See* Shockey, ITU-T, *supra* note 4, slide 13. NSI / VeriSign also does not view number portability as a crucial ENUM issue. *See* ENUMWorld FAQs (n.d.) *at* <http://www.enumworld.com/faqs.html#9>. *See also* NeuStar FAQ, *supra* note 4, p. 6 (stating "ENUM is not intended to service this function . . .), *at* <http://www.enum.org/information/files/enum_faq.pdf>.

126. *See* NeuStar FAQ, *supra* note 4, p. 6 (stating "It is likely that the service provider that allocated the number(s) to the user will be involved in the process of authentication."), *at* <http://www.enum.org/information/files/enum_faq.pdf>.

127. P. Pfautz, IETF Informational Draft, Administrative Requirements for Deployment of ENUM in North America (Sept. 2000), *at* <http://www.ietf.org/internet-drafts/draft-pfautz-na-enum-01.txt>.

128. *See* notes 116–121 and accompanying text.

129. *See* Liaison, *supra* note 18, *at* <http://www.itu.int/infocom/enum/wp1-39_rev1.htm>. *See also* Lind, Callflows, *supra* note 4, Sec. 5.3 (noting further work on issue before the ITU), *at* <http://www.ietf.org/internet-drafts/draft-lind-enum-callflows-01.txt>.

130. *See* NeuStar FAQ, *supra* note 4, p. 5 (stating "Emergency numbers are generally considered "access codes" and are outside of E.164 and ENUM services. If the user dials an emergency number from a SIP phone, the phone will recognize that it cannot make a SIP connection and will open a gateway to the PSTN."), *at* <http://www.enum.org/information/files/enum_faq.pdf>. *See also* Contribution of NeuStar, Inc., US Study Group A Ad-Hoc, *supra* note 4, p. 13 (recommending that these types of numbers not be populated into ENUM database).

131. *See* Shockey, ITU-T, *supra* note 4, slide 13 (stating "ENUM does not change the Numbering Plan"); Contribution of NeuStar, Inc., US Study Group A Ad-Hoc, *supra* note 4, pp. 13–14; *See* NeuStar FAQ, *supra* note 4, p. 1 (stating "ENUM does not change the Numbering Plan and does not change telephony numbering or its administration in any way. ENUM will not drain already scarce numbering resources because it uses existing numbers.").

132. Shockey, ITU-T, *supra* note 4, slide 13; Shockey, SGA, *supra* note 10, slide 15, *at* <http://www.itu.int/infocom/enum/workshopusafeb12–13/shockey.htm>.

133. Shockey, ITU-T, *supra* note 4, slide 13.

134. *See* Lind, ENUM Administration Issues, *supra* note 100, slide 15 (enables "network by-pass").

135. Ad Hoc ENUM Report, *supra* note 2, Sec. 7.2 (discussing privacy concerns), *at* <http://www.cybertelecom.org/library/enumreport.htm>.

136. Ad Hoc ENUM Report, *supra* note 2, Secs. 4.3 & 7.2, *at* <http://www.cybertelecom.org/library/enumreport.htm>; Faltstrom, ENUM Technical Issues, *supra* note 9, slide 29; Shockey, ITU-T, *supra* note 4, slide 14, *at* <http://www.itu.int/infocom/enum/workshopjan01/annex4-shockey.ppt>;

NeuStar FAQ, *supra* note 4, p. 7 (stating "ENUM would be a subscriber-controlled 'opt-in' system . . ."), *at* <http://www.enum.org/information/files/enum_faq.pdf>.

137. NeuStar claims that ENUM is consistent with the EC Privacy Policy. Shockey, ITU-T, *supra* note 4, slide 14, *at* <http://www.itu.int/infocom/enum/workshopjan01/annex4-shockey.ppt>; Shockey, SGA, slide 16, *at* <http://www.itu.int/infocom/enum/workshopusafeb12–13/shockey.htm>. However, the conclusion is not substantiated.

3

On Target? The Shifting Standards for Determining Internet Jurisdiction

Michael A. Geist

I. Introduction

The Internet has no territorial boundaries. To paraphrase Gertrude Stein, as far as the Internet is concerned, not only is there perhaps "no there there," the "there" is everywhere where there is Internet access.[1]

> *Judge Nancy Gertner,*
> *Digital Equipment Corp. v. Altavista Technology, Inc., 1997*

We order the company YAHOO! Inc. to take all measures to dissuade and make impossible any access via Yahoo.com to the auction service for Nazi objects and to any other site or service that may be construed as constituting an apology for Nazism or contesting the reality of Nazi crimes. . . .[2]

> *Judge Jean-Jacques Gomez,*
> *UEJI et LICRA v. Yahoo! Inc. et Yahoo France, May 2000*

As business gravitated to the Internet in the late 1990s, concern over the legal risks of operating online quickly moved to the fore, as legal issues inherent in selling products, providing customer service, or simply maintaining an information-oriented website began to emerge.[3] Certain legal risks, such as selling defective products or inaccurate information disclosure, were already well-known to business, as these risks are encountered and addressed daily in the offline world.[4]

The unique challenge presented by the Internet is that compliance with local laws is rarely sufficient to assure a business that it has limited its exposure to legal risk. Since websites are instantly accessible worldwide, the prospect that a website owner might be haled into a courtroom in a far-off jurisdiction is much more than a mere academic exercise; it is a very real possibility.[5] Businesses seeking to embrace the promise of a global market at the click of a mouse must factor into their analysis the prospect of additional compliance costs and possible litigation.

The risks are not limited to businesses, however. Consumers anxious to purchase online must also balance the promise of unlimited choice, greater access to information, and a more competitive global marketplace with the fact that they may not benefit from the security normally afforded by local consumer protection laws. Although such laws exist online, just as they do offline, their effectiveness is severely undermined if consumers do not have recourse within their local court system or if enforcing a judgment requires further proceedings in another jurisdiction.[6]

Moreover, concerns over the legal risks created by the Internet extend beyond commercial activities. Public interest information-based websites on controversial topics may face the prospect of prosecution in far-away jurisdictions despite their legality within the home jurisdiction.[7] Meanwhile, anonymous posters to Internet chat sites face the possibility that the target of their comments will launch legal action aimed at uncovering their anonymous guise.[8]

In recent years, adoption of the *Zippo* legal framework has exacerbated the challenge of adequately accounting for the legal risk arising from Internet jurisdiction.[9] In the *Zippo* framework, commonly referred to as the passive versus active test, courts gauge the relative interactivity of a website to determine whether assertion of jurisdiction is appropriate. At one end of the spectrum lies "passive" websites—minimally interactive information-based websites.[10] At the other end of the spectrum lies "active" websites, which feature greater interactivity and end-user contacts.[11] The *Zippo* test suggests that courts should refrain from asserting jurisdiction over passive sites, while jurisdiction over active sites is appropriate.

In light of the various standards being applied by courts in establishing jurisdictional rights in the online environment, this paper examines the effectiveness of the current approaches and recommends possible reforms. I argue that the passive versus active test established in *Zippo* has, with time, become increasingly outdated and irrelevant. It has been surpassed in practice by an effects-based analysis that poses even greater danger to legal certainty and the prospect for "over-regulation" of Internet-based activities. I argue instead for the adoption of a three-factor targeting test that includes analysis of contract, technology, and knowledge as the standard for assessing Internet jurisdiction claims.

Part II contains a review of recent Internet jurisdiction jurisprudence in both the United States and Canada, beginning with the development of and subsequent approval of the *Zippo* passive versus active test. It identifies the subtle changes that have been occurring since late 1999, as courts begin to find the *Zippo* test too constraining and shift their analysis toward an effects-based paradigm.

Having argued that the *Zippo* test should be replaced, Part III presents an alternative, proposing a targeting-based test for Internet jurisdiction which is supported by the growing acceptance of targeting in both case law and international policy levels. It then advocates the adoption of a three-factor approach to targeting that includes assessments of any contractual provisions related to jurisdiction, the technological measures employed to identify the targeted jurisdiction, and the actual or implied knowledge of the website operator with respect to targeted jurisdictions.

II. The Rise and Fall of the *Zippo* Test

Since 1996, United States courts have regularly faced litigation that includes an Internet jurisdiction component. As courts grapple with the issue, the jurisprudence has shifted first toward the *Zippo* passive versus active test, then more recently toward an effects-based test with elements of targeting analysis.

A. The Emergence of the *Zippo* Passive versus Active Test

The first North American application of jurisdictional principles to the Internet traces back to 1996 and *Inset Systems, Inc. v. Instruction Set, Inc.*, a Connecticut district court case.[12] In this instance, Inset Systems, a Connecticut company, brought a trademark infringement action against Instruction Set, a Massachusetts company, arising out of its use of the domain name "Inset.com."[13] Instruction Set used the domain name to advertise its goods and services on the Internet, a practice to which Inset objected since it was the owner of the federal trademark "Inset."[14] The legal question before the court was one of jurisdiction. Did Instruction Set's activity, the establishment of a website, properly bring it within the jurisdiction of Connecticut under that state's long-arm statute? Did Inset's conduct meet the minimum contacts standard outlined by the United States Supreme Court in *World-Wide Volkswagen*?[15]

The *Inset* court concluded that it could properly assert jurisdiction, basing its decision on Instruction Set's use of the Internet.[16] Likening the Internet to a continuous advertisement, the court reasoned that Instruction Set had purposefully directed its advertising activities toward Connecticut on a continuous basis and therefore could reasonably have anticipated being sued there.[17]

The court's decision was problematic for several reasons. First, its conclusion that creating a website amounts to a purposeful availment of every jurisdiction distorts the fundamental principle of jurisdiction.[18] Second, the court did not analyze the Internet itself, but merely drew an analogy between the Internet and a more traditional media form, in this case a continuous advertisement.[19] If the court was correct, every court, everywhere, could assert jurisdiction where a website was directed toward its forum. This decision would stifle future Internet growth, as would-be Internet participants would be forced to weigh the advantages of the Internet with the potential of being subject to legal jurisdiction throughout the world. Third, the court did not assess Instruction Set's actual activity on the Internet.[20] The mere *use* of the Internet was sufficient for this court to establish jurisdiction.[21] In fact, the court acknowledged that Instruction Set did not maintain an office in Connecticut nor did it have a sales force or employees in the state.[22]

A more complete analysis of the underlying facts would have included an assessment of precisely what was happening on the Internet. Was Instruction Set selling products directly to people in Connecticut through its website? Was it providing a service directly through its website? Was it actively soliciting the participation of potential users by encouraging correspondence? What was the approximate number of Connecticut users who actually accessed the website? Asking these and similar questions would have provided the court with a much stronger basis for holding that Instruction Set had purposefully directed its activity toward Connecticut. Moreover, it would have developed a framework that would not allow courts to differentiate Internet activity for jurisdictional purposes.

While several U.S. cases followed the *Inset* approach,[23] a New York district court case stands out as an important exception.[24] The Blue Note was a small Columbia, Missouri club operated by Richard King. King promoted his club by establishing a website that included information about the club, a calendar of events, and ticketing information.[25] New York City was also home to a club named The Blue Note, this one operated by the Bensusan Restaurant Corporation, who owned a federal trademark in the name.[26] King was familiar with the New York Blue Note as he included a disclaimer on his website that stated: "The Blue Note's Cyberspot should not be confused with one of the world's finest jazz club[s], [the] Blue Note, located in the heart of New York's Greenwich Village. If you should find yourself in the Big Apple give them a visit."[27]

Within months of the establishment of King's Blue Note website, Bensusan brought a trademark infringement and dilution action in New York federal court.[28] Once again, the court faced the question of personal jurisdiction in a trademark action arising out of activity on the Internet. Unlike the *Inset* line of cases, however, the court considered the specific uses of the website in question. It noted that King's website was passive rather than active in nature—several affirmative steps by a New York resident would be necessary to bring any potentially infringing product into the state.[29] Specifically, tickets could not be ordered online, so that anyone wishing to make a purchase would have to telephone the box office in Missouri, only to find that the Missouri club did not mail tickets.[30] The purchaser would have to travel to Missouri to obtain the tickets.[31] Given the level of passivity, the court ruled that the website did not infringe Bensusan's trademark in New York.[32] The court argued "[t]he mere fact that a person can gain information on the allegedly infringing product is not the equivalent of a person advertising, promoting, selling or otherwise making an effort to target its product in New York."[33]

The *Bensusan* decision, which the Court of Appeals for the Second Circuit affirmed in September 1997,[34] provided an important step toward the development of deeper legal analysis of Internet activity. Although the decision did not attempt to reconcile the *Inset* line of cases, it provided the groundwork for a new line of cases.[35] However, by the end of 1996, the majority of Internet-related decisions evidenced little genuine understanding of activity on the Internet. Rather, most courts were unconcerned with the jurisdictional implications of their rulings and instead favored an analogy-based approach in which the Internet was categorized en masse.[36]

In early 1997, a new approach emerged, led by a Pennsylvania district court decision, *Zippo Manufacturing Co. v. Zippo Dot Com, Inc.*[37] It was with this decision that courts gradually began to appreciate that activity on the Internet was as varied as that in real space, and that all-encompassing analogies could not be appropriately applied to this new medium. *Zippo* Manufacturing was a Pennsylvania based manufacturer of the well-known *"Zippo"* brand of tobacco lighters.[38] Zippo Dot Com was a California based Internet news service that used the domain name "Zippo.com" to provide access to Internet newsgroups.[39] Zippo Dot Com offered three levels of subscriber service—free, original, and super.[40] Those subscribers desiring the original or super level of service were required to fill out an online application form and submit a credit card number through the Internet or by telephone.[41] Zippo Dot Com's contacts with Pennsylvania occurred almost exclusively on the Internet because the company maintained no offices, employees, or agents in the state.[42] Dot Com had some success in attracting Pennsylvania subscribers; at the time of the action, approximately 3,000, or two percent of its subscribers, resided in that state.[43] Once again, the issue before the court was one of personal jurisdiction arising out of a claim of trademark infringement and dilution.[44]

Rather than using Internet analogies as the basis for its analysis, the court focused on the prior, somewhat limited Internet case law.[45] The court, which clearly used the *Bensusan* decision for inspiration, determined that, although few cases had been decided, the likelihood that personal jurisdiction can be constitutionally exercised is *directly proportionate to the nature and quality of commercial activity that an entity conducts over the Internet.*[46]

The court proceeded to identify a sliding scale based on Internet commercial activity:

At one end of the spectrum are situations where a defendant clearly does business over the Internet. If the defendant enters into contracts with residents of a foreign jurisdiction that involve the knowing and repeated transmission of computer files over the Internet, personal jurisdiction is proper. At the opposite end are situations where a defendant has simply posted information on an Internet Web site, which is accessible to users in foreign jurisdictions. A passive Web site that does little more than make information available to those who are interested in it is not grounds for the exercise of personal jurisdiction. The middle ground is occupied by interactive Web sites where a user can exchange information with the host computer. In these cases, the exercise of jurisdiction is determined by examining the level of interactivity and commercial nature of the exchange of information that occurs on the Web site.[47]

Although the court may have conveniently interpreted some earlier cases to obtain its desired result, its critical finding was that the jurisdictional analysis in Internet cases should be based on the nature and quality of the commercial activity conducted on the Internet. There is a strong argument that prior to *Zippo*, jurisdictional analysis was based upon the mere use of the Internet. Courts relying solely on the inappropriate analogy between the Internet and advertisements developed a legal doctrine poorly suited to the reality of Internet activity. In the aftermath of the *Zippo* decision, Internet legal analysis underwent a significant shift in perspective.

B. Post-*Zippo* Case Law

In the years following *Zippo*, the passive versus active approach has been cited with approval in numerous cases.[48] For example, in *Cybersell, Inc. v. Cybersell, Inc.,* the Ninth Circuit considered whether it could exercise jurisdiction over a website containing an allegedly infringing service mark.[49] Both Cybersell Arizona, the owner of the "Cybersell" federal service mark, and Cybersell Florida provided Internet marketing and consulting services.[50] Cybersell Florida's presence in Arizona was limited to a website advertising its services and inviting interested parties to contact it for additional information.[51] The court, in determining the appropriateness of exercising jurisdiction, noted:

[N]o court has ever held that an Internet advertisement alone is sufficient to subject the advertiser to jurisdiction in the plaintiff's home state. Rather, in each, there has been "something more" to indicate that the defendant purposefully (albeit electronically) directed his activity in a substantial way to the forum state.[52]

The court followed the *Zippo* approach by attempting to ascertain the nature and quality of Cybersell Florida's web-based activity.[53] The court considered the passive nature of the site, the fact that no Arizonian other than Cybersell Arizona visited the site, and the lack of evidence that any Arizonians had entered into a contractual relationship with Cybersell.[54] On these facts, the court concluded that it could not properly assert jurisdiction in this matter.[55]

The widespread approval for the *Zippo* test should come as little surprise. The uncertainty created by the Internet jurisdiction issue led to a strong desire for a workable solution that provided a fair balance between the fear of a lawless Internet and one burdened by over-regulation. The *Zippo* test seemed the best available alternative. This is particularly true in light of the *Inset* line of cases, which illustrated that the alternative might well be the application of jurisdiction by any court, anywhere. The court in *Neato v. Stomp L.L.C.*, a 1999 federal court case in California, aptly summarized the competing policy positions of consumers and businesses: protecting consumers and encouraging the development of Internet commerce, respectively.[56] The court chose to side squarely with consumers, noting that businesses can choose to sell their goods only to consumers in a particular geographic location:

When a merchant seeks the benefit of engaging in unlimited interstate commerce over the Internet, it runs the risk of being subject to the process of the courts of those states.[57]

The *Zippo* passive versus active test is grounded in traditional jurisdictional principles. The analysis conducted as part of the test draws heavily from a foreseeability perspective, suggesting that it is not foreseeable for the owner of a passive website to face the prospect of being sued in multiple jurisdictions worldwide. Conversely, as the court in *Neato* recognized, the active e-commerce website owner must surely foresee the possibility of disputes arising in other jurisdictions, and recognize that those courts are entitled to protect local residents by applying local law and asserting jurisdiction.

Most important, however, in an emphatic repudiation of the "Internet as a separate jurisdiction[al]" approach, the *Zippo* case made it explicit that local law still applies to the Internet. Although it is at times difficult to discern precisely whose law applies, there is little doubt that at least one jurisdiction, if not more, can credibly claim jurisdiction over any given Internet dispute. With this principle in hand, the *Zippo* court sent a clear signal to the Internet community: courts were willing to establish a balanced approach to Internet jurisdiction.

C. The Shift Away from *Zippo*

Despite the widespread acceptance of the *Zippo* doctrine (and indeed the export of the test to foreign countries, including Canada), limitations of the test began to appear late in 1999. In fact, closer examination of the case law indicates that by 2001, many courts were no longer strictly applying the *Zippo* standard, but were using other criteria to determine when assertion of jurisdiction was appropriate.[58]

Numerous judgments reflect that courts in the United States moved toward a broader, effects-based approach when deciding whether or not to assert jurisdiction in the Internet context. Under this new approach, rather than examining the specific characteristics of a website and its potential impact, courts focused their analysis on the actual effects that the website had in the jurisdiction. Indeed, courts are now relying increasingly on the effects doctrine established by the United States Supreme Court in *Calder v. Jones*.[59]

The effects doctrine holds that personal jurisdiction over a defendant is proper when: a) the defendant's intentional tortious actions b) expressly aimed at the forum state c) cause harm to the plaintiff in the forum state, which the defendant knows is likely to be suffered.[60] In *Calder*, a California entertainer sued a Florida publisher for libel in a California district court.[61] In ruling that personal jurisdiction was properly asserted, the Court focused on the effects of the defendant's actions.[62] Reasoning that the plaintiff lived and worked in California, spent most of her career in California, suffered injury to her professional reputation in California, and suffered emotional distress in California, the Court concluded that the defendant had intentionally targeted a California resident and thus it was proper to sue the publisher in that state.[63]

The application of the *Calder* test can be seen in the Internet context in *Blakey v. Continental Airlines, Inc.*,[64] an online defamation case involving an airline employee. The employee filed suit in New Jersey against her co-employees, alleging that they published defamatory statements on the employer's electronic bulletin board, and against her employer, a New Jersey-based corporation, alleging that it was liable for the hostile work environment arising from the statements.[65] The lower court granted the co-employees' motion to dismiss for lack of personal jurisdiction and entered summary judgment for the employer on the hostile work environment claim.[66]

In reversing the ruling, the New Jersey Supreme Court found that defendants who published defamatory electronic messages with the knowledge that the messages would be published in New Jersey could properly be held subject to the state's jurisdiction.[67] The court applied the effects doctrine and held that while the actions causing the effects in New Jersey were performed outside the state, this did not prevent the court from asserting jurisdiction over a cause of action arising out of those effects.[68]

The broader effects-based analysis has moved beyond the defamatory tort action at issue in *Calder* and *Blakey* to a range of disputes including intellectual property and commercial activities. On the intellectual property front, *Nissan Motor Co. Ltd. v. Nissan Computer Corp.*,[69] typifies the approach. The plaintiff, an automobile manufacturer, filed a complaint in a California district court against a Massachusetts-based computer seller. Prompting the complaint was an allegation that the defendant altered the content of its "nissan.com" website to include a logo that was similar to the plaintiff's logo and links to automobile merchandisers and auto-related portions of search engines.[70] In October 1999, the parties met to discuss the possibility of transferring the "nissan.com" domain name.[71] These negotiations proved unsuccessful.[72] The defendant brought a motion to dismiss for lack of personal jurisdiction and improper venue, and the plaintiff brought a motion for a preliminary injunction in March 2000.[73]

In considering the defendant's motion, the court relied on the effects doctrine, ruling that the defendant had intentionally changed the content of its website to exploit the plaintiff's goodwill and to profit from consumer confusion.[74] Moreover, since the plaintiff was based in California, the majority of the harm was suffered in the forum state.[75] The court rejected the defendant's argument that it was not subject to personal jurisdiction because it merely operated a passive website.[76] Although the defendant did not sell anything over the Internet, it derived advertising revenue through the intentional exploitation of consumer confusion.[77] This fact, according to the court, satisfied the *Cybersell* requirement of "something more," in that it established that the defendant's conduct was deliberately and substantially directed toward the forum state.[78]

Courts have also refused to assert jurisdiction in a number of cases where insufficient commercial effects were found. For example, in *People*

Solutions, Inc. v. People Solutions, Inc.,[79] the defendant, a California-based corporation, moved to dismiss a trademark infringement suit brought against it by a Texas-based corporation of the same name. The plaintiff argued that the suit was properly brought in Texas because the defendant owned a website that could be accessed and viewed by Texas residents.[80] The site featured several interactive pages that allowed customers to take and score performance tests, download product demonstrations, and order products online.[81]

The court characterized the site as interactive but refused to assert jurisdiction over the matter.[82] Relying on evidence that no Texans had actually purchased from the website, the court held that "[p]ersonal jurisdiction should not be premised on the mere possibility, with nothing more, that defendant may be able to do business with Texans over its website."[83] Instead, the plaintiff had to show that the defendant had "purposefully availed itself of the benefits of the forum state and its laws."[84]

Although the case law illustrates that there is no single reason for the courts to shift away from the *Zippo* test, a number of themes do emerge. First, the test simply does not work particularly well in every instance. For example, with courts characterizing chat room postings as passive in nature,[85] many might be inclined to dismiss cases involving allegedly defamatory or harassing speech on jurisdictional grounds. Such speech may often be targeted toward a particular individual or entity located in a jurisdiction different from the poster or the chat site itself. Characterizing this act as passive does not result in a desirable outcome since the poster knows or ought to know that the effect of his posting will be felt most acutely in the home jurisdiction of the target. If the target is unable to sue locally due to a strict adherence to the passive versus active test, the law might be seen as encouraging online defamatory speech by creating a jurisdictional hurdle to launching a legal claim.

The *Zippo* test also falls short when active sites are at issue, as the court in *People Solutions* recognized.[86] That court's request for evidence of actual sales within the jurisdiction illustrates that the mere potential to sell within a jurisdiction does not necessarily make a website active.[87] While the owner of an active website may want to sell into every jurisdiction, the foreseeability of a legal action is confined primarily to those places where actual sales occur. The *Zippo* test does not distinguish between actual and potential sales, however, but rather provides that the mere existence of an active site is sufficient to assert jurisdiction.

The problems with the *Zippo* test are not limited to inconsistent and often undesirable outcomes. The test also encourages a perverse behavior that runs contrary to public policy related to the Internet and e-commerce. Most countries have embraced the potential of e-commerce and adopted policies designed to encourage the use of the Internet for commercial purposes.[88] The *Zippo* test, however, inhibits e-commerce by effectively discouraging the adoption of interactive websites. Prospective website owners who are concerned about their exposure to legal liability will rationally shy away from developing active websites because such sites increase the likelihood of facing lawsuits in far-off jurisdictions. Instead, the test encourages passive websites that feature limited legal exposure and therefore present limited risk. Since public policy aims to increase interactivity and the adoption of e-commerce (and in doing so, enhance consumer choice and open new markets for small and medium sized businesses), the *Zippo* test acts as a barrier to that policy approach.

One of the primary reasons for the early widespread support for the *Zippo* test was the desire for increased legal certainty for Internet jurisdiction issues. While the test may not have been perfect, supporters felt it offered a clear standard that would allow businesses to conduct effective legal risk analysis and make rational choices with regard to their approach to the Internet.[89]

In the final analysis, however, the *Zippo* test simply does not deliver the desired effect. First, the majority of websites are neither entirely passive nor completely active. Accordingly, they fall into the "middle zone," that requires courts to gauge all relevant evidence and determine whether the site is "more passive" or "more active." With many sites falling into this middle zone, their legal advisors are frequently unable to provide a firm opinion on how any given court might judge the interactivity of the website.

Second, distinguishing between passive and active sites is complicated by the fact that some sites may not be quite what they seem. For example, sites that feature content best characterized as passive, may actually be using cookies or other data collection technologies behind the scenes unbeknownst to the individual user.[90] Given the value of personal data,[91] its collection is properly characterized as active, regardless of whether it occurs transparently or surreptitiously.[92] Similarly, sites such as online chatrooms may appear to be active, yet courts have consistently characterized such sites as passive.[93]

Third, it is important to note that the standards for what constitutes an active or passive website are constantly shifting. When the test was developed in 1997, an active website might have featured little more than an email link and some basic correspondence functionality. Today, sites with that level of interactivity would likely be viewed as passive, since the entire spectrum of passive versus active has shifted upward with improved technology. In fact, it can be credibly argued that owners of websites must constantly re-evaluate their positions on the passive versus active spectrum as web technology changes.

Fourth, the *Zippo* test is ineffective even if the standards for passive and active sites remain constant. With the expense of creating a sophisticated website now easily in excess of $100,000,[94] few organizations will invest in a website without anticipating some earning potential. Since revenue is typically the hallmark of active websites, most new sites are likely to feature interactivity, and therefore be categorized as active sites. From a jurisdictional perspective, this produces an effect similar to that found in the *Inset* line of cases—any court anywhere can assert jurisdiction over a website because virtually all sites will meet the *Zippo* active benchmark.

In light of the ever-changing technological environment and the shift toward predominantly active websites, the effectiveness of the *Zippo* doctrine is severely undermined no matter how it develops. If the test evolves with the changing technological environment, it fails to provide much needed legal certainty. On the other hand, if the test remains static to provide increased legal certainty, it risks becoming irrelevant as the majority of websites meet the active standard. In the next section, this paper will offer an alternative test.

III. Toward a Trio of Targets

Given the inadequacies of the *Zippo* passive versus active test, a new standard is needed to determine jurisdiction over Internet contacts. This section sketches the components of a targeting test by focusing on three factors: contracts, technology, and actual or implied knowledge.

A. Advantages of a Targeting Approach

The *Zippo* experience suggests that the new test should remain technology neutral so as to: a) remain relevant despite ever-changing web technologies, b) create incentives that, at a minimum, do not discourage online interactivity, and c) provide sufficient certainty so that the legal risk of operating online can be effectively assessed in advance.

The solution submitted here is to move toward a targeting-based analysis. Unlike the *Zippo* approach, a targeting analysis would seek to identify the intentions of the parties and to assess the steps taken to either enter or avoid a particular jurisdiction. Targeting would also lessen the reliance on effects-based analyses, the source of considerable uncertainty because Internet-based activity can ordinarily be said to cause effects in most jurisdictions.

A targeting approach is not a novel idea. Several United States courts have factored targeting considerations into their jurisdictional analysis of Internet-based activities. The strongest indication of a move toward a targeting test for Internet jurisdiction came in April 2001 in *American Information Corp. v. American Infometrics, Inc.,* a Maryland district court case.[95] The court left little doubt that targeting was a central consideration in its jurisdictional analysis, stating that:

> In the case at bar, non-customers cannot interact with the website except to submit their contract information to inquire about available services or jobs, according to Goreff, and no one from Maryland has ever inquired, or been a customer of American Infometrics. On a company's website, neither the "mere existence of an e-mail link, without more," nor "receiving . . . an indication of interest," without more, subjects the company to jurisdiction. The ability of viewers to ask about the company's services, particularly in the absence of any showing that anyone in Maryland has ever done so, does not subject the company to jurisdiction here.[96]

Fourth Circuit cases on minimum contacts supported the view that the American Informetrics' website did not create jurisdiction in Maryland. A company's sales activities focusing "generally on customers located throughout the United States and Canada without focusing on and targeting" the forum state did not yield personal jurisdiction.[97] A web presence that permits no more than basic inquiries from Maryland customers that has never yielded an actual inquiry from a Maryland customer, and that does not target Maryland in any way, similarly, should not yield personal jurisdiction.[98]

Targeting-based analysis has also become increasingly prevalent among international organizations seeking to develop global minimum legal standards for e-commerce. The OECD Consumer Protection Guidelines refer to the concept of targeting, stating that "business should take into account the global nature of electronic commerce and, wherever possible, should consider various regulatory characteristics of the markets they target."[99] Similarly, a recent draft of the Hague Conference on Private International Law's Draft Convention on Jurisdiction and Foreign Judgments includes provisions related to targeting.[100]

The American Bar Association Internet Jurisdiction Project, a global study on Internet jurisdiction released in 2000, also recommended targeting as one method of addressing the Internet jurisdiction issue.[101] It was noted in the report:

[E]ntities seeking a relationship with residents of a foreign forum need not themselves maintain a physical presence in the forum. A forum can be "targeted" by those outside it and desirous of benefiting from a connecting with it via the Internet . . . . Such a chosen relationship will subject the foreign actor to both personal and prescriptive jurisdiction, so a clear understanding of what constitutes targeting is critical.[102]

It is the ABA's last point—that a clear understanding of what constitutes targeting is critical—that requires careful examination and discussion. Without universally applicable standards for assessment of targeting in the online environment, a targeting test is likely to leave further uncertainty in its wake. For example, the ABA's report refers to language as a potentially important determinant for targeting purposes. That criterion overlooks the fact that the development of new language translation capabilities may soon enable website owners to display their site in the language of their choice, safe in the knowledge that visitors around the world will read the content in their own language through the aid of translation technologies.[103]

B. The Targeting Test

Targeting as the litmus test for Internet jurisdiction is only the first step in the development of a consistent test that provides increased legal certainty. The second, more challenging step is to identify the criteria to be used in assessing whether a website has indeed targeted a particular jurisdiction. This article cites three factors: contracts, technology, and actual or implied knowledge. Forum selection clauses found in website terms of use agreements or transactional clickwrap agreements allow parties to mutually determine an appropriate jurisdiction in advance of a dispute. They therefore provide important evidence as to the foreseeability of being haled into the courts of a particular jurisdiction. Newly emerging technologies that identify geographic location constitute the second factor. These technologies, which challenge widely held perceptions about the Internet's architecture, may allow website owners to target their content by engaging in "jurisdictional avoidance." The third factor, actual or implied knowledge, is a catch-all that incorporates targeting knowledge gained through the geographic location of tort victims, offline order fulfillment, financial intermediary records, and web traffic.

Although all three factors are important, no single factor should be determinative. Rather, each must be analyzed to adequately assess whether the parties have fairly negotiated a governing jurisdiction clause at a private contract level, whether the parties employed any technological solutions to target their activities, and whether the parties knew, or ought to have known, where their online activities were occurring. While all three factors should be considered as part of a targeting analysis, the relative importance of each will vary. Moreover, in certain instances, some factors may not matter at all. For example, a defamation action is unlikely to involve a contractual element, though evidence from the knowledge factor is likely to prove sufficient to identify the targeted jurisdiction.

It is important to also note that the targeting analysis will not determine exclusive jurisdiction, but rather identify whether a particular jurisdiction can be appropriately described as having been targeted. The test does not address which venue is the *most* appropriate of the jurisdictions that meet the targeting threshold.

1. Contracts

The first of the three factors for the recommended targeting test considers whether either party has used a contractual arrangement to specify which law should govern. Providing parties with the opportunity to limit their legal risk by addressing jurisdictional concerns in advance can be the most efficient and cost-effective approach to dealing with the Internet jurisdiction issue. The mere existence of a jurisdictional clause within a contract, however, should not, in and of itself, be determinative of the issue, particularly when consumer contracts are involved. In addition to considering the two other targeting factors, the weight accorded to an online contract should depend upon the method used to obtain assent and the reasonableness of the terms contained in the contract.

Courts in the United States have upheld the per se enforceability of an online contract,[104] commonly referred to as a clickwrap agreement. In *Kilgallen v. Network Solutions, Inc.*,[105] the court faced a dispute over the re-registration of a domain name. The plaintiff claimed that Network Solutions, the defendant, was in breach of contract when it transferred its domain name to a third party.[106] Network Solutions defended its actions by countering that the plaintiff had failed to make the annual payment necessary to maintain the domain.[107] Moreover, it sought to dismiss the action on the grounds that the registration agreement specified that all disputes were to be resolved in the Eastern District of Virginia.[108] The federal court in Massachusetts agreed, ruling that forum selection clauses are enforceable unless proven unreasonable under the circumstances.[109]

Notwithstanding the apparent support for enforcing forum selection clauses within clickwrap agreements, the presence of such a clause should only serve as the starting point for analysis. A court must first consider how assent to the contract was obtained. If the agreement is a standard clickwrap agreement in which users were required to positively indicate their agreement by clicking on an "I agree" or similar icon, the court will likely deem this to be valid assent. Many jurisdictional clauses are not found in a clickwrap agreement, however, but rather are contained in the terms of use agreement on the website. The terms typically provide that users of the website agree to all terms contained therein by virtue of their use of the website.

The validity of this form of contract, in which no positive assent is obtained and the website visitor is unlikely to have read the terms, stands on shakier ground. Three recent United States cases have considered this form of contract with the consensus moving toward nonenforcement. In *Ticketmaster v. Tickets.com*,[110] a dispute over links between rival event ticket sites, the court considered the enforceability of the terms and conditions page found on the Ticketmaster site and concluded that the forum selection clause was not enforceable.[111] The terms and conditions set forth on the Ticketmaster home page provided that users going beyond the home page were prevented from making commercial use of the information and were prohibited from deep linking.[112] Ticketmaster defended on the grounds that courts enforce "shrink-wrap licenses" where "packing on the outside of the CD stated that opening the package constitutes adherence to the license agreement . . . contained therein."[113]

The court found that Ticketmaster's system of notification did not create a binding contract on the user.[114] Unlike the agreement on the Ticketmaster site, "the 'shrink-wrap license agreement' is open and obvious and in fact hard to miss."[115] Ticketmaster's terms and conditions did not require the user to "click on 'agree' to the terms and conditions before going on" as many websites do.[116] The court further noted that customers were required "to scroll down the home page to find and read" the terms and conditions.[117] Given this system, "[m]any customers . . . are likely to proceed to the event page of interest rather than reading the 'small print.' *It cannot be said that merely putting the terms and conditions in this fashion necessarily creates a contract with any one using the website.*"[118] This case suggests that mere inclusion of a forum selection or other jurisdictional clause, within the terms and conditions, may not be enforceable because the term is not brought sufficiently to the attention of the user.

Several months after the Ticketmaster decision, another federal court adopted a different approach in *Register.com, Inc. v. Verio, Inc.*[119] This case involved a dispute over Verio's use of automated software to access and collect the domain name registrant's contact information contained in the Register.com WHOIS database. Verio collected the data to use for marketing purposes.[120] Register.com provided the following terms and conditions for those wishing to access its WHOIS database:

By submitting a WHOIS query, you agree that you will use this data only for lawful purposes and that, under no circumstances will you use this data to: (1) allow, enable, or otherwise support the transmission of mass unsolicited, commercial advertising or solicitations via direct mail, electronic mail, or by telephone; or (2) enable high volume, automated, electronic processes that apply to Register.com (or its systems). The compilation, repackaging, dissemination or other use of this data is expressly prohibited without the prior written consent of Register.com. Register.com reserves the right to modify these terms at any time. By submitting this query, you agree to abide by these terms.[121]

Unlike the *Ticketmaster* case, the court in Register.com ruled that these terms were binding on users, despite the absence of a clear manifestation of assent.[122] The court relied on the users' willingness to engage with the website, by using the WHOIS database, as evidence that the user could implicitly be considered to have agreed to the terms of the contract.

Most recently, in *Specht v. Netscape Communications Corp.*,[123] the same federal court in New York distinguished between clickwrap contracts, which it argued features positive assent in the form of clicking "I agree", and browsewrap contracts, in which the user is merely alerted to the existence of a contract through a disclaimer or other notice. The court ruled that the latter form of contract, employed in this case by Netscape Communications, was not binding against the user since Netscape had failed to obtain the user's positive assent. Netscape argued "the mere act of downloading indicates assent."[124] As the court noted, however, "downloading is hardly an unambiguous indication of assent" because "[t]he primary purpose of downloading is to obtain a product, not to assent to an agreement."[125] The court criticized Netscape for not drawing the user's attention to the clickwrap contract, for not requiring an affirmative manifestation of assent, and for only making a "mild request" that the user review the terms of the licensing agreement.[126]

While the form of assent may call into question the validity of an online contract, the actual terms of the contract itself are of even greater consequence. Courts are required to consider the reasonableness of the terms of a contract as part of their analysis. Within the context of a jurisdictional inquiry, several different scenarios may lead the court to discount the importance of the contract as part of a targeting analysis. A court may simply rule that the forum selection clause is unenforceable in light of the overall nature of the contract.

This occurred in *Mendoza v. AOL,*[127] a recent California case involving a disputed ISP bill. After Mendoza sued AOL in California state court, AOL responded by seeking to have the case dismissed on the grounds that the AOL service contract contains a forum selection clause that requires all disputes arising from the contract to be brought in Virginia.[128] The court surprised AOL by refusing to enforce the company's terms of service agreement on the grounds that "it would be unfair and unreasonable because the clause in question was not negotiated at arm's length, was contained in a standard form contract, and was not readily identifiable by plaintiff due to the small text and location of the clause at the conclusion of the agreement."[129] Though cases such as *Mendoza* are the exception rather than the rule, they do point to the fact that a forum selection clause will not always be enforced, particularly in consumer disputes where the provision may be viewed by a court as too onerous given the small amount at issue.[130]

Courts may also be unwilling to enforce such clauses where the court perceives the clause to be an attempt to contract out of the jurisdiction with the closest tie to the parties. Courts must be vigilant to ensure that forum selection clauses are not used to create a "race to the bottom" effect whereby parties select jurisdictions with lax regulations in an attempt to avoid more onerous regulations in the home jurisdictions of either the seller or purchaser.[131]

Contracts must clearly play a central role in any determination of jurisdiction targeting since providing parties with the opportunity to set their own rules enhances legal certainty. As the foregoing review of recent Internet jurisdiction case law reveals, however, contracts do not provide the parties with absolute assurance that their choice will be enforced, particularly in a consumer context. Rather, courts must engage in a detailed analysis of how consent was obtained as well as consider the reasonableness of the terms. The results of that analysis should determine what weight to grant the contractual terms when balanced against the remaining two factors of the proposed targeting analysis.

2. Technology

The second targeting factor focuses on the use of technology to either target or avoid specific jurisdictions. Just as technology originally shaped the Internet, it is now reshaping its boundaries by quickly making geographic identification on the Internet a reality. The rapid emergence of these new technologies challenges what has been treated as a truism in cyberlaw—that the Internet is borderless and thus impervious to attempts to impose on it real-space laws that mirror traditional geographic boundaries.[132]

Courts have largely accepted the notion that the Internet is borderless as reflected by their reluctance to even consider the possibility that geographic mapping might be possible online. In *American Libraries Ass'n v. Pataki,*[133] a Commerce Clause challenge to a New York state law targeting Internet content classified as obscene, the court characterized geography on the Internet in the following manner:

The Internet is wholly insensitive to geographic distinctions. In almost every case, users of the Internet neither know nor care about the physical location of the Internet resources they access. Internet protocols were designed to ignore rather than document geographic location; while computers on the network do have "addresses," they are logical addresses on the network rather than geographic addresses in real space. The majority of Internet addresses contain no geographic clues and, even where an Internet address provides such a clue, it may be misleading.[134]

Although the ALA court's view of the Internet may have been accurate in 1997, the Internet has not remained static. Providers of Internet content increasingly care about the physical location of Internet resources and the users that access them, as do legislators and courts who may want real space limitations imposed on the online environment.[135] A range of companies have responded to those needs by developing technologies that provide businesses with the ability to reduce their legal risk by targeting their online presence to particular geographic constituencies. These technologies also serve the interests of governments and regulators who may now be better positioned to apply their offline regulations to the online environment.[136]

Since both business and government share a vested interest in bringing geographic borders to the online environment (albeit for different reasons), it should come as little surprise that these technologies have so quickly arrived onto the marketplace. In fact, they have become available before the Internet community has engaged in a current discussion on the benefits, challenges, and consequences of creating borders or "zoning" the Internet with these new technologies.[137] This is most unfortunate since geographic bordering technologies raise important privacy considerations that have, as yet, attracted little debate.[138]

Although critics often point to the inaccuracy of these technologies, few users of the technology actually demand perfection.[139] Businesses want either to target their message to consumers in a specific jurisdiction or to engage in "jurisdictional avoidance."[140] Effective jurisdictional avoidance provides the means to exclude the majority of visitors who cannot be verified as residing in the desired jurisdiction. For example, iCraveTV, a Canadian webcaster, did not use identifying technologies, choosing instead to rely on the user clickwrap agreements.[141] JumpTV, a newer Canadian entry into the webcasting market, has indicated that it will use identifying technologies to ensure that only Canadians access its signal.[142] While this may exclude some Canadians who cannot be positively identified as coming from Canada, it will provide the company with a greater level of assurance in meeting its goal of limiting its online signal.

Government, on the other hand, may often want to engage in jurisdictional identification so that it can more easily identify when its laws are triggered. For example, Nevada recently enacted legislation that paves the way for the Nevada Gaming Commission to legalize online gambling.[143] Central to the new legislation is jurisdiction identification. Section 3(2) provides:

> The commission may not adopt regulations governing the licensing and operation of interactive gaming until the commission first determines that:
>
> (a) Interactive gaming can be operated in compliance with all applicable laws;
>
> (b) Interactive gaming systems are secure and reliable, and provide reasonable assurance that players will be of lawful age and communicating only from jurisdictions where it is lawful to make such communications.[144]

To reach the determination required by subsection (b), an analysis of available geographic identification technology will be necessary.

Geographic identification technologies can be grouped into at least three categories: a) user identification, which is typically based on IP address identification; b) self-identification, which often occurs through attribute certificates; and c) offline identification.

a) User Identification

User identification has been utilized on a relatively primitive scale for some time. For example, for many years, in order to comply with United States regulations prohibiting the export of strong-encryption web browsers, Microsoft has used Internet Protocol (IP) lookups, which determine user locations by cross-checking their IP address against databases that list Internet service provider locations.[145] Although imperfect, the process was viewed as sufficiently effective to meet the standards imposed by the regulations. Recently, several companies, including Infosplit, NetGeo, Akamai, Quova, and Digital Envoy, have begun offering more sophisticated versions of similar technologies.

b) Self-identification

Unlike user identification technologies, which identify the user's geographic location without requesting permission to do so, self-identification uses technologies that enable users to provide geographic identification directly to the website. This is most frequently accomplished through the use of attribute certificates, which, as Michael Froomkin explains, provide information about the attributes of a particular user without revealing his actual identity:

> Although identifying certificates are likely to be the most popular type of certificate in the short run, in the medium term CAs are likely to begin certifying attributes other than identity. An authorizing certificate might state where the subject resides, the subject's age, that the subject is a member in good standing of an organization, that the subject is a registered user of a product, or that the subject possesses a license such as bar membership.[146]

Froomkin points out that attribute certificates have many potential applications, chief among them geographic identification.[147] Self-identification technology represents a middle ground between user identification, which puts the power of identification solely in the hands of the website, and self-declaration, in which the user declares where they reside but without any independent or technological verification of the accuracy of the declaration. The danger with self-identification technologies is that if they become popular, they may also quickly cease to be voluntary since businesses may begin to require that their users supply the data contained in an attribute certificate in order to obtain service.[148]

c) Offline Identification

Offline identification combines an online presence with certain offline knowledge to form a geographic profile of a user. The best example of offline identification is credit card data. Since credit cards remain the preferred payment mechanism for most online transactions, sellers are regularly asked to verify the validity of a user's credit card. The verification process for online purchases includes an offline component, as the address submitted by the user is cross-checked with the address on file to confirm a match prior to authorization of the charge.[149] This process provides websites with access to offline data such as the user's complete address—which is confirmed through a third party, the financial intermediary.

While this system may be effective for sites actively engaged in e-commerce and for those whose geographic risks are confined strictly to those circumstances when they are selling into a particular jurisdiction, the use of credit-card data is of limited utility to those who do not actively sell online or those who are concerned about jurisdictional issues prior to the submission of a credit card number and address information. This would include sites such as JumpTV, which use an advertiser-supported model so that they do not require users to provide credit card data, yet are concerned with the availability of the site outside Canada.

Though clearly limited in scope, offline identifiers have the advantage of being the most inexpensive method of identifying geographic location because they rely on offline data collected independently of online activities. Precisely because they merge offline and online, these technologies raise profound privacy concerns, creating the prospect of personally identifiable information being transferred along with nonidentifiable geographic data.

d) Targeting and Technology

Given the development of new technologies that allow for geographic identification with a reasonable degree of accuracy, a targeting test must include a technology component that places the onus on the party contesting or asserting jurisdiction to demonstrate what technical measures, including offline identifiers, it employed to either target or avoid a particular jurisdiction. The suitability of such an onus lies in the core consideration of jurisdiction law—that is, whether jurisdiction is foreseeable under the circumstances. Geographic identifying technologies provide the party that deploys the technology with a credible answer to that question at a cost far less than comparable litigation expenses. Since parties can identify who is accessing their site, they can use technical measures to stop people from legally risky jurisdictions, including those jurisdictions where a site owner is reluctant to contest potential litigation or face regulatory scrutiny, from doing so. A fair and balanced targeting jurisdiction test demands that they do just that.

It is important to note that parties are not typically required to use geographic identification technologies.[150] In many instances, they do not care who accesses their site and thus will be unwilling and may not have the incentive to incur the expense of installing such systems. In other instances, the party may be acutely aware of the need to identify users from a jurisdiction that bans access to certain content or certain activities. In such instances, the party may wish to limit access to those users it can positively identify from a safe jurisdiction.

The inclusion of technology into the targeting test does not, therefore, obligate parties to use the technology. Rather, it forces parties to acknowledge that such technologies are available and that prudence may dictate using them in some capacity. Moreover, the test does not prescribe any specific technology—it only requires that consideration be given to the technologies used and available at a particular moment in time. This technology neutral prong of the targeting test, which does not prescribe a particular type of technology but rather the outcome, also provides an effective counterbalance to the contract and knowledge factors. It removes the ability to be willfully blind to users who enter into a clickwrap contract stating that they are from one jurisdiction, while the technological evidence suggests something else entirely.

3. Actual or Implied Knowledge

The third targeting factor assesses the knowledge the parties had or ought to have had about the geographic location of the online activity. Although some authors have suggested that the Internet renders intent and knowledge obsolete by virtue of the Internet's architecture,[151] the geographic identification technologies described above do not support this view. This factor ensures that parties cannot hide behind contracts and/or technology by claiming a lack of targeting knowledge when the evidence suggests otherwise.

The implied knowledge factor is most apparent in the defamation tort cases that follow from the *Calder* decision. In those cases, courts have accepted that the defaming party is or should be aware that the injury inflicted by her speech would be felt in the jurisdiction of her target. Accordingly, in such cases a party would be unable to rely on a contract that specifies an alternate jurisdiction as the choice of forum.

The court's desire to dismiss any hint of willful blindness is evident in the *People v. World Interactive Gaming* case, referred to earlier.[152] In that case, the online casino argued that it had limited access to only those users that had entered an address of a jurisdiction where gambling was permitted. The court saw through this ruse, however, firmly stating that:

[t]his Court rejects respondents' argument that it unknowingly accepted bets from New York residents. New York users can easily circumvent the casino software in order to play by the simple expedient of entering an out-of-state address. Respondents' violation of the Penal Law is that they persisted in continuous illegal conduct directed toward the creation, establishment, and advancement of unauthorized gambling.[153]

The relevance of a knowledge-based factor extends beyond reliance on contracts that the parties know to be false. In an e-commerce context, the knowledge that comes from order fulfillment is just as important. For example, sales of physical goods such as computer equipment or books, provide online sellers with data such as a real-space delivery address, making it relatively easy to exclude jurisdictions that the seller does not wish to target.

Courts have also begun to use a knowledge-based analysis when considering jurisdiction over intellectual property disputes. In *Starmedia Network v. Star Media, Inc.,*[154] an April 2001 federal case from New York, the court asserted jurisdiction over an alleged out-of state trademark infringer, noting that:

[t]he defendant knew of plaintiff's domain name before it registered "starmediausa.com" as its domain name. Therefore, the defendant knew or should have known of plaintiff's place of business, and should have anticipated being haled into New York's courts to answer for the harm to a New York plaintiff caused by using a similar mark.[155]

Although the application of the knowledge principle is more complex when the sale involves digital goods for which there is no offline delivery, the seller is still customarily furnished with potentially relevant information. As discussed above, most telling may be credit card data that the purchaser typically provides to the seller. In addition to the credit card number and expiration date, the purchaser is often also required to supply billing address information so that the validity of the card can be verified before authorization. Since the seller is supplied with a real-space billing address for digital transactions, there remains the opportunity to forego the sale if there is a jurisdictional concern. For example, the Washington Capitals hockey team recently rejected attempts by rival fans from Pittsburgh to purchase tickets on the team's website. The site was set to reject purchase attempts from customers entering a Pittsburgh-area code.[156] While some sellers may be loathe to use consumer payment information in this fashion, the approach reflects a more general trend toward recognizing the important role that payment intermediaries such as credit card companies play in the consumer e-commerce process.[157]

IV. Conclusion

With courts increasingly resisting the *Zippo* passive versus active approach to Internet jurisdiction, the time for the adoption of a new targeting-based test has arrived. Unlike the *Zippo* test, which suffers from a series of drawbacks including inconsistent and undesirable outcomes as well as the limitations of a technology-specific approach, a targeting-based analysis provides all interested parties—including courts, e-commerce companies, and consumers—with the tools needed to conduct more effective legal risk analysis.

Under the three-factor targeting test, it is important to note that no single factor is determinative. Analysis will depend on a combined assessment of all three factors in order to determine whether the party knowingly targeted the particular jurisdiction and could reasonably foresee being haled into court there. In an e-commerce context, the targeting test ultimately establishes a trade-off that should benefit both companies and consumers. Companies benefit from the assurance that operating an e-commerce site will not necessarily result in jurisdictional claims from any jurisdiction worldwide. They can more confidently limit their legal risk exposure by targeting only those countries where they are compliant with local law.

Consumers also benefit from this approach since they receive the reassurance that online companies that target them will be answerable to their local law. The test is sufficiently flexible to allow companies to deploy as many or as few precautions as needed. For example, if the company is involved in a highly regulated or controversial field, it will likely want to confine its activities to a limited number of jurisdictions, avoiding locations with which it is unfamiliar. Under the targeting test, the company could adopt a strategy of implementing technological measures to identify its geographic reach, while simultaneously incorporating the desired limitations into its contract package. Conversely, companies with fewer legal concerns and a desire to sell worldwide can still accomplish this goal under the targeting test analysis. These companies would sell without the technological support, incurring both the benefits and responsibilities of a global e-commerce enterprise.

Notwithstanding the advantages of a targeting test, there are, nevertheless, some potential drawbacks. First, the test accelerates the creation of a bordered Internet. Although a bordered Internet carries certain advantages, it is also subject to abuse because countries can use bordering technologies to keep foreign influences out and suppress free speech locally.[158] Second, the targeting test might also result in less consumer choice since many sellers may stop selling to consumers in certain jurisdictions where risk analysis suggests that the benefits are not worth the potential legal risks.

Although the targeting test will not alter every jurisdictional outcome, it will provide all parties with greater legal certainty and a more effective means of conducting legal risk assessments. The move toward using contract and technology to erect virtual borders may not answer the question of whether there is a there there, but at least it will go a long way in determining where the there might be.

Acknowledgments

The author would like to thank the Uniform Law Conference of Canada and Industry Canada for their financial support in sponsoring this paper; Teresa David and William Karam for their research assistance; Vaso Maric, Rene Geist, Harvey Goldschmid, Ted Killheffer, Denis Rice, as well as the participants at the Consumer Measures Committee/Uniform Law Conference of Canada April 2001 Workshop on Consumer Protection and Jurisdiction in Electronic Commerce, the TPRC 2001 Conference, and the Georgetown University Advanced E-commerce Institute, for their comments on earlier versions of this paper; and to the editors of the BERKELEY TECHNOLOGY LAW JOURNAL for their excellent work in bringing the paper upon which this is based to publication. Any errors or omissions remain the sole responsibility of the author.

Notes

1. Digital Equip. Corp. v. Altavista Tech. , Inc., 960 F. Supp. 456, 462 (D. Mass. 1997).
2. Yahoo!, Inc. v. LICRA, C-00-21275 JF, 2001 U.S. Dist. LEXIS 18378, at *6,

7 (N.D. Cal. Nov. 7, 2001) (citing the French court's decision in UEJF et LICRA v. Yahoo! Inc. et Yahoo France).

3. *See, e.g.,* Louis Trager, *Unhappy Holidays at Toys "R" Us,* ZDNET INTERACTIVE WK., January 12, 2000, *at* <http://www.zdnet.com/filters/printerfriendly/-0,6061,2421416-35,00.html>.

4. *See, e.g.,* Cornell Law School Legal Information Institute, Products Liability Law: An Overview, *at* <http://www.law.cornell.edu/topics/products_liability.html> (last visited Nov. 26, 2001).

5. *See, e.g.,* UEJF et LICRA v. Yahoo! Inc. et Yahoo France, T.G.I. Paris, May 22, 2000, N° RG: 00/05308 [hereinafter *Yahoo!France*]; *see also* Braintech, Inc. v. Kostiuk, [1999] 171 D.L.R. (4th) 46, 63–64 (B.C.C.A.).

6. The U.S. Federal Trade Commission has noted:

> Shifting to a pure country-of-origin approach to address challenges inherent in the current system risks undermining consumer protection, and ultimately consumer confidence in e-commerce. The same would be true under a "pre-scribed-by-seller" approach to the extent it would allow contractual choice-of-law and choice-of-forum provisions dictated by the seller to override the core protections afforded to consumers in their home country or their right to sue in a local court.

United States Federal Trade Commission, Bureau of Consumer Protection, Consumer Protection in the Global Electronic Marketplace: Looking Ahead (Staff Report), *available at* <http://www.ftc.gov/bcp/icpw/lookingahead/electronicmkpl.pdf> (Sept. 2001).

7. *See Yahoo!France, supra* note 5; *see also Yahoo! Ordered to Bar French from Nazi Sites,* REUTERS, Nov. 20, 2000, *available at* <http://www.zdnet.co.uk/ news/2000/-46/ns-19192.html>.

8. In Canada, see *Irwin Toy Ltd. v. Doe* [2000] O.J. no. 3318 (Ont.). In the United States see *J. Erik Hvide v. "John Does 1–8,"* no. 99-22831-CA01 (Fla. Cir. Ct. Jun. 14, 2001). *See also* John Doe, also known as Aquacool_2000 v. Yahoo! Inc., no. 00-20677 (Cal. Super. Ct. filed May 11, 2000); *see generally* C. S. Kaplan, *Judge Says Online Critic Has No Right to Hide,* N.Y. TIMES CYBER L. J., June 9, 2000 (on file with author).

9. Zippo Mfg. Co. v. Zippo Dot Com, Inc., 952 F. Supp. 1119, 1122–23 (W.D. Pa. 1997).

10. *Id.* at 1124.

11. *Id.* at 1127.

12. Inset Sys., Inc. v. Instruction Set, Inc., 937 F. Supp. 161 (D. Conn. 1996).

13. Internet domain names, which have become a ubiquitous part of commercial advertising, enable users to access websites simply by typing in a name such as "www.inset.com" in their web browser. The "www" portion of the address identifies that the site is part of the World Wide Web; the "Inset" portion is usually the name of a company or other identifying words; and "com" identifies the type of institution, in this case a company. Domain names, the subject of several

other litigated cases, are administered in the United States by a government appointed agency, Network Solutions Inc. (NSI) and are distributed on a first come, first served basis. *See* Cynthia Rowden & Jeannette Lee, *Trademarks and the Internet: An Overview,* Nov. 4, 1998, *at* <http://www.bereskinparr.com/art-pdf/TM&InternetOverview.pdf>.

14. *Inset,* 937 F. Supp. *at* 163.

15. World-Wide Volkswagen Corp. v. Woodson, 444 U.S. 286, 291–92 (1980).

16. *Inset,* 937 F. Supp. *at* 160.

17. *Id.* at 165.

18. *Id.*

19. *Id.*

20. *Id.*

21. *Id.*

22. *Id.* at 162–63.

23. *See, e.g.,* Heroes, Inc. v. Heroes Found., 958 F. Supp. 1, 5 (D.D.C. 1996) (citing Inset with approval in finding that a website sustained contact with the District of Columbia); Panavision Int'l, L.P. v. Toeppen, 938 F. Supp. 616 (C.D. Cal. 1996) (finding that use of a trademark infringing domain name in Illinois was an act expressly directed *at* California).

24. Bensusan Rest. Corp. v. King, 937 F. Supp. 295 (S.D.N.Y. 1996), *aff'd* 126 F.3d. 25 (2d Cir. 1997).

25. *Id.* at 297.

26. *Id.* at 298.

27. *Id.* at 297–98.

28. *Id.* at 297.

29. *Id.* at 299.

30. *Id.*

31. *Id.*

32. *Id.*

33. *Id.*

34. Bensusan Rest. Corp. v. King, 126 F.3d 25, 29 (2d Cir. 1997).

35. *See, e.g.,* Hearst Corp. v. Goldberger, no. 96 Civ. 3620 PKL AJP, 1997 WL 97097, *at* *15 (S.D.N.Y. Feb. 26, 1997). The *Goldberger* court relied heavily upon the *Bensusan* analysis in refusing to assert personal jurisdiction in a trademark infringement matter involving the domain name "Esqwire.com." *Id.* The *Goldberger* court carefully reviewed Internet case law to that point, noted its disagreement with decisions such as *Inset, Maritz,* and *Panavision,* and cautioned that:

> [w]here, as here, defendant has not contracted to sell or actually sold any goods or services to New Yorkers, a finding of personal jurisdiction in New

York based on an Internet website would mean that there would be nation-wide (indeed, worldwide) personal jurisdiction over anyone and everyone who establishes an Internet website. Such nationwide jurisdiction is not con-sistent with traditional personal jurisdiction case law nor acceptable to the court as a matter of policy.

Id. at *13.

36. Michael Geist, *The Reality of Bytes: Regulating Economic Activity in the Age of the Internet*, 73 WASH. L. REV. 521, 538 (1998).

37. 952 F. Supp. 1119, 1126 (W.D. Pa. 1997).

38. *Id.* at 1121.

39. *Id.*

40. *Id.*

41. *Id.*

42. *Id.*

43. *Id.*

44. *Id.*

45. One case omitted from the discussion but relied upon by the *Zippo* court was *Compuserve Inc. v. Patterson*, 89 F.3d 1257 (6th Cir. 1996). Although the *Zippo* court refers to the decision as an Internet case, in fact, the activity in ques-tion did not involve the use of the Internet. Rather, Patterson used Compuserve's proprietary network to distribute certain shareware programs. Accordingly, Patterson's contacts with Ohio, Compuserve's headquarters and the location of the litigation, were confined to an offline contractual agreement and the posting of shareware on a Compuserve server that was available to users of its propri-etary network (not Internet users *at* large).

46. *Zippo*, 952 F. Supp. at 1127.

47. *Id.* at 1124 (internal citations omitted).

48. *See, e.g.*, Am. Eyewear, Inc. v. Peeper's Sunglasses and Accessories, Inc., 106 F. Supp. 2d 895 (N.D. Tex. 2000); Am. Online, Inc. v. Huang, 106 F. Supp. 2d 848 (E.D. Va. 2000); Citigroup v. City Holding Co., 97 F. Supp. 2d 549 (S.D.N.Y. 2000); Standard Knitting, Ltd. v. Outside Design, Inc., no. 00-2288, 2000 WL 804434 (E.D. Pa. Jun. 23, 2000); Decker v. Circus Circus Hotel, 49 F. Supp. 2d 748 (D. N.J. 1999); Hasbro, Inc. v. Clue Computing, Inc., 66 F. Supp. 2d 117 (D. Mass. 1999); Blumenthal v. Drudge, 992 F. Supp. 44 (D.D.C. 1998); Mallinkrodt Med., Inc. v. Sonus Pharm., Inc., 989 F. Supp. 265 (D.D.C. 1998); Resuscitation Techs., Inc. v. Cont. Health Care Corp., no. IP 96-1457-C-M/S, 1997 WL 148567 (S.D. Ind. Mar. 24, 1997); Smith v. Hobby Lobby Stores, Inc., 968 F. Supp. 1356 (W.D. Ark. 1997); TELCO Communications v. An Apple A Day, 977 F. Supp. 404 (E.D. Va. 1997); Conseco, Inc. v. Hickerson, 698 N.E.2d 816 (Ind. App. 1998); State by Humphrey v. Granite Gate Resorts, Inc. (Minn. App. 1997).

49. 130 F.3d. 414 (9th Cir. 1997).

50. Interestingly, the principals behind Cybersell Arizona were Laurence Canter and Martha Siegel, attorneys who are infamous among web users as the first Internet "spammers" or junk e-mailers. *Id.* at 415.

51. *Id.* at 419.

52. *Id.* at 418.

53. *Id.*

54. *Id.*

55. *Id.* at 420.

56. Stomp, Inc. v. Neato LLC, 61 F. Supp. 2d 1074 (C.D. Cal. 1999). The court also recognized that:

> [S]uch a broad exercise of personal jurisdiction over defendants who engage in commerce over the Internet might have devastating effects on local merchants and small businesses that seek to expand through the Internet. These small businesses make up the backbone of the American economy and should not have to bear the burden of defending suits in distant fora when they intend only to sell to local consumers their wares from the convenience of their own homes. This concern must be balanced against the ability of a distant consumer to press its cause against a defendant who uses the Internet to do business within the forum while remaining outside the boundaries of the jurisdiction.

Id. at 1080–81.

57. *Id.*

58. In addition to the cases discussed *infra*, see also Panavision Int'l., L.P. v. Toeppen, 141 F.3d 1316, 1320 (9th Cir. 1998); Compuserve v. Patterson, 89 F.3d 1257 (6th Cir. 1996); Neogen Corp. v. Neo Gen Screening, Inc., 109 F. Supp. 2d 724, 729 (W.D. Mich. 2000); Search Force v. Data Force Intern., 112 F. Supp. 2d 771, 777 (S.D. Ind. 2000); Uncle Sam's Safari Outfitters, Inc. v. Uncle Sam's Navy Outfitters—Manhattan, Inc., 96 F. Supp. 2d 919, 923 (E.D. Mo. 2000); Bochan v. La Fontaine, 68 F. Supp. 2d 692, 701–02 (E.D. Va. 1999); Rothschild Berry Farm v. Serendipity Group LLC, 84 F. Supp. 2d 904, 908 (S.D. Ohio 1999).

59. 465 U.S. 783 (1984).

60. *Id.* at 789.

61. *Id.* at 784.

62. *Id.* at 789.

63. *Id.* at 789–90.

64. 751 A.2d 538 (N.J. 2000).

65. *Id.* at 543–48.

66. *Id.*

67. *Id.* at 543.

68. *Id.* at 556.

69. 89 F. Supp. 2d 1154 (C.D. Cal. 2000).

70. *Id.* at 1157.

71. *Id.*

72. *Id.* at 1158.

73. *Id.*

74. *Id.* at 1160.

75. *Id.*

76. *Id.*

77. *Id.*

78. *Id.* at 1159.

79. no. Civ. A. 399-CV-2339-L, 2000 WL 1030619 (N.D. Tex. Jul. 25, 2000).

80. *Id.* at *2.

81. *Id.* at *1.

82. *Id.* at *4.

83. *Id.* at *4.

84. *Id.*

85. *See* Braintech, Inc. v. Kostiuk [1999] 171 D.L.R. (4th) 46, 61 (B.C.C.A.); *see also* Barrett v. Catacombs Press, 44 F. Supp. 2d 717, 728 (E.D. Pa. 1999).

86. People Solutions, Inc. v. People Solutions, Inc., no. Civ. A. 399-CV-2339-L, 2000 WL 1030619, *at* *4 (N.D. Tex. Jul. 25, 2000).

87. *Id.*

88. The Canadian government's e-commerce policy is stated as follows:

> On September 22, 1998, the Prime Minister announced Canada's Electronic Commerce Strategy, outlining initiatives designed to establish Canada as a world leader in the adoption and use of electronic commerce. Working in close collaboration with the private sector, the federal government has concentrated on creating the most favorable environment possible in areas which are critical to the rapid development of e-commerce.

Industry Canada, Electronic Commerce in Canada: Canadian Strategy, *at* <http://www.ecom.ic.gc.ca/english/60.html> (last modified Feb. 14, 2001).

The U.S. government shares a similar e-commerce policy:

> Commerce on the Internet could total tens of billions of dollars by the turn of the century. For this potential to be realized fully, governments must adopt a non-regulatory, market-oriented approach to electronic commerce, one that facilitates the emergence of a transparent and predictable legal environment to support global business and commerce. Official decision makers must respect the unique nature of the medium and recognize that widespread competition and increased consumer choice should be the defining features of the new digital marketplace.

A Framework for Global Electronic Commerce, Jul. 1, 1997, *at* <http://www. ecommerce.gov/framewrk.htm>.

89. John Gedid noted the following at an international conference on Internet jurisdiction:

> The *Zippo* opinion is comprehensive, thorough and persuasive . . . . The court's review of precedents is sweeping and thorough, and its logic is compelling. The *Zippo* court fully understood and explained difficult precedents, so that they could be understood in terms of the *International Shoe* criteria. While there are some who would question the approach on the theories that it does not go far enough or that it goes too far, nevertheless, it is an attempt *at* stating a more comprehensive and coherent approach to Internet jurisdiction cases. The result was that the *Zippo* opinion is probably the most persuasive and influential opinion that has been published on the subject of cyberspace jurisdiction.

John L. Gedid, *Minimum Contacts Analysis in Cyberspace—Sale Of Goods And Services,* Jul. 1997, *at* <http://ilpf.org/events/jurisdiction/presentations/gedid_ addl.htm>.

See generally, Charles H. Fleischer, *Will The Internet Abrogate Territorial Limits on Personal Jurisdiction?,* 33 TORT & INS. L.J. 107 (1997); Michael J. Sikora III, *Beam Me into Your Jurisdiction: Establishing Personal Jurisdiction Via Electronic Contacts in Light of the Sixth Circuit's Decision in* Compuserve, Inc. v. Patterson, 27 CAP. U. L. REV. 163, 184–85 (1998).

90. Jerry Kang, *Information Privacy in Cyberspace Transactions,* 50 Stan. L. Rev. 1193, 1226–29 (1998).

91. *Id.*

92. Zippo Mfg. Co. v. Zippo Dot Com, Inc., 952 F. Supp. 1119, 1126 (W.D. Pa. 1997).

93. *See, e.g.,* Barrett v. Catacombs Press, 64 F. Supp. 2d 440 (E.D. Pa. 1999).

94. David Legard, *Average Cost to Build E-commerce Site: $1 Million,* THE STANDARD, May 31, 1999 (on file with author).

95. 139 F. Supp. 2d 696 (D. Md. 2001).

96. *Id.* at 700.

97. *Id.*

98. *Id.*

99. Organization for Economic Cooperation and Development, *Recommendation of the OECD Council Concerning Guidelines for Consumer Protection in the Context of Electronic Commerce,* at 5, *at* <http://www.oecd.org/dsti/sti/it/ consumer/prod/-CPGuidelines_final.pdf> (last visited Nov. 26, 2001).

100. Hague Conference on Private International Law, *Preliminary Draft Convention on Jurisdiction and Foreign Judgments in Civil and Commercial Matters,* Oct. 30, 1999, *at* <http://www.hcch. net/e/conventions/draft36e.html>.

101. *See* American Bar Association, *Achieving Legal and Business Order in Cyberspace: A Report on Global Jurisdiction Issues Created By the Internet* (on file with author). In the interests of full disclosure, it should be noted that the

author was chair of the Sale of Services Working Group, one of nine working groups tasked with developing Internet jurisdiction recommendations.

102. *Id.*

103. Currently in beta, Google offers searchers the ability to configure their Google searching to translate automatically any results that appear in a foreign language. *See* Google, *at* <http://www.google.com/machine_translation.html> (last visited Nov. 26, 2001).

104. Graves v. Pikulski, 115 F. Supp. 2d 931 (S.D. Ill. 2000); Kilgallen v. Network Solutions, 99 F. Supp. 2d 125 (D. Mass. 2000); Rudder v. Microsoft Corp., [1999] 2 C.P. R. (4th) 474 (Ont.).

105. *Kilgallen,* 99 F. Supp. *at* 129.

106. *Id.* at 126.

107. *Id.*

108. *Id.*

109. *Id.* at 129.

110. no. CV 99-7654 HLH, 2000 WL 525390 (C.D. Cal. Mar. 27, 2000).

111. *Id.*

112. *Id.* at *3.

113. *Id.*

114. *Id.*

115. *Id.*

116. *Id.*

117. *Id.*

118. *Id.* (emphasis added)

119. 126 F. Supp. 2d 238 (S.D.N.Y. 2000).

120. *Id.* at 252.

121. *Id.* at 242–43.

122. *Id.*

123. 150 F. Supp. 2d 585 (S.D.N.Y. 2001).

124. *Id.* at 595.

125. *Id.*

126. Furthermore, unlike the user of Netscape Navigator or other click-wrap or shrink-wrap licensees, the individual obtaining SmartDownload is not made aware that he is entering into a contract. SmartDownload is available from Netscape's website free of charge. Before downloading the software, the user need not view any license agreement terms or even any reference to a license agreement, and need not do anything to manifest assent to such a license agreement other than actually taking possession of the product. From the user's vantage point, SmartDownload could be analogized to a free neighborhood newspaper, readily obtained from a sidewalk box or supermarket counter without any exchange with

a seller or vendor. It is there for the taking. The only hint that a contract is being formed is one small box of text referring to the license agreement, the text that appears below the screen used for downloading and that a user need not even see before obtaining the product: "Please review and agree to the terms before downloading and using the software for the Netscape Smart Download software license agreement." Couched in the mild request, "[p]lease review," this agreement reads as a mere invitation, not as a condition. The language does not dictate that a user must agree to the license terms before downloading and using the software. While clearer language appears in the License Agreement itself, the language of the invitation does not require the reading of those terms or provide adequate notice either that a contract is being created or that the terms of the License Agreement will bind the user. *Id.* at 595–96.

127. Mendoza v. AOL (Cal. Super. Ct.) (unreported, on file with author).

128. *Id.*

129. *Id.*

130. For another example in which a Massachusetts state court refused to enforce the AOL forum selection clause in a class action suit over AOL system software see *Williams v. AOL,* no. 00-0962 (Mass. Super. Ct. Feb 2001) (on file with author).

131. For example, the *Wall Street Journal* reports that Bermuda has become a haven for dot-com operations seeking to avoid tax and other regulatory measures in North America. Michael Allen, *As Dot-Coms Go Bust in the U.S., Bermuda Hosts a Little Boomlet,* WALL ST. J., Jan. 8, 2001, at A4.

132. *See generally* David R. Johnson & David G. Post, *Law and Borders: The Rise of Law in Cyberspace,* 48 STAN. L. REV. 1367 (1996).

133. Am. Libraries Ass'n v. Pataki, 969 F. Supp. 160 (S.D.N.Y. 1997).

134. *Id.* at 170.

135. Bob Tedeschi, *E-commerce: Borders Returning to the Internet,* N.Y. TIMES, Apr. 2, 2001 (on file with author).

136. In addition to the discussion below, *see* Jack L. Goldsmith & Alan O. Sykes, *The Internet and the Dormant Commerce Clause,* 110 Yale L.J. 785, 810–12 (2001).

137. Although in fairness, there are some that saw these developments coming many years ago. For example, Professor Lawrence Lessig, in the same Stanford Law Review issue featuring Post's and Johnson's *Law and Borders* article, *supra* note 132, commented that:

> In its present design, cyberspace is open, and uncontrolled; regulation is achieved through social forces much like the social forms that regulate real space. It is now unzoned: Borders are not boundaries; they divide one system from another just as Pennsylvania is divided from Ohio. The essence of cyberspace today is the search engine—tools with which one crosses an infinite space, to locate, and go to, the stuff one wants. The space today is open, but only because it is made that way. Or because we made it that way. (For whatever is true about society, *at* least cyberspace is socially constructed.)

It could be made to be different, and my sense is that it is. The present architecture of cyberspace is changing. If there is one animating idea behind the kinds of reforms pursued both in the social and economic spheres in cyberspace, it is the idea to increase the sophistication of the architecture in cyberspace, to facilitate boundaries rather than borders. It is the movement to bring to zoning to cyberspace.

Lawrence Lessig, *The Zones of Cyberspace*, 48 STAN. L. REV. 1403, 1408–9 (1996) [hereinafter Lessig, *Zones*]; *see also*, LAWRENCE LESSIG, CODE AND OTHER LAWS OF CYBERSPACE 56–57 (1999).

138. Stefanie Olsen, *Geographic Tracking Raises Opportunities, Fears*, CNET NEWS.COM, Nov. 8, 2000, *at* <http://news.cnet.com/news/0-1005-200-3424168.html>.

139. As Lessig points out, "[a] regulation need not be absolutely effective to be sufficiently effective." Lessig, *Zones, supra* note 137, *at* 1405. The same applies to bordering technologies; whether used for targeted marketing or to ensure legal compliance, they need not be perfect.

140. *See* Tedeschi, *supra* note 135.

141. Twentieth Century Fox Film Corp. v. iCraveTV, no. 00-121, 2000 U.S. Dist. LEXIS 1013 (W.D. Pa. Jan. 28, 2000).

142. Matthew Fraser, *Jump TV Takes On Vested Interests*, FIN. POST, Jan. 29, 2001, at C02.

143. *Nevada Governor Signs Internet Gambling Bill*, SAN JOSE MERCURY NEWS, June 15, 2001, *available at* <http://www.siliconvalley.com/docs/news/tech/060919.htm>.

144. H.R. 466, 71st Ass., Reg. Sess., (Nev. 2001), *available at* <http://www.leg. state.nv.us/71st/bills/AB/-AB446_EN.html>.

145. Anick Jesdanun, *The Potential and Peril of National Internet Boundaries*, S.F. EXAMINER, Mar. 4, 2001, *available at* <http://www.examiner.com/business/-default.jsp?story=b.net.0107>.

146. A. Michael Froomkin, *The Essential Role of Trusted Third Parties in Electronic Commerce*, 75 OR. L. REV. 49, 62 (1996).

147. It is illegal to export high-grade cryptography from the United States without advance permission from the federal government, but there are no legal restrictions on the distribution of strong cryptography to resident aliens or United States citizens in the United States. The lack of a reliable means to identify the geographical location of a person from an Internet address creates a risk of prosecution for anyone making cryptographic software available over the Internet. For example, if Alice is making high-grade cryptography available for distribution over the Internet, she might protect herself from considerable risk by requiring that Bob produce a valid certificate from a reputable CA, stating that he is a United States citizen or green card holder residing in the United States, before allowing him to download the cryptographic software. *Id.*

148. *See* LESSIG, *supra* note 137, at 42.

149. *Credit Card Fraud Crippling Online Merchants,* E-COMMERCE TIMES, Mar. 20, 2000, *at* <http://www.ecommercetimes.com/news/articles2000/000320-2.shtml> ("At present, credit card companies only verify if a credit card number is correct and then match the number against the customer's billing address.").

150. Except where as required by law. *See, e.g.,* Anick Jesdanun, *The Potential and Peril of National Internet Boundaries,* S. F. EXAMINER, Mar. 4, 2001, *available at* <http://www.examiner.com/business/ default.jsp?story=b.net.0107>.

151. *See, e.g.,* Martin H. Redish, *Of New Wine and Old Bottles: Personal Jurisdiction, The Internet, and the Nature of Constitutional Evolution,* 38 Jurimetrics J. 575 (1998). Redish notes:

> The most effective defense of an Internet exception to the purposeful avail-ment requirement is not that state interest should play an important role only in Internet cases, but rather that the technological development of the Internet effectively renders the concept of purposeful availment both conceptually incoherent and practically irrelevant. An individual or entity may so easily and quickly reach the entire world with its messages that it is simply not help-ful to inquire whether, in taking such action, that individual or entity has con-sciously and carefully made the decision either to affiliate with the forum state or seek to acquire its benefits.

Id. at 605–06.

152. People v. World Interactive Gaming, 714 N.Y.S.2d 844 (Sup. Ct. 1999).

153. *Id.*

154. No. 00 Civ. 4647 (DLC), 2001 WL 417118 (S.D.N.Y. Apr. 23, 2001).

155. *Id.* at *4.

156. Thomas Heath, *Capitals Owner Puts Pittsburgh Fans on Ice,* THE WASH. POST, Apr. 14, 2001 (on file with author).

157. In March 2001, the *Electronic Commerce and Information, Consumer Protection Amendment and Manitoba Evidence Amendment Act* (S.M. 200, c. E55. 77) and the *Internet Agreements Regulations* (Man. Reg. 176/2000) took effect within the province. Designed to foster an online environment where con-sumer confidence will flourish, the new laws apply exclusively to the online retail sale of goods or services or the retail lease-to-own of goods between buyers and sellers. Under the new rules, binding e-commerce transactions require the seller to provide certain obligatory information to the buyer under threat of a pur-chaser contract cancellation remedy.

158. *Cf.* Joel R. Reidenberg, *The Yahoo Case and the International Democratization of the Internet* (Fordham Law & Econ. Working Paper no. 11, 2001) (arguing that online bordering facilitates democracy by allowing demo-cratically elected governments to implement policy choices that affect their citi-zens both offline and online), *available at* <http://papers.ssrn.com/paper. taf?ABSTRACT_ID=267148> (last visited Nov. 26, 2001).

II

Digital Democracy: Prospects and Possibilities

4

Security Considerations for Remote Electronic Voting over the Internet

Avi Rubin

Introduction

The right of individuals to vote for our government representatives is at the heart of the democracy that we enjoy in the United States. Historically, great effort and care has been taken to ensure that elections are conducted in a fair manner such that the candidate who should win the election based on the vote count actually does. Of equal importance is that public confidence in the election process remain strong. In the past changes to the election process have proceeded deliberately and judiciously, often entailing lengthy debates over even the minutest of details. These changes are approached so sensitively because a discrepancy in the election system threatens the very principles that make our society free, which in turn, affects every aspect of the way we live.

Times are changing. We now live in the Internet era, where decisions cannot be made quickly enough, and there is a perception that anyone who does not jump on the technology bandwagon is going to be left far behind. Businesses are moving online at astonishing speed. The growth of online interaction and presence can be witnessed by the exponential increase in the number of people with home computers and Internet access. There is a prevailing sentiment that any organization that continues in the old ways is obsolete. So, despite the natural inclination to treat our election process as the precious, delicate and fragile process that it is, the question of using the new advances in technology to improve our elections is natural. The 2000 presidential election in the United States, and the controversy that was created by the ballot problem in Florida generated demand for using computers more in the election process.

The feasibility of *remote electronic voting* in public elections was studied by the National Science Foundation by request of the president of the United States (see *http://www.netvoting.org/*). The group produced a report.[1] There have been other studies as well, including the Caltech-MIT study,[2] the Democracy Online Project,[3] and the National Commission on Federal Election Reform.[4] Remote electronic voting refers to an election process whereby people can cast their votes over the Internet, most likely through a web browser, from the comfort of their home, or possibly any other location where they can get Internet access. There are many aspects of elections besides security that bring this type of voting into question. The primary ones are

coercibility   the danger that outside of a public polling place, a voter could be coerced into voting for a particular candidate.

vote selling   the opportunity for voters to sell their vote.

vote solicitation   the danger that outside of a public polling place, it is much more difficult to control vote solicitation by political parties at the time of voting.

registration   the issue of whether or not to allow online registration, and if so, how to control the level of fraud.

The possibility of widely distributed locations where votes can be cast changes many aspects of our carefully controlled elections as we know them. The relevant issues are of great importance, and could very well influence whether or not such election processes are desirable. However, in this paper, we focus solely on the security considerations as they relate to conducting online public elections. In particular, we look at remote online voting, as opposed to online voter registration, which is a separate, but important and difficult problem. We also focus solely on public elections, as opposed to private elections, where the threats are not as great, and the environment can be more controlled.

The importance of security in elections cannot be overstated. The future of our country, and the free world for that matter, rests on public confidence that the people have the power to elect their own government. Any process that has the potential to threaten the integrity of the system, or even the perceived integrity of the system, should be treated with the utmost caution and suspicion.

The Voting Platform

The type of remote electronic voting that we discuss in this paper involves regular Internet users with personal computers and standard operating systems and software. For the sake of the discussion, we focus on Intel machines running Microsoft operating systems with Microsoft or Netscape browsers, and voters participating from home, communicating over a TCP/IP network attached to the Internet. While this is a simplification, it is representative of the vast majority of users under consideration. In this discussion, we refer to the voting platform simply as a *host*.

Threats to hosts can be described as *malicious payload* and *delivery mechanism* (A malicious payload is software or configuration information designed to do harm.). Both of these have advanced in sophistication and automation in the past couple of years. The attacks are more sophisticated in the sense that they can do more damage, are more likely to succeed, and disguise themselves better than before. They are more automated in that more and more toolkits have been developed to enable unsophisticated computer users to launch the attacks.

Malicious Payload

There are literally hundreds of attack programs that we could discuss in this section. One only needs to visit the web site of any number of security software vendors to see the long lists of exploits that affect hosts to various degrees. The fact of the matter is that on the platforms currently in the most widespread use, once a malicious payload reaches a host, there is virtually no limit to the damage it can cause. With today's hardware and software architectures, a malicious payload on a voting host can actually change the voter's vote, without the voter or anyone else noticing, regardless of the kind of encryption or voter authentication in place. This is because the malicious code can do its damage before the encryption and authentication is applied to the data. The malicious module can then erase itself after doing its damage so that there is no evidence to correct, or even detect the fraud. To illustrate, we focus the discussion on two particular malicious payloads that each exemplify the level of vulnerability faced by hosts. Such code may run in stealth mode, which means that it was carefully designed to be very difficult to detect. Such programs do not appear in the Task Menu of running processes, and are designed so that even an experienced administrator would have a difficult time discovering that it is on a computer. A stealth program is difficult to detect even while it is running.

The first program we describe, Backorifice 2000 (BO2K) is packaged and distributed as a legitimate network administration toolkit. In fact, it is very useful as a tool for enhancing security. It is freely available, fully open source, extensible, and stealth. The package is available at http://www.bo2k.com/. BO2K contains a remote control server that when installed on a machine, enables a remote administrator (or attacker) to view and control every aspect of that machine, as though the person were actually sitting at the console. This is similar in functionality to a commercial product called PCAnywhere. The main differences are that BO2K is available in full source code form and it runs in stealth mode.

The open source nature of BO2K means that an attacker can modify the code and recompile such that the program can evade detection by security defense software (virus and intrusion detection) that look for known *signatures* of programs. A signature is a pattern that identifies a particular known malicious program. The current state of the art in widely deployed systems for detecting malicious code does not go much beyond comparing a program against a list of attack signatures. In fact, most personal computers in peoples' houses have no detection software on them. BO2K runs in stealth mode.

There can be no expectation that an average Internet user participating in an online election from home could have any hope of detecting the existence of BO2K on his computer. At the same time, this program enables an attacker to watch every aspect of the voting procedure, intercept any action of the user with the potential of modifying it without the user's knowledge, and to further install any other program of the attacker's desire, even ones written by the attacker, on the voting user's machine. The package also monitors every keystroke typed on the machine and has an option to remotely lock the keyboard and mouse. It is difficult, and most likely impossible, to conceive of an application that could prevent an attacker who installs BO2K on a user's machine from being able to view and/or change a user's vote.

The second malicious payload that is worth mentioning is the CIH virus, also known as the Chernobyl virus. There are two reasons why we choose this example over the many other possible ones. The first is that the malicious functionality of this virus is triggered to activate on a particular day. April 26, 1999 was a disastrous day in Asia, where the virus had not been that well known, and thousands of computers were affected. This raises concern because election dates are known far in advance. The second reason for choosing this example is that the damage that it caused was so severe, that it often required physically taking the computer to the shop for repair. The code modified the BIOS of the system in such a way that it could not boot. The BIOS is the part of the computer that initializes and manages the relationships and data flow between the system devices, including the hard drive, serial and parallel ports, and the keyboard. A widespread activation of such a virus on the day of an election, or on a day leading up to an election could potentially disenfranchise many voters, as their hosts would not be usable. This threat is increased by the possibility that the spread of the virus could be orchestrated to target a particular demographic group, thus having a direct effect on the election, and bringing the integrity of the entire process into question.

It does not take a very sophisticated malicious payload to disrupt an election. A simple attack illustrates how easy it is to thwart a web application such as voting. Netscape Navigator and Internet Explorer, the two most common browsers have a setting in which all web communication takes place via a *proxy*. A proxy is a program that is interposed between the client and the server. It has the ability to completely control all Internet traffic between the two. Proxies are useful for many Internet applications and for sites that run certain kinds of firewalls. The user sets a proxy by making a change in the preferences menu. The browser then adds a couple of lines to a configuration file. For example, in Netscape, the existence of the following lines in the file

```
c:\program_files\netscape\prefs.js
```

delivers all web content to and from the user's machine to a program listening on port 1799 on the machine www.badguy.com.

```
user_pref("network.proxy.http", "www.badguy.com");
user_pref("network.proxy.http_port", 1799);
```

If an attacker can add these two lines (substituting his hostname for www.badguy.com) to the preferences file on somebody's machine, he can control every aspect of the web experience of that user. There are also ways of doing this without leaving a trail that leads directly to the attacker. While proxies cannot be used to read information in a secure connection, they can be used to spoof a user into a secure connection with the attacker, instead of the actual voting server, without the user realizing it. The next section explains various ways that an attacker could effect changes on a voter's computer.

Delivery mechanism

The previous section gave three examples of what an attacker could do to disrupt an election if the attacker could install code of his choosing on voters' computers. This section deals with how this installation could happen.

The first, and most obvious mechanism is physical installation. Most people do not keep their computers in a carefully controlled, locked environment. Imagine someone who develops an application to attack the voting system, such as the two described above, prepares a floppy disk with the code on it, and then installs it on as many machines as possible. This could be accomplished by breaking into houses, by accessing machines in someone's house when visiting, by installing the program on public machines in the library, etc. The bottom line is that many people can obtain physical access to many other peoples' computers at some point leading up to an election. Then, malicious code can be delivered that can trigger any action at a later date, enable future access (as in the case of BO2K), or disrupt normal operation at any time. Considering that many of the attack programs that we are seeing these days run in stealth mode, malicious code could be installed such that average computer users cannot detect its presence.

While the physical delivery of malicious code is a serious problem, it is nowhere near as effective as remote automated delivery. By now, most people have heard of the Melissa virus and the I Love You bug. These are the better-known ones, but many such attacks happen all the time. In fact, the most widespread of the e-mail viruses, Happy99, has received very little media attention. Typically, these attacks cause temporary disruption in service, and perform some annoying action. In most of the cases, the attacks spread wider and faster than their creators ever imagined. One thing that all of these attacks have in common is that they install some code on the PCs that are infected. There is a misconception by many people that users must open an attachment in order to activate them. In fact, one virus called Bubbleboy was triggered as soon as a message was previewed in the Outlook mailer, requiring no action on the part of the user. Any one of these e-mail viruses could deliver the attack code described in the previous section.

It is naïve to think that we have seen the worst of the Internet viruses, worms, and bugs. In the last several months, the incidents of new attacks have grown much faster than our ability to cope with them. This is a trend that is likely to continue.

E-mail viruses are not the only way that malicious code can be delivered to hosts. The computers in most peoples' houses are running operating systems with tens of thousands of lines of code. These systems are known to be full of operational bugs as well as security flaws. On top of these platforms, users are typically running many applications with security problems. These security flaws can be exploited remotely to install malicious code on them. The most common example of such a flaw is a buffer overflow. A buffer overflow occurs when a process assigns more data to a memory location than was expected by the programmer. The consequence is that that attacker can manipulate the computer's memory to cause arbitrary malicious code to run. Although there are ways to check for and prevent this in a program, buffer overflows are the most common form of security flaw in deployed systems today.

Perhaps the most likely candidate for delivering a widespread attack against an election is an ActiveX control, downloaded automatically and unknowingly from a Web server, which installs a Trojan horse (hidden program) that later interferes with voting. Several documented attacks against Windows systems operated exactly this way. In fact, any application that users are lured into downloading can do the same. This includes browser plug-ins, screen savers, calendars, and any other program that is obtained over the Internet. Another danger is that the application itself may be clean, but the installer might install a dynamically linked library (DLL) or other malicious module, or overwrite operating system modules. Most users are not aware of the dangers when they add software to their computers. As long as there are people out there who download and install software over the Internet onto today's personal computers running today's operating systems, it will be easy for attackers to deliver code that changes their votes.

User's who open attachments and download software from the network are not the only ones putting their votes at risk. AOL, for instance, is in a position to control a large fraction of the total votes, because all of their users run AOL's proprietary software. There are dozens of software vendors whose products run on many peoples' home machines. For example, there are millions of personal computers running Microsoft office, Adobe Acrobat, RealPlayer, WinZip, Solitaire, and the list goes on. These vendors are in a position to modify any configuration file and install any malicious code on their customers' machines, as are the computer manufacturers and the computer vendors. Even if the company is not interested in subverting an election, all it takes is one rogue programmer who works for any of these companies. Most of the software packages require an installation procedure where the system registry is modified, libraries are installed, and the computer must reboot. During any stage of that process, the installation program has complete control of all of the software on that machine.

In current public elections, the polling site undergoes careful scrutiny. Any change to the process is audited carefully, and on election day, representatives from all of the major parties are present to make sure that the integrity of the process is maintained. This is in sharp contrast to holding an election that allows people to cast their votes from a computer full of insecure software that is under the direct control of several dozen software and hardware vendors and run by users who download programs from the Internet, over a network that is known to be vulnerable to total shutdown at any moment.

The Communications Infrastructure

A network connection consists of two endpoints and the communication between them. The previous section dealt with one of the endpoints, the user's host. The other endpoint is the elections server. While it is in no way trivial, the technology exists to provide reasonable protection on the servers. This section deals with the communication between the two endpoints.

Cryptography can be used to protect the communication between the user's browser and the elections server. This technology is mature and can be relied upon to ensure the integrity and confidentiality of the network traffic. This section does not deal with the classic security properties of the communications infrastructure; rather, we look at the *availability* of the Internet service, as required by remote electronic voting over the Internet.

Most people are aware of the massive distributed denial of service (DDOS) attack that brought down many of the main portals on the Internet in February, 2000.[5] While these attacks brought the vulnerability of the Internet to denial of service attacks to the mainstream public consciousness, the security community has long been aware of this, and in fact, this attack was nothing compared to what a dedicated and determined adversary could do. The February attack consisted of the installation and execution of publicly available attack scripts. Very little skill was required to launch the attack, and minimal skill was required to install the attack.

The way DDOS works is that a program called a *daemon* is installed on many machines. Any of the delivery mechanisms described above can be used. One other program is installed somewhere called the *master*. These programs are placed anywhere on the Internet, so that there are many, unwitting accomplices to the attack, and the real attacker cannot be traced. The system lies dormant until the attacker decides that it is time to strike. At that point, the attacker sends a signal to the master, using a publicly available tool, indicating a target to attack. The master conveys this information to all of the daemons, who simultaneously flood the target with more Internet traffic than it can handle. The effect is that the target machine is completely disabled.

We experimented in the lab with one of the well known DDOS programs called Tribe Flood Network (TFN), and discovered that the attack is so potent, that even one daemon attacking a Unix workstation disabled it to the point where it had to be rebooted. The target computer was so overwhelmed that we could not even move the cursor with the mouse.

There are tools that can be easily found by anyone with access to the web that automate the process of installing daemons, masters, and the attack signal. People who attack systems with such tools are known as *script kiddies*, and represent a growing number of people. In an election, the adversary is more likely to be someone at least as knowledgeable as the writers of the script kiddy tools, and possibly with the resources of a foreign government.

There are many other ways to target a machine and make it unusable, and it is not too difficult to target a particular set of users, given domain name information that can easily be obtained from the online registries such as Register.com and Network Solutions, or directly from the WHOIS database. The list of examples of attacks goes on and on. A simple one is the *ping of death*, in which a packet can be constructed and split into two fragments. When the target computer assembles the fragments, the result is a message that is too big for the operating system to handle, and the machine crashes. This has been demonstrated in the lab and in the wild, and script kiddy tools exist to launch it.

The danger to Internet voting is that it is possible that during an election, communication on the Internet will stop because attackers cause routers to crash, election servers to get flooded by DDOS, or a large set of hosts, possibly targeted demographicly, to cease to function. In some close campaigns, even an untargeted attack that changes the vote by one percentage point could sway the election.

Social Engineering

Social Engineering is the term used to describe attacks that involve fooling people into compromising their security.[5] Talking with election officials, one discovers that one of the issues that they grapple with is the inability of many people to follow simple directions. It is surprising to learn that, for example, when instructed to circle a candidate's name, people will often underline it. While computers would seem to offer the opportunity to provide an interface that is tightly controlled and thus less subject to error, this is counter to the typical experience most users have with computers. For non-Computer Scientists, computers are often intimidating and unfamiliar. User interfaces are often poor and create confusion, rather than simplifying processes.

A remote voting scheme will have some interface. The actual design of that interface is not the subject of this paper, but it is clear that there will be some interface. For the system to be secure, there must be some way for voters to know that they are communicating with the election server. The infrastructure does exist right now for computer security specialists, who are suspicious that they could be communicating with an imposter, to verify that their browser is communicating with a valid election server. The SSL protocol and server side certificates can be used for this. While this process has its own risks and pitfalls, even if we assume that it is flawless, it is unreasonable to assume that average Internet users who want to vote on their computers can be expected to understand the concept of a server certificate, to verify the authenticity of the certificate, and to check the active ciphersuites to ensure that strong encryption is used. In fact, most users would probably not distinguish between a page from an SSL connection to the legitimate server and a non-SSL page from a malicious server that had the exact same look as the real page.

There are several ways that an attacker could spoof the legitimate voting site. One way would be to send an e-mail message to a user telling that user to click on a link, which would then bring up the fake voting site. The adversary could then collect the user's credentials and in a sense, steal the vote. An attacker could also set up a connection to the legitimate server and feed the user a fake web page, and act as a man in the middle, transferring information between the user and the web server, with all of the traffic under the attacker's control. This is probably enough to change a user's vote, regardless of how the application is implemented.

A more serious attack is possible by targeting the Internet's Domain Name Service (DNS). The DNS is used to maintain a mapping from IP addresses, which computers use to reference each other (e.g., 135.207.18.199) to domain names, which people use to reference computers (e.g., *www.research.att.com*). The DNS is known to be vulnerable to attacks, such as cache poisoning, which change the information available to hosts about the IP addresses of computers. The reason that this is serious is that a DNS cache poisoning attack, along with many other known attacks against DNS, could be used to direct a user to the wrong web server when the user types in the name of the election server in the browser. Thus, a user could follow the instructions for voting, and yet receive a page that looked exactly like what it is supposed to look like, but actually is entirely controlled by the adversary. Detailed instructions about checking certificate validity are not likely to be understood nor followed by a substantial number of users.

Another problem along these lines is that any computer under the control of an adversary can be made to simulate a valid connection to an election server, without actually connecting to anything. So, for example, a malicious librarian or cyber café operator could set up public computers that appear to accept votes, but actually do nothing with the votes. This could even work if the computers were not connected to the Internet, since no messages need to be sent or received to fool a user into believing that their vote was cast. Setting up such machines in districts known to vote a certain way could influence the outcome of an election.

Specialized Devices

One potential enabler at our disposal is the existence of tamper-resistant devices, such as smart cards. Cryptographic keys can be generated and stored on these devices, and they can perform computations, such that proper credentials can be exchanged between a voting host and a voting server. However, there are some limitations to the utility of such devices. The first is that there is not a deployed base of smart card readers on peoples' personal computers. Any system that involves financial investment on the part of individuals in order to vote is unacceptable. Some people are more limited in their ability to spend, and it is unfair to decrease the likelihood that such people vote. It would, in effect, be a poll tax. This issue is often referred to as the *digital divide*.

Even if everybody did have smart card readers on their computers, there are security concerns. The smart card does not interact directly with the election server. The communication goes through the computer. Malicious code installed on the computer could misuse the smart card. At the very least, the code could prevent the vote from actually being cast, while fooling the user into believing that it was. At worst, it could change the vote.

Other specialized devices, such as a cell phone with no general-purpose processor, equipped with a smart card, offer more promise of solving the technical security problems. However, they introduce even greater digital divide issues. In addition, the user interface issues, which are fundamental to a fair election, are much more difficult. This is due to the more limited displays and input devices. Finally, while computers offer some hope of improving the accessibility of voting for the disabled, specialized devices are even more limiting in that respect.

Is There Hope?

Given the current state of insecurity of hosts and the vulnerability of the Internet to manipulation and denial of service attacks, there is no way that a public election of any significance involving remote electronic voting could be carried out securely. So, is there any hope that this will change?

For this to happen, the next generation of personal computers that are widely adopted must have hardware support to enable a *trusted path* between the user and the election server. There must be no way for malicious code to be able to interfere with the normal operation of applications. Efforts such as the Trusted Computing Platform Alliance (TCPA) (see *http://www.trustedpc.org/home/home.htm*) must be endorsed. The challenge is great because to enable secure remote electronic voting, the vast majority of computer systems need to have the kind of high assurance aspired to by the TCPA. It is not clear whether or not the majority of PC manufacturers will buy into the concept. The market will decide. While it is unlikely that remote electronic voting will be the driving force for the design of future personal computers, the potential for eliminating the hazards of online electronic commerce could potentially fill that role.

One reason that remote electronic voting presents such a security challenge is that any successful attack would be very high profile, a factor that motivates much of the hacking activity to date. Even scarier is that the most serious attacks would come from someone motivated by the ability to change the outcome without anyone noticing. The adversaries to an election system are not teenagers in garages but foreign governments and powerful interests at home and abroad. Never before have the stakes been so high.

Conclusions

A certain amount of fraud exists in the current offline election system. It is tolerated because there is no alternative. The system is localized so that it is very unlikely that a successful fraud could propagate beyond a particular district. Public perception is that the system works, although there may be a few kinks in it here and there. There is no doubt that the introduction of something like remote electronic voting will, and should, come under careful scrutiny, and in fact, the system may be held up to a higher standard. Given the current state of widely deployed computers in peoples' homes, the vulnerability of the Internet to denial of service attacks, and the unreliability of the Domain Name Service, we believe that the technology does not yet exist to enable remote electronic voting in public elections.

There is a difference between *public* elections and *private* elections. Private elections, such as a stock proxy vote, or a board of directors vote within a company, are usually only of interest to a particular group of people. The threat faced by these organizations is typically well understood and relatively small. Also, the consequences of a successful attack are typically quite limited. In contrast public elections are the cornerstone of our democracy, and there is great incentive for well-financed parties to disrupt them.

Acknowledgments

We thank all of the participants of the Internet Policy Institute e-voting workshop for a wonderful exchange of ideas. Special thanks go to Lorrie Cranor, Andrew Hume, and David Jefferson for valuable input.

Notes:

1. *Report on the National Workshop on Internet Voting,* Sponsored by the National Science Foundation, March, 2001.

2. *Voting: What Is; What Could Be,* Caltech-MIT voting technology project, July, 2001.

3. *Voting in the Information Age: The Debate Over Technology,* The Democracy Online Project, January, 2001.

4. *To Assure Pride and Confidence in the Electoral Process,* National Commission on Federal Election Reform, August, 2001.

5. Avi Rubin, *White-Hat Security Arsenal,* Addison-Wesley Inc, June, 2001.

5

Signing Initiative Petitions Online: Possibilities, Problems, and Prospects

Walter Baer

1 Introduction

"The Internet changes everything" is a mantra familiar to technologists, entrepreneurs, and the media.[1] Indeed, the Internet has already transformed many organizations and business sectors and profoundly affected others. These trends suggest to many that the Internet will inevitably change American politics—most likely in the direction of increasing direct citizen participation and forcing government officials to respond more quickly to voters' concerns. Certainly the dramatic vote counting problems in the 2000 presidential election have brought new calls for using the Internet in state and federal elections.[2] Although attention has focused primarily on Internet voting, efforts are also under way to authorize the use of electronic signatures over the Internet to qualify candidates, initiatives, and other ballot measures. Petitions for one such initiative, called by its backers the "Smart Initiatives Initiative," were circulated in California in 2001 but failed to qualify for the 2002 election.[3]

Petition signing on the Internet would draw on the technologies and processes developed for electronic commerce ("e-commerce"). It would also draw on the growing use of the Internet for disseminating government information and facilitating online communications and transactions between citizens and government ("e-government"). Its proponents claim that Internet signature gathering will significantly lower the cost of qualifying initiatives and thereby reduce the influence of organized, well-financed interest groups. They also maintain that Internet petition signing will increase both public participation in the political process and public understanding about specific measures. However, questions about security and access pose significant problems for Internet signature gathering, as they do for casting and counting ballots using the Internet.[4] Some observers also express concern that Internet petition signing would make qualifying initiatives too easy and thus further distance the initiative process from the deliberative political discourse envisioned by the framers of the U.S. and California constitutions.

This paper explores the prospects for and issues surrounding Internet petition signing, focusing primarily on recent experience in California. After describing how voters would use the Internet to "sign" petitions and how their electronic or digital signatures could be verified, it goes on to discuss security, cost, access, and equity issues that pose significant obstacles to online petition signing. It then outlines trends in Internet voting, e-commerce, and e-government that may affect the development of Internet petition signing. The final section discusses some broader implications of the Internet for the initiative process, summarizes the arguments pro and con, and concludes that while Internet petition signing is not ready to be implemented in the next election cycle, public pressure to authorize it will continue to build and could prove unstoppable over the next few years.

2   How Would Internet Petition Signing Work?

Initiative petitions must receive a specified number of valid signatures from registered voters to be placed on the ballot.[5] Proposals of Internet petition signing would change existing election laws to permit registered voters to sign petitions on a computer and transmit their signatures over the Internet to be counted toward the required total. Nearly all such proposals would permit signing at any computer, so long as proper security procedures were followed. At least for the foreseeable future, however, Internet petition signing would complement rather than supplant conventional methods of gathering written signatures.

Internet signature gathering requires at least the following three technical components:

- One or more websites that display the text of the proposed initiative on the public Internet;
- Means for voters to sign the initiative petition and transmit their signatures to the officials certifying them; and

• Means to authenticate the signatures and check them against the lists of registered voters.

Such websites could be run either by the initiative proponent or by state election officials. Under current California law, no changes in a proposed initiative are permitted once it has been approved by the Attorney General's office for signature gathering. Of course, these websites must be secured against hacker intrusion, denial of service attacks,[6] and other abuses;[7] but these problems appear to be less critical than those of securely gathering and authenticating voters' signatures on the Internet.

Electronic and Digital Signatures

Internet petition signing would build on the acceptance of electronic signatures for contracts and many other transactions as authorized under the 1999 California Uniform Electronic Transactions Act[8] (UETA) and the federal Electronic Signatures in Global and National Commerce (E-SIGN) Act of 2000.[9] These laws basically state that a signature, document, or record may not be denied legal effect or enforceability solely because it is in electronic form.[10] The laws deliberately do not specify the methods to be used for electronic signatures or the level of security required.

California's UETA statute broadly defines an electronic signature as "an electronic sound, symbol or process attached to or logically associated with an electronic record and executed or adopted by a person with the intent to sign the electronic record."[11] Thus, a customer can make a legally binding purchase simply by clicking on an icon shown on the computer screen so long as the parties have agreed to conduct the transaction using electronic media.[12] This kind of arrangement underlies much of the consumer commerce conducted on the Internet.

The term "digital signature," although often used as a synonym for "electronic signature," more precisely denotes a technical approach for binding an electronic signature to a particular electronic record that includes protections against alteration or other abuse.[13] Digital signatures use a mathematically robust method of encryption, known as "public key cryptography," associated with a "public key infrastructure" (PKI), to ensure the integrity of electronic signatures and records transmitted over the Internet.[14] Thus, for security reasons, many proponents of Internet voting and petition signing would mandate the use of digital signatures.

To use digital signatures for petition signing, registered voters would be assigned a unique pair of private and public cryptographic keys by a public agency such as the Department of Motor Vehicles (DMV) or an approved private "certification authority."[15] The private key would be downloaded onto the voter's computer or stored on a "smart card" containing a microchip, while the public key would be registered with the certification authority. A voter could then use his or her private key to sign a petition—either on the voter's computer or on another computer or device with a smart card reader—and send the digital signature[16] to the initiative website. Signatures would be decrypted using the public key registered with the certification authority and verified by election officials against the current voter list.

Despite their mathematical complexity, digital signatures are now used in some e-commerce and e-government transactions with relatively little added burden to either party. Private firms have established themselves as certification authorities, and several have been approved by the California secretary of state for use by public agencies. The digital signature approach to Internet petition signing thus appears technically feasible, although it raises a number of security, cost, and access issues which are discussed in the next section.

3   Security, Cost, and Access Issues

Security Issues Surrounding Internet Petition Signing

Newspapers regularly report the exploits of hackers who have broken in to supposedly secure computer networks, reminding us that perfect security will never be achieved in computer systems or any other human endeavor.[17] Internet petition signing is potentially vulnerable at several points and levels of the process. Websites displaying initiatives can be altered, "spoofed," or made unreachable for extensive periods of time. Private keys are usually protected by passwords that may be all-too-easily accessible or otherwise compromised. Thus, a voter's private key can be willingly or unwittingly given to someone else or copied remotely by a sophisticated intruder, who can then use it to sign petitions.[18] Viruses or other malicious code can be introduced to copy a private key or substitute another. Smart card readers can be similarly compromised. Individuals working for a certification authority, or election officials can be corrupted. The list of possible security breaches goes on.

These vulnerabilities are similar to those identified in numerous prior reports and discussions about Internet voting, such as the January 2000 final report of the California Internet Voting Task Force and the report from a National Science Foundation sponsored workshop on Internet voting held in October 2000. [19] The California Task Force concluded that "technological threats to the security, integrity and secrecy of Internet ballots are significant" and recommended against early implementation of remote Internet voting from home and office computers. Although the Task Force "did not consider Internet petition signing at any great length," its Technical Committee was concerned about the possibility of large-scale, computerized, "automated fraud" if individuals could register to vote remotely over the Internet without appearing personally and showing some sort of identification.[20] Regarding Internet petition signing, the Technical Committee report commented:

Systems that would allow online petition signing from a home or office PC are vulnerable to malicious code or remote control attacks on the PC that might prevent the signing of a petition, or spy on the process, or permit additional petitions to be signed that the voter did not intend to sign, all without detection. Hence, for the same reasons that we do not recommend Internet voting from machines not controlled by election officials, we cannot recommend similar systems for petition-signing until such time as there is a practical solution to the general malicious code problem and the development of a system to electronically verify identity.

While there are similarities between voting and petition signing, it is important to note that the two are not identical and they have somewhat different cost and security properties:

- Petition signing is a year-round activity, whereas voting occurs during a limited time window. Hence, servers and other infrastructure needed to support petition signing would need to be running year-round, instead of just during a time window before election day. This may dramatically increase the total cost of managing the system.
- While it is reasonable to expect voters, for security reasons, to submit a signed request for Internet voting authorization each time before they vote (similar to a request for an absentee ballot), it is not reasonable to expect voters to submit such a request each time they wish to sign a petition. As a result, voters who wish to sign petitions electronically would likely have to be issued authorization (means of authentication) that is open-ended in time. The longer such authorizations are valid, the more likely it is that some of them will be compromised, or sold, reducing the integrity of the petition-signing system over time.
- Voters can sign any number of petitions in an election cycle. Hence, a compromised authorization to sign petitions would be usable for signing any number of petitions, magnifying the damage to the system's integrity.[21]

Although these three bulleted objections should not be minimized, other factors may well make online petition signing less risky than online voting. First, because petition signing takes place over an extended period of time, denial of service attacks pose less of a threat to initiatives than to voting. More important, the voting process disconnects the voter's identity from the recorded vote; it must not be possible to reconstruct after-the-fact who voted for which candidates or measures. In contrast, petition signing deliberately links the signer with the measure, so that signatures can be verified when they are counted.

Compared to present methods, Internet petition signing should improve the verification of voter signatures. In California, county clerks now examine a random sample of 500 signatures or 3 percent of the total, whichever is higher. The results by county are given to the secretary of state, who uses them to project a statewide total of valid signatures.[22] With online petition signing, every digital signature, not just a sample, can be checked when decrypted to verify that the signer is a registered voter and has not previously signed the petition.[23] Consequently, statewide results should be more accurate and available more quickly. For added security, an automated query might be sent to a sample of electronic signers at their registered postal or e-mail addresses, asking them to confirm by return mail or e-mail that they actually had signed the petition.

Finally, the political stakes seem considerably less for petition signing than for actual voting, with commensurately less motivation to corrupt or obstruct the process. The risks involved in Internet petition signing may be closer to those associated with private elections or e-commerce, where online systems mostly use passwords and encrypted transmission (see Section 4). Of course, private firms can apply risk management concepts and tools to keep losses from security lapses at an acceptable level, whereas public trust in the initiative process may well require a higher standard. The questions then become: How secure must Internet petition signing be to gain voters' trust, and can that level of security be achieved at acceptable cost?

The Costs of Internet Petition Signing

Advocates of Internet petition signing forecast dramatically lower costs both for initiative proponents and for county and state offices that process their petitions. Using paid signature gatherers, proponents now typically spend more than $1 million to qualify a statewide initiative in California.[24] According to Marc Strassman, Executive Director of the Smart Initiatives Project, that expense could fall "to the ten thousand dollars needed to build a first-class website, thereby allowing individuals and groups without million dollar budgets to participate in the initiative process."[25] However, initiative proponents would still incur the costs of circulating other petitions for handwritten signatures and of managing the campaigns of initiatives that qualified for the ballot.[26] Nevertheless, significant cost savings are plausible once the infrastructure for Internet petition signing is in place.

How much would the infrastructure cost, and who would pay for it? Strassman estimates that the initial cost to the state of providing smart cards and digital certificates for roughly 25 million California adults would be less than $200 million, or about $8 per person.[27] This figure does not include the cost of smart card readers, which are widely available in cell phones and point-of-sale terminals in Europe and parts of Asia but not yet in the United States. The U.S. lag results in large part from our pervasive use of credit cards that are routinely and inexpensively checked over the telephone network for each transaction. This practice has so far obviated the need for more costly smart cards.

A smart card reader costs between $40 and $80 if bought as a separate unit but only $10 to $20 each if purchased in large quantities and integrated into cell phones or personal computers (PCs).[28] Hardly any PCs sold in the U.S. now come equipped with smart card readers, however, and PC manufacturers are unlikely to include them as standard features in the next few years. Using a cell phone or other mobile device equipped with a smart card reader to access the Internet is a likely scenario for consumer transactions; but this scenario is rather less likely for petition signing. As a consequence, ensuring general public access to smart card readers might require the state to purchase thousands of card readers, which it would then connect to the Internet at public kiosks, libraries, government offices, and other places where petitions could be signed.

Once a PKI infrastructure is in place, there will be continuing costs to manage the certification process for digital signatures. Certificates should be renewed on a regular basis to deter the potential fraud problems identified by the California Internet Voting Task Force. If an individual's private key is lost or compromised, it must be revoked and a new key pair and certificate issued. Moreover, the list of revoked certificates must be distributed promptly to election officials and anyone else who might rely on their authenticity. These recurring costs are difficult to estimate today because no PKI system of the proposed size is operational. The costs could be significantly lower if the key pairs and certificates issued for petition signing were also used for other public or private transactions, but this arrangement would further increase the risks of compromise and fraud.[29]

Developing secure, up-to-date, and Internet-accessible voting lists for checking and verifying digital signatures represents another cost to state and county government. Satisfying all three criteria is not a trivial task and would likely involve substantial expense. However, it is not wholly unprecedented; Michigan has recently built an integrated statewide computer system for cross-checking voter records.[30] California's voting lists also appear to be in better shape than those of many other states. Once Internet-accessible voter lists were available and election officials were trained to use them, the cost of verifying signatures should drop appreciably below that for the existing labor-intensive method.[31]

Access and Equity Issues

A persistent objection to Internet petition signing is that it would create further disadvantages for the poor, minorities, and people with disabilities who do not have easy access to computers and the Internet. If online signature gathering makes it cheaper and easier to qualify initiatives, the argument goes, it will favor the wealthy, highly educated, and mostly white voters who already have Internet connections at home and work.

Overall, Californians rank well above the national averages in terms of computer and Internet use. Surveys conducted by the Public Policy Institute of California (PPIC) indicate that as of October 2000, 68 percent of California adults were using the Internet compared with 60 percent of all U.S. adults.[32] More than half (51 percent) of the adults surveyed reported that they went online "often," a substantial increase from 43 percent in December 1999.

Even so, the most recent national[33] and California[34] data show substantial differences in computer ownership and Internet use according to

Table 5.1
Percentage of California Adults Using Computers and the Internet

Category	Computer Users	Internet Users
All California adults	78*%	68*%
Race/Ethnicity		
Non-Hispanic White	80*	71*
Asian	91	82
Black	76	60
Latino	71*	56*
Income		
Under $20,000	48	33
$20,000 – 59,000	76	62
$60,000 and above	93	85
Education		
High school or less	56	39
Some college	81	68
College graduate	89	81
Age		
18–64	83	70
65+	39	28
Region		
San Francisco Bay Area	82	72
Los Angeles County	74	59
Southern California	77	66
Central Valley	72	61

*PPIC survey data from October 2000. All other figures are averages from seven PPIC surveys between September 1999 and October 2000.

race or ethnicity, income, education level, age, and region. Among California adults, differences of more than 10 percent in Internet use separate Blacks and Latinos from Asians and non-Hispanic whites (table 5.1). And to no one's surprise, Internet use is characterized by a large generation gap: Californians between the ages of 18 and 64 are two and a half times more likely to use the Internet than those over 65.

In many respects, however, the "digital divide" has narrowed appreciably in the past two years. According to national data, the gender gap among Internet users has essentially disappeared.[35] In California, the gap between Latinos and non-Hispanic whites who have been to college has nearly closed, although it remains for those without some college education.[36] The generation gap is also shrinking steadily, but it will probably take two to four years before more than half of Californians age 65 and over are Internet users.[37] Given these remaining disparities, any near-term implementation of Internet petition signing should include access provisions for those who are not connected to the Internet.

4   Is Internet Petition Signing Inevitable? Trends in internet Voting, E-Commerce, and E-Government

Proponents of Internet signature gathering argue that the Internet is an unstoppable force that is transforming all private and public sector activities and will soon be used for petition signing, voting, and other political processes. Because this outcome is inevitable, they contend, citizens and government officials should start planning to integrate Internet petition signing into the political system in ways that will best support core democratic values. This section discusses trends and developments in Internet voting, e-commerce, and e-government and the extent to which they may spur public interest in and acceptance of Internet petition signing.

Internet Voting in Government Elections

Internet voting in U.S. general elections dates back to 1997, when astronaut David Wolf had his ballot e-mailed from his local election district in Texas to the Russian space station Mir, where he was temporarily assigned.[38] Three years later, few Internet votes were officially counted in the 2000 elections, but the topic is receiving considerable attention in the press and among citizen groups and public officials.

In a pilot project conducted by the Department of Defense, some 84 overseas military service personnel cast absentee ballots over the Internet in the 2000 presidential election. Using secure circuits developed for military communications, the encrypted ballots were sent electronically to voting officials in four states—Florida, South Carolina, Texas and Utah—and were counted along with other absentee ballots. Although criticized in Congress for its high cost, the pilot project "maintained the integrity of the electoral process, and in many respects posed fewer risks to election integrity than the current [overseas] absentee by-mail process," according to a DOD sponsored assessment.[39] The project director called it "a resounding success."

A significantly larger test took place in the March 2000 Arizona Democratic primary, in which nearly 40,000, or 46 percent, of the 86,000 votes were cast over the Internet.[40] Registered Democrats received a unique Personal Identification Number (PIN) in the mail and could vote from computers at 124 public polling places as well as from their homes or offices. Internet voters entered their PINs along with their names and addresses when they logged onto the primary website, and the information was checked against the voter registration list and assigned PINs. Digital signatures were not used. The binding primary election was administered by election.com, a for-profit firm specializing in Internet voting. Some technical problems arose during the four-day period for Internet voting;[41] but according to the company, no significant security breaches occurred. Voter participation was substantially higher than that for the 1996 presidential primary, and the Arizona Democratic Party seems quite satisfied with the results. Others, however, have criticized the Arizona Democratic primary for its lack of strong security measures and election official oversight of those who voted online from remote computers.[42]

California has taken a more cautious approach. Citing the security concerns of the Internet Voting Task Force report issued in January 2000, Governor Gray Davis vetoed a bill in September that would have authorized binding trials of Internet voting in state and local elections. Instead, prior to the November 2000 election, four California counties— Contra Costa, Sacramento, San Mateo and San Diego—conducted non-binding tests of Internet voting from computers located at polling places. According to VoteHere.net, the firm administering the trials in Sacramento and San Diego counties,[43] voters found the system easy to use, "8 out of 10 said they preferred Internet voting to the current system, and . . . 65 percent said they would vote from home if they thought the system was secure."[44]

As a result of the slow counts and other problems encountered with absentee ballots in the November 2000 election, some Internet voting advocates are now focusing on allowing absentee voters to use the Internet rather than the mails. This would be consistent with the conclusion reached by the Internet Voting Task Force that "it is technologically possible to utilize the Internet to develop an additional method of voting that would be at least as secure from vote-tampering as the current absentee ballot process in California."[45] Improving the security and integrity of absentee voting seems a high priority for election reform,[46] which may create an opening for early tests of Internet voting by absentees. Given that the percentage of California absentee ballots has grown from 6 percent in 1980 to 24.5 percent in 2000,[47] Internet voting would have the potential to grow rapidly once authorized. Oregon, where the November 2000 election was conducted entirely by mail, is also looking into the possibility of online voting.

Internet Voting in Nongovernment Elections
Meanwhile, Internet voting has found new niches in the private and nonprofit sectors. Many publicly traded U.S. corporations, which are required to conduct annual shareholder elections for directors and on other proposals, now permit and encourage proxy voting over the Internet. The number of investors voting online has more than doubled each year for the past three years and in 2000 constituted about 15 percent of all voting shareholders.[48]

Other organizations such as credit unions, labor unions, professional societies, and university student governments are beginning to hold their elections online. Probably the largest such effort to date was the October 2000 direct election of five at-large members to the international governing board of the nonprofit Internet Corporation for Assigned Names and Numbers (ICANN). The Markle Foundation gave $500,000 to ICANN and other organizations to support the Internet vote, which was managed by election.com. Anyone at least 16 years old could register with ICANN by providing a permanent mailing address and e-mail address. ICANN then mailed an encrypted PIN to the individual, which functioned as a password to verify that the person was registered when he or she logged on to vote.

Of the 76,000 individuals who registered as ICANN at-large members, 34,035 or nearly 45 percent voted during the 10-day voting period. Frank Fatone, Chief of Election Services for election.com, commented: "45% represents a significantly higher turnout than other private sector elections. . . . We usually see 13–18% . . . turnout in elections of this type. Use of the Internet clearly had a positive impact on participation in the ICANN election."[49] However, some technical glitches occurred:

During the first twelve hours of the 10-day voting period, some 2,800 of the 76,000+ At Large members encountered an error message when attempting to submit their votes. The difficulty was caused by the interaction of election.com's voting system with ICANN's encryption routine. . . . The situation was identified and corrected within the first 12 hours of the voting period. ICANN members that were affected by the situation were notified immediately via e-mail, and were directed to log on and cast their vote. Of the 2,800 people who received an error on their first attempt, 2,685 returned to the site and successfully cast their votes.[50]

The ICANN election shows that Internet voting with passwords can work with large numbers of dispersed voters, but also that technical problems are likely to arise in the early implementations. These problems would have to be solved before online voting is used widely in binding government elections. As Zoe Baird, president of the Markle Founda-tion, said afterwards: "[The ICANN election was] far from perfect. . . . It is now imperative that the data from this election experiment be thor-oughly analyzed and available for public scrutiny so that the dialogue can continue and the system can be improved."[51]

Managing Internet voting for corporations and nongovernment organ-izations represents an important near-term source of learning and rev-enue for electon.com and other firms such as Election Systems and Software, Safevote, Inc. and VoteHere.net. These firms expect to apply their experience to online government elections, and they would be well positioned to bid on support contracts for Internet petition signing as well.

Online Security for E-Commerce and E-Government Applications
Despite well-publicized failures of online retailers, Internet shopping continues to grow. A UCLA survey conducted in Spring 2000 found that more than half (51 percent) of U.S. Internet users have made purchases online.[52] The PPIC survey in October 2000 reported that 59 percent of California adults who use the Internet went online "to purchase goods or services."[53] For many young (and some older) adults, Internet shop-ping has become a familiar part of their daily lives.

As consumer online purchasing expands, e-commerce firms are seri-ously investing in identification and encryption to enhance security and generate customer trust. Shopping websites typically use registered pass-words for identification and "secure socket layer" (SSL) encryption for transmitting credit card or other payment information.[54] Websites that offer high-value transactions such as securities purchases, mortgages, and insurance may add PKI digital signatures backed by third-party certification authorities to verify customers' identities. As a next step, online identification systems using biometric methods to recognize fingerprints, faces, or voices are under development and appear likely to find acceptance among consumers.[55]

Over the next few years, digital signatures and certification authorities developed for e-commerce will likely be used for such e-government applications as filing taxes, obtaining licenses or permits, and bidding for government procurement contracts, which still require written signatures. This change may require government approval of the certification authorities used in these transactions, which the office of the California secretary of state has already initiated under its 1998 regulations.[56] Japan is also preparing regulations for ministerial approval of "certification services" under its recently passed digital signature law.[57]

Europe is well ahead of the United States in its use of smart cards for e-commerce and e-government applications. The European Commission is overseeing a formal plan to develop smart card requirements for a common "European Citizen Digital ID Document." According to one Commission report, this development

will promote European commerce and online payments. Moreover, it will be a very important step towards e-government in the European member states. Another benefit is enhanced data security. The qualified citizen's certificate enables strong authentication, encryption and digital signatures.[58]

Europeans have been more comfortable than Americans with government identity cards, and the European Citizen Digital ID Document represents both a modernization and harmonization of existing national paper ID documents into a common European Union digital format. No similar trend toward using smart cards for identification is apparent in the U.S., although credit card issuers continue to experiment with them.[59] It is quite possible that the U.S. credit card industry will replace existing magnetic-stripe cards with smart cards sometime within this decade, in large part to improve security for online transactions. However, the actual timing of such a move is difficult to predict.

5   Discussion, Conclusions, and Recommendations

To this observer, Internet petition signing does not yet seem ready for implementation in California or other states, but pressures for it seem likely to increase as more people use the Internet regularly to pursue their personal and professional interests, e-commerce, and interactions with government.

Current Obstacles and Ameliorating Trends

Security, access, and cost remain the principal obstacles to implementation of Internet petition signing. The security concerns associated with signing a petition on a remote computer are very real and appear difficult, but not impossible, to resolve satisfactorily. The continuing growth of e-commerce and new experiments with Internet voting will bring with them considerably more experience with digital signatures, biometrics, and other security approaches over the next few years. Given the commercial pressure to reduce risks and losses from large numbers of online transactions, identification and security methods will undoubtedly improve, and it seems highly likely that the commercial world will find workable solutions. Whether and when such solutions will be adequate to maintain public trust in remote signing of initiative petitions remains to be seen.

As costs decrease and a new, Internet-savvy generation reaches voting age, equity and access concerns will diminish but not disappear. Market and demographic forces alone will not bring all adults online. Consequently, any decision to permit Internet petition signing should include access arrangements for those who are not connected at home, school, or work. These arrangements would be consistent with the recommendations of the California Internet Voting Task Force to provide Internet kiosks for registration or initiative signature gathering. They would also have obvious cost implications for government.

State and local government seems unlikely to pay for the needed security and access infrastructure solely for Internet petition signing. However, the growing interest in California and other states in using the Internet for government operations and services will go a long way toward building that infrastructure. In his State of the State address on

January 8, 2001, Governor Davis officially launched a new state web-site—<http://my.ca.gov>—that provides a portal to e-government services such as registering vehicles, making state park campsite reservations, and checking the status of state income tax refunds. Hackers will surely test the privacy and security measures put in place for these e-government applications. As a result, it will be important to monitor, document, and analyze the ongoing security experience with e-government services, both to make these applications more secure and to inform any subsequent efforts to develop online voting or petition signing.

Election reforms in the aftermath of last November's problems may also have implications for petition signing. One such reform could be to update and maintain official voting lists online, with offline backup in the case of outage, intrusion, or other problems. Although initial voter registration would still require tangible proof of identity, such as a driver's license or social security card, subsequent changes could be processed online. Michigan's decision to link voter registration records to drivers' licenses, so that a DMV address change will automatically trigger a similar change on the voting rolls, also seems likely to spread to other states. Although such developments will not lead directly to Internet petition signing, they would provide much of the infrastructure needed for it.

The growth of remote Internet voting in the private and nonprofit sectors, along with more field trials in government elections, may further encourage other Internet applications in the political process such as petition signing. Despite the forecast by one well-respected consulting firm that "all states [will] have some form of Internet-based electronic voting by 2004,"[60] Internet voting must overcome many obstacles before it becomes widespread. Still, many voters say they favor online voting from home or work.[61] Moreover, absentee-voting reforms may include steps toward Internet voting. The issues surrounding Internet voting are closely intertwined with those for Internet petition signing, and future studies of or proposals for Internet voting should therefore consider the implications for initiative signature gathering on the Internet.

Broader Impacts of the Internet on the Initiative Process

Although the real effects of Internet signature gathering on the overall initiative process are as yet unknown, its proponents and opponents have focused on a few key points. Proponents have emphasized the Internet's potential to lower the cost and reduce the time required to qualify an initiative. Opponents usually stress the security and access concerns discussed above. Beyond these issues, however, lie more philosophical questions about how the Internet might influence initiatives and direct democracy generally.

One important question is whether the Internet could improve the quality of, as well as voters' actual use of, information about initiatives. Critics of the initiative process cite the scarcity and superficiality of information available to voters on television and radio.[62] In principle, the Internet is an ideal medium for presenting detailed information about specific initiatives and the groups supporting or opposing them. Internet websites can also link this information to relevant commentaries and other sources. Voters who seek information in greater depth than ballot pamphlets[63] and the mass media provide would be able to find it on the Internet.[64] As one example, California now requires all committees supporting and opposing ballot propositions that raise or spend $50,000 or more to file lists of contributors and contributed amounts electronically. This information is then made publicly available on the secretary of state's website.[65]

A related question is whether and to what extent the Internet will encourage greater and more informed public participation in the initiative process. Initiative websites could include interactive message boards that stimulate public discussion and debate, as other websites now offer on nearly every conceivable topic. It is certainly true that website message boards often spiral down into banal chatter or diatribe; nevertheless, many examples of sustained, spirited discussions on serious topics also can be found. The Internet's capacity to allow substantial numbers of people to interact over an extended period of time could counter another central criticism of initiatives: that they do not foster a structured, deliberative political process so essential to representative democracy.

An interesting recent proposal would use the Internet for public discussion of initiatives during the drafting process so that the proposed language could be debated and modified before seeking ballot qualification.[66] This proposal would require major changes in the current legislation governing initiatives as a way of developing a forum "in which the mix of professional and public voices could create a deeply deliberative process of public law."[67] Of course, others will make precisely the opposite argument, contending that the Internet favors nondeliberative, emotional responses that only exacerbate the flaws of initiatives and other tools of direct democracy. In all likelihood, the Internet can and will be used in both ways simultaneously.

Perhaps the most significant question raised by Internet petition signing is whether its chief effect would be to worsen current problems surrounding the initiative process itself. Lowering the cost to qualify an individual initiative could inundate voters with ballot measures at every election and might, in fact, increase the total sum spent on initiatives. Along with sheer number of items to be voted on, the influence of money and organized interest groups could increase.[68]

Such concerns about intensifying the negative aspects of direct democracy, like the hopes for a positive Internet role in spurring informed public participation, are conjectural. We lack good data or systematic studies on these points[69] and simply do not understand the full implications of using the Internet for petition signing or voting. The Internet can help level the political playing field among candidates and initiative proponents, but it could also exacerbate the influence of well-heeled contributors and organized interest groups. It can inform and encourage participation among voters in ways other media cannot, but it could also stimulate and reward superficial, emotional responses. It can be used for serious deliberation and debate on proposed initiatives among informed citizens, but it could also lead to an explosion of easy-to-qualify ballot measures with disastrous results for representative government.

We can be fairly sure, however, that Internet signature gathering, like Internet voting, will have unintended consequences. That prospect may be reason enough for many to oppose its early implementation in California, but it will not make the concept disappear. Its proponents will likely gain strength as more young people who have grown up with the Internet reach voting age and see no reason why they should not engage in political activities online as they do in all other areas.

Internet petition signing seems an idea whose time is not yet ripe but is clearly ripening. Its emergence on the political horizon should spur reformers of the initiative process to get on with their work before they are overtaken by events in cyberspace.

Acknowledgments

An earlier version of this paper was presented to the Speaker's Commission on the California Initiative Process in January 2001. The author has benefited from helpful comments from Robert Anderson, Mark Baldassare, Lorrie Faith Cranor, Max Neiman, Joyce Peterson, Fred Silva, Willis Ware, and Jeri Weiss. I also thank the Public Policy Institute of California for its support.

Notes

1. An early example of this now-popular phrase comes from Amy Cortese, "The Software Revolution: The Internet Changes Everything," *Business Week,* December 4, 1995 <http://www.businessweek.com/1995/49/b34531.htm>.

2. For example, see Audrey Cooper, "Legislator Proposes Online Voting for California," Associated Press, December 5, 2000; and John Chambers, "Can Technology Fix Balloting Problems? Yes; Harness Strength of the Internet," *USA Today,* December 19, 2000.

3. "Digital Signature. Election Petitions. Public and Private Transactions. Initiative Statute," State of California, SA2000RF0023, 2001.

4. The Final Report of the California Internet Voting Task Force, convened by Secretary of State Bill Jones, provides a detailed discussion of security and related issues. See Secretary of State, State of California, *Final Report of the California Internet Voting Task Force, Appendix A,* January 18, 2000; available at <http://www.ss.ca.gov/executive/ivote/>.

5. California requires signatures equivalent to 5 percent of the vote in the most recent gubernatorial election for statutory initiatives and 8 percent for constitutional initiatives. Based on the 1998 vote, the required numbers are 419,260 and 670,816, respectively; see Secretary of State, State of California, "1998 General Election Returns," <vote98.ss.ca.gov/Final/sov/summary.pdf>.

6. Although denial of service attacks are very real threats to election websites, they pose a more serious problem to Internet voting, which is conducted over a short period of time, than to initiative signature gathering, which is carried out over several months.

7. For example, hackers may be able to divert traffic from a legitimate website to one with a similar look that they have created; they could then fool users into revealing passwords or other personal information.

8. *Uniform Electronic Transactions Act: California Civil Code,* California Senate Bill 820, Enacted September 16, 1999.

9. *Electronic Signatures in Global and National Commerce Act,* P. L. 106–229, Enacted June 30, 2000.

10. Wills, testamentary trusts, and certain other specified transactions are excluded under UETA and E-SIGN.

11. *Uniform Electronic Transactions Act,* op. cit.

12. E-SIGN, §101(c), states that the parties must have "affirmatively consented" to the electronic transaction.

13. Information Security Committee, "Digital Signature Guidelines," American Bar Association, Section of Science and Technology, Electronic Commerce and Information Technology Division, 1996, <http://www.abanet.org/scitech/ec/isc/digital_signature.html>.

14. Computer Science and Telecommunications Board, *The Internet's Coming of Age,* Washington, DC: National Academy Press, 2000, pp. 5/15–19; and Fred B. Schneider, *Trust in Cyberspace,* Washington, D.C., National Academy Press, 1999, pp. 124–132. California regulations approved in 1998 for digital signatures valid for use by public entities also permit the use of a technical method known as "Signature Dynamics," which requires special hardware and expert handwriting analysis. Because Signature Dynamics is more cumbersome and expensive and less secure than PKI, this discussion assumes that the PKI approach would be used for petition signing with digital signatures. See Secretary of State, State of California, "California Digital Signature Regulations," June 12, 1998, <www.ss.ca.gov/digsig/regulations.htm>.

15. The list of private certification authorities approved by the California Secretary of State can be found at <www.ss.ca.gov/digsig/cert1.htm>.

16. Technically, the "signature" is the result of a mathematical calculation using the bits contained in the private key and the electronic record (petition).

17. For a sensible and accessible introduction to computer security, see Scott Culp, "The Ten Immutable Laws of Security," October 2000, <www.microsoft.com/technet/security/10imlaws.asp>.

18. As computer security experts have pointed out, digital signatures can only verify that a private key assigned to an individual was securely linked by a computer to a particular electronic document or record. It does not prove that the individual intended to sign the document, or that he or she was even present when the document was signed. See Bruce Schneier, "Why Digital Signatures Are Not Signatures," *CRYPTO-GRAM,* November 15, 2000 <http://www.counterpane.com/crypto-gram-0011.html>.

19. *Final Report of the California Internet Voting Task Force,* op. cit.; Internet Policy Institute, "Report of the National Workshop on Internet Voting," March 6, 2001, <http://www.internetpolicy.org/research/e_voting_report.pdf>.

See also Michael Ian Shamos, "Electronic Voting: Evaluating the Threat," 1993, <http://www.cpsr.org/conferences/cfp93/shamos.html>; Mercuri, Rebecca, "Electronic Voting," <http://www.notablesoftware.com/evote.html>; and Rubin, Avi, Chapter 4, this volume.

20. *Final Report of the California Internet Voting Task Force,* op. cit., Appendix A, pp. 9–12.

21. *Ibid,* Appendix A, pp. 13–14.

22. "The Secretary of State projects the rate [of signatures qualifying] for each county, totals the projected valid signatures from all 58 counties, and qualifies the initiative if there are 110 percent or more of the needed signatures. If the total falls between 95 and 110 percent, each signature must be individually verified; below 95 percent, the initiative does not qualify." Charlene Simmons, "California's Initiative Process: A Primer," California Research Bureau, California State Library, CRB-97-006, May 1997, p. 10

23. This verification process assumes that counties and the state maintain up-to-date computer voting lists, and that the digital signatures have not themselves been compromised.

24. Simmons, op. cit., p. 9.

25. Marc Strassman, "After Florida, What?" Smart Initiatives Online Newsletter, November 12, 2000.

26. The Internet can also serve as a fundraising and organizing tool for initiative proponents (and opponents) once a measure has been qualified. Both political candidates and organized interest groups are already making effective use of the Internet for these purposes.

27. Marc Strassman, "Fuzzy Math for Smart Initiatives," Smart Initiatives Online Newsletter, December 14, 2000.

28. Donald Davis, "Where There's A Web, There's A Way," *CardTechnology.com,* October 2000 <http://www.ct-ctst.com/CT/>.

29. Computer Science and Telecommunications Board, *Trust in Cyberspace,* op. cit., p. 131.

30. John Harwood, "Fixing the Electoral System: Lessons From States Hold Hope for Reform," *The Wall Street Journal,* December 22, 2000.

31. Strassman, "Fuzzy Math . . . ," reports cost estimates from California county officials of 60 cents to one dollar per signature for manual checking and verification.

32. The results from seven statewide surveys of California adults from September 1999 to October 2000 are available on the PPIC website <http://www.ppic.org>.

33. National Telecommunications and Information Administration (NTIA), *Falling through the Net: Toward Digital Inclusion,* U.S. Department of Commerce, 2000, <http://search. ntia.doc.gov/pdf/fttn00.pdf>.

34. Public Policy Institute of California (PPIC), "California's Digital Divide," November 2000, <http://www.ppic.org/facts/digital.nov00.pdf; "PPIC Statewide Survey: Californians and Their Government—October 2000," pp. 27–28, <http://www/ppic.org/publications/CalSurvey15/survey15.pdf>.

35. Results from a national survey conducted in August 2000 showed only a 0.2 percent difference between men and women using the Internet. National Telecommunications and Information Administration, *op. cit.,* p. xvi.

36. Public Policy Institute of California, "California's Digital Divide," op. cit. The NTIA study finds that, among Blacks and Hispanic households at the

national level, lower income and education appear to account for about two thirds of the reported gaps. National Telecommunications and Information Administration, *op. cit.,* pp. 14–15.

37. According to the NTIA national data, in the 20 months between December 1998 and August 2000, Internet use among those aged 62 to 65 increased by more than 60 percent. *Ibid.,* figure II–2, p. 36. Applying this growth rate to Californians aged 62 to 65, whose participation is already greater than 28 percent, suggests that a majority of Californians aged 65 and over will be Internet users within three years.

38. Counting Wolf's vote required passage of special legislation by the Texas legislature. See "Hurtling Toward Cyber-Elections," Voting Integrity Project, 1999, <http://www.voting-integrity.org/projects/votingtechnology/internetvoting/ivp_3_hurtling.shtml>.

39. Department of Defense, "Voting Over the Internet: Pilot Project Assessment Report," June 2001, p. 4–2, <http://www.fvap. ncr.gov/voireport.pdf>.

40. election.com, "Arizonans Register Overwhelming Support for Online Voting," March 12, 2000, <http://votation.com/us/pressroom/pr2000/0312.htm>. Besides the 46 percent who used the Internet, 32 percent voted by mail and 24 percent went in person to the polls.

41. Anick Jesdanun, "Resistance Continues for Web Voting," *San Jose Mercury News,* October 26, 2000.

42. For example, see L. Scott Tillett, "Will Internet Improve Voting?" Internet Week Online, November 17, 2000, <http://www.internetweek.com/lead/lead111700.htm>.

43. Safevote, Inc., and Election Systems and Software ran the Internet voting trials in Contra Costa and San Mateo counties, respectively.

44. John Schwartz, "E-Voting: Its Day Has Not Come Just Yet," *The New York Times,* November 27, 2000 <http://www.nytimes.com/2000/11/27/technology/27CHAD.html>.

45. *Final Report of the California Internet Voting Task Force,* op. cit., p. 1.

46. Absentee voting has relatively little protection against fraud and other abuses. See, for example, Simpson, Glenn R., and Evan Perez, "'Brokers' Exploit Absentee Voters; Elderly Are Top Targets for Fraud," *The Wall Street Journal,* December 19, 2000.

47. Miguel Bustillo, "Rise in Use of Absentee Ballot Alters Tactics as Election Day Nears," *Los Angeles Times,* November 3, 2000; Secretary of State, State of California, "Jones Officially Certifies California Election Results," December 15, 2000. <http://www.ss.ca.gov/executive/press_releases/2000/00-131.htm>.

48. Sara Nathan, "More Investors Click to Cast Proxy Votes," *USA Today,* March 27, 2000.

49. election.com, "ICANN and election.com Announce Results for First Worldwide Online Vote," October 10, 2000, <http://www.election.com/us/pressroom/pr2000/1010.htm>.

50. Ibid.

51. Markle Foundation, "ICANN Elections: An Important Moment for Internet Governance," October 11, 2000, <http://www.markle.org/news/Release.200010111248.1872.html>.

52. "The UCLA Internet Report: Surveying the Digital Future," UCLA Center for Communication Policy, November 2000, p. 10, <http://www.ccp. ucla.edu>.

53. Public Policy Institute of California "PPIC Statewide Survey: Californians and Their Government—October 2000," op. cit., p. 28.

54. Computer Science and Telecommunications Board, *The Internet's Coming of Age,* op. cit., p. 5/16.

55. See, for example, Carol Power, "Consumers Favor Fingerprint Scans in ID-Verification Tests," *American Banker,* December 22, 2000.

56. Secretary of State, "California Digital Signature Regulations, op. cit.

57. Government of Japan, "Law Concerning Electronic Signatures and Certification Services," enacted May 24, 2000. <http://www.meti.go.jp/english/special/E-Commerce/index.html>.

58. Information Society Technologies Programme, "eEurope Smart Cards: Common Requirements," Brussels, European Commission, December 11, 2000, §7.1.1, <http://europa.eu.int>.

59. In September 1999, American Express launched "Blue," a smart card targeted to "technology-minded individuals." As of mid-2001, it appears to have had only modest success. See "American Express Launches Blue," September 8, 1999, <http://home3.americanexpress.com/corp/latestnews/blue.asp>.

60. Gartner Group, " Gartner Says All States in the United States to Have Some Form of Internet-Based Electronic Voting by 2004," Press Release, April 11, 2000.

61. "A poll by ABC News found that 61% of 18–34-year-olds would like to vote online." Chambers, op. cit.

62. David Broder, *Democracy Derailed,* New York: Harcourt, 2000; Philip P. Frickey, "Representative Government, Direct Democracy, and the Privatization of the Public Sphere," *Willamette Law Review,* 34, 421, 1998. See also Thomas Cronin, *Direct Democracy: The Politics of Initiative, Referendum and Recall,* New York: Twentieth Century Fund, 1989.

63. A California ballot pamphlet for the November 2000 election, with information about each initiative, was available online before the election at <http://vote2000.ss.ca.gov/VoterGuide>. The state also spent about $6.5 million to mail pamphlets to 10 million voter households. Harwood, op. cit.

64. As of August 2000, 29 percent of California adults reported they went online "to visit the web sites of elected officials, political candidates, political parties, or political causes." Public Policy Institute of California, "PPIC Statewide Survey: Californians and Their Government—August 2000," <http://www.ppic.org/publications/CalSurvey13/survey13.pdf>.

65. California Automated Lobbying and Campaign Contribution & Expenditure Search System (CAL-ACCESS), <http://CAL-ACCESS.ss.ca.gov>.

66. Jay Worthington, "A Wider Hillside: Direct Democracy, Information Deficits and the Net," unpublished manuscript, 2000, pp. 27–28.

67. Ibid., p. 28.

68. As one example noted by a reviewer of an earlier draft of this paper, a well-financed group could pay individuals to place messages on initiative websites and thereby spin the discussion toward the group's point of view.

69. Bruce Bimber, "The Internet and Political Transformation: Populism, Community and Accelerated Pluralism," *Polity* 35, no. 1 (fall 1998): 133–160. For examples of speculative scenarios about the Internet and direct democracy, both positive and negative, see Corrado, Anthony and Charles M. Firestone, eds, *Elections in Cyberspace: Toward a New Era in American Politics*, Washington, D.C.: The Aspen Institute, 1996.

6

Efficient Choice, Inefficient Democracy? The Implications of Cable and Internet Access for Political Knowledge and Voter Turnout

Markus Prior

People face dramatically different media choices today than two or three decades ago. Television used to be broadcast only on three to five channels. Today, cable provides easily ten times as many channels and offers around-the-clock news coverage. The Internet further offers an unquantifiable amount of additional media options, including numerous newspapers, magazines, TV programs, and other political information. Few doubt that more information is available as a result of recent changes in the media environment. Does that imply that people are better informed? The present study attempts to answer this question by comparing people who have access to cable television and the Internet to those who do not. Results suggest that some people with new media access may indeed be better informed than those with limited or no access. But other new media users actually know less about the political process than otherwise similar users of "old" media. The knowledge gap (Tichenor, Donohue, and Olien 1970) between the most informed and the least informed is larger among new media users than among people without access to cable or Internet. This larger gap, I argue, is the result of the parallel increase of news *and entertainment* options for new media users. Cable viewers and Internet users can watch, read or listen to abundant information, but they can also avoid news better than people with no Internet and only broadcast television. The challenge is to predict who will indulge in news and who will ignore it.

In a broadcast environment, audiences are considered "captive." When referring to broadcasts of presidential addresses, Baum and Kernell (1999, 101) maintain that "a viewer's 'captive' status results from the combination of limited channels, an unwillingness to turn off the set, and the networks' joint suspension of commercial programming during a presidential appearance." While these simultaneous network broadcasts represent an extreme case, broadcast viewers face a comparable situation every day in the early evening, when most, if not all, broadcast channels offer local and national news for at least an hour. At these times, programming strategies effectively force broadcast viewers to choose between watching news and turning off the TV. Cable and Internet access remove these constraints by making more content and content types available overall and at any point in time. For people with access to new media, content preferences should determine exposure more directly than for the still-captive viewer without cable or Internet access.

Content preferences condition the effects of media use, and the power of this conditional effect increases with the number of media choices. Baum (1999; Baum and Kernell 1999) introduces a model of television watching, in which people's expectation about the utility they can gain from different programs determines their program choice. People weigh the benefits of obtaining information against the transaction costs of obtaining the information and the opportunity costs of not being able to use their attention differently. Baum argues that people do not tune in to hard news programs because opportunity costs (in form of forfeiting payoffs from entertainment) are too high. With more soft news programs, this utility calculation changes and more people maximize their utility by watching soft news (i.e., a mix of news and entertainment), because it provides a sufficient amount of entertainment. This paper applies a similar logic to the more general (and simplified) choice between news and entertainment content, focusing not only on changes due to increased program availability on cable television, but also the impact of the Internet.

One of the conclusions from Baum's model is that exposure to news and political awareness of certain events is not always the intended consequence of people viewing decisions, but can occur as a "byproduct." News-watching is not only determined by people's desire for information, but also by the entertainment programs they miss while watching news. The amount of news people watch is in part a function of the availability of nonpolitical programs and people's liking of these nonpolitical programs, as compared to news. Since news exposure leads to learning (Neuman, Just, and Crigler 1992), political knowledge can be a byproduct of a viewer's more general "utility" calculation, one which is not intentionally focused on obtaining political information. I argue that since cable viewers and Internet users can better match their content preferences to their content choices, their opportunity to obtain political knowledge as a secondary consequence or "byproduct" is reduced. In this paper, I develop hypotheses about the effects of new media on people's political knowledge and likelihood to vote. The hypotheses are tested using existing survey data. Despite difficulties in creating a measure of motivation from available data, empirical tests support the hypothesis that content preference is a better predictor of political knowledge and vote likelihood for new media users than it is for people with limited or no access to new media. People who enjoy watching entertainment more than news *and have access to cable television and the Internet* are less knowledgeable and less likely to vote than any other group of people.

Political Learning in a Media Environment with Increased Choice

Numerous studies, most of them in the uses-and-gratifications tradition (Katz, Blumler and Gurevitch 1973; Katz, Gurevitch and Haas 1973), have shown that people use media for different reasons. One of the most basic distinctions is between entertainment-focused and information-focused media use (e.g., Rubin 1984). Most entertainment exposure is motivated by the expectation of immediate, diversionary gratification. People do watch entertainment programs on television to gain knowledge about social behavior or fashion, among other things, but "[t]hese guidance motives are generally moderate in importance, ranking below enjoyment-oriented reasons" (Atkin 1985, 87,88). According to one recent analysis of survey data, more people give as their reason for watching television "to be entertained" than "to learn something" or "to keep up with what's going on." For roughly forty percent, being entertained is the primary reason for watching. Another fifty percent mention both being entertained and informed (Campbell, Yonish and Putnam

1999). Similar results were obtained by other studies (e.g., Comstock and Scharrer 1999; Graber 2001).

Yet while a sizable segment of the population watches television primarily to be entertained, and not to obtain political information, this does not necessarily imply that this segment is not also exposed to news. When only broadcast television is available, the audience is captive and, to a certain extent, watches whatever is offered. Audience research has confirmed a two-stage model according to which people first decide to watch television and then pick the available program they like best. Klein (1972, 77) aptly called this model of television the "Theory of Least Objectionable Program." Empirical evidence for the two-step model comes from analysis of audience data showing repeat-viewing rates of around 50 percent (Barwise, Ehrenberg, and Goodhardt 1982). That is, only about half the viewers of a particular program watch the same program on the following day. Repeat-viewing rates are low for all program types and do not increases when repeat-viewing of genres instead of particular programs is evaluated (Barwise and Ehrenberg 1988, 40). During the heyday of broadcast television, one study showed that only a third of all programs are watched from beginning to end by at least 80 percent of the people watching the programs at some point. Forty percent of the respondents reported watching programs because it came on the channel they were already watching or because someone else wanted to see it (LoSciuto 1972). Hence, a major share of television viewing does not seem to follow a deliberate choice of a program, but convenience, availability of spare time and the decision to spend that time watching television (see also Comstock and Scharrer 1999; Neuman 1991, 94).

It follows from the "two-stage" viewing behavior that news audiences should be larger when no (or few) alternatives are offered on other channels. Indeed, local news audiences tend to be larger when no competing entertainment programming is scheduled (Webster 1984; Webster and Newton 1988; Webster and Wakshlag 1983). Based on the analysis of commercial audience data, Barwise and Ehrenberg (1988, 57) conclude that restriction of choice due to simultaneous scheduling of news programs on all networks coincides "with lower audience appreciation among those viewing at these times (i.e., *they did not all necessarily want to watch news then*)" (emphasis added). As cable viewers can easily evade simultaneous news programs on all or most broadcast channels, audiences for entertainment programs should increase at the expense of news among people with cable access. Weimann (1996) documents that the introduction of cable in Israel caused increased watching of movies and MTV-like music channels (see also Katz 1996). Correlational research for the United States suggests that cable subscribers watch more entertainment programs than nonsubscribers (Becker, Creedon, Blood, and Fredin 1989). The most convincing evidence that high news ratings among broadcast viewers are explained by lack of alternatives rather than preference comes from a study by Baum and Kernell (1999) who show that cable subscribers, especially the less educated among them, are less likely to watch the presidential debates than people who receive only broadcast television. Far from being conclusive, these studies do suggest that viewers without cable access are constrained by the limited opportunities to watch entertainment programs and that they would prefer to tune in to entertainment more frequently than the offerings on broadcast channels allows them to do. And hence, "[a]lthough cable has fostered a core of "news junkies" who immerse themselves in CNN and C-SPAN, its more significant effect has been to contribute to a steep decline in the overall size of the news audience." (Patterson 2000, 247)

When exposed to television news, people learn about politics (e.g., Neuman et al. 1992; Zhao and Bleske 1995; Zhao and Chaffee 1995). Exposure alone leads to learning; attention is not necessary to pick up at least basic facts from the news (Keeter and Wilson 1986; Zukin and Snyder 1984). Zukin and Snyder (1984) show that even many politically uninterested New Jersey citizens who received their broadcast news from New York City stations recalled the names of New York's mayoral candidates, even though they could not vote for any of the candidates. Hence, broadcast viewers are likely to learn about politics even in the absence of political interest. Even those who would prefer to watch entertainment programs rather than news acquire at least basic political knowledge more or less "accidentally," because they happened to turn on their television at a time when only news was on.

This kind of accidental exposure and passive learning is much less likely among cable viewers. With plenty of entertainment options at all times of the day, cable viewers do not have to settle for news as their "least objectionable" program choice. Hence, for viewers who prefer entertainment to news, political knowledge should be lower if they have cable access than if they can only watch over-the-air channels. On the other hand, cable viewers with a preference for news have the opportunity to watch more news than broadcast viewers with the same preference. Therefore, their political knowledge should be higher than that of otherwise similar viewers without cable access. In short, theoretical considerations lead me to predict an interaction effect between cable access and content preference on political knowledge.

Much of this section focused on television viewing behavior because decades of research have produced relatively firm understanding of what people like about watching television and how they decide what to watch. Research on Internet use has not yet developed as far, in part because the medium itself changed quickly in its first decade. Consequently, predictions about the effects of Internet access cannot rely on an equally developed theoretical understanding of user behavior. With respect to one key property, however, the Internet is very similar to cable television: Both increase the availability of media content considerably. To the extent that greater availability and greater choice explain the effect on political knowledge derived above, the effect of the Internet may be very similar to that of cable television. Chance encounters with political information (beyond the occasional headline) may be equally infrequent on the Internet. Active searching for political information driven by a preference for news may be required for people to learn about politics. Avoiding politics may be as easy (if not easier) on the Internet as it is on cable television. The following analysis should be understood as a first test of the proposition that increased content availability and choice on cable TV and the Internet have similar effects, *not* as an argument that cable television and Internet are equivalent *in all respects*.

In the second part of this paper, the analysis is extended to turnout. Since an individual's likelihood to vote in an election increases with her level of political knowledge (Tan 1980; Verba, Burns, and Schlozman 1997; Verba, Schlozman, and Brady 1995, ch. 12), the same interaction between new media access and content preferences should occur for models of turnout. All other things equal, new media users with a preference for news should be more likely to vote in an election than people with the same news preferences, but limited or no new media access. Analogously, people with access to new media and a preference for entertainment should be less likely to vote compared to otherwise similar individuals without new media access.

The Data

The survey data to test the hypothesis comes from two different sources: The National Election Studies (1996, 2000) and the Pew Media Consumption Surveys (1996, 1998, 2000).

Relative Entertainment Preference

Testing the hypotheses requires a measure of people's relative preferences for entertainment over news. Since respondents are not directly asked about their preferences in any of these surveys, preferences have to be assessed indirectly by the actual program types they report watching. In particular, relative entertainment preference is measured as the share of entertainment viewing, or:

$$\text{Relative Entertainment Preference} = \frac{\text{Entertainment Viewing}}{\text{Entertainment Viewing} + \text{News Viewing}}$$

Entertainment viewing is measured slightly differently for each of the surveys used here. While consistency was the goal in creating the scales, the available items differ from survey to survey. For the NES 2000, entertainment viewing is based on two items about *Jeopardy* and *Wheel of Fortune*. Entertainment viewing is measured by the mean daily viewing of both shows. For the NES 1996, entertainment viewing is the mean frequencies of watching games shows (*"Jeopardy"* or *Wheel of Fortune"*) and *Dr. Quinn, Medicine Woman* (measured on a four-point scale and standardized to the 0–1 interval). For the Pew Media Consumption Surveys, entertainment viewing is operationalized as watching *Entertainment Tonight* (MCS 2000), *Entertainment Tonight* and MTV (MCS 1998), and *Hardcopy* and MTV (MCS 1996). All items used four-point response formats ("regularly," "sometimes," "hardly ever," "never").

News viewing is operationalized as average daily viewing of local and national news for all data sets.[2] Relative Entertainment Preference cannot be computed for respondents who reported no information and entertainment viewing at all. These respondents are excluded from the analysis (2.5% in MCS 1996, 2.8% in MCS 1998, 5.4% in MCS 2000,

5% in NES 1996, 11% in NES 2000). A summary of the relative entertainment preference scales and descriptive statistics is in table 6.6.

Obviously, the entertainment programs on which the scales are based
are arbitrary. Arguably, game shows are not a viable entertainment options for many people, not even in times of severe boredom. Given that
this study is limited by the availability of secondary data, there is no fix
for this problem. Using a number of different entertainment programs in
different surveys, however, should ease fears that results are based only
on the idiosyncrasies of game show viewers. In order to assess the seri-
ousness of these inevitable problems, the next section provides a validity
check for the measures of relative entertainment preferences.

Validating the Index of Relative Entertainment Preference

The basic premise of this paper is that people, if given the opportunity,
expose themselves to media content that they like. This idea is simplified
here to distinguish people who prefer news from those who prefer entertainment. Since no direct measure of content preferences is available, the
index of relative entertainment preference (REP) was created as a ratio
of self-reported exposure to news and entertainment (news) programs. In
this section, I present some evidence that the REP index, while created
differently for different data sets, is consistently and in intuitive ways
related to other relevant variables.

Table 6.6 shows bivariate correlations of REP with various measures
of attention to news. For the NES 1996 and 2000, REP is negatively
related to local and national news attention. Consistent with the notion
that national news tend to be more serious, the bivariate correlation is
slightly larger for attention to national news. For the Pew data sets, table
6.6 contains bivariate correlations of the REP index with respondents'
self-reported tendency to follow general news and entertainment news in
particular. For all three data sets, REP is negatively related to following
news. More importantly, however, the correlations of the REP index
with following entertainment news are distinctly more positive, indicating that the REP index distinguishes people with a preferences for hard
news from those with a preference for entertainment aspects of news, if
not entertainment per se. (The Pew studies do not include any measure
of viewing entertainment shows, so the relation of REP and entertainment programming cannot be assessed.)

The second way to validate the REP index is to examine its relation to television news exposure. Theoretically, news exposure is the mediating variable between REP and political knowledge. The prediction that the knowledge gap between information- and entertainment-seekers is larger for cable subscribers is based on the intuition that information-seekers can watch more news when they have cable access, while entertainment-seekers with cable can avoid news more effectively. Thus, the interaction of cable and REP should be negative in its effect on news exposure.

Table 6.7 presents empirical tests of the prediction for various measures of television news exposure. In order to validate the REP index, the exposure measures have to be general enough not to mention a particular news program or even "network news," as such measures would have different meanings for people with and without cable access. (A person without cable access who reports watching little network news is unlikely to be exposed to a lot of national news, whereas this conclusion would be invalid for someone with access to cable.) Pew's 1996 MCS includes a 5-point scale of time spent watching television news on the day before the interview, as well as the question whether the respondent watches more news than before. In the 2000 MCS, respondents were simply asked whether they watch news regularly or not. For the NES 1996 and 2000, finally, composite news exposure measures were built from self-reported watching of the presidential debates and "programs about the campaign" (alpha = .68, r = .52 for NES 2000; alpha = .69, r = .52 for NES 1996).

Results in table 6.7 are very consistent. Exposure to television news is lowest among people with cable access and a strong preference for entertainment. Access to cable television increases the effect of entertainment preference on news viewing. This interaction is significant at p<.10 or better in four of the five models and has a p-value of .19 for the fifth model.[3] The consistently very low R^2s, however, should caution against overinterpreting these results. They do provide indication that the REP index indeed measures the concept of relative content preferences.

Information and Participation Measures

The dependent variables in this paper are a set of information measures about congressional elections and voting in House and presidential elections. The NES 1996 and 2000 include the traditional questions on name recall for House candidates in the respondent's district. The number of correctly recalled candidate names is counted so that the measure ranges from zero (no recall) to two (recall of both candidates' names). Indices of incumbent-specific information are created in the NES data sets from four items. In 1996, respondents were asked whether the incumbent voted for or against welfare reform, how often the incumbent supported President Clinton's legislative proposals, and how well the incumbent "keeps in touch with the people in your district." The number of times that the respondent gave an answer other than "don't know" was counted. The forth item was the respondent's knowledge of who the incumbent candidate in her district was. For the 2000 index, the first two items were different: Respondents were asked whether they remembered anything the incumbent had done for their district and whether they knew the number of years the incumbent was in office.

Vote measures were created for self-reported vote in presidential and House elections (post-election interview) for the 1996 NES.[4] The Pew Media Consumption Surveys in 1996, 1998, and 2000 use retrospective questions on voting in the last presidential election. Any specific candidate named is coded as 1; "did not vote," "don't know," and not remembering which candidate the vote was cast for are coded as 0.[5]

Cable Access and Control Variables

Cable access is coded as a dummy variable based on the question "Do you have either cable or satellite television?" (Hence, "cable access" subsumes satellite services.) To test whether the effect of cable and the effect of new media more generally are similar, a measure of new media access is created. Respondents with access to either cable television or the Internet are scored 1, while respondents with access to both are scored 2. People without access to either receive a score of 0.

Two possible confounding factors have to be considered carefully in the present study design. First, new media access as an explanatory factor has to be distinguished from the influence of other variables that might explain information and turnout, and *that are correlated with having new media access*. Most importantly, cable and Internet access is not affordable for all Americans. This leads to correlations between cable access and other demographic variables, notably income, education and campaign interest. While a cross-sectional design is certainly not optimal to disentangle these influences, the present study uses several demographic control variables, including income, education, and campaign interest.

The second possible confound results from the self-selection of cable subscribers and people with Internet connections. Some people might be more interested in political affairs (and already more knowledgeable) and obtain new media access only as a result of their existing higher interest. This concern is eased by including a variety of variables that control for possible difference between cable subscribers and broadcast viewers. These control variables include campaign interest, political information, frequency of discussing politics, group membership, trust, internal and external efficacy, and the strength of the respondent's partisan identification. Hence, the analysis compares the effect of new media access among otherwise (in a statistical sense) similar individuals—similarly interested in, and informed about, politics; similarly trusting in government; and similarly engaged in the political process.

Differences in knowledge might be explained simply by different media use patterns that happen to correlate with new media access. In order to minimize this possibility, controls are included for respondents' frequency of watching national and local news, reading the newspaper, and listening to talk radio. Since different media uses tend to be positively correlated, this also controls for the possibility that people with new media access simply spend more time using media and are better informed as a result of their long watching or web-surfing hours, not their cable or Internet access as such. To be even more certain that the length of media use does not confound the analysis, a control variable is included for the time that respondents spent working. Some controls were not available for all data sets used in this study. Using a variety of control variables reduces the danger of attributing effects to new media access and entertainment preferences that are in fact caused by correlates of those factors.[6]

Results

According to my hypothesis, viewing preferences should prove a better predictor of political knowledge for people with greater access to new media. Consequently, the interaction effect of REP and new media access in regressions of the different information measures should be negative and significant, whereas the main effect of REP should be insignificant. In particular, knowledge should be lowest for people who have both maximum access to new media and a strong preference for entertainment, as these people are most likely to use new media to avoid news exposure. In the following analysis, the predicted values on the knowledge scales obtained from the regression models should be lowest for this group.

This section presents the results both for the effect of cable television only and for the effect of new media. For recall of House candidates, results from OLS regressions are shown in table 6.1. The interaction term is significant at $p < .10$ in three of four models, and marginally significant at $p = .14$ in the fourth. To interpret the results correctly, main and interaction effects need to be considered together. To this end, figure 6.1 graphs the predicted values by new media access for the range of possible values that relative entertainment preference can take, while holding all other independent variables at their means. (Only results from the new media models are graphed.) The models include controls for a variety of factors that would otherwise confound the impact of new media access and entertainment preference. Most importantly, respondents' overall political knowledge, as measured by interviewer assessment, and campaign interest are held constant. In other words, candidate knowledge is lower among respondents with greater new media access and a preference for entertainment than among equally informed and interested respondents with less access. Controls are also included for respondents' media use habits and frequency of political discussions. That is, people know less about the candidates when they have an entertainment preference and new media access, even if they report watching the same amount of local and national news, reading newspapers with a similar frequency, listening to talk radio for equally long periods, and discussing just as often. Finally, the models control for factors such as age, gender, income, and working hours that might affect media use.

The graphs in the first row of figure 6.1 provide support for the hypothesis: Among people who prefer entertainment, greater access to new media is associated with lower knowledge about politics. The reverse is not apparent in the results: People with a preference for news and access to new media do not recall candidate names better than people with a news preference but no or only limited access to new media. One graph (NES 1996) also suggest a slight *increase* in recall and familiarity at higher levels of entertainment preference for people without new media

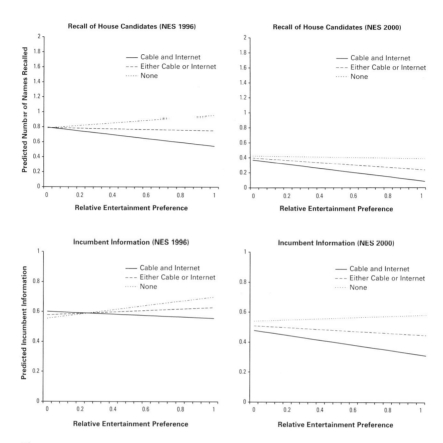

Figure 6.1
Political Knowledge

access. This main effect of the REP index is positive in some of the models, sometimes at statistically significant levels. One explanation is that the measure of entertainment preference picks up the amount of media use to some degree, as shown above.[7] With respect to cable television, it is not inconceivable that political advertising, which is often most heavily targeted toward prime-time (i.e., noncable) programs, affects broadcast viewers with high relative entertainment preference disproportionally. Given the limitations of the available measures, it is difficult to interpret the absolute predicted values. Their relative magnitude, however, shows that a high preference for entertainment translates into below-average political knowledge *only for people with access to new media.*

Table 6.1
Candidate Name Recall (NES 1996, 2000)

	NES 1996		NES 2000	
	Model 1	Model 2	Model 1	Model 2
Entertainment Preference	.30 (.15)**	.17 (.14)	.11 (.12)	-.021 (.067)
Cable	.052 (.065)	—	-.024 (.045)	—
New Media	—	.0039 (.046)	—	-.025 (.025)
Ent. Pref. X Cable	-.47 (.18)***	—	-.19 (.13)	—
Ent. Pref. X New Media	—	-.21 (.13)*	—	-.12 (.060)*
Party ID	.0092 (.011)	.0090 (.011)	-.0080 (.0093)	-.0084 (.0093)
Incumbent Cand. ID	-.039 (.025)	-.039 (.025)	.010 (.018)	.011 (.018)
Open Race	-.0031 (.074)	-.0043 (.074)	.095 (.060)	.094 (.059)
Strong Party Identifier	.19 (.088)**	.19 (.088)**	.081 (.055)	.077 (.055)
Weak Party Identifier	.13 (.084)	.13 (.084)	.010 (.048)	.0079 (.049)
Independent Leaner	.12 (.087)	.12 (.072)	.016 (.049)	.016 (.049)
Education	.064 (.017)***	.067 (.017)***	.041 (.013)***	.042 (.013)***
Income	.013 (.0042)***	.013 (.0043)***	.0088 (.0060)	.0087 (.0058)
Gender	-.054 (.046)	-.06 (.046)	.0034 (.033)	.0043 (.033)
Black	-.42 (.066)***	-.43 (.067)***	-.15 (.054)***	-.14 (.053)***
Hispanic	—	—	-.11 (.053)**	-.12 (.054)**
Other Non-White	-.31 (.15)**	-.30 (.15)**	-.0073 (.067)	-.0021 (.068)
Age	.019 (.0073)***	.019 (.0074)**	.0032 (.0050)	.0026 (.0051)
Age^2	-.0002 (.0001)***	-.0002 (.0001)***	-.00002 (.00005)	-.00002 (.00005)
South	-.073 (.045)	-.068 (.048)	-.027 (.034)	-.025 (.034)
Weekly Working Hours	-.002 (.0012)	-.0020 (.0013)	-.0018 (.00085)**	-.0019 (.00086)**
Religious Attendance	.13 (.058)**	.12 (.059)**	.096 (.043)**	.10 (.044)**
Political Information	.49 (.11)***	.47 (.12)***	.35 (.074)***	.37 (.075)***

Table 6.1
(continued)

	NES 1996		NES 2000	
	Model 1	Model 2	Model 1	Model 2
Campaign Interest	.17 (.073)**	.18 (.073)**	.022 (.054)	.27 (.054)
Discuss Politics	-.07 (.085)	-.062 (.086)	.049 (.043)	.48 (.043)
Group Memberships	.018 (.016)	.019 (.016)	.036 (.013)***	.37 (.013)***
Trust	.049 (.069)	.063 (.070)	-.0067 (.049)	-.0064 (.049)
Internal Efficacy	.086 (.079)	.081 (.080)	.082 (.054)	.090 (.055)*
External Efficacy	.089 (.063)	.095 (.063)	-.037 (.045)	-.035 (.045)
Live in Community	.22 (.055)***	.22 (.055)***	.099 (.025)***	.096 (.025)***
Watch National News	-.017 (.072)	-.0090 (.073)	.014 (.051)	.010 (.051)
Watch (Early/Late) Local News	.022 (.068)	.027 (.069)	.027 (.050) /	.021 (.050) /
Read Newspaper	.14 (.057)**	.13 (.057)**	.013 (.0058)**	.013 (.0059)**
Listen to Talk Radio	-.0076 (.048)	-.0044 (.048)	.032 (.037)	.032 (.037)
Time of Interview	-.0078 (.0027)***	-.0078 (.0027)***	-.0044 (.0014)***	-.0044 (.0014)***
Constant	-.96 (.22)***	-.92 (.22)***	-.39 (.14)***	-.35 (.14)**
N (with MV imputations)	1448	1441	1358	1347
N (without MV imputations)	1260	1259	1083	1078
R^2	.24	.23	.22	.22

*** $p < .01$, ** $p < .05$, * $p < .10$

Note: Models are OLS regressions estimated on five imputed data sets created by AMELIA (Honaker, et al. 1999). The coefficient estimate is the mean of the five separate estimates. The robust standard error (in parentheses) is based on the variance across the five imputed data sets plus the variance within each data set. For details, see King et al. (2001).

The table lists the number of observations with and without multiple imputations of missing values. Goodness-of-fit statistics are only available for non-imputed estimations.

The second measure of political knowledge employed here focuses on incumbent-specific information. This measure includes information about the incumbent's identity and her record while in office. Results for 1996 and 2000 are presented in table 6.2. The interaction effect is in the predicted (negative) direction and significant at $p < .05$ for three of four models. The specification that included both cable and Internet in measuring new media access performs better than the cable-only model. The second row of graphs in figure 6.1 illustrates results graphically by showing predicted knowledge levels, while holding other variables at their means. Again, knowledge decreases with REP only for people with new media access, and more so if they have access to both cable and the Internet. However, as for recall, there is no discernable effect for low REP and the main effect of REP is again positive for the NES 1996 data. In sum, the analysis can only support a weaker version of the hypothesis for political knowledge: The more people have access to new media, the less they know about (congressional) politics, if they prefer entertainment. The reverse does not find support: Among people who like news, access to new media does not appear to increase political knowledge.

Since politically knowledgeable people are more likely to vote (e.g., Verba et al. 1997; Verba et al. 1995, ch. 12), viewing preferences should also be a better predictor of turnout for those with greater new media access. If, as results suggests, people with a strong entertainment preference and maximum new media access are indeed the least knowledgeable segment of the electorate, they may also be the least likely to vote. Table 3 presents tests of this second prediction for voting in the 1996 presidential and House elections based on data from the NES 1996. Support for the hypothesis comes from voting in the House election. Figure 6.2 graphs the likelihood of voting by new media access for the range of the entertainment preference variable while holding other variables at their means. The shape of the interaction for the 1996 NES Study, while in the predicted direction, is somewhat unexpected, since it appears to be driven mostly by changes among viewers without new media access. As in the discussion of the information results, the relative differences are more insightful than the absolute values. Among people with a strong relative entertainment preference, the likelihood to vote decreases with access to new media.

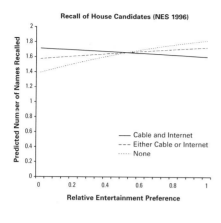

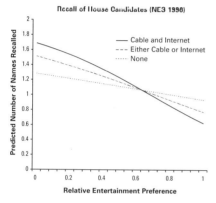

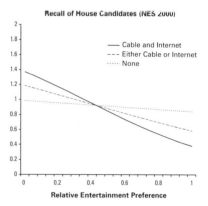

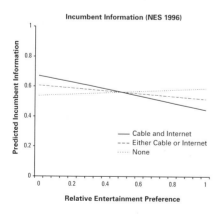

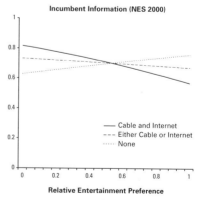

Figure 6.2
Vote Likelihood

Table 6.2
Knowledge of Incumbent House Candidates (NES 1996, 2000)

	NES 1996		NES 2000	
	Model 1	Model 2	Model 1	Model 2
Entertainment Preference	.15 (.056)***	.14 (.053)***	.0083 (.061)	.041 (.041)
Cable	.029 (.024)	—	-.039 (.023)*	—
New Media	—	.023 (.016)	—	-.029 (.013)
Ent. Pref. X Cable	-.13 (.066)**	-.094 (.045)**	—	—
Ent. Pref. X New Media	—	—	—	-.098 (.046)**
Party ID	-.0025 (.0036)	-.0021 (.0037)	-.0072 (.0043)	-.0077 (.0043)*
Incumbent Cand. ID	.0088 (.0080)	.0085 (.0080)	.020 (.0090)**	.020 (.0089)**
Strong Party Identifier	.077 (.029)***	.075 (.029)***	.042 (.026)	.039 (.026)
Weak Party Identifier	.070 (.027)**	.069 (.027)**	.028 (.026)	.025 (.026)
Independent Leaner	.087 (.029)***	.088 (.028)***	.045 (.026)*	.043 (.026)*
Education	.0032 (.0059)	.0028 (.0059)	.017 (.0061)***	.018 (.0062)***
Income	-.0017 (.0016)	-.0022 (.0017)	.0030 (.0025)	.0046 (.0028)
Gender	-.041 (.015)***	-.042 (.015)***	-.021 (.017)	-.018 (.017)
Black	-.058 (.030)*	-.059 (.030)**	-.094 (.028)***	-.098 (.027)***
Hispanic	—	—	-.082 (.040)**	-.084 (.040)**
Other Non–White	-.039 (.059)	-.039 (.060)	-.046 (.034)	-.040 (.034)
Age	.012 (.0027)***	.012 (.0027)***	.011 (.0028)***	.010 (.0028)***
Age²	-.0001 (.00003)***	-.0001 (.00003)***	-.0001 (.00003)***	-.0001 (.00003)***
South	.0053 (.016)	.0063 (.016)	-.039 (.018)**	-.040 (.018)**
Weekly Working Hours	-.00068 (.00042)	-.00069 (.00042)*	-.00046 (.00043)	-.00045 (.00043)
Religious Attendance	.022 (.019)	.023 (.019)	.0091 (.021)	.012 (.021)
Political Information	.24 (.036)***	.23 (.036)***	.23 (.038)***	.24 (.038)***
Campaign Interest	.057 (.025)**	.060 (.025)**	.046 (.029)	.048 (.029)*

Table 6.2
(continued)

	NES 1996		NES 2000	
	Model 1	Model 2	Model 1	Model 2
Discuss Politics	.047 (.029)	.045 (.029)	.030 (.022)	.033 (.022)
Group Memberships	.0084 (.0050)*	.0088 (.0050)*	.013 (.0048)***	.013 (.0048)***
Trust	.015 (.023)	.017 (.023)	-.0013 (.025)	.0027 (.025)
Internal Efficacy	.042 (.027)	.043 (.027)	.040 (.026)	.048 (.026)*
External Efficacy	.011 (.021)	.011 (.021)	.024 (.022)	.021 (.022)
Live in Community	.094 (.022)***	.093 (.022)***	.063 (.019)***	.057 (.020)***
Watch National News	.013 (.024)	.011 (.024)	.013 (.026)	.0081 (.026)
Watch (Early/Late) Local News	.053 (.024)**	.056 (.024)**	.049 (.024)** /	.048 (.024)* /
			.020 (.022)	.016 (.022)
Read Newspaper	.046 (.020)**	.044 (.020)**	.012 (.0032)***	.012 (.0032)***
Listen to Talk Radio	.027 (.016)*	.026 (.016)	.013 (.017)	.013 (.017)
Time of Interview	-.0001 (.00093)	-.00016 (.00094)	-.0003 (.00076)	-.00021 (.00075)
Constant	-.20 (.084)**	-.20 (.084)**	-.23 (.080)***	-.22 (.079)***
N (with MV imputations)	1315	1309	1352	1341
N (without MV imputations)	1135	1136	1083	1076
R^2	.22	.24	.26	.33

*** $p < .01$, ** $p < .05$, * $p < .10$

Note: Models are OLS regressions estimated on five imputed data sets created by AMELIA (Honaker, et al. 1999). The coefficient estimate is the mean of the five separate estimates. The robust standard error (in parentheses) is based on the variance across the five imputed data sets plus the variance within each data set. For details, see King et al. (2001).

The table lists the number of observations with and without multiple imputations of missing values. Goodness-of-fit statistics are only available for non-imputed estimations.

Table 6.3
Voting in 1996 Presidential and House Elections (NES 1996)

	House Election		Presidential Election	
	Model 1	Model 2	Model 1	Model 2
Entertainment Preference	1.63 (.56)***	1.45 (.55)***	.99 (.61)	.7⁻ (.61)
Cable	.70 (.24)***	—	.26 (.27)	.2⁻ (.20)
New Media	—	.47 (.18)**	—	—
Ent. Pref. X Cable	-1.47 (.66)**	—	-.36 (.74)	—
Ent. Pref. X New Media	—	-.92 (.49)*	—	.0⁻55 (.58)
Party ID	.058 (.045)	.056 (.045)	-.017 (.049)	-.0⁻6 (.048)
Incumbent Cand. ID	.088 (.089)	.098 (.089)	-.065 (.097)	-.0⁻1 (.096)
Open Race	.32 (.24)	.31 (.24)	-.14 (.25)	-.1⁻ (.25)
Strong Party Identifier	1.65 (.31)***	1.60 (.31)***	1.77 (.32)***	1.7⁻ (.33)***
Weak Party Identifier	.83 (.28)***	.80 (.28)***	.87 (.29)***	.8⁻ (.27)***
Independent Leaner	.58 (.30)*	.58 (.30)*	.77 (.31)**	.7⁻ (.31)**
Education	.18 (.065)***	.16 (.066)**	.27 (.073)***	.2⁻ (.074)***
Income	.051 (.016)***	.051 (.016)***	.066 (.017)***	.0⁻3 (.017)***
Gender	.31 (.17)*	.30 (.17)*	.19 (.18)	.1⁻ (.18)
Black	-.32 (.26)	-.30 (.26)	-.28 (.26)	-.2⁻ (.26)
Other Non-White	-.69 (.50)	-.76 (.51)	-.48 (.62)	-.4⁻ (.62)
Age	.060 (.028)**	.069 (.028)**	.021 (.031)	.0⁻6 (.031)
Age²	-.00043 (.00027)	-.00051 (.00027)*	-.000066 (.00030)	-.00011 (.00030)
South	-.25 (.17)	-.26 (.17)	-.43 (.18)**	-.44 (.18)**
Weekly Working Hours	.0012 (.0049)	.00092 (.0048)	-.0065 (.0054)	-.0⁻62 (.0055)
Religious Attendance	1.12 (.22)***	1.11 (.23)***	1.13 (.24)***	1.1⁻ (.24)***
Political Information	1.52 (.41)***	1.46 (.41)***	1.79 (.43)***	1.7⁻ (.44)***
Campaign Interest	.76 (.27)***	.80 (.27)***	1.30 (.29)***	1.33 (.29)***

Table 6.3
(continued)

	House Election		Presidential Election	
	Model 1	Model 2	Model 1	Model 2
Discuss Politics	.87 (.32)***	.84 (.33)**	.76 (.34)**	.74 (.35)**
Group Memberships	.10 (.079)	.096 (.077)	.082 (.099)	.080 (.098)
Trust	-.091 (.25)	-.039 (.25)	-.12 (.26)	-.038 (.26)
Internal Efficacy	-.012 (.30)	.0091 (.30)	-.18 (.32)	-.20 (.32)
External Efficacy	.41 (.23)*	.36 (.23)	.47 (.26)*	.45 (.26)*
Live in Community	.75 (.23)***	.73 (.23)***	.36 (.21)*	.33 (.21)*
Watch National News	.62 (.25)**	.60 (.25)**	.28 (.26)	.25 (.27)
Watch Local News	.086 (.27)	.12 (.26)	-.16 (.27)	-.14 (.27)
Read Newspaper	.16 (.21)	.16 (.21)	.33 (.22)	.33 (.22)
Listen to Talk Radio	.042 (.18)	.045 (.18)	.16 (.19)	.17 (.19)
Time of Interview	-.0039 (.0094)	-.0047 (.0096)	.0043 (.010)	.0041 (.010)
Constant	-7.98 (.98)***	-7.98 (1.00)***	-5.86 (.95)***	-5.92 (.97)***
N (with MV imputations)	1437	1430	1448	1441
N (without MV imputations)	1260	1249	1250	1259
R²	.32	.30	.30	.32

*** p <.01, ** p <.05, * p <.10

Note: Models are logit regressions estimated on five imputed data sets created by AMELIA (Honaker, et al. 1999). The coefficient estimate is the mean of the five separate estimates. The robust standard error (in parentheses) is based on the variance across the five imputed data sets plus the variance within each data set. For details, see King et al. (2001).

The table lists the number of observations with and without multiple imputations of missing values. Goodness-of-fit statistics are only available for non-imputed estimations.

As table 6.3 also shows that the hypothesis is not supported for voting in the 1996 presidential election, results from the NES 1996 are mixed. In order to provide additional tests, models of vote likelihood are estimated on data from the Pew Media Consumption Surveys conducted in 1996, 1998, and 2000. Tables 6.4 and 6.5 present results for logistic regression models of voting in the last presidential or House election prior to the survey. Graphic illustrations of the coefficients are in figure 6.2. Of the eight models, six yield significant interactions at $p < .10$ or better, while the coefficients in the two other models approach significance at $p = .12$ and $p = .15$. These results provide the clearest support for the hypothesis. Entertainment preference affects the likelihood to vote very little among people without any access to new media. Among people with access to cable and the Internet, on the other hand, the REP index is strongly related to vote likelihood.

Moreover, the effect among people with a high news preference is more symmetric than for the models of political knowledge. While news-seekers with new media access were not discernibly more knowledgeable than those without, people with the same high preference for news are indeed more likely to vote when they have access to new media. As in the knowledge models, the reverse is true for people with a preference for entertainment. While a drop in knowledge and turnout among people with both high REP and access to new media is clearly apparent throughout this analysis, more empirical tests are required to establish whether the additional news offerings on cable and Internet have a positive effect on these variables among people with a preference for news.

New media access, then, appears to increase the effect of relative entertainment preference on political knowledge and vote likelihood. But how certain can we be that this reflects the increased media choice for cable subscribers and Internet users, and not some other characteristic that they share? One way to guard against such a confound is the use of control variables. But the controls used in this study cannot entirely rule out the possibility that the technological savvy or lifestyle of new media users account for the observed results. To examine this claim, I made use of a number of variables in the MCS 2000 that asked respondents whether they owned a cell phone, a pager, a DVD player, and a palm pilot. The same model of vote likelihood as in table 6.5 was run with these variables instead of new media access. While the coefficient for the interaction with new media access was significant at $p < .01$, none of the interactions of the REP index with the other technological devices produce results that even approach significance. Consequently, increased media choice, not some other aspect related to new media technology or its users, is likely to cause the observed effects.

It would be possible that the results presented here simply showed that more politically interested people watch more news and become more informed if they have access to new media. Entertainment, in this view, does not matter at all and the results occur regardless of the role of entertainment content. I tested this counter-hypothesis in two ways. If the above were true, running the analyses with an interaction of new media and political interest instead of the REP index should produce comparable, if not stronger, results. However, interaction terms of new media access with political interest (or education) do not reach statistical significance. Second, if entertainment preferences did not have any effect on knowledge or turnout, the effect of the REP index should be similar to the effect of news viewing alone. However, including an interaction of new media with news viewing instead of the complete REP index did not produce significant estimates in any of the models. The negative results indicate that political interest by itself does not explain the effect of new media on knowledge and vote likelihood. Rather, entertainment as a competing choice, its relatively greater availability, and its appeal to some media users drive the observed results *in conjunction with the motivation to follow politics.* The relative balance between preferences for these two broad types of content, news and entertainment, explains people's viewing decisions better than either one by itself.

This result was to be expected given that political interest and entertainment preference are largely independent. A person who reports to be highly interested in politics does not necessarily watch or read a lot of news, because the same person could also be very attracted to entertainment content. Similarly, if you are not very interested in politics, you may still be exposed to news if entertainment is even more boring to you. That neither the new media × political interest interaction nor the new media × news viewing interaction produces significant results, while the new media × REP interaction does, suggests that new media users with a preference for entertainment know less about politics because they like entertainment, not because they are uninterested in politics.

Table 6.4
Voting in 1992 Presidential and 1994 House Elections (Pew MCS 1996)

	Voted in 1992 Presidential Election		Voted in 1994 House Election	
	Model 1	Model 2	Model 1	Model 2
Entertainment Preference	-.72 (.61)	-.71 (.59)	.20 (.66)	-.27 (.65)
Cable	.62 (.25)*	—	.55 (.25)**	—
New Media	—	.56 (.19)***	—	.40 (.17)**
Ent. Pref. X Cable	-1.16 (.74)	—	-1.91 (.80)**	—
Ent. Pref. X New Media	—	-.88 (.52)*	—	-.96 (.54)*
Party ID	.095 (.040)**	.095 (.040)**	-.072 (.039)*	-.075 (.039)*
Strong Party Identifier	1.27 (.21)***	1.25 (.21)***	.92 (.23)***	.88 (.23)***
Weak Party Identifier	.87 (.23)***	.84 (.22)***	.76 (.24)***	.74 (.24)***
Education	.22 (.045)***	.22 (.045)***	.21 (.045)***	.21 (.045)***
Income	.035 (.038)	.028 (.038)	.089 (.041)**	.083 (.041)*
Gender	-.31 (.12)**	-.31 (.13)**	-.018 (.130)	-.017 (.13)
Age	.10 (.021)***	.11 (.021)***	.10 (.025)***	.10 (.025)***
Age2	-.0007 (.0002)***	-.0008 (.0002)***	-.0006 (.0003)**	-.0006 (.0003)**
Black	-.13 (.21)	-.13 (.21)	-.17 (.24)	-.13 (.23)
Other Non-White	-.70 (.24)***	-.68 (.24)***	-.69 (.26)***	-.65 (.26)**
Owns Home	.21 (.15)	.21 (.15)	.20 (.16)	.19 (.16)
Employment Status	.20 (.14)	.20 (.14)	-.35 (.14)**	-.35 (.14)***
Size of Town	-.016 (.060)	-.010 (.060)	.020 (.063)	.028 (.063)
Watch National News	-.067 (.21)	-.089 (.21)	-.26 (.22)	-.25 (.22)
Watch Local News	.058 (.26)	.093 (.26)	.34 (.29)	.36 (.29)
Read Newspaper	.13 (.15)	.12 (.15)	.31 (.16)**	.30 (.16)*
Listen to Talk Radio	.31 (.18)*	.30 (.18)*	.61 (.19)***	.60 (.19)***
Reads Magazines	.042 (.19)	.011 (.19)	.21 (.20)	.18 (.20)

Table 6.4
(continued)

	Voted in 1992 Presidential Election		Voted in 1994 House Election	
	Model 1	Model 2	Model 1	Model 2
Follows News	.71 (.36)**	.72 (.36)**	1.11 (.37)***	1.14 (.37)***
Constant	−4.91 (.63)***	−5.12 (.63)***	−6.34 (.71)***	−6.39 (.71)***
N (with MV imputations)	1708	1708	1585	1585
N (without MV imputations)	1521	1521	1424	1424
Pseudo R^2	.16	.16	.20	.20

*** p <.01, ** p <.05, * p <.10

Note: Models are logit regressions estimated on five imputed data sets created by AMELIA (Honaker, et al. 1999). The coefficient estimate is the mean of the five separate estimates. The robust standard error (in parentheses) is based on the variance across the five imputed data sets plus the variance within each data set. For details, see King et al. (2001).

The table lists the number of observations with and without multiple imputations of missing values. Goodness-of-fit statistics are only available for non-imputed estimations.

Table 6.5
Voting in 1996 Presidential Election (Pew MCS 1998, 2000)

	Pew MCS 1998		Pew MCS 2000	
	Model 1	Model 2	Model 1	Model 2
Entertainment Preference	.12 (.41)	.20 (.42)	.20 (.32)	.62 (.39)
Cable	.17 (.15)	—	.43 (.16)***	—
New Media	—	.28 (.11)***	—	.43 (.11)***
Ent. Pref. X Cable	-.68 (.48)	—	-1.03 (.40)**	—
Ent. Pref. X New Media	—	-.57 (.32)*	—	-.91 (.27)***
Party ID	.096 (.029)***	.097 (.029)***	-.038 (.033)	-.040 (.033)
Strong Party Identifier	1.53 (.14)***	1.52 (.14)***	1.10 (.14)***	1.09 (.14)***
Weak Party Identifier	.80 (.16)***	.80 (.16)***	.45 (.16)***	.45 (.16)***
Education	.22 (.033)***	.21 (.034)***	.32 (.038)***	.30 (.039)***
Income	.054 (.028)*	.044 (.029)	.037 (.039)	.025 (.040)
Gender	.0041 (.094)	-.0017 (.094)	.053 (.11)	.046 (.11)
Age	.066 (.015)***	.067 (.015)***	.11 (.015)***	.11 (.016)***
Age²	-.0004 (.0002)***	-.0004 (.0002)***	-.0007 (.0002)***	-.0007 (.0002)***
Black	.032 (.14)	.038 (.15)	.64 (.19)***	.66 (.19)***
Other Non-White	-.22 (.24)	-.22 (.24)	-.51 (.21)**	-.53 (.21)**
Owns Home	.39 (.11)***	.41 (.11)***	.43 (.12)***	.44 (.12)***
Employment Status	.18 (.11)	.17 (.11)	.16 (.12)	.17 (.12)
Size of Town	-.072 (.045)	-.064 (.045)	-.020 (.051)	-.011 (.051)
Watch National News	.13 (.14)	.13 (.14)	.17 (.15)	.19 (.15)
Watch Local News	-.071 (.18)	-.087 (.18)	.059 (.19)	.060 (.19)
Read Newspaper	.36 (.11)***	.35 (.11)***	.22 (.11)**	.22 (.11)**
Listen to Talk Radio	-.048 (.094)	-.047 (.094)	.22 (.12)*	.21 (.12)*
Reads Magazines	.20 (.14)	.19 (.14)	.078 (.16)	.040 (.16)

Table 6.5
(continued)

	Pew MCS 1998		Pew MCS 2000	
	Model 1	Model 2	Model 1	Model 2
Follows News	1.01 (.24)***	1.00 (.24)***	1.09 (.21)***	1.05 (.21)***
Constant	−5.30 (.45)***	−5.40 (.45)***	−6.27 (.48)***	−6.53 (.49)***
N (with MV imputations)	2918	2918	2736	2736
N (without MV imputations)	2426	2426	2260	2260
Pseudo R^2	.18	.19	.24	.24

*** p <.01, ** p <.05, * p <.10

Note: Models are logit regressions estimated on five imputed data sets created by AMELIA (Honaker, et al. 1999). The coefficient estimate is the mean of the five separate estimates. The robust standard error (in parentheses) is based on the variance across the five imputed data sets plus the variance within each data set. For details, see King et al. (2001).

The table lists the number of observations with and without multiple imputations of missing values. Goodness-of-fit statistics are only available for non-imputed estimations.

Table 6.6
A.1 Measuring Relative Entertainment Preference

Ent.	Items used to measure... Entertainment Viewing	Information Viewing	N	Mean	Stand. Dev.	Percentiles 25th	50th	75th	Campaign Interest	Correlation with... Attention to News	Follow News
NES 2000	*Jeopardy, Wheel of Fortune*	Early Local News, National News	1356	.18	.26	.00	.00	.31	-.13	-.24[1] / -.13[2]	
NES 1996	*Jeopardy or Wheel of Fortune, Dr. Quinn*	Local News, National News	1446	.21	.24	.00	.18	.35	-.12	-.21[1] / -.17[2]	
Pew MCS 2000	*Entertainment Tonight*	Local News, National News	2964	.28	.26	.00	.28	.50		-.09[3]	.30
Pew MCS 1998	*Entertainment Tonight, MTV*	Local News, National News	2918	.25	.21	.00	.25	.40		-.09[3]	.30
Pew MCS 1996	*Hardcopy, MTV*	Local News, National News	1708	.30	.19	.17	.33	.40		-.07[3]	.18

Note: Number of cases are based on unweighted samples. Means and standard deviations are calculated using weights.

[1] Attention to national news
[2] Attention to local news
[3] Composite index of following several different news stories

Table 6.7

A.2 Relative Entertainment Preference and Exposure to News

	Pew MCS 1996		Pew MCS 2000	NES 1996	NES 2000
	Time Watching News	More news than before	Watch News Regularly[2]	News Exposure	News Exposure
Entertainment Preference	.054 (.10)	.47 (.19)**	.40 (.35)	.0064 (.065)	.037 (.078)
Cable	.14 (.043)***	.23 (.062)***	.36 (.15)**	-.0034 (.025)	.10 (.028)***
Ent. Pref. X Cable	-.35 (.13)***	-.70 (.21)***	-.74 (.43)*	-.098 (.074)	-.15 (.088)*
Education	.00068 (.0072)	-.0085 (.0092)	-.048 (.030)	.035 (.0053)***	.040 (.0061)***
Employment Status[1]	-.085 (.023)***	-.045 (.029)	-.42 (.098)***	-.0022 (.00038)***	-.0013 (.00042)***
Black	.099 (.040)**	.062 (.046)	.58 (.19)***	.0027 (.026)	-.081 (.027)***
Hispanic	—	—	—	—	-.030 (.039)
Other Non-White	-.011 (.040)	-.052 (.057)	-.068 (.19)	-.020 (.044)	-.025 (.040)
Constant	.48 (.047)***	.55 (.064)***	1.43 (.18)***	.35 (.031)***	.36 (.039)***
Adj. R²	.0024	.035	.016	.057	.07
N	1679	829	2903	1431	1336

***p <.01, **p <.05, *p <.10

Note: Models are estimated by OLS regression. Cell entries are unstandardized coefficient estimates and robust standard errors in parentheses. All models are calculated using sample weights.

[1]Weekly working hours for NES 1996 and 2000.

[2]Logit regression since dependent variable is dichotomous.

Conclusion

Andrew Kohut (quoted in Marks 2000), the director of the Pew Research Center, recently asserted that "[c]able is the political conduit of the air. If you don't have that cable coming in your house, you're getting a whole heck of a lot less information about politics." This study suggests that having "that cable" or new media in general "coming in your house" does not automatically make people better informed, and, in fact, may lower political knowledge for some of them. The simple reason is that new media bring the opportunity to learn about politics at every hour of the day, but also offer the chance to avoid politics entirely:

> The period since the late 1980s is often considered the beginning of the "information age." . . . What has been mostly overlooked is that the indicated technological development toward increasingly rich media environments carries with it a previously unimaginable wealth of entertainment choices. In fact, entertainment offerings obtrusively dominate media content and are bound to do so in the foreseeable future. This circumstance, together with the apparent growing public demand on entertainment provisions, land equal justification to characterizing the present times as the "entertainment age." (Zillmann and Vorderer 2000, vii)

The current period may be information age for some; for others, it is the entertainment age. This study demonstrates that we need to know people's content preferences in order to assess the political implications of the information/entertainment age. I have tried to measure this preference through an index of relative entertainment preference (REP). Built from existing data not collected with this goal in mind, the REP has several weaknesses. It is based on self-reported exposure to entertainment and information programs. The selection of these programs is necessarily arbitrary and severely restricted by the available data. Ideally, an index of REP would not rely on exposure measures at all, but ask respondents about their relative preference for different types of content.

The operationalization of REP has some empirically undesirable qualities. Since few people report watching a lot of entertainment programs but little or no news (and since people tend to exaggerate their news consumption), the index is right-skewed. Moreover, it is slightly correlated with the overall amount of television viewing. Therefore, the interpretation of the absolute predicted values obtained from the models estimated here cannot be entirely conclusive. Some models, notably of political knowledge, indicate a trend toward slightly increased knowledge among people with a preference for entertainment and no access to new media. Future research will have to create a more reliable measure of REP to determine whether this trend is a measurement artifact or an observation that is stable across measures.

Despite these weaknesses, the results in this study provide consistent empirical support for the hypothesis. In an attempt to compensate for the inherent arbitrariness of the operationalizations, a number of different data sets are used to test the hypotheses. Data collected by different organizations (NES and Pew) and for different election contexts support the hypotheses consistently and at acceptable levels of statistical significance given the imprecision of the main independent variable. Moreover, while caution is warranted when interpreting the absolute predicted values, confidence in the relative effects of new media access and entertainment preference is much higher. Throughout the analysis, people with a preference for entertainment were less likely to recall candidates, less likely to know political facts, and less likely to vote, *only when they had access to new media.* Cable and Internet access, in other words, provide people who want to avoid politics with the means to do so. According to Baum (1999, 18), "the highly segmented modern television marketplace presumably allows individuals to escape political news more effectively than was the case in prior decades." This study suggests that escaping politics is made even easier with access to the Internet. While it would be premature to conclude that the impact of cable and the Internet is additive in this respect, the analysis does suggest that access to both of these new media leads to a stronger interaction with entertainment preference than access to any one of them.

In their study of the effects of different media environments, Delli Carpini et al. (1994, 454) emphasize that "learning requires not only the will to learn, but the opportunity to do so." For all practical purposes, people with access to new media have endless opportunity to learn about politics. But at the same time, people's "will to learn" becomes much more important. The results of this study suggest that for some people, political learning in the broadcast era was not driven by the "will to learn," but simply by the lack of other ways to satisfy their desire to be entertained. Knowledge and vote likelihood of people with a high entertainment preference was lower for new media users across different data sets and operationalizations of the concept of entertainment preference.

To turn Delli Carpini et al.'s above statement on its head, avoiding news requires not only the will to watch something else, but also the opportunity to do so.

Support for the other side of the interaction effect is more ambiguous. People who prefer news and have new media access do not appear to know more about politics than similar respondents lack this access and the chance to watch or read news at any time. This result does not seem to be explained by a ceiling effect. It is all the more puzzling since the likelihood to vote among people with a news preference is indeed higher for new media users. Future research will have to resolve the details of this argument. The results concerning turnout are more conclusive. They clearly suggest that the gap between people who prefer entertainment and people who like news better widens as people gain access to new media.

Content preferences are better predictors of political knowledge and turnout among new media users in the present cross-sectional analysis. It is tempting to infer that the growth of new media is the cause of lower news audiences and declining knowledge and turnout among people who prefer entertainment programming. Direct evidence for this could only come from panel data covering people's transition from broadcast viewers to cable and Internet users. But the likely chain of events is obvious: Most people do not watch television to follow a particular program. They decide to watch and then select the best available program. During the broadcast era, simultaneous broadcast of news on the three networks led most people to watch some news, even those who were not particularly interested in politics and would have turned to entertainment in a heartbeat, had that been possible. In Neuman's (1996, 19) words, people watched "politics by default." Cable television and the Internet have removed these constraints and enabled subscribers to better match content preferences to content. News audiences have declined over the course of a decade or two, but not necessarily because people became dramatically less interested in news and politics. While that may be part of the explanation, the present study suggests a different cause. A segment of the electorate was never particularly interested and watched news merely out of habit and for lack of better options. When cable subscribers and Internet users were offered greater content choice, the consequence was a decline in knowledge and turnout among people who only watched news because they were "captive." This argument leads to the uncomfortable conclusion that even the mediocre levels of political knowledge during the broadcast era (e.g., Delli Carpini and Keeter 1996) were, in part, a result of de facto restrictions of people's freedom to watch what they want.

Notes

1. One of the earliest references on the subject of "passive learning" is Krugman and Hartley (1970) who discuss learning from television among children.

2. The 2000 NES asked separately about early and late local news. Only the frequency of watching early local news is used here.

3. In addition, table 6.7. suggests a positive effect of entertainment preference on news viewing for respondents without cable. The effect is significant and sizable in only two of the five models, but does indicate the possibility that the REP index picks up the amount of TV consumption in addition to the relative preference for entertainment.

There is some evidence for this from the two other NES pilot studies that contain measures of overall viewing (but not data on internet access). The correlations between REP and total viewing at night and during the day are r = .17/ r = .16 for 1995 and r = .09/r = .09 for 1998. For the purpose of testing my model, this possibility is not a severe problem since, to the extent that high REP is correlated with watching a lot of television, the estimated effect of REP will be biased downwards.

4. Unlike before, one half of the 2000 NES interviews were conducted by telephone. Interview mode affects responses. For example, 76 percent of the respondents interviewed by phone reported voting in the 2000 presidential election, while only 68 percent of the people interviewed face-to-face did. The different degrees of overreporting as a result of different interview modes affect the estimation of the vote model for the NES 2000 considerably. In fact, the coefficients for the interaction effect are opposite for phone and face-to-face interviews, and the explained variance is lower by a third in the phone condition. For the remaining half-sample interviewed face-to-face, the effect is in the predicted direction, but does not reach significance. Since it is unclear how to treat the different interview modes, I decided not to include the NES 2000 in the analysis of turnout effects.

5. Respondents who did not know whether they voted or who refused to answer (1996: 3.8%, 1998: 6.1%, 2000: 7.3%) could be excluded from the analysis. Respondents who reported voting, but did not remember whom they voted for (1996: 5.1%, 1998: 6.7%, 2000: 8.8%), could be coded as not having voted. The results change very little for these alternative specifications for the 1996 and 1998 MCS.

In the 2000 MCS, Pew used a modified coding scheme, reporting mention of other candidates than Clinton, Dole or Perot. This new category is coded as having voted. The analysis for the 2000 MCS turns out to be somewhat sensitive to the coding of respondents that reported voting but do not remember the candidate they voted for. For the 2000 MCS only, results are reported for coding these respondents as having voted because it improves the fit of the regression as measured by the explained variance. While coding them as not having voted (as in the MCS 1996 and 1998) reduces the size of the interaction coefficient and the significance level (from $p < .01$ to $p < .10$), the hypothesis is supported either way.

6. Most of the control variables are almost completely observed, but a considerable number of respondents refused to answer questions about their income. On average about 15 percent of the respondents have missing data on this variable in the data sets used here. Since cable and Internet access may not be affordable to respondents with lower income, including income as a control variable is important. The failure to do so might lead to the incorrect attribution of knowledge differences to new media access, when in fact income differences are the causal factor. Excluding all respondents with missing value on the income variable, however, introduces a different bias if refusing to answer questions on income is systematically related to other characteristics of the respondent. A solution to this problem is to impute values for respondents that failed to answer a question. Based on other information about the respondent, the best estimate of their income (and a measure of the uncertainty of this estimate) is created. This is done through multiple imputation (King, Honaker, Joseph and Scheve 2001).

For this analysis, missing data on all independent variables except for the REP index and access to cable and new media are replaced by imputed values using the EMis algorithm implemented in AMELIA (Honaker, Joseph, King, Scheve and Singh 1999). Missing values on REP, new media access or any of the dependent variables are not imputed since their relationship to other variables in the data sets that could be used for imputation is unclear. When missingness is "nonignorable" (NI), that is, a variable with missing data is not related to any other variable in the data set, listwise deletion outperforms multiple imputation. While this cannot be directly tested with only the observed data, not imputing missing values on REP, new media access, and the dependent variables seems the more conservative approach. (New media access and the dependent variables have very little missing data anyway.) The following tables give the number of observations included in the analyses with and without multiple imputation. Using multiple imputation increases the number of cases by between ten and twenty percent and helps to avoid bias from nonrandom deletion of cases.

7. See note 3.

References

Atkin, Charles K. 1985. "Informational Utility and Selective Exposure to Entertainment Media." In *Selective Exposure to Communication*, ed. Dolf Zillmann and Jennings Bryant (pp. xii, 251). Hillsdale N.J.: L. Erlbaum Associates.

Barwise, T. P., and A. S. C. Ehrenberg. 1988. *Television and Its Audience, Sage Communications in Society Series*. London; Newbury Park Calif.: Sage Publications.

Barwise, T. P., A. S. C. Ehrenberg, and G. J. Goodhardt. 1982. "Glued to the Box. Patterns of TV Repeat-Viewing." *Journal of Communication* 32: 22–29.

Baum, Matthew A. 1999. "A Paradox of Public Opinion: Why a Less Interested Public Is More Attentive to War." Unpublished manuscript.

Baum, Matthew A., and Samuel Kernell. 1999. "Has Cable Ended the Golden Age of Presidential Television?" *American Political Science Review* 93: 99–114.

Becker, Lee B., Pamela J. Creedon, R. Warwick Blood, and Eric S. Fredin. 1989. "United States: Cable Eases Its Way into the Household." In *Audience Responses to Media Diversification: Coping with Plenty*, ed. Lee B. Becker, Klaus Schoenbach and et al. (pp. 291–331). Hillsdale: Lawrence Erlbaum Associates Inc.

Campbell, David E., Steven Yonish, and Robert D. Putnam. 1999. "Tuning in, Tuning out Revisited: A Closer Look at the Causal Links between Television and Social Capital." Paper presented at the Annual Meeting of the American Political Science Association, Atlanta

Comstock, George A., and Erica Scharrer. 1999. *Television : What's on, Who's Watching, and What It Means*. San Diego: Academic Press.

Delli Carpini, Michael X., and Scott Keeter. 1996. *What Americans Know About Politics and Why It Matters*. New Haven [Conn.]: Yale University Press.

Delli Carpini, Michael X., Scott Keeter, and J. David Kennamer. 1994. "Effects of the News Media Environment on Citizen Knowledge of State Politics and Government." *Journalism Quarterly* 71: 443–456.

Graber, Doris A. 2001. *Processing Politics : Learning from Television in the Internet Age, Studies in Communication, Media, and Public Opinion*. Chicago: University of Chicago Press.

Honaker, James, Anne Joseph, Gary King, Kenneth Scheve, and Naunihal Singh. 1999. Amelia: A Program for Missing Data (Windows Version). Harvard University, Cambridge, M.A.

Katz, Elihu. 1996. "And Deliver Us from Segmentation." *The Annals of the American Academy of Political and Social Science* 546: 22–33.

Katz, Elihu, Jay G. Blumler, and Michael Gurevitch. 1973. "Uses and Gratifications Research. " *Public Opinion Quarterly* 37: 509–523.

Katz, Elihu, Michael Gurevitch, and Hadassah Haas. 1973. "On the Use of the Mass Media for Important Things." *American Sociological Review* 38: 164–181.

Keeter, Scott, and Harry Wilson. 1986. "Natural Treatment and Control Settings for Research on the Effects of Television." *Communication Research* 13: 37–53.

King, Gary, James Honaker, Anne Joseph, and Kenneth Scheve. 2001. "Analyzing Incomplete Political Science Data: An Alternative Algorithm for Multiple Imputation." *American Political Science Review* 95: 49.

Klein, Paul. 1972. "The Television Audience and Program Mediocrity." In *Mass Media and Society*, ed. Alan Wells (pp. 76–79). Palo Alto, Calif.: National Press Books.

Krugman, Herbert E., and Eugene L. Hartley. 1970. "Passive Learning from Television." *Public Opinion Quarterly* 34: 184–190.

LoSciuto, Leonard A. 1972. "A National Inventory of Television Viewing Behavior." In *Television and Social Behavior. Television in Day-to-Day Life: Patterns of Use*, ed. Eli A. Rubinstein, George A. Comstock and John P. Murray (pp. 33–86). Washington, D.C.: U.S. Government Printing Office.

Marks, Peter. 2000. "Networks Cede Political Coverage to Cable," *New York Times,* April 7, A16.

Neuman, W. Russell. 1991. *The Future of the Mass Audience.* Cambridge [England] ; New York: Cambridge University Press.

Neuman, W. Russell. 1996. "Political Communication Infrastructure." *The Annals of the American Academy of Political and Social Science* 546: 9–21.

Neuman, W. Russell, Marion R. Just, and Ann N. Crigler. 1992. *Common Knowledge: News and the Construction of Political Meaning.* Chicago: University of Chicago Press.

Patterson, Thomas E. 2000. "The United States: News in a Free-Market Society." In *Democracy and the Media,* ed. Richard Gunther and Anthony Mughan (pp. 241–265). Cambridge, U.K.: Cambridge University Press.

Rubin, Alan M. 1984. "Ritualized and Instrumental Television Viewing." *Journal of Communication* 34: 67–77.

Tan, Alexis S. 1980. "Mass Media Use, Issue Knowledge and Political Involvement." *Public Opinion Quarterly* 44: 241–248.

Tichenor, Philip J., George A. Donohue, and Calice A. Olien. 1970. "Mass Flow and Differential Growth in Knowledge." *Public Opinion Quarterly* 34: 149–170.

Verba, Sidney, Nancy Burns, and Kay Lehman Schlozman. 1997. "Knowing and Caring About Politics: Gender and Political Engagement." *Journal of Politics* 59: 1051–1072.

Verba, Sidney, Kay Lehman Schlozman, and Henry E. Brady. 1995. *Voice and Equality: Civic Voluntarism in American Politics.* Cambridge, Mass.: Harvard University Press.

Webster, James G. 1984. "Cable Television's Impact on Audience for Local News." *Journalism Quarterly* 61: 419–422.

Webster, James G., and Gregory D. Newton. 1988. "Structural Determinants of the Television News Audience." *Journal of Broadcasting & Electronic Media* 32: 381–389.

Webster, James G., and Jacob J. Wakshlag. 1983. "A Theory of Television Program Choice." *Communication Research* 10: 430–446.

Weimann, Gabriel. 1996. "Cable Comes to the Holy Land: The Impact of Cable TV on Israeli Viewers." *Journal of Broadcasting & Electronic Media* 40: 243–257.

Zhao, Xinshu, and Glen L. Bleske. 1995. "Measurement Effects in Comparing Voter Learning from Television News and Campaign Advertisements." *Journalism and Mass Communication Quarterly* 72: 72–83.

Zhao, Xinshu, and Steven H. Chaffee. 1995. "Campaign Advertisements Versus Television News as Sources of Political Issue Information." *Public Opinion Quarterly* 59: 41–65.

Zillmann, Dolf, and Peter Vorderer, eds. 2000. *Media Entertainment: The Psychology of Its Appeal, Lea's Communication Series.* Mahwah: Lawrence Erlbaum Associates Inc. Publishers.

Zukin, Cliff, and Robin Snyder. 1984. "Passive Learning: When the Media Environment Is the Message." *Public Opinion Quarterly* 48: 629–638.

III

Monopoly and Competition in Communications Markets

7

Assessing the Effectiveness of Section 271 Five Years after the Telecommunications Act of 1996

Daniel R. Shiman and Jessica Rosenworcel[1]

I Introduction

This paper examines the effectiveness of section 271 of the Telecommunications Act of 1996 (the Act) in achieving Congress' goals of increasing competition in the local and long distance telephone markets. In section 271, Congress developed an incentive structure whereby incumbent Bell Operating Companies (BOCs) are rewarded with entry into long distance markets in their territory if they can demonstrate to the Federal Communications Commission (FCC) that they have opened their local wireline markets to competition. In this paper we examine the logic behind this structure, to determine if it is a reasonable means of achieving increased competition in both the local and long distance markets.[2] We also provide an update on the extent of competitive entry in the local exchange market five years after enactment of the Act.

Some commentators have claimed that the section 271 process is unnecessary, alleging that it is a superfluous regulatory scheme that unnecessarily duplicates the market-opening provisions of section 251 (e.g., Hausman and Sidak 1999, 430). There has also been extensive debate about the consequences of delayed BOC entry into the long distance market, with some economists arguing that immediate entry would provide the greatest benefit to consumers (e.g., Crandall and Hazlett 2000, Crandall 1999). After analyzing the industry's technical and economic structure, and the legal and informational constraints under which regulators operate, we conclude that section 271 is a reasonably effective incentive mechanism for opening the local exchange market to competition, and is superior to other regulatory alternatives that are available. We also agree with those who argue that the use of entry into the long distance market as a prize for the BOCs will benefit the long distance market by adding an additional competitor only when that competitor's ability to vertically leverage its market power has been significantly reduced. Delaying entry until the local market is open to competition provides an appropriate safeguard against potential BOC discrimination against competitors in the long distance market (Schwartz 2000).

In section II we summarize the structure of sections 271 and 251 of the Act, and review the interrelation of section 271 and the market-opening provisions of section 251, in light of the history of the line-of-service restriction imposed by the Modification of Final Judgement. In section III we examine the economic, institutional and legal environment in which regulators operate, and discuss whether section 271 is likely to be an effective means of opening local telecommunications markets to competition, and whether BOC entry into the long distance market should be linked to local market access obligations. Section IV provides a statistical assessment of the development of local competition across the country, using available data, while section V offers some concluding remarks.

II Development of Section 271 of the Telecommunications Act of 1996

A The Local Exchange Market Prior to the Act

For over half a century AT&T's telecommunications network, which included both local and long-distance services, effectively was treated as a natural monopoly. In 1974 the Department of Justice initiated a lawsuit against AT&T under the Sherman Antitrust Act, alleging that AT&T used its local exchange monopoly to prevent competitive entry into the long distance and equipment manufacturing markets. The trial ended in a 1982 settlement known as the Modification of Final Judgment (MFJ). Under a key feature of the MFJ, AT&T divested itself of its local exchange telephone companies in 1984. These local exchange companies were organized into seven regional BOCs. The BOCs were subject to line-of-service restrictions that, among other things, prohibited them from competing in the long distance market.

The rationale underlying the divestiture was that AT&T would be unable to exercise monopoly control over the long distance market once it had lost control of the local exchange market. Moreover, without the line-of-service restriction prohibiting BOC entry into the long distance market, the BOCs would have the incentive to misallocate costs and subsidize competitive long distance services with their monopolized local exchange services, and degrade the quality of access received by interexchange carriers (552 F.Supp 131, 162, 165, 170–75).

Under section VIII(C) of the MFJ, a BOC could petition for relief from the line-of-service restriction prohibiting BOC entry into the long distance market, if it could successfully demonstrate to the court "that there is no substantial possibility that it could use its monopoly power to impede competition in the market it seeks to enter." No BOC, however, successfully petitioned under the MFJ to provide long distance services.[3]

B   The Interrelationship of Sections 251 & 271 of the Act

The Telecommunications Act of 1996 fundamentally altered the regulation of local telecommunications markets in the United States. It replaced the MFJ's restrictions on the BOCs with a new set of regulations,[4] and provided a means for the BOCs to enter the long-distance market. In the Act Congress also directed the FCC to remove the barriers that historically protected incumbent BOC local exchange carrier monopolies from competition and to develop regulatory policies that promote competition in local exchange markets. Two key elements of the Act supply the framework for opening up the BOCs' networks to competitors: section 251 and section 271. Both are briefly reviewed below.

1   *Section 251*

Section 251 imposed a new set of requirements on local exchange companies (LECs), including the duty to provide for number portability, dialing parity, reciprocal compensation, resale of all services provided, and access to rights of way it owns (47 U.S.C. sect. 251(b)). LECs classified as incumbent local exchange carriers (ILECs), which are firms that have traditionally provided local exchange service in a local area and presumably have substantial market power in their local exchange market (47 U.S.C. sect. 251(h)), have an additional set of obligations to open up their networks for use by competitors.

Under section 251, ILECs are required to provide resold services to competitive local exchange carriers (CLECs) (47 U.S.C. sect. 251(c)).

Thus, a CLEC can purchase the same services an ILEC makes available to its end-user customers at a discount that reflects the retail price minus avoided costs.

In addition, section 251 requires ILECs to provide access to the piece parts of their networks as separate, unbundled network elements (UNEs). In effect, this allows a CLEC to lease only those portions of the ILEC's network it wishes to use as inputs in providing its own telecommunications services to its own end-user customers. At present the FCC requires ILECs to provide UNE access to 7 UNEs, including loops (the transmission facilities between the demarcation point at the end-user's premises and the ILEC's central office), local circuit switching (equipment that determines the routing of local calls), and dedicated and shared transport (interoffice transmission facilities) (47 C.F.R. sect. 319).[5] These UNEs must be offered at cost-based prices, based on the pricing standards in section 252 of the Act, which the FCC has implemented as the marginal cost of offering the element in a hypothetical, technologically efficient network under the TELRIC (Total Element Long-Run Incremental Cost) standard.[6] CLECs may order these elements on an individual basis or as part of a complete package known as the UNE platform (UNE-P). In addition, an ILEC is required to permit interconnection at any technically feasible point, and provide for the collocation of equipment necessary for a competitor's interconnection or access to UNEs.

Finally, ILECs are required to negotiate in good faith interconnection agreements with competitors wishing to arrange interconnection and collocation, and purchase the ILECs' services through resale and purchase of UNEs. The process and deadlines for negotiating agreements, and for state arbitration of open issues, are laid out in section 252. State public utility commissions (PUCs) are given substantial responsibility for applying sections 251, 252, and the FCC's rules implementing those sections, to arrangements and interconnection agreements in their states.

Thus section 251 effectively provides for three modes of entry for CLECs: full facilities-based, partially facilities-based, and resale of the ILEC's services. Full facilities-based entry, in which the CLEC provides its own facilities and only needs interconnection and rights of way from the ILEC, has the potential to provide significant benefits to consumers, because CLECs are incented to develop new services, and bring new technologies to market, in order to differentiate their product offerings from the ILEC. Yet, scale economies outside of populated, downtown areas rich with business customers are unlikely to justify the cost of deploying new network facilities. The ability to enter using partial facilities-based entry allows for efficient choices regarding network duplication. Thus, CLECs may be able to rely on those UNEs, such as the local loop, where the economies of scale and scope are large and make entry difficult, and combine them with their own complementary facilities where deployment costs are justified by potential revenues, such as switching (an entry strategy known as UNE-Loop or UNE-L). This allows them the limited ability to provide their own set of unique services, without incurring the significant costs of duplicating bottleneck facilities.[7] Finally, entry through resale of the ILEC's services (which includes UNE-P) requires that the CLEC provide no transmission facilities of its own, allowing CLECs to reach customers for whom the cost of building facilities to serve them is too high to be practical, but limits them to providing the same services that are offered by the ILEC, over the same facilities.[8]

2   Section 271

If in section 251 Congress supplied the basic principles for local competition, by describing the terms and conditions for interconnection, resale, and access to unbundled network elements, then in section 271, Congress supplied the structured incentive for the largest ILECs, the BOCs, to abide by these principles and demonstrate their compliance.

Under section 271, a BOC must meet four requirements in order to receive authority from the FCC to provide in-region long distance services. Under the first of these four requirements, known as the Track A/Track B test, a BOC must show that either a facilities-based competitor currently exists within its market (Track A) or that the BOC has offered to provide competitors with access and interconnection to its network but no alternative provider has chosen to accept the offer (Track B).[9]

Under the second requirement, a BOC must demonstrate compliance with a 14-point competitive checklist. This checklist features a list of 14 discrete access requirements that reflect the basic interconnection principles of section 251. Among other items, the checklist requires that a BOC demonstrate that it provides interconnection, nondiscriminatory access to the UNEs required under section 251 at cost-based prices, local dialing parity, and the poles, ducts, conduits, and rights of way owned by the BOC. The checklist also requires that a BOC demonstrate that it makes its own retail services available for resale.

Under section 271's third requirement, a BOC must demonstrate how it will comply with section 272 of the Act, which requires that any BOC long distance services be provided through a separate affiliate, with separate books, officers and employees, and with all transactions between the BOC and the affiliate conducted at arm's length. These structural safeguards amount to a congressional acknowledgement that following section 271 approval, a BOC may still have an incentive to discriminate in providing exchange access services and facilities that rival interexchange carriers (IXCs) need to compete (FCC 1996b, 21911–13). Finally, the fourth requirement under section 271 requires that the FCC determine that a BOC's entry into the long distance market in a particular state is in the public interest (47 U.S.C. sect. 271(d)(3)(C)).

The FCC is required to make its determination on an application within 90 days of filing. Section 271 also specifically requires that the FCC consult with the Department of Justice and the state commission, and give "substantial weight" to the Department of Justice's evaluation of the BOC's filing.

As of this writing, the BOCs have filed a total of 20 section 271 applications with the FCC. During the first three years following enactment, the FCC denied 5 applications and 1 applicant chose to withdraw its filing. In 1999, the FCC approved its first section 271 application, for Bell Atlantic New York. Since that time, the FCC has approved 7 applications and 3 applicants have chosen to withdraw their filings. In addition, as of this writing, 4 applications are pending at the FCC.[10]

III Section 271 as an Appropriate Market-Opening Mechanism and Safeguard Against Discrimination

To determine whether the incentive structure of section 271 is an appropriate mechanism for increasing the competitiveness of local telecommunications markets, we examine two issues in this section of the paper: (1) whether section 271 is the best means of achieving the market-opening goals of section 251, given the informational and legal constraints regulators labor under; and (2) whether it is rational to link BOC entry into the long distance market to BOC success in opening the local market to competition.

A Increasing Competition in the Local Market: Is Section 271 the Best Method of Achieving the Goals of Section 251?

1 Background—The Challenge Facing Policymakers

This paper does not concern itself with the question of whether the goals of section 251 are economically desirable. Given the ILECs' enormous costs of opening up their networks to competition, the significant scale economies involved in providing local telecommunications services, and the regulatory costs involved in forcing reluctant incumbent providers to open their networks to competitors, it is at this point unclear whether the future benefits of increased competition will outweigh the costs of implementing section 251. For the sake of this paper, we assume that section 251's goals are achievable and economically desirable, and that the long-run expected net benefits to society and to consumers from implementing such a scheme is positive.[11] The legislator's/regulator's problem is to design an incentive mechanism to best achieve these goals.

There is a substantial theoretical and empirical literature on the design of incentive mechanisms for the communications industry (see, e.g., Berg and Foreman 1996; Laffont and Tirole 2000). These mechanisms solve the basic principal-agent problem, in which the regulator is attempting through an appropriate monitoring and reward structure to elicit a desired kind of behavior from a regulatee. Crucial factors involved in determining which type of mechanism is most efficient is the information the regulator has about the company's costs and capabilities, the regulator's ability to monitor the actions of the company, and the tools the regulator has available to provide incentives to achieve the right behavior (Laffont and Tirole 1993, ch. 1). As we show later, the nature of the informational asymmetries must be carefully considered before deciding which mechanism will be most effective.

Two key well-known characteristics of the industry make opening up the local telecommunications market to competition difficult. First, the telecommunications industry is characterized by large network effects. The value of the network depends on the number of subscribers, making larger networks more valuable to join. Thus interconnection with the incumbent LEC is essential for new entrants and small carriers to be able to survive and compete. Second, local telecommunications networks have large fixed costs for certain parts of their operations, leading to significant economies of scale.[12] As a result, there are bottlenecks in the production of local exchange services for many kinds of customers. For instance, it is generally believed that for the majority of subscribers, the scale economies involved make duplicating the local loop by CLECs pro hibitively expensive under current technologies.

Section 251 attempts to enable competition in the local exchange market in the face of these network effects and scale economies by requiring all ILECs to interconnect and to provide nondiscriminatory access to the piece parts of their networks as separate, unbundled network elements at cost-based prices, as well as provide their services for resale (47 U.S.C. sect. 251(c)). By providing the means for three kinds of entry strategies (resale, full facilities-based, and partial facilities-based), section 251 increases the likelihood that competition will develop for all customers.[13]

Nonetheless, several factors make the implementation of the section 251 scheme difficult for regulators, particularly the technical complexity and closed architectures of the ILEC systems, and the lack of incentives for ILECs to cooperate. The technical complexity of the ILECs' internal operations means regulators need a large amount of information to properly monitor and evaluate ILEC progress in making required changes to their systems. The informational demands on regulators are further increased by the rapid rate of technological change, which forces frequent reassessment of the situation.[14]

Meanwhile, many critical aspects of ILEC networks, organizational structures, and back-end systems used to provision service are closed architectures. By closed architectures, we mean systems designed to operate efficiently internally, but not designed for outside use or access to the intermediate stages of production and consumption. Many of these architectures were developed prior to the Act, and therefore were constructed based on the assumption that services would only be used internally. Consequently, to meet the requirements of section 251, ILECs are obligated to resolve a large number of technical and organizational problems, including: designing and implementing changes to their systems so CLECs can interconnect with their networks and utilize their network elements;[15] finding and constructing space for CLEC collocation of equipment; developing standardized interfaces and organizational procedures for CLECs to use to access their OSS computer systems to place orders and trouble tickets; generating technical documentation and building a support staff to support CLEC use of ILEC systems; creating new organizational structures to support the ILECs' wholesale operations, for example to manually process orders and handle troubles with CLEC lines; and working out new contractual and informational arrangements with CLECs.[16] Thus, rather than view the Act's requirements as creating a static obligation for the ILECs to allow access to their networks by competitors, a more appropriate view might be to think of the Act as initiating a massive engineering project to convert the ILEC systems from closed to open architectures.[17]

Two important consequences follow from the technical complexity and closed architecture of the ILECs' networks. First, there is substantial uncertainty as to the time, effort and expense needed to complete the process of opening up the ILEC systems. Second, the regulator must possess an enormous amount of information to be able to assess whether the ILEC is implementing the processes appropriately. Thus it becomes difficult for a regulator, who often lacks the first-hand knowledge and detailed technical expertise of the ILEC, to determine whether the ILEC is making appropriate progress in making changes to its systems.

Usually regulators are able to rely on the regulated firm's natural incentives to provision a good.[18] ILECs, however, lack the incentive to open up their networks to their competitors. Not only is opening up their networks perceived as an additional and costly burden, but their success undermines the source of their market power (Economides 1999).[19] The development of a new contractual relationship between two firms normally requires significant effort and expense by the two firms to negotiate the terms and conditions of the contract, and to solve technical problems that may arise. Here ILECs potentially lack the incentive to negotiate in good faith, and to devote the physical and managerial resources needed to resolve the considerable number of problems that can be expected to arise from opening up their closed architecture network. When one side has a vested interest in preventing agreement, negotiations can bog down and be delayed indefinitely.[20] Regulators, therefore, must monitor the negotiation and interconnection process, but lack reliable tools for measuring good faith effort.[21] Marius Schwartz points out that it is easier for regulators to monitor existing arrangements than the negotiation and development of new ones (Schwartz 2000). The development of an appropriate monitoring and incentive mechanism thus becomes essential if regulators want to ensure that the ILECs' network is opened up to competitors in a timely manner.

2   Alternative Schemes

Congress had the freedom to choose which method it wanted to use to ensure that the BOCs, who were operating under the MFJ, would comply with section 251's requirements. When a new requirement is imposed on regulated companies, some thought must be given to developing a scheme to ensure efficient compliance. Taking into consideration the market characteristics just discussed, we next review a variety of alternatives to the section 271 incentive structure that might have been used to induce compliance with the market-opening provisions of section 251.

Penalties for Observed Infractions   One alternative incentive structure involves monitoring ILECs' behavior and imposing penalties for observed infractions. Kinds of penalties available include fines payable to the federal government, liquidated damages paid to affected CLECs, and suspension of an ILEC's participation in the in-region long distance market. Any fine or penalty used would need to be set large enough to deter noncompliance (Ford and Jackson 1999). This sort of scheme is the most common and most direct means of ensuring compliance with new laws and regulations. It is most effective when the requirements for compliance are clear, monitoring compliance is easy, and imposing fines or other enforcement penalties can be done directly and quickly.

For the purpose of implementing section 251, however, this method has significant drawbacks. The technical complexity of the network, and the substantial work needed to open up the ILEC's network and negotiate agreements for access and interconnection, makes it very difficult for a regulator to attempt to impose detailed requirements concerning what the ILEC must do, continually monitor the efforts made by the ILEC to comply, and spot and penalize every small violation. The regulator operates at a significant informational disadvantage, because of his lack of first-hand knowledge, resources, and equivalent technical expertise. The FCC's implementation of its Open Network Architecture (ONA) scheme —which predates the Act but similarly involves ILEC obligations to supply "unbundled" telecommunications inputs to third parties—illustrates how difficult it is for the regulator to resolve, as one commentator observed, "disputes over the details of what has—and has not—actually been implemented" (Schwartz 2000, 270).

In addition, the regulator has the burden of demonstrating that a fine or other enforcement action is warranted. The imposition of penalties for infractions will only be effective when both the standards for section 251 compliance and the evidence of malfeasance are clear. Because this kind of clarity is rare in the context of having to monitor ILECs' work on their networks and their negotiations with CLECs, which is complicated further by political pressures and the threat of legal challenges, it would be difficult to initiate the frequent, quick, decisive enforcement actions necessary to ensure compliance.

Deadlines   For regulators, outcomes are often easier to observe than the process. As a result, some of the disadvantages of the informational asymmetries facing regulators may be ameliorated if a deadline-oriented scheme is used. A deadline could be set by Congress, or the FCC could be allowed to set a deadline and/or grant extensions, with perhaps some penalty for noncompliance.

Determining how long a task should take, and setting the appropriate deadline, however, can be tricky, particularly if the task is technically complex. Regulators also may have a difficult time determining the merits of a regulated company's request for extension. For example, thirty-one carriers have asked for a waiver of the FCC's October 1, 2001 implementation deadline for wireless carriers to provide the locations of customers calling 911 (Stern, E1). The FCC has faced similar requests for an extension of the September 30, 2000 deadline for carriers to comply with packet-mode communications electronic surveillance requirements under the Communications Assistance for Law Enforcement Act (FCC 2001b). Regulators have the additional problem of deciding whether the company's actions are sufficient to be considered to have met the deadline. The pressure to pass may be considerable if an automatic penalty results from a declaration of noncompliance.

Allow the States to Devise Their Own Schemes   Alternatively, Congress could have encouraged the states to experiment with different regulatory structures in order to identify the market-opening schemes that generate the most benefits to consumers. Yet there are drawbacks to such a scheme. If each state has a different set of interconnection and unbundling rules, the ILECs would bear the significant costs of implementing a different scheme in each state. This scheme would also significantly raise the costs for CLECs attempting national or regional entry strategies, since they would have to develop different internal OSS systems to support a different scheme in each state, engage in more state specific negotiations with the ILEC, and lobby in each state to achieve the desired system. In addition, many state PUCs lack the resources to design and implement an efficient scheme, and some state PUCs are more susceptible to lobbying from various parties, particularly the ILEC. Before passage of the Act only a few states had taken steps to open their local markets to competition.[22]

Provide Direct Financial Compensation to the ILECs for Unbundling Congress and/or the FCC alternatively could have provided a greater direct financial incentive for ILECs to interconnect and unbundle their networks. This could be achieved by setting the rates of unbundling at the cost of interconnection and provisioning the element, plus the full opportunity cost to the ILEC of providing the element. This pricing scheme is known as the Efficient Component Pricing Rule (ECPR), and was proposed by a number of economists in order to induce efficient levels of investment by entrants (Laffont and Tirole 2000; Baumol and Sidak 1994). It provides an incentive to the ILEC to provision UNEs to competitors when they are more efficient in provisioning complementary elements. The FCC rejected this rule, however, partly on efficiency grounds, because "the ECPR does not provide any mechanism for moving prices toward competitive levels; it simply takes prices as given" and "application of ECPR would result in input prices that would be either higher or lower than those which would be generated in a competitive market and would not lead to efficient retail pricing" (FCC 1996a, 15859–60).[23]

Deregulatory Contracting Approach Congress could have chosen a deregulatory approach to the local exchange market. Unbundled access to network elements, interconnection, and resale could all be available only as a matter of private contracts between the ILECs and new entrants.

Although the simplicity of this approach and the corresponding decrease in regulatory costs has some appeal, ILECs lack the incentive to enter into contracts at prices that would permit competitors to compete. New Zealand adopted this scheme in 1987, and competition has failed to develop there (Economides 1999).

3 Section 271: A Prize for Compliance

In the scheme adopted by Congress, requirements for interconnection and unbundling for ILECs are set out in section 251, and a large "prize" is given to the BOCs for demonstrating compliance in section 271.[24] The prize, of course, is allowing BOC entry into the long distance market, a market the BOCs were prohibited from entering under the MFJ. The BOCs are likely to enjoy significant profits from entry into the long distance market, due to the scope economies involved in provisioning both local and long distance services, resulting in substantial savings in administrative, marketing and overhead costs in serving long distance customers relative to the IXCs, and the low network costs involved, estimated at about one cent per minute (Schwartz 2000; Crandall and Waverman 1995; MacAvoy 1998).[25]

The use of a prize as a tool for ensuring compliance has several advantages over other incentive mechanisms available, especially penalties based on observed infractions and deadlines. First, it reduces the need for the regulator to monitor the pace of changes, or determine appropriate deadlines. Assuming clear and observable outcomes can be determined in advance, the BOC will have an incentive to meet those objectives, and therefore the need for the regulator to monitor progress, and determine if any delays are unwarranted, is greatly reduced.

Second, the regulator has an advantage legally in terms of the burden of proof. When awarding a prize, the burden of proof rests on the applicant to show that it has complied with the conditions of the prize. The imposition of fines or other enforcement penalties, on the other hand, requires the regulator to demonstrate that the penalty is warranted. While equal-sized penalties and rewards should have a symmetric impact on a firm's incentive to comply, the legal system's asymmetric treatment of penalties and rewards makes the use of rewards less cumbersome and potentially more effective. This is particularly the case with complicated and technically complex regulations, when the regulators' inherent incomplete information about the regulated firm makes it difficult to prove a violation has occurred. Use of a reward gives the company an incentive to provide information to the regulator in order to demonstrate it has complied. It also gives the regulator the flexibility to determine what proof the company needs to provide.

Third, utilizing a prize can be superior to threatening penalties if the legislator/regulator is fairly certain about the benefits of the new regulations, but is uncertain as to their cost, and therefore is unsure whether to mandate the change. If the total social cost from the change is equal to the company's private cost of implementing it, then by setting the prize equal to the total benefit to society from the new regulations, the company will have an incentive to implement the necessary changes only if the social benefit exceeds the social cost of making the change. In the case of section 271, however, the benefit of increased local competition from unbundling and interconnection is very likely to differ from the "prize" offered of entry into long distance, thus possibly leading to a suboptimal outcome. The use of a direct monetary prize might have been more efficient, but is politically difficult to offer.[26]

Section 271 provides the prize of long distance entry if the BOCs demonstrate to the FCC that they have taken the necessary steps to open up their networks to interconnection with CLECs, and have implemented the processes necessary to provision UNEs to CLECs in a nondiscriminatory manner. Because it is difficult to observe a BOC's internal processes, the FCC has used the limited amount of freedom the Act gives it in choosing how to evaluate an application to urge that section 271 applicants submit evidence that make compliance more easily observable.[27] For instance, applicants rely on the submission of performance metric data, measuring the BOC's performance in providing service to CLECs, to demonstrate that they are provisioning services to the CLECs in a timely and nondiscriminatory manner.[28] The FCC has also encouraged the use of independent third party tests to demonstrate that the BOC's OSS are readily accessible to the CLECs, for those areas of the BOC's operation difficult to measure with performance metrics (e.g., the quality of help documentation), and for areas where commercial volumes are too low to evaluate using performance metrics. Once 271 approval is granted the carrot for ensuring compliance is gone, but monitoring of post-approval compliance is made easier with the requirement that the BOCs continue to submit performance metric reports to the FCC.[29] The danger of post-approval backsliding has also been much reduced by the establishment of performance assurance plans, generally created by state commissions, that generate automatic payments by the BOC for poor performance to CLECs when indicated by the performance metrics.[30]

In addition, the section 271 process depends heavily on actions by state PUCs. Under sections 251 and 252 the state PUCs arbitrate interconnection agreements, and can also help develop a statement of generally available terms in order to expedite interconnection negotiations. Section 271 requires that the FCC consult with the state PUC before making its determination, and the FCC has encouraged state PUCs to play an active role in the 271 process, by providing an independent evaluation of BOC compliance with the checklist, developing a third-party test of the BOC's OSS, creating performance metrics to measure BOC performance and provide for an independent audit of the BOC's data, and developing a performance assurance plan to prevent post-approval backsliding.[31] The BOCs have cooperated with state PUC efforts partly because the FCC's section 271 precedent relies heavily on the development of this kind of evidence, but also because state PUC endorsement of their section 271 application has proven to be helpful in seeking approval at the FCC. This has given the state PUCs some leverage to develop their own rules, and to develop a performance assurance plan.[32] Thus, the Act allows the state PUCs some room for experimentation, within the confines of the Act and FCC regulations. To a large extent, the success or failure of the Act to bring local competition to each state depends on the actions of the state PUC to arbitrate interconnection agreements, set wholesale prices, monitor BOC performance to CLECs, fix any deficiencies that appear in the performance metrics and the performance assurance plan, and handle complaints and take enforcement action if problems with BOC performance appear.

B   Impact on the long distance market: Should BOC entry into long distance be linked to the BOC's implementation of Section 251?

While the use of a prize may be a superior solution to the problem of how to efficiently ensure BOC compliance with new interconnection and unbundling obligations, letting entry into long distance be the prize could prove costly if harm is done to the long distance market. Harm can occur from an unnecessary delay of entry into long distance, by eliminating an entrant capable of providing additional competition to the long distance marketplace, or from premature entry, allowing a BOC to vertically leverage its market power from the local to the long distance market. Some economists have argued that the long distance market is dominated by an oligopoly which has maintained prices above long-run incremental cost through tacit collusion, and suggest that delaying BOC entry to achieve some unrelated goal of opening up the local market denies consumers the benefit from adding a potentially powerful competitor to the long distance market (MacAvoy 1998; Crandall and Hazlett 2000).

There is, however, a long-standing concern on the part of regulators about the ability of a firm to vertically leverage its market power from one market to another through a vertical price squeeze or some other means. In the development of the MFJ, and in various proceedings of the FCC including the Competitive Carrier Proceedings, the ability of ILECs to vertically leverage their market power from the local market into other markets has been taken very seriously (FCC 1997). With a regulated monopoly in the local exchange market, BOCs will have an incentive to discriminate against rivals in the long distance market once they are granted entry in order to raise prices and reap the benefits of their market power (Schwartz 2000; Economides 1999).[33] BOC entry into long distance without adequate safeguards could cause harm to the long distance market and lower consumer welfare, if the BOCs are able to vertically leverage their market power into the long distance market.

BOC discrimination against rivals can happen in a variety of ways, including by footdragging in initiation of service or providing new features, by offering price structures that appear to be nondiscriminatory but in fact favor the BOC's affiliate, or by degrading the quality of a rival's service.[34] These forms of discrimination might be indistinguishable from legitimate conduct and difficult for regulators to detect or correct. Cooperation between interexchange carriers and their local exchange access supplier becomes more important over time as new technologies and the development of new call forward and distributing services make interconnection more complex and more difficult to arrange.

We won't get into a lengthy discussion in this paper of the long distance market and whether market prices reflect vigorous competition or collusive oligopoly. However, we believe that the potential for vertical leveraging of market power in the local exchange market into long distance is real, and that this threat outweighs any possible benefits from adding one more competitor to the long distance market. Therefore the preferred policy is to add a powerful entrant to that market, but only after ensuring that it is unable to vertically leverage its market power into the long distance market. This is best achieved by requiring the BOCs to open up their local market to competition before allowing them into the long distance market. If the BOC attempts to degrade the quality of interconnection with competitive IXCs, the IXCs' customers will have the opportunity to switch their local service to another local exchange provider that provides good quality interconnection services. Attempts to discriminate against competitive IXCs will then likely accelerate the BOC's loss of market share in the local market. Thus section 271 not only serves as an effective prize for opening up the local market, but also acts as a long-term guarantee that the BOC will lack the incentive to discriminate against its long distance rivals.

Section 271 just conditions BOC entry on the local market being open to competition, not on there being ubiquitous and pervasive competitive entry (such as would be required with a market share test). This can be justified by observing that it is the ability of consumers to switch local exchange companies that limits the BOCs' incentives to discriminate in the long distance market (Schwartz 2000). In addition, in many BOC markets CLEC entry may be slow to occur for a variety of reasons, such as a high cost of entry, low retail prices, and the level of demand in those markets. However, requiring the FCC and the state PUCs to certify that the market is open to competition places a heavy regulatory burden on these agencies. They must conduct detailed analyses to determine that the checklist has been met, and thereby demonstrate that there are no barriers to entry attributable to BOC failure to make the necessary changes to its systems and offerings or to state regulations. A market share test would have been much easier to apply, but would have delayed BOC entry for many markets that are less desirable to CLECs.[35]

IV Statistics on the Development of Local Competition

While local competition has grown more slowly than many have desired, there has been a steady increase in CLEC market share. According to data submitted in Form 477 to the FCC, and provided in the FCC's report "Local Telephone Competition· Status as of December 31, 2000," CLECs had 16.4 million lines for a market share of 8.5 percent of all switched end-user lines in the United States as of December 31, 2000. This was 97 percent higher than one year earlier. Data for total CLEC lines is unavailable for the period before December 1999, but data provided by the largest ILECs for lines provided to CLECs shows that the lines they have sold to CLECs, as resale and UNEs, have climbed rapidly, with an annual average growth rate of 62 percent for December 1997 to December 2000 (FCC 2001a).[36] Growth appears to have slowed recently, with the estimated number of loops provided by ILECs to CLECs for plain old telephone service (POTS) growing by 13 percent during the period from December 2000 to June 2001, for an annual growth rate of 28 percent.[37] This may be due to the well-documented woes of the CLEC industry, with many CLECs cutting back operations or filing for bankruptcy (Crandall 2001).

The level of competition across the country varies significantly, with CLECs gaining a market share as high as 20 percent in New York and 12 percent in Texas. The breakdown of CLEC market shares by state is provided in figure 7.1, for those states with publicly available data (FCC 2001a).[38] States for which the FCC has approved a BOC's 271 application are shaded.[39]

While we have only limited publicly available information about the total number and location of CLEC lines in each state, we have better publicly available information about the number of lines purchased for POTS service from the BOCs and their affiliates, obtained from the performance metric reports that the BOCs file with state PUCs and with the FCC, for various purposes.[40] Using this data, we provide in table 7.1 the breakdown by state of CLEC purchases of BOC services for providing POTS lines according to the type of facilities purchased, whether resale, UNE-P, or UNE-L for June 2001.[41]

Figure 7.2 shows the breakdown by state for June 2001. While this table and figure does not include full facilities-based competition, and

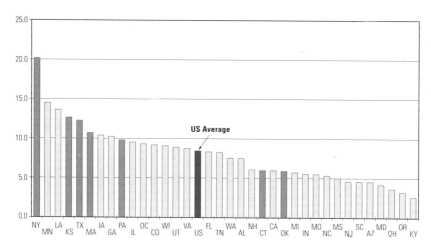

Figure 7.1
CLEC Market Share as of Dec. 2000 for States with Public Data
(States with granted 271 approval as of October 2001 shaded darker)

thus cannot be used to determine CLEC penetration, it does provide an indication of the extent of competition in each state.

The volume of lines provisioned to CLECs by ILECs can be considered a measure of how effectively ILECs have opened their systems and have set wholesale prices that allow for entry. It is generally more difficult for ILECs to meet their unbundling and resale obligations (because they may require major system changes) than it is for them to meet the needs of full facilities-based CLECs, which may only require basic interconnection similar to that already provided to IXCs. Consequently, this paper's data on lines purchased by CLECs may actually provide a better indication of how far the BOCs have progressed in meeting their Section 251 obligations than CLEC market share data. The percentage of lines provisioned to CLECs for resale, UNE-P and UNE-L for the larger ILECs for which data is publicly available is provided in table 7.2, and shown in figure 7.3 for December 2000. The much larger proportion of BOC lines ordered by CLECs in states with 271 approval (13.1% of BOC lines), or even in states that are eligible for 271 approval (4.2%), than for ILECs for whom section 271 does not apply (2.0% of ILEC lines), supports the argument that section 271 has been successful in providing an incentive for BOCs to open up their networks and allow for greater entry.[42]

Table 7.1
Percentage of BOC Switched Lines Purchased by CLECs, by Type of Line, for June 2001

State	BOC	Total BOC Lines	BOC % of ILEC Lines	Percent Resale	Percent UNE-P	Percent UNE-L	Percent Total	Total Lines
							Lines Purchased by CLECs	
Alabama	BellSouth	1,997,723	79.3	2.2	1.8	0.6	4.7	93,048
Arizona	Qwest	2,959,467	93.4	1.7	0.3	0.5	2.5	73,272
Arkansas	SBC-SWBT	1,048,587	69.2	3.3	0.5	1.6	5.4	56,340
California	SBC-PacTel	18,810,937	78.2	1.0	0.3	1.6	2.9	552,391
Colorado	Qwest	2,845,889	95.6	2.0	1.7	0.8	4.6	130,480
Connecticut	Verizon-BA North	57,893	99.0	3.5	0.0	0.9	4.4	2,547
Delaware	Verizon-BA South	595,708	100	1.8	0.0	2.9	4.7	28,061
District of Columbia	Verizon-BA South	1,019,026	100	7.8	0.0	0.9	3.7	89,023
Florida	BellSouth	6,850,656	59.1	3.0	1.4	1.6	5.0	408,159
Georgia	BellSouth	4,264,151	83.3	2.7	3.1	1.5	7.4	313,869
Idaho	Qwest	583,168	72.2	1.8	0.1	0.0	1.9	11,013
Illinois	SBC-Ameritech	6,880,696	85.1	3.9	1.9	3.0	8.8	607,957
Indiana	SBC-Ameritech	2,256,736	61.9	1.5	0.0	1.6	3.2	71,381
Iowa	Qwest	1,143,962	64.9	1.0	11.0	0.8	12.8	146,145
Kansas	SBC-SWBT	1,389,742	84.0	5.7	3.9	0.3	9.9	137,041
Kentucky	BellSouth	1,264,064	56.6	2.4	1.4	0.3	4.0	50,859
Louisiana	BellSouth	2,439,723	92.7	3.8	0.6	0.4	4.8	115,929
Maine	Verizon-BA North	749,853	83.3	5.3	0.2	1.2	6.8	50,868
Maryland	Verizon-BA South	4,051,759	99.8	5.5	0.1	1.0	6.6	267,007
Massachusetts	Verizon-BA North	4,636,622	99.9	5.8	0.6	1.8	8.2	378,294
Michigan	SBC-Ameritech	5,397,189	84.4	2.0	3.2	2.3	7.5	403,613
Minnesota	Qwest	2,342,669	73.2	3.1	3.4	2.1	8.7	203,010
Mississippi	BellSouth	1,359,773	93.4	4.4	1.0	0.3	5.7	77,687
Missouri	SBC-SWBT	2,605,726	74.9	4.1	2.3	0.3	6.7	173,384
Montana	Qwest	386,624	68.1	3.2	0.1	0.4	3.6	14,067
Nebraska	Qwest	507,263	50.5	2.2	0.4	1.3	3.9	20,035
Nevada	SBC-PacTel	380,616	27.2	2.1	0.0	1.6	3.8	14,285

Table 7.1
(*continued*)

State	BOC	Total BOC Lines	BOC % of ILEC Lines	Lines Purchased by CLECs				
				Percent Resale	Percent UNE-P	Percent UNE-L	Percent Total	Total Lines
New Hampshire	Verizon-BA North	816,322	93.5	5.5	0.3	2.9	8.8	71,801
New Jersey	Verizon-BA South	6,914,330	96.6	2.9	0.1	0.5	3.5	240,290
New Mexico	Qwest	863,377	85.0	1.1	0.0	0.4	1.5	13,250
New York	Verizon-BA North	12,050,789	89.5	3.0	14.5	2.2	19.6	2,365,206
North Carolina	BellSouth	2,603,650	50.0	2.3	1.2	1.4	4.9	128,832
North Dakota	Qwest	218,651	60.8	4.8	11.1	1.5	17.4	38,038
Ohio	SBC-Ameritech	4,063,464	59.0	1.3	0.7	2.4	4.5	181,924
Oklahoma	SBC-SWBT	1,660,815	82.7	3.2	1.5	0.3	4.9	81,690
Oregon	Qwest	1,460,169	65.5	1.7	2.6	2.2	6.5	94,355
Pennsylvania	Verizon-BA South	6,366,128	77.1	2.0	3.7	2.4	8.1	516,057
Rhode Island	Verizon-BA North	670,464	100	4.8	0.3	3.4	8.5	57,113
South Carolina	BellSouth	1,543,218	64.5	3.3	1.2	0.7	5.1	79,358
South Dakota	Qwest	280,799	65.3	3.9	6.2	0.4	10.6	29,676
Tennessee	BellSouth	2,764,068	79.6	1.8	1.2	1.6	4.6	125,973
Texas	SBC-SWBT	8,947,790	77.4	3.3	13.3	1.1	17.7	1,586,888
Utah	Qwest	1,165,099	95.0	1.9	0.2	0.8	2.8	33,070
Vermont	Verizon-BA North	368,392	84.6	4.9	0.1	0.1	5.1	18,898
Virginia	Verizon-BA South	3,800,149	76.2	3.3	0.0	3.1	6.5	245,516
Washington	Qwest	2,607,757	67.4	1.4	1.2	1.1	3.8	98,557
West Virginia	Verizon-BA South	897,968	83.7	1.4	0.0	1.0	2.4	21,407
Wisconsin	SBC-Ameritech	2,160,922	63.5	5.4	0.0	5.0	10.4	223,866
Wyoming	Qwest	261,266	83.2	1.0	8.2	0.0	9.1	23,900
Nationwide BOC		141,311,809	75.8	2.8	3.2	1.6	7.6	10,765,430

Source: FCC's ARMIS database, BOC Performance Metric Reports.

Note: For BellSouth and SBC-PacTel states CLEC purchased lines data is for June 1, not June 30. BOC is Bell Operating Company for that state, separated out by subsidiary corresponding to original 7 BOCs (Ameritech, Bell Atlantic, BellSouth, NYNEX, PacTel, Southwestern Bell, US West). NYNEX is now Verizon-BA North. Bell Atlantic is now Verizon-BA South. US West is now Qwest. Ameritech, SWBT, and PacTel are now part of SBC.

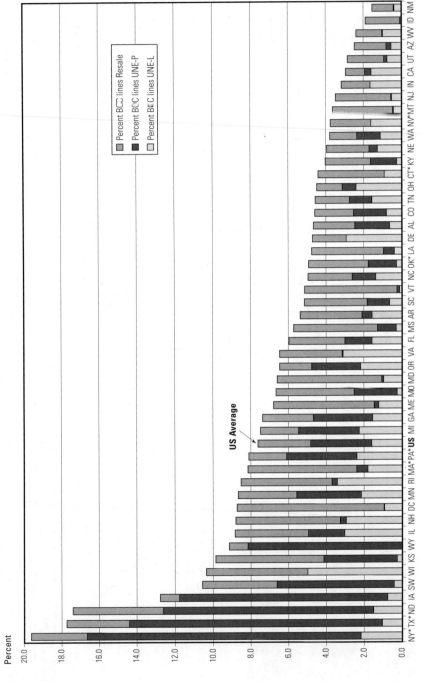

Figure 7.2
BOC Lines purchased by CLECs for POTS as Percent of BOC Lines, June 2001
(States with granted 271 approval as of October 2001 marked with*)

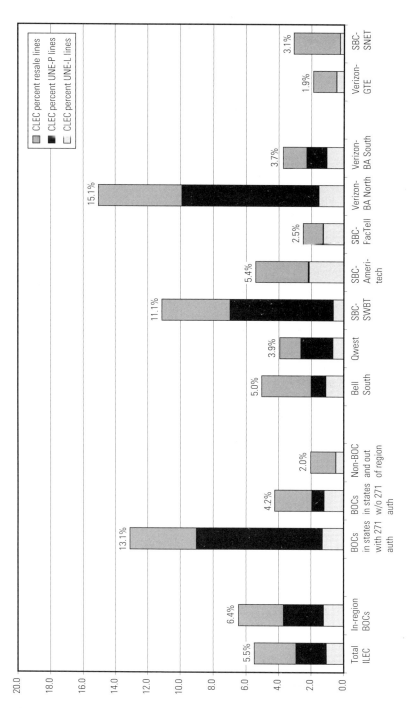

Figure 7.3
ILEC Lines Purchased by CLECs for POTS as Percent of ILEC Lines, Dec. 2000

The drawback to using this data is that the FCC's review of Section 271 applications, under the standard set by Congress, is not based on the extent of CLECs' penetration in the market, but instead whether the BOC has met the section 271 requirements, which effectively mean the market is open to competition. Thus, sections 251 and 271 do not guarantee that all forms of entry will be financially viable by efficient entrants, only that the cost of accessing the BOC's OSS systems, whole sale prices, the ability to get an interconnection agreement, and state and federal regulations will not be a hindrance to entry. Other factors have a major impact on the level of competitive entry in a state, including the level of retail prices, the quality and diversity of the ILEC's retail products, demand characteristics such as the wealth and density of customers and the number of businesses buying telecom services, the aggressiveness of the state commission in promoting competition, and the level of CLEC entrepreneurial activity in a state. For example, lower levels of CLEC entry into non-BOC ILECs' territories could be because smaller ILECs are usually located in rural areas, which may be less attractive markets to entrants.

From figures 2 and 3 it is clear that in states with section 271 authority or with significant levels of CLEC purchases of lines, CLECs have tended to rely heavily on UNE-P as an entry strategy, especially in New York and Texas. As of June 2001 UNE-P loops have been 65 percent of the lines purchased from BOCs in states with 271 approval versus 22 percent without it. When UNE-P prices provide a substantial discount from retail prices, which resale does not, UNE-P becomes an attractive means of reaching customers, especially price-sensitive residential customers who will only switch to achieve a significant savings.[43] Meanwhile, resale is a fairly popular entry strategy in most states.[44] In addition, while much has been made of CLEC's "cream-skimming" business customers while avoiding serving residential customers, data available suggests that CLECs are going after residential customers. Forty-one percent of CLEC lines in December 2000 were reported to be provided to residential and small business customers (FCC 2001a). In New York the state PUC reported that 52 percent of CLEC lines went to residential customers (New York Public Service Commission 2001).

We lack comparable consistent statistics measuring the growth of BOC entry on the long distance market, due to the recency of the BOCs' 271 approvals. However, Verizon reported in August 2001 it had signed up 6 million long distance customers, and had a market share of 31 percent in New York and 16 percent in Massachusetts (Verizon Press Release). SBC reported in July 2001 that it had gained 2.8 million customers in Texas, Kansas, and Oklahoma (SBC Press Release).

V   Conclusion

Section 271 has generated more controversy in the press and in political debate than it has in the economics literature. We hope that will change, because it represents a bold attempt to provide a strong incentive for ILECs to open up their networks, and cooperate with regulators, while providing protection for the long distance market. Sections 251 and 271 are part of an experiment to see if competition and rapid innovation can be brought to a market that has been considered a natural monopoly, and that historically has been slow to change in technology and products. There is much to learn from the successes and failures of this experiment, and future and foreign regulators could benefit from the insights gained by economists here.

The slow development of local competition has concerned many observers, but as section IV pointed out, there has been significant and continuous growth already. The process of opening up such a technologically complex industry with closed systems should have been expected to take many years. There were unrealistic expectations by many of the players (including CLECs, regulators, legislators, and investors) about how fast competition would develop. This process has been delayed further by litigation, conflicting court rulings, and disputes over who has the proper jurisdiction over each part of the process. A key part of the process is having all parties accept a common set of ground rules, and even now, this could be derailed by political pressures, new court challenges, regulatory fatigue, and the volatility of financial markets and the economy.

Based on our analysis of the industry's technical and economic structure, and the constraints under which regulators operate, we believe that section 271 is a more effective incentive structure for opening the local market to competition than other typically used regulatory alternatives. We also believe that it is an appropriate safeguard for protecting competition in the long distance market after ROC entry has occurred. While full assessment will only be possible after twenty or thirty years,

Table 7.2
Percentage of ILEC Lines Purchased by CLECs, by Type of Line and Type of ILEC

	Total ILEC Switched Access Lines	Percent of US Switched Access Lines	CLEC Lines Purchased as Percent of ILEC Lines				Total CLEC Lines Purchased
			% Resale	% UNE-P	% UNE-L	% Total	
December 2000							
Total ILEC	186,501,328	100	2.6	1.9	1.1	5.5	10,243,113
In-region BOCs	141,311,809	75.8	2.7	2.5	1.2	6.4	9,110,970
BOCs in states with 271	35,109,779	18.8	4.1	7.7	1.3	13.1	4,598,121
BOCs in states w/o 271	106,202,030	56.9	2.3	0.7	1.2	4.2	4,512,849
NonBOCs	44,970,534	24.1	1.5	0.0	0.5	2.0	913,158
BellSouth	25,087,026	13.5	3.0	0.9	1.1	5.0	1,264,846
Qwest	17,626,160	9.5	1.3	2.0	0.7	3.9	696,126
SBC-SWBT	15,652,660	8.4	4.2	6.3	0.7	11.1	1,743,935
SBC-Ameritech	20,759,007	11.1	3.2	0.1	2.1	5.4	1,126,259
SBC-PacTell	19,191,553	10.3	1.2	0.0	1.3	2.5	483,610
Verizon-BA North	19,350,335	10.4	5.1	8.4	1.6	15.1	2,912,404
Verizon-BA South	23,645,068	12.7	1.4	1.2	1.1	3.7	883,790
Verizon-GTE	20,020,554	10.7	1.4	0.0	0.4	1.9	377,387
SBC-SNET	2,449,914	1.3	2.9	0.0	0.2	3.1	75,708

Table 7.2
(*continued*)

	Total ILEC Switched Access Lines	Percent of US Switched Access Lines	CLEC Lines Purchased as Percent of ILEC Lines				Total CLEC Lines Purchased
			% Resale	% UNE-P	% UNE-L	% Total	
June 2001							
Total ILEC	186,501,328	100	N/A	N/A	N/A	N/A	N/A
Ir-region BOCs	141,311,809	75.8	2.8	3.2	1.6	7.6	10,765,430
BOCs in states with 271	35,109,779	18.8	3.4	9.3	1.7	14.4	5,067,723
BOCs in states w/o 271	106,202,030	56.9	2.6	1.2	1.6	5.4	5,697,707
NonBOCs	44,970,534	24.1	N/A	N/A	N/A	N/A	N/A
BellSouth	25,087,026	13.5	2.8	1.6	1.2	5.6	1,393,714
Qwest	17,626,160	9.5	2.0	2.3	1.0	5.3	928,868
SBC-SWBT	15,652,660	8.4	3.7	8.5	0.8	13.0	2,035,343
SBC-Ameritech	20,759,007	11.1	2.8	1.6	2.8	7.2	1,488,741
SBC-PacTell	19,191,553	10.3	1.0	0.3	1.6	3.0	566,676
Verizon-BA North	19,350,335	10.4	4.0	9.2	2.1	15.2	2,944,727
Verizon-BA South	23,645,068	12.7	3.3	1.0	1.6	6.0	1,407,361
Verizon-GTE	20,020,554	10.7	1.2	0.0	0.5	1.7	348,539
SBC-SNET	2,449,914	1.3	3.1	0.0	0.6	3.8	92,477

Source: ARMIS, BOC Performance Metric Reports, FCC 2001a.

Note: For BellSouth and SBC-PacTel states CLEC purchased lines data is for the beginning of the month. Total BOC lines assumed to be the same for December and June. BOCs in states with 271 approval as of October 2001. BOC is Bell Operating Company for that state, separated out by subsidiary corresponding to original 7 BOCs (Ameritech, Bell Atlantic, BellSouth, NYNEX, PacTel, Southwestern Bell, US West). NYNEX is now Verizon-BA North. Bell Atlantic is now Verizon-BA South. US West is now Qwest. Ameritech, SWBT, and PacTel are now part of SBC. NonBOCs GTE is now a subsidiary of Verizon, and SNET is now a subsidiary of SBC.

N/A = Not Available.

the statistical evidence we have five years after enactment of the Act suggests that the section 271 incentive mechanism has accelerated the process of opening local exchange markets to competition.

Notes

1. Daniel R. Shiman is an Economist and Jessica Rosenworcel an Attorney-Advisor in the Policy and Program Planning Division of the Common Carrier Bureau at the Federal Communications Commission. Opinions expressed are those of the authors alone, and do not represent the views or policies of the FCC or its commissioners.

2. We do not address the appropriate level of prices associated with competitive entry in the local exchange market.

3. Thus, the court generally concluded that the efficiency losses that would likely result from the BOCs' ability to engage in anti-competitive conduct outweighed the benefit of the BOCs' presence in the long distance market. *See generally BellSouth v. FCC*, 162 F.3d 678, 681 (D.C. Cir. 1998).

4. The Act provided that "[a]ny conduct or activity that was, before the date of enactment [of the Act], subject to any restriction or obligation imposed by the [MFJ] shall, on and after such date, be subject to the restrictions and obligations imposed by the [Act] and shall not be subject to the restrictions and the obligations imposed by [the MFJ]" (Pub. L. no. 104–04, sect. 601(a)(1), 110 Stat. 56, 143).

5. The other UNEs the FCC required to be unbundled are the Network Interface Device or NID, signalling and call-related databases, Operations Support Systems, and the high frequency portion of the loop (47 C.F.R. sect. 319).

6. See 47 U.S.C. sect. 252(d); 47 C.F.R. sect. 51.501 *et seq.; Implementation of the Local Competition Provisions in the Telecommunications Act of 1996*, First Report and Order, 11 FCC Rcd 15499, 15844–47 (1996). Although the United States Court of Appeals for the Eighth Circuit stayed the FCC's pricing rules in 1996, the Supreme Court restored the FCC's pricing authority on January 25, 1999, and remanded to the Eighth Circuit for consideration of the merits of the challenged rules. *Iowa Utils. Bd. v. FCC*, 109 F.3d 418 (8th Cir. 1996), 120 F.3d 753, 800, 804–06 (8th Cir. 1997), *aff'd in part, rev'd in part sub nom., AT&T Corp. v. Iowa Utils. Bd.*, 525 U.S. 366, 397 (1999). On remand from the Supreme Court, the Eighth Circuit concluded that certain FCC pricing rules are contrary to congressional intent. *Iowa Utils. Bd. v. FCC*, 219 F.3d 744 (8th Cir. 2000), *cert. granted sub nom. Verizon Communications, Inc. v. FCC*, 121 S.Ct. 877 (2001). The Eighth Circuit has stayed the issuance of its mandate pending review by the Supreme Court. *Iowa Utils. Bd. v. FCC*, no. 96–3321 et al. (8th Cir., Sept. 25, 2000).

7. Many CLECs serving medium-sized business customers will purchase a high capacity (DS1 or higher) loop and transport to that customer and will aggregate the voice and data traffic onto that circuit.

8. Resale is often used to serve business customers, especially those willing to pay extra for better customer service or in locations that the CLEC's network does not yet reach, and residential customers who have failed to pay their bills to the ILEC.

9. Thus, through the Track B test, a BOC operating in a state where there are no CLECs pursuing entry, may nonetheless be eligible to apply for section 271 authority.

10. The list of all applications that have been processed by the FCC is located in the FCC's *Statistics of Communications Common Carriers,* and on the FCC's website for the Competition Policy Division of the Wireline Competition Bureau (formerly called the Policy and Program Planning Division of the Common Carrier Bureau) at <http://www.fcc.gov/Bureaus/Common_Carrier/in-region_applications>.

11. It is possible that because of the ILEC's scale economies and low retail prices, and the presence of other barriers and difficulties hindering CLEC entry, that effective local competition could never develop. This paper assumes that effective local competition can be achieved through the right set of incentive and regulatory mechanisms.

12. Because of these scale economies the local exchange market has been considered to be a natural monopoly, and regulated as such.

13. Arguably, full-facilities based competition would yield the most benefits to consumers, not because it will lower prices the most, but because the potential long-term gains from innovation are greatest, including working around the bottleneck. However, CLECs may not find it economically feasible to use their own facilities to serve many kinds of customers.

14. For example, technological changes may change the location of bottlenecks, may change the cost of unbundling particular elements, and may change the speed with which requirements may be implemented.

15. Some parts of the network are difficult to unbundle for CLECs' use, such as digital loop carrier systems, which have been frequently employed in place of the traditional copper loop.

16. This is only a partial list of the actions an ILEC must take to open its network to competitors' use. For a more detailed discussion, see FCC 1996a and the FCC's various orders in response to section 271 applications.

17. The ambitious nature of the Act makes it highly regulatory in certain aspects, requiring detailed regulations governing the ILECs wholesaling of their networks and services, but with the goal of reducing regulation at the retail level. A similar purpose was served by Part 68 of the Code of Federal Regulations, which provides detailed rules governing the connection of customers premise equipment (CPE) to the network, in order to improve competition in the CPE market.

18. Usually the regulators' task is to set retail prices for a good for which the firm has some market power, and so long as the regulators choose a price that is above marginal cost, the firm will have an incentive to produce it. From an historical

perspective the Act has created an unusual situation, in which firms are required to go to a great deal of effort to produce a good they do not want to sell.

19. As has been widely recognized, there are circumstances in which upstream monopolists who are competing downstream will not want to discriminate against users of their inputs, such as when they can extract their monopoly profits upstream, or when the downstream users are much more efficient, but those circumstances do not generally apply to ILECs (Laffont & Tirole 1999; Schwartz 2000). In addition, ILECs gain two benefits from degrading competitors' access, one from reducing their loss of retail customers, and the second from saving money by not developing the needed facilities for unbundling and interconnection.

20. For a discussion of problems of this sort, see Morris and Preece 1982.

21. It is very difficult to set performance standards and benchmarks concerning the negotiation of new arrangements and the working out of technical details. The Act provides for the use of arbitration and regulatory rule-making to resolve outstanding issues, but this process can be slow.

22. New York and Illinois were early states to promote competition in the local exchange market (Tomlinson 2000, 169).

23. ECPR was also rejected because it was inconsistent with the Act, since "the existing retail prices that would be used to compute incremental opportunity costs under ECPR are not cost-based" (FCC 1996a, 15859).

24. The remainder of this section concentrates on the BOCs, since section 271 only pertains to them. They were the only ILECs prohibited from entering the long distance market under the MFJ, so Congress had the unique opportunity to use long distance entry as a prize for them. The BOCs are by far the largest ILECs, and have about 75% of the nation's access lines.

25. Indeed, in states where it has been permitted to sell long distance service, SWBT only offers long distance service to customers that are also taking its local service.

26. Tax credits, however, are sometimes used as a prize for undertaking some action such as an investment.

27. The Act requires that the FCC process a lot of information about the BOCs' systems, since the requirement is only that the BOCs systems be open to competitors, and not that the market is competitive.

28. "Non-discriminatory service" is interpreted to mean that service to CLEC customers is of the same quality and timeliness as service to the BOC's retail customers, when the same service is provided to both sets of customers.

29. Under section 271(d)(6) the FCC has authority to take an enforcement action if the BOC's performance were to decline post-approval.

30. This comports with Marius Schwartz's argument that the section 271 prize is needed so long as new arrangements are being made. Once the arrangements are established and reporting mechanisms in place, routine enforcement should be sufficient to prevent discrimination against CLECs (Schwartz 2000).

31. The FCC has encouraged the use of open collaboratives, in which CLECs

can participate and voice their concerns, in the state process. Where state PUCs lack the requisite resources to accomplish all of these tasks, they often rely on the efforts of large state PUCs in their BOC region to accomplish the more difficult region-wide tasks, such as conduct a third party test, or in some cases have pooled their resources with other state PUCs in the region.

32. Many state PUCs lack the statutory authority to impose a plan that provides for automatic fines levied against the BOC, so with the FCC's encouragement, the BOCs have voluntarily submitted to a state-developed performance assurance plan.

33. According to economic theory, a firm with an unregulated monopoly in one market will be unlikely to discriminate against rivals in a vertically related market, since the firm should be able to extract all possible monopoly profits by raising prices in the monopolized market. However, there is an incentive to vertically leverage the market power if the monopolized market is regulated, such that the firm is unable to raise prices and extract monopoly profits from it.

34. Degradation of a rival's service can occur by allowing interconnection to deteriorate, thus allowing more calls to be blocked to an IXC than calls to its own long distance affiliate. One BOC engineer has said that in the past it set up its tandem switches to have lower blocking (i.e., fewer calls unable to get through at peak calling times) for long distance calls than for local calls, since carrying long distance calls was much more profitable.

35. A market share test would also have given CLECs owned by the IXCs the opportunity to game the process, by limiting their own entry into the local market to prevent BOC entry into long distance. The IXCs have been seen as natural entrants into the local market, and have aggressively entered many local exchange markets through a variety of entry strategies.

36. We use the terms "purchased" and "sold" for convenience, although the lines are in fact being leased, if obtained as a UNE, or the services on that line are being resold by the CLEC.

37. This estimate was based on numbers taken from the performance metric reports, discussed below. The number of UNE loops provisioned for DSL grew at about the same rate for this period.

38. The data was withheld for about a third of the states for confidentiality reasons (FCC 2001a).

39. The states counted as having section 271 approval for this section are those states with approval as of October 2001: New York, Texas, Kansas, Oklahoma, Massachusetts, Connecticut and Pennsylvania. Note that this graph includes all ILEC lines in the state, while 271 approval applies only to the BOC territory in these states. The data used comes from FCC 2001a, and is the number of switched access lines reported by each CLEC divided by the total number of switched access lines (CLEC plus ILEC) in the state. FCC approval is not based on market share lost to CLECs, which explains why some states with lower levels of CLEC entry have received section 271 approval.

40. These reports show the level of performance by the BOC to the CLECs in a

variety of areas and product lines, and compare it to performance to their own customers, where possible, or to a benchmark. The reports were developed for section 271 applications, and to meet the conditions of a merger approval. See <http://www.fcc.gov/ccb/mcot/> for performance metric data filed for the SBC-Ameritech and Bell Atlantic-GTE mergers. The total number of CLEC lines for a particular product category for a state were taken from the December 2000 and June 2001 reported CLEC volumes (i.e., the denominator used) for the network trouble report rate metrics, which measure the percentage of all lines in a product category that had a reported trouble for that month. We consider this data to be more reliable than the form 477 data, since for both section 271 applications and for the merger conditions an audit of the data was required.

41. We assumed that the number of ILEC lines remained the same as for December 2000 (according to FCC ARMIS data, growth of BOC access lines appears to have been about zero for 1999–2000). By the term "BOC" we are referring to states classified as in-region territories for section 271 purposes. Companies subsequently merged into the BOCs, such as SNET (now a part of SBC) and GTE (now a part of Verizon), are considered separately for the purposes of this discussion. Section 271's requirements do not apply for BOC affiliates in states the BOCs were not in when the Act was passed.

42. The data for "BOCs in states with section 271 authority" are for the BOCs in all states that currently (as of October 2001) have 271 authorization, for both December 2000 and June 2001. See note 39 for the list of those states.

43. The long-term economic benefits from CLECs offering UNE-P and resale, however, are likely to be much less than those from CLECs investing in their own facilities, for full or partial facilities-based competition.

44. Statistics available indicate that resale is used to serve business customers more—about 55% of resale POTS lines went to business customers in June 2001, from data for all of the BOCs except Verizon. In New York 90% of all resale lines went to business customers. Resale can be an easy and useful means of providing service to small and medium-sized businesses who are willing to pay extra for customized billing and additional customer care.

References

Baumol, William J., and J. Gregory Sidak 1994. *Toward Competition in Local Telephony.* MIT Press.

BellSouth v. FCC 1998. 162 F.3d 678, 681 (D.C. Cir.).

Berg, Sanford V., and Dean Foreman 1996. "Incentive Regulation and Telco Performance: A Primer," *Telecommunications Policy,* 20, no. 9, 641.

Crandall, Robert W. 2001. "An Assessment of the Competitive Local Exchange Carriers Five Years after the Passage of the Telecommunications Act." Criterion Economics, L.L.C.

Crandall, Robert W. 1999. "Managed Competition in U.S. Telecommunications," Working Paper 99-1, AEI-Brookings Joint Center for Regulatory Studies.

Crandall, Robert W., and Thomas Hazlett 2000. "Telecommunications Policy Reform in the United States and Canada," Working Paper 00-9, AEI-Brookings Joint Center for Regulatory Studies.

Crandall, Robert W., and Leonard Waverman 1996. *Talk is Cheap: The Promise of Deregulation in North American Telecommunications.* Brookings Institution Press.

Economides, Nicholas 1999. "The Telecommunications Act of 1996 and its Impact." *Japan and the World Economy.*

FCC 1996a. *Implementation of the Local Competition Provisions of the Telecommunications Act of 1996,* First Report and Order, 11 FCC Rcd 15499.

FCC 1996b. *Implementation of the Non-Accounting Safeguards Standards of Sections 271 and 272,* First Report and Order, 11 FCC Rcd 21905.

FCC 1997. *Regulatory Treatment of LEC Provision of Interexchange Services Originating in LEC's Local Exchange Area and Policy and Rules Concerning the Interstate, Interexchange Marketplace,* Second and Third Report and Order, 12 FCC Rcd 15756.

FCC 2001a. *Local Competition: Status as of December 31, 2000,* Report. <http://www.fcc.gov/Bureaus/Common_Carrier/Reports/FCCState_Link/comp.html>.

FCC 2001b. *Communications Assistance for Law Enforcement Act,* CC Docket No. 97-213, adopted Sept. 18, 2001.

Ford, George S., and John D. Jackson 1999. "Effective Enforcement of Non-Discriminatory Performance by Incumbent Local Exchange Carriers." Unpublished manuscript.

Hausman, Jerry A., and Gregory Sidak 1999. "A Consumer-Welfare Approach to the Mandatory Unbundling of Telecommunications Networks," 109 Yale L.J.417.

Laffont, Jean-Jacques, and Jean Tirole 2001. *Competition in Telecommunications.* MIT Press.

Laffont, Jean-Jacques, and Jean Tirole 1998. *A Theory of Incentives in Procurement and Regulation.* MIT Press.

MacAvoy, Paul W. 1998. "Testing for Competitiveness of Markets for Long Distance Telephone Services: Competition Finally?," *Review of Industrial Organization,* Vol. 13, No. 3, 295.

Morris, Roy L., and Robert S. Preece 1982. "Negotiating for Improved Interconnection," FCC OPP Working Paper Series, No. 7.

New York Public Service Commission 2001. *Analysis of Local Exchange Service Competition in New York State: Reflecting Company Reported Data and Statistics as of December 31, 2001.*

SBC Press Release Aug. 20, 2001. <http://www.swbell.com/About/NewsCenter>.

Schwartz, Marius 2000. "The Economic Logic for Conditioning Bell Entry into Long Distance on the Prior Opening of Local Markets," *Journal of Regulatory Economics,* 18:3 247–288.

Stern, Christopher and Yuki Noguchi Sept. 19, 2001. *Attacks renew Calls for 911 System to Locate Cell Phones,* Washington Post, E1.

Tomlinson, Richard G. 2000. *Tele-Revolution: Telephone Competition at the Speed of Light.* Penobscot Press.

United States v. Amer. Tel. & Tel. Co. 1982. 552 F.Supp 131 (D.D.C.), *aff'd sub nom., Maryland v. United States* (1983), 460 U.S. 1003.

Verizon Press Release Aug. 1, 2001. <http://www.newscenter.verizon.com>.

8

A Competitive Analysis of International Long Distance

Sean F. Ennis

1 Introduction

The structure of the U.S. long distance telecommunications market has changed dramatically since MCI began providing switched long distance service in 1974. Prior to that time, AT&T was the primary provider of U.S. long distance service. In the late 1970s, U.S. regulators encouraged competition in long distance service by prompting AT&T to negotiate temporary access tariffs that allowed long distance carriers to interconnect with its local facilities on standard terms. Since that time, regulators have continued to encourage competition through various means, including separating AT&T's long distance arm from its local divisions and setting mandatory conditions of interconnection between long distance and local companies. The fundamental rationale for policy makers to encourage competition has been the belief that competition leads to lower prices. While this belief is in accord with common economic theory, and U.S. long distance rates have indeed fallen by as much as 80 percent since 1984, there is surprisingly little direct evidence to support the view that competition is related to lower prices.

The reason that price reductions could be so dramatic and yet not indicate active competition is that costs themselves have fallen substantially. Domestic U.S. long distance costs have been affected by regulatory actions that have led to considerable reductions in the per-minute access charges that are paid by U.S. long distance carriers to local carriers for the origination and termination of a call. Access charges have fallen from a total of 17.3 cents per minute in 1984 to 2.8 cents per minute in 2000 (Industry Analysis Division (2000), pp. 1–4, nominal values).

A similar cost-reducing phenomenon has occurred with international long distance. The most significant element of international costs consists of a country-specific access charge that is called the settlement rate and that is paid by the U.S. carrier to the foreign carrier for U.S.-originated calls and by a foreign carrier to the U.S. carrier that completes a foreign-originated long distance call. For international long distance, the cost of sending a call overseas from the United States has fallen as much as 90 percent.

In the face of dramatic cost reductions, prices would likely decline even in the absence of competition both for domestic and for international long distance. That is, a monopolist or a cartel would lower prices if costs were reduced. Thus the fact that prices have fallen may simply reflect lower costs rather than increased competition.

The economic work analyzing the relationship between long distance competition and prices deals primarily with domestic U.S. pricing (see Edelman [1997], MacAvoy [1995, 1996, and 1998], Taylor and Taylor [1993], and Taylor and Zona [1997]). One prominent line of work, exemplified by MacAvoy (1995 and 1998), examines "basic rate" price changes between 1985 or 1987 and the early 1990s to show that prices have decreased less quickly than costs. MacAvoy has been instrumental in pointing out the possibility that lower costs, on their own, might explain all the price declines observed in long distance rates. MacAvoy argues that margins have increased while costs have fallen and concludes that domestic competitors are essentially operating as a cartel.

This work faces two primary limitations. The first of these limitations is that its measure of price typically focuses on the highest price plan (or "basic" plan). This plan is the default rate received by a consumer who signs up for no special long distance plan. Focusing on the basic rate is justified by the fact that a high proportion of users are covered by the basic rate plan. However, the rationale for focusing on the basic rate is weakened by the fact that major long distance companies have customers on a variety of different plans, and a minority of calls are actually covered by a basic rate plan. Focusing on the basic rate plan thus ignores the majority of usage that might be indicative of actual price competition. At any given time, long distance companies typically offer a flagship plan that provides much lower per-minute rates for calling than the basic plan.

The second limitation of the work is that it consists primarily of a graphical analysis of trends, and thus its statistical strength is somewhat limited. This difficulty is inherent in the data and not a criticism of the approach. Comparing basic rates to costs yields a time series of prices and costs that may be a complete characterization of the relationship between basic rates and costs. However, once the results for basic rates are claimed to apply more broadly, the extent to which behavior of basic rates mimics that of other plans becomes critical. Given that there is no reliable measurement that weights all the different domestic calling plans, and that there is limited variation in any measurement of the change in competition over time, an approach to the problem of domestic competition that contains more statistical variation would be desirable.

In this paper, we suggest that international routes provide significant variation in price, costs, and market structure over time. We can use such variation to analyze whether price reductions are occurring solely as costs decline or whether price reductions are related also to other factors, such as declining concentration on routes. As with domestic long distance data, costs and prices are relatively clearly defined. However, the international data has a feature not found in available domestic data: significant variation in the levels of concentration on routes. To the extent that concentration is related to varying physical capacities to provide service, concentration may be considered a reasonable proxy for competition. International data will allow for a direct test of the relationship between concentration and price.

Previous work focusing on international pricing is relatively limited (see Acton and Vogelsang [1992], Bewley and Fiebig [1988], Cave and Donnelly [1996], and Madden and Savage [2000]) and has not focused on the impact of competition, except for Madden and Savage. They analyze a limited number of countries and focus primarily on the thesis that prices fall as markets become more symmetric in their levels of competition and private ownership.[1]

One of the two primary hypotheses we analyze is whether prices decrease most on routes when concentration decreases the most. This hypothesis is consistent with the standard view that competition is associated with lower prices. In particular, we examine how price changes varied depending on the change in concentration on country-pair routes between 1992 and 1998. Over this time, the number of competitors and their capacities on many routes increased considerably, but to different degrees in different countries at different times. This data provides variation in all the variables of interest.

The second primary hypothesis we consider is whether there is any relationship of the dispersion between basic and flagship rates and the level of competition on a route. The differences between rates in the high-price basic plan and the low-price flagship plan can be dramatic. Calls made with a basic plan can easily cost as much as ten times more than calls made on a flagship plan. Intuitively, one might imagine this price dispersion is most likely to survive under monopolistic industry structure, but less likely to survive as the structure grows more competitive, since a competitor will likely have the incentive to offer a plan type that is, in some sense, intermediate between those of its competitors when its competitors attempt to segment the market into two or more customer types.

An increasing body of literature finds that price dispersion may exist for reasons unrelated to cost differences (see, for example, Borenstein [1985], Shepard [1991], Borenstein [1991], Borenstein and Rose [1994], and Sorenson [2000]). These papers analyze products that are relatively, but not perfectly, homogeneous and that contain multiple sellers, such as gasoline and air travel. A common theory underlying the body of work is that consumer search costs explain the price dispersion. As the expected gains from search grow, price dispersion will fall. In line with this theory, Sorenson (2000) finds that repeatedly purchased pharmaceutical prescriptions, for which one would expect the greatest benefit from search, have significantly lower price dispersion than other types of prescriptions.

Little research has focused on the relation between price dispersion and competition. Most surprisingly, Borenstein and Rose (1994) note that there is a significant positive effect of competition on price dispersion. That is, on a more competitive airline route, prices on the route tend to exhibit more dispersion. This result is particularly interesting because it suggests that price dispersion may not only exist in competitive markets but rather may on occasion be greater in competitive markets than in more monopolistic ones, contrary to the intuition above. The result is based on a cross-sectional analysis of airline fares in the second quarter of 1992.

International telecommunications data is well constructed for examining the question of whether, over time, price dispersion increases as competition increases in international long distance. In addition, the telecommunications market benefits from having a relatively simple measure of dispersion, namely the difference between flagship and basic rates, since there are two main international long distance prices offered to residential customers by a typical long distance carrier. As a result, this analysis can provide a relatively crisp characterization of the relationship between dispersion and competition.

The variable costs of providing international long distance can be measured with a relatively high degree of precision and thus their effect on price can be reasonably disentangled from the effect of concentration. Between 1992 and 1998, the long distance companies' costs of making international long distance calls have fallen dramatically in measurable ways. The cost to a long distance company of completing a call to a foreign country is made up of three primary parts: a local access charge paid to the local U.S. telephone company, the network cost of bringing the call to another country, and a per-minute settlement rate that is paid to the foreign carrier that completes the call. The settlement rate has typically been negotiated by AT&T and foreign carriers under a regulatory framework that governs the allocation of return calls between carriers and the rate paid and received by a provider for sending and receiving calls. The rate negotiated by AT&T is then applied to all U.S. carriers. From the perspective of a carrier besides AT&T, these rate changes can be viewed as exogenous cost shocks. Generally, the settlement charges constitute the vast majority of the cost of completing a call overseas.

The settlement mechanism includes a rule that when traffic is sent to the U.S. from a foreign carrier, the foreign carrier pays a per-minute settlement rate to the U.S. carrier that is equivalent to the rate the U.S. carrier pays for sending a call to the foreign carrier. In addition, the foreign carrier must return traffic to U.S. carriers in proportion to the number of minutes sent to that carrier's country by the U.S. carrier. For example, if Sprint sends 25 percent of the traffic from the U.S. to a foreign country, that foreign country's carrier must return 25 percent of its U.S.-bound traffic through Sprint. While a long distance carrier incurs charges for completing a call to a foreign country, it generates counterbalancing revenue when it receives traffic from that foreign carrier. Thus, from the

U.S. long distance carrier's perspective, the net cost of making calls overseas includes the settlement rates from both outgoing and incoming calls. Since the number of outgoing minutes from the U.S. generally exceeds the number of incoming minutes, the U.S. carriers generally face a positive per-minute cost per call.[2]

In the late 1990s, the rules governing the international settlement process changed to reflect the fact that many foreign countries had competing long distance carriers. In fact, rates to some countries (e.g., Canada) can be lower than many domestic long distance rates in the United States. The Federal Communications Commission (FCC) has recently set target settlement rates for different countries which, when achieved, allow nondominant carriers in those countries to opt out of the international settlement process. In addition, the FCC introduced in 1994 International Simple Resale (ISR) for countries that met certain competitiveness criteria within the country and which had settlement rates below particular target rates. ISR service is the provision of international switched traffic services over international private lines. ISR service allows the U.S.-originating carrier and end-country receiving carrier to avoid the traditional settlements system.

There were significant changes in the international environment over the time period of analysis, in particular with the formation of the World Trade Organization (WTO) in 1995 and with the full or partial implementation of the WTO telecommunications agreement in selected WTO countries in 1998. Clearly it is of policy interest to see whether there have been price impacts of WTO membership, so variables reflecting these changes will also be considered.

The rest of this paper is organized as follows: Section 2 discusses the competitive model. Section 3 discusses the data that is used in this paper, including the method of estimating costs, and presents descriptive statistics. Section 4 presents the empirical results. Section 5 then concludes.

2　Model

The first question considered here is whether increasing competition on a route is associated with reductions in prices on that route. The second question considered is whether price dispersion increases or decreases as competition increases. These questions implicitly assume that pricing for different country pairs is largely governed by country-specific conditions. Given that international pricing plans typically provide a set of prices for all countries, it is not obvious that separating prices on a route-by-route basis is appropriate. If we find that concentration levels on a route are related to prices on that route, then the fact that prices for international calling are typically bundled together does not imply that international calls are in fact a bundled product.

Since this study focuses on the actions of common firms in one industry facing common, route-specific cost shocks, the panel data set approach holds considerable promise. Costs are known with great precision because the vast majority of international long distance costs arise from observable, regulated settlement rates.

We might expect that, assuming constant costs, if competition increases (or concentration decreases), industry-wide prices will fall. For simplicity, we assume that this time period is exemplified primarily by changes in supply conditions, as the average cost of calls fell by about 50 percent. This assumption is most reasonable when the time period of analysis is short, the number of foreign-born residents is little changed, and the amount of U.S. trade with a foreign country is little changed.[3]

Our model relates prices over time to concentration levels over time, as well as to cost and regulatory variables. We will estimate this model in a panel framework with fixed effects for countries. That is,

$$p_{it} = \beta_0 + \beta_{1i}D_i + \beta_2 h_{it} + \beta_3 c_{it} + \beta_4 ISR_{it} + \beta_5 WTO_{it}$$

where

p_{it}: price in country i in period t
D_i: dummy set to 1 for country i
h_{it}: concentration in country i in period t
c_{it}: cost in country i in period t
ISR_{it}: ISR status dummy variable in country i in period t
WTO_{it}: WTO status dummy variables in country i in period t

The costs include the payment made by the U.S. carrier to overseas carriers for completing calls, the payments made to U.S. local carriers for originating or completing calls, and the actual physical cost to the carrier of carrying the call.

The model will be estimated for overall average prices by all U.S. carriers between 1992 and 1998.

3   Data

In order to estimate the equations above, we use measures of price, cost, concentration, the WTO status of countries, and the FCC-determined ISR status of countries. We measure price as either an average price or a plan specific price. Average price to a country is calculated by taking the domestic revenue from all international calling to a country and dividing by the number of minutes of calling to that country. Plan-specific prices detail the flagship rates of a carrier to a specific country or the basic rates charged by a carrier when consumers call a specific country.

The average price measures are calculated for the combination of all facilities-based carriers providing international telephone service, as reported in FCC international data gathered according to section 43.61 of FCC regulations (FCC 1994, 1996, 1997, 1998, 1999, and 2000). For the average data, the time period begins in 1992 because 1992 is the first year for which the FCC data is readily available.

To calculate price dispersion, we contrast flagship and basic rate data for MCI and Sprint. These data are submitted to the FCC in regular tariff filings by each carrier.[4] The flagship and basic rate comparison begins in 1994, because that is the first year the price data is readily available. International flagship rates are calculated based on the lowest marginal rate available for calls to a foreign country.[5]

The average price across all carriers for sending a call to each of the top 10 country destinations is shown for 1992 and 1998 in table 8.1. The average per-minute price fell by 60 percent over this time period. All price measures are adjusted for inflation with the CPI-U index from the Bureau of Labor Statistics (Bureau of Labor Statistics, 2000). They are then logged.

The primary data source for cost and concentration consists of the FCC international data. Between 1992 and 1998, all facilities-based carriers had to report figures for traffic carried over their international facilities, including revenues, payments, and outgoing and incoming minutes on a route-by-route basis.

In order to calculate the costs of sending traffic to a given country, we begin with the net amount paid by U.S. carriers to overseas carriers from that country and from the revenues of their return traffic from that country. From this, the cost of originating, terminating, and carrying calls to

Table 8.1
Average Price for International Long Distance Minutes to the Top 10 Countries

Country	1992 Price ($)	1998 Price ($)	Change ($)
Mexico	0.95	0.51	−0.44
Canada	0.39	0.27	−0.13
United Kingdom	0.91	0.32	−0.59
Germany	1.08	0.39	−0.69
Japan	1.32	0.40	−0.93
India	2.13	0.70	−1.43
Philippines	1.52	0.64	−0.88
Korea, South	1.46	0.69	−0.77
Dominican Republic	0.97	0.39	−0.58
China	2.02	0.77	−1.25

Source: Calculations from FCC 43.61 Data. Top 10 by revenue.
Values deflated by CPI-U to 1992 dollars.

the international meeting point is subtracted to calculate the costs for Message Telephone Service (MTS) traffic to specific countries.

The settlement costs between a carrier and the carriers of a foreign country are determined by a formula that returns traffic to the U.S.-based carrier in proportion to its share of the minutes sent to the foreign country. Thus revenues derived from incoming minutes counterbalance the costs of sending outgoing minutes. Represent the total cost to carrier i of transmitting O_i outgoing minutes to a country as C_i. Then

$$C_i = s \left(O_i - \frac{O_i}{O} I \right)$$

where

O_i = the number of outgoing minutes of carrier i
O = the total number of outgoing minutes from the U.S.
I = the total number of incoming minutes to the U.S.
s = the settlement rate

As an illustrative example, suppose that Sprint sends 50 of the United States's 200 minutes a year to France and that France send 100 minutes a year back to the U.S. Sprint then has a 25 percent share of the U.S. outgoing minutes and derives, by the rule of proportionate returns, 25 minutes in return from France.[6] Suppose the settlement rate is $1 per minute and that completing a call or originating a call costs $0.10 per minute.

The marginal cost of traffic may seem like $1. However, that ignores the fact that sending over a marginal minute increases the amount of traffic that is sent back to Sprint and that this new overseas traffic generates revenue for Sprint. For clarity, let us complete the reasoning about what Sprint's costs will be from sending traffic to France. The cost of the outgoing calls to France, for Sprint, will amount to $50 from settlement and $5 from local access and network costs. By virtue of sending 25 percent of the traffic that goes to France, Sprint will receive back 25 minutes of traffic. From these 25 minutes, it will receive revenue of $25 but experience costs of $2.50. Sprint's net cost of sending these minutes to France will then be $32.50 and Sprint's net cost per minute will be $0.65. The point of this example is that, despite the assumed settlement rate of $1.00 per minute, Sprint will act as though its marginal cost of sending traffic is considerably below this level. Thus we do not use settlement rates for calculating the cost of international traffic, but rather the difference between incoming and outgoing international revenue to a country.

The cost for originating and terminating access is derived from the FCC's table of originating and terminating charges, multiplied by the number of outgoing minutes (for the originating charge) and incoming minutes for the terminating charge. In addition, transport costs are estimated as 1 cent per minute, falling to 0.5 cents per minute by 1998. These estimates are intended to capture a known trend whose impact on route costs varied by route according to the relative traffic ratio between the United States and the country at the other end of the route. This transport cost decline assumption does not affect the results. All financial variables are adjusted for inflation with the CPI-U and then logged.

Concentration measures are calculated using the Hirschman-Herfindahl Index (HHI) and are based on minutes of traffic, as opposed to firm revenues and thus limit the direct impact of price on HHI.[7] This means the HHI is not calculated from revenue information. The HHI provides a good measure of facilities-based concentration but provides an imperfect view of firm shares in the end-consumer marketplace because the FCC reports are solely for facilities-based providers. The reports exclude resellers who might sell minutes to end-consumers, to avoid double counting of minutes. Thus, the HHI statistics provide a better measure of capacity concentration than retail concentration. In measuring potential competition between different facilities-based providers,

Table 8.2
Concentration Measures for International Long Distance Minutes to the Top
10 Countries

Country	1992 HHI	1998 HHI	Change
Mexico	5,793	3,594	–2,199
Canada	4,581	4,028	–553
United Kingdom	4,963	2,345	–2,618
Germany	5,754	2,932	–2,821
Japan	4,689	2,565	–2,124
India	4,953	3,251	–1,702
Philippines	5,348	2,644	–2,704
Korea, South	4,899	3,192	–1,707
Dominican Republic	5,716	1,839	–3,877
China	4,404	2,243	–2,161

Source: Calculations from FCC 43.61 Data.

focusing on capacity concentration may be preferable. Importantly, HHI values have exhibited substantial variation between 1992 and 1998. These values are shown in table 8.2. For these 10 countries, the average HHI has fallen by more than 2,200 points on a HHI scale of 10,000.

In addition, we include data on the ability to carry traffic over international private lines, as represented by whether the FCC has designated a country as an ISR country, and on the impact of international WTO membership of the destination country.[8] The ISR and WTO information is represented by dummy variables that are 0 in the period prior to the change and then 1 in the period of change and thereafter. For instance, if a country were among the original WTO signatories, WTO membership would be indicated by a dummy set to 1 in 1995, when the WTO agreement went into effect, 1 in later years, and 0 in years prior to 1995. Summary statistics are provided in table 8.3.

4 Data Analysis

The time period of analysis is 1992–1998. We look at the 100 countries with the most U.S.-based spending on international calling. We perform a regression that relies on a fixed-effect for each country. The estimates for a regression of logged average price on HHI and logged cost per minute are:

$$p = -0.423 + 1.006h_{it} + 0.286c_{it} - 0.236ISR_{it} - 0.099WTO_{it}$$
$$\quad\;\; (-6.65) \quad\;\; (12.34) \quad\quad (9.40) \quad\quad\;\; (-4.91) \quad\quad\quad (-5.15)$$

$R^2 = 0.63$

$n = 700$

$groups = 100$

t-statistics are in parentheses.

When considering average prices across carriers, concentration has a positive and significant relationship to price, suggesting that reductions in concentration are associated with reductions in price. These results are consistent with the view that telecommunications competition leads to lower prices for consumers, even after adjusting for changes in the costs of making telephone calls.

Apart from cost and U.S.-based concentration relationships, it is important to consider the impacts of regulatory variables. We must be cautious in the interpretation of results relating to the regulatory variables due to the difficulty of interpreting the meaning of regulatory and membership decisions.

ISR designation is associated with significantly lower prices. This may arise from the fact that ISR designations indicate a higher degree of competition in destination countries. Alternately, this might be an indication that freeing some negotiations from the strictures of the international settlements policies leads to lower costs of traffic exchange. The broadness of this conclusion is limited because the ISR-designated countries are thought to have significant domestic long distance competition. In countries without such competition, eliminating the international settlements policies may not lead to lower prices.

WTO membership appears to be associated with lower prices for international traffic. This may reflect a general pro-competition bias on the part of governments that are WTO members relative to those that are not.

Table 8.4 reports the extent of price dispersion between flagship and basic plans for MCI and for Sprint. One of the more interesting implications of this data is that basic rates are typically 2–3 times higher than flagship rates to a country. This table shows that price dispersion has increased over time while competition has also increased. These results suggest that a regression analysis of dispersion patterns may yield interesting findings. However, such empirical work is beyond the scope of the current study.

Table 8.3
Summary Statistics for 1994 and 1998

Variable	Obs	Mean	Std. Dev.	Min	Max
pri92	100	1.299	0.324	0.391	2.254
pri98	100	0.669	0.213	0.265	1.681
hhi92	100	0.598	0.121	0.378	0.999
hhi98	100	0.333	0.082	0.176	0.716
costpm92	100	0.573	0.269	0.102	1.313
costpm98	100	0.312	0.165	0.044	0.711
isr92	100	0.000	0.000	0.000	1.000
isr98	100	0.160	0.368	0.000	1.000
wto92	100	0.000	0.000	0.000	0.000
wto98	100	0.820	0.386	0.000	1.000

Dollar figures are deflated by CPI–U to 1992 dollars and not logged.

Table 8.4
Price Dispersion Between 1992 and 1998

Variable	1994	1998	Change
HHI	0.473	0.333	–0.140
MCI flagship price	0.714	0.543	–0.171
MCI basic price	1.363	1.987	0.624
MCI price dispersion	0.649	1.444	0.795
Sprint flagship price	0.828	0.546	–0.282
Sprint basic price	1.364	1.987	0.623
Sprint price dispersion	0.536	1.441	0.905

Dollar figures are deflated by CPI-U to 1992 dollars and not logged.

The finding that price dispersion has increased at a time when concentration has fallen is consistent with a carrier setting lower rates on its plan designed for the most price-elastic consumers as competition increases on a route, but at the same time raising the rates for the most inelastic consumers. The relationship between price and concentration could arise because increased competition at the low-rate side of the spectrum, due to prepaid cards, leads to lower flagship rates. As flagship rates fall, the expected benefits of search increase, leading the more price-sensitive basic rate consumers to leave for better plans. As the remaining group of basic rate consumers is more inelastic than before, it is most profitable to actually raise prices to that group at a time when concentration is generally decreasing. This suggests that at least one significant and relatively discrete set of consumers may suffer from increased levels of competition in international long distance.

Given the inverse movement of prices on the basic rate and flagship plans, it is important to consider whether, overall, increased competition hurts or helps consumers. Data limitations prevent us from knowing the quantity of minutes provided under the basic rates and under flagship plan rates. Thus, the simplest approach to answering the question of the overall impact of competition on consumers may be to examine the impact of changes in concentration on the average prices charged by a carrier. The fact that the lower average prices from providers are associated with lower concentration levels suggests that, on net, the negative impact on the basic rate consumers is outweighed by the beneficial impact on other consumers from decreased levels of concentration.

5   Conclusion

The results strongly suggest that international pricing varies on a country-by-country basis in a way that reflects the costs of sending traffic to a given country and the level of competition to that country. This finding is interesting because generally, when consumers purchase international flagship plans, they sign up for a bundle of rates to all foreign countries. Thus one might consider that international traffic should be analyzed as a bundled product. However, the pricing relationships found here suggest that it is appropriate to consider each international route individually when evaluating competition. Particularly given that much international calling is generated by foreign-born residents calling their relatives and friends in the nation of their birth, we might expect that demand for an international plan, with its bundle of prices, is frequently governed by considerations of solely one of those prices.

Given that international routes are best viewed as unbundled products, analysis of international long distance calling can help to evaluate the extent to which competitive forces are at work in a domestic setting. This is because domestic carriers are the ones competing to provide international long distance with each other, and they are competing for U.S.-based customers.

An analysis of the international data suggests that decreases in concentration are associated with lower average prices for international long distance. This initial finding certainly merits further investigation. To the extent possible, it would be desirable to analyze long distance competition for specific types of plans.

In our simple means-based analysis of plan-specific pricing, we find that pricing displays high and increasing price dispersion. During the time period under analysis, which has been a time period of reduced concentration on almost all country-specific routes, the dispersion increases between flagship plan prices and basic plan prices.[9] The fact that prices can move in opposite directions in plans offered by the same carrier suggests the complex nature of the demand for telecommunications services. More generally, however, this increased dispersion represents an interesting example of how offering a better deal for one plan, in response to competition, may shift the distribution of customers between the offered plans, so that raising prices for the other plan becomes profitable, as the consumers remaining in the other plan are, on average, less price-sensitive than before.

International long distance data holds great potential for measuring the relationship between telecommunications competition and prices. The reason is that international data allows for a panel data set analysis that involves far more variation than any purely domestic analysis could provide. While these findings relate strictly to international telephone calling, they actually reflect competition between domestic U.S. carriers to carry domestically originated international calls and thus can be viewed broadly as findings about domestic U.S. competition. Overall, these results suggest that pro-competitive policies may have beneficial impacts, whether implemented by domestic policy makers or by international organizations such as the WTO.

Acknowledgments

The opinions expressed here are those of the author and do not necessarily reflect those of the U.S. Department of Justice. I thank Joe Farrell, John Harkrider, Jim Lande, Bob Majure, Carl Willner and seminar participants at the FCC, ENST, and TPRC for their comments. Special thanks for aid with data to Linda Blake, Mark Heuritsky, Jim Lande, and Carl Willner.

Notes

1. The interpretation of their competitiveness variables is somewhat unclear since they are all multiplied by the number of minutes of traffic even though the dependent variable of price is apparently not quantity-adjusted.

2. This unusual mechanism of cost imposition was created to counterbalance the possibility that foreign carriers would charge high rates for traffic to their countries, and then negotiate low rates for return traffic with just one of the competing U.S. carriers, leading to a higher telecom trade imbalance than already exists between the United States and foreign countries (the trade imbalance for IMTS calls was about $4.8 billion in 1998 (Industry Analysis Division, 2000.) For a further discussion of the International Settlement Process, its distortions, and a proposal for a less distorted process, see Malueg and Schwartz (1998).

3. In order to maintain our assumption that changes found in this data are primarily related to supply conditions, countries where we might expect that demand conditions have changed considerably over the time period of analysis are excluded from the data set. These include Vietnam and Eastern European countries. Their exclusion, however, does not affect the results.

4. AT&T is excluded from the analysis because it changed the structure of its flagship plan significantly during the time period.

5. For years when there was time-of-day pricing, the cheapest time period was selected.

6. The U.S. almost always sends more minutes overseas than it receives.

7. The HHI is defined as the sum of the squared shares of firm output. If firm i is one of I firms and produces output q_i, then the HHI is defined by:

$$HHI = \sum_{i=1}^{I} (\frac{q_i}{\sum_{i=1}^{I} q_i})^2 .$$

8. Traffic that is carried under the ISR system is still reportable under section 43.61 of FCC regulations. Thus the data relied on for much of this analysis should reflect a complete record of reported minutes and accounting payments to foreign countries over the time period in question.

9. This finding may help to explain MacAvoy's finding of basic rate increases during periods of cost and concentration reductions, while at the same time suggesting that, on average, lower levels of concentration are indeed associated with lower rates.

References

Acton, J. P., and Vogelsang, I. (1992). Telephone demand over the atlantic: Evidence from country-pair data. *Journal of Industrial Economics,* XL, 305–323.

Bewley, R., and Fiebig, D. (1988). Estimation of price elasticities for an international telephone demand model. *Journal of Industrial Economics,* XXXVI, 393–409.

Borenstein, S. (1985). Price discrimination in free-entry markets. *Rand Journal of Economics,* 16, 380–397.

Borenstein, S. (1991). Selling costs and switching costs: Explaining retail gasoline margins. *Rand Journal of Economics,* 22, 354–369.

Borenstein, S., and Rose, N. (1994). Competition and price dispersion in the U.S. airline industry. *Journal of Political Economy,* 102, 653–683.

Bureau of Labor Statistics. (2000). CPI-U Index. web download from <http://www.bls.gov/datahome.htm>.

Cave, M., and Donnelly, M. P. (1996). The pricing of international telecommunications services by monopoly operators. Information Economics and Policy, 8, 107–123.

Edelman, S. (1997). The FCC and the decline in AT&T's long distance residential rates, 1980–1992: Did price caps do it? Review of Industrial Organization, 12, 537–553.

Federal Communications Commission. (1994). International communications traffic data for 1992. Washington, D.C.

Federal Communications Commission. (1996). International communications traffic data for 1994. Washington, D.C.

Federal Communications Commission. (1997). International communications traffic data for 1995. Washington, D.C.

Federal Communications Commission. (1998). International communications traffic data for 1996. Washington, D.C.

Federal Communications Commission. (1999). International communications traffic data for 1997. Washington, D.C.

Federal Communications Commission. (2000). International communications traffic data for 1998. Washington, D.C.

Industry Analysis Division. (2000). Trends in telephone service. Washington, D.C.

MacAvoy, P. W. (1995). Tacit collusion under regulation in the pricing of interstate long distance telephone services. Journal of Economics and Management Strategy, 4 (2), 147 185.

MacAvoy, P. W. (1996). *The failure of antitrust and regulation to establish competition in long-distance telephone services.* Cambridge, MA and Washington, D.C.: MIT Press and AEI Press.

MacAvoy, P. W. (1998). Testing for competitiveness of markets for long distance telephone services: Competition finally? *Review of Industrial Organization,* 13, 295–319.

Madden, G., and Savage, S. (2000). Market structure, competition, and pricing in United States international telephone service markets. *Review of Economics and Statistics,* 82, 291 296.

Malueg, D., and Schwartz, M. (1998). Where have all the minutes gone? Asymmetric telecom liberalization, carrier alliances, and gaming of international settlements. (Georgetown University Department of Economics,Working Paper 98-08)

Shepard, A. (1991). Price discrimination and retail configuration. *Journal of Political Economy,* 99, 30–53.

Sorenson, A. (2000). Equilibrium price dispersion in retail markets for prescription drugs. *Journal of Political Economy,* 108, 833–850.

Taylor, W. E., and Taylor, L. D. (1993). Postdivestiture long-distance competition in the united states. *American Economic Review,* 83, 185–189.

Taylor, W. E., and Zona, J. D. (1997). An analysis of the state of competition in long-distance telephone markets. *Journal of Regulatory Economics,* 11, 227–255.

9

Ownership Concentration and Product Variety in Daily Newspaper Markets

Lisa Megargle George

Introduction

Regulation of media markets in the U.S. historically emphasized content and content variety rather than consumer or advertiser prices. This focus accompanies a strong presumption that a larger numbers of owners and products in a market leads to better outcomes. Limits on the number of radio stations in a market owned by a single firm, protection of newspaper joint operating agreements, a prohibition against cross-ownership of broadcast and print media products in a market, and active antitrust enforcement against newspaper mergers all attest to this presumption.

Yet, it is far from obvious that more owners give rise to greater variety. Media markets offer differentiated products produced with large fixed costs and advertiser finance. It is well known that such markets can deliver too much, or too little, variety.[1] In economic terms, "too much" variety means duplication of fixed investments to produce products that are largely undistinguishable from each other. Duplication might arise in media markets if revenue from capturing only a fraction of one consumer type covers fixed costs, since multiple firms could earn positive profits by catering to the tastes of these consumers (Steiner, 1952). At the same time, markets can fail to provide specialized coverage. If advertising revenue obtained from targeting particular groups is less than the cost of developing new content (Spence and Owen, 1977), or if individuals in these groups are willing to consume less-preferred products (Beebe, 1977), these groups may not be served.

Ownership concentration matters because the incentives to produce variety change when firms enter and exit a market, and when firms merge.[2] Multi-product firms do not want their products to compete with each other, so mergers can lead owners to eliminate duplicative products and change the content of others. Various production economies, as well as higher revenues, brought about by consolidation can also make new content viable. For example, a newspaper owner who acquires a local competitor's paper similar to his own would likely not continue to operate both papers in their previous forms. Rather, the owner would either differentiate them by altering their content, or close one of the papers altogether. Differentiation might take the form of simply eliminating duplicative content from one paper, replacing duplicative content with new material, or shifting emphasis among reporting topics. In closing one of the papers, the owner might add content to the remaining product to prevent competitor entry into a formerly viable niche or to attract new readers. Hence even mergers that reduce the number of newspapers would not necessarily reduce content variety. The effect of ownership concentration on variety is thus an empirical question.

Despite the fact that theory alone cannot determine the effect of ownership concentration on variety, there is relatively little empirical evidence on the question. The most relevant evidence comes from Berry and Waldfogel (2001), who examine the effects of ownership concentration on programming variety in radio broadcasting. They find that consolidation triggered by the Telecommunications Act of 1996 reduced entry but increased the number of radio formats broadcast both absolutely and relative to the number of stations. In newspaper markets, a substantial literature in sociology and communications examines the relationship between ownership and content, broadly defined.[3] However, most of these studies consider small samples with cross-sectional data, producing few clear, robust results. A few papers offer suggestive evidence of the effect of ownership concentration. Lacy (1991), one of the more extensive studies in this literature, finds that chain-owned papers contain shorter articles and devote less space to news and editorial beats than independently owned papers, but that they also devote more staff resources for a given allocation of space. Hicks and Featherstone (1978) find evidence that newspapers under common ownership tend to produce less overlapping content.

A more comprehensive analysis of the effect of ownership concentration on product variety would use content measures comparable across a large sample of papers and consistent over time. George (2001) uses data on reporter assignments to characterize the amount of variety available in a market. The notion that more variety in reporter assignments corresponds to more variety in coverage is highly intuitive. Does a market have a travel editor or not? A music critic? A political analyst? The presence or absence of coverage in a particular topical area is directly related to choices available to readers and hence constitutes a reasonable measure of content variety. The results of George (2001), summarized in this chapter, reveal that a decrease in the number of owners in a market leads to an increase in the number of topical reporting beats covered per market. There is also evidence that the additional coverage brought about by consolidation increases readership. Although policy may be concerned with aspects of diversity beyond the number of topics covered by newspapers, these results suggest that from the standpoint of variety, increased concentration does not harm readers.

The chapter proceeds as follows. The first section characterizes changes in ownership concentration and product variety in daily newspaper markets over time. The second section presents empirical tests of the relationship between ownership concentration, product variety and readership in daily newspaper markets. The third section concludes the paper.

Market Characteristics

Ownership Concentration
In many ways, the effects of ownership concentration in daily newspaper markets is a study of economic history rather than modern markets. During the 20th century, the invention of substitutes for newspapers in the form of radio and television dramatically altered the audience for newspapers at the same time that technological innovation increased scale economies in production. The resulting consolidation was enormous, with the number of cities supporting competing daily newspapers declining from 502 to 137 over the years 1923 to 1943, leaving close to 90 percent of U.S. cities with local newspaper monopolies. By the early 1970s, the percentage had increased to 98 percent.[4] With only a handful of cities with competing newspapers, debate over the effects of consolidation may no longer seem relevant.

But in another sense, newspaper ownership in the U.S. is not highly concentrated. More than 1,500 daily newspapers are published by 136

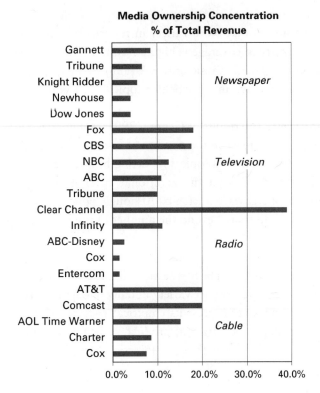

Figure 9.1
Media Ownership Concentration, Percent of Total Revenue
Source: Dirks, Van Essen & Murray, "The More Things Change. . .Top 25 Newspaper Groups 1975 vs. 2001," *Newspaper Acquisitions,* 2001.

newspaper groups and several hundred independent owners across the U.S. Today, the top five groups account for only about one third of total daily newspaper circulation. Ownership concentration in daily newspapers is also far less concentrated than in other media industries. For example, the five largest newspaper companies in the U.S. generate about 25 percent of total industry revenue, while the five largest radio firms generate about 55 percent of industry revenue. Concentration among the five largest firms in cable and broadcast television is even higher, exceeding 65 percent in both industries.[5] Ownership shares by the five largest firms in newspapers, television, radio and cable are shown in figure 9.1.

The diversity of newspaper ownership suggests that policy debate on the effects of increased concentration is not strictly academic. And although overall concentration in the market for daily newspapers is low compared to other media, the 1990s did see considerable increases in ownership concentration at the market level. The consolidation wave was fueled by a booming economy and regulatory changes in media ownership rules that altered incentives for media firms to own newspapers vis-à-vis broadcast products across markets.[6] Figure 9.2 shows the number of newspaper acquisitions each year since 1980. In all but one case, the number of newspapers changing hands each year since 1993 has exceeded the number sold each year since 1980. Unlike transactions in earlier decades, most transactions in the 1990s have been among ownership groups seeking geographic consolidation.[7] Between the start of the

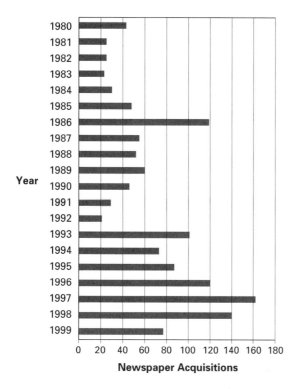

Figure 9.2
Newspaper Acquisitions per Year, 1980–1999
Source: Dirks, Van Essen & Associates, "Near-Record Number of Daily Newspapers Sold in 1996," *Newspaper Acquisitions*, 1997 and Dirks, Van Essen & Associates, "Clustering: Growing Regional Groups Retaining Readers as Industry Circulation Slips," *Newspaper Acquisitions*, 1998.

boom in 1993 and 1999, the number of owners per market decreased by about 8 percent overall and more than 15 percent in the 20 largest markets.[8]

Product Variety in Daily Newspaper Markets

What can be said about product variety in daily newspaper markets over this period? Reporter data from *Burrelle's Media Directory* can be used to characterize the types of content available at individual newspapers and newspaper markets. Burrelle's reports newspaper-level data on the assignment of reporters and editors to topical beats. The 2000 edition of the directory maps the job title of about 20,000 reporters and editors (e.g., "Travel Editor") into about 150 topical reporting beats at 1,500 daily newspapers in 1999. The 1994 *Directory* reports job titles for 1993, which can be linked individually to beat codes in the 2000 edition. For tractability, the beats identified by Burrelle's are collapsed into 50 more general beat categories, then aggregated to the market level.[9]

Figure 9.3 shows the average number of reporters per paper assigned to each consolidated beat. Figure 9.4 shows the percentage of markets in which each beat is covered in 1999. General news, sports, national news, entertainment, and opinion are the largest beats covered in all markets by virtually all papers. Topics such as business, food, fashion, and travel are also available in most markets although only at about 20–25 percent of papers. Computing, gardening, and science reporting are more specialized: coverage is available only in a few percent of papers in about half of the markets. Specialized industry coverage, arts, and multicultural reporting are produced only by a small number of reporters in the very largest markets.

It is also interesting to explore the differences between large and small papers. Figure 9.5 shows the allocation of reporters to the top 15 beats at the smallest 20 percent and largest 20 percent of daily newspapers. Staff allocations differ significantly, with small papers devoting a much larger fraction of resources to basic topics such as general news, sports, and classifieds. Larger papers assign a greater fraction of reporters to standard topics such as food and education as well as to a large number of specialty topics, listed as "other" in the figure. These differences suggest that, to the extent mergers and acquisitions produce larger papers, the number of topics covered may increase.

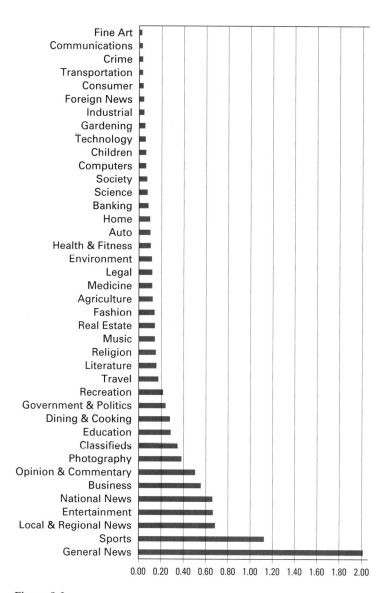

Figure 9.3

Average Reporters per Newspaper, 40 Largest Consolidated Beats (1999)

Source: George (2001).

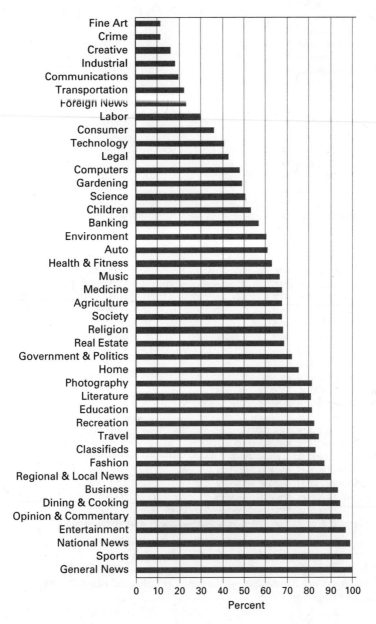

Figure 9.4
Percent of Markets Covered, 40 Largest Consolidated Beats (1999)
Source: George (2001).

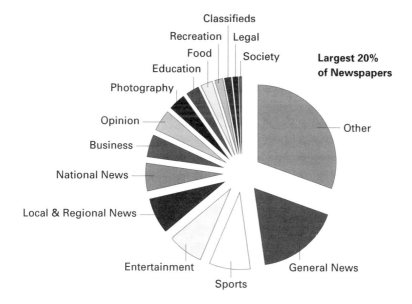

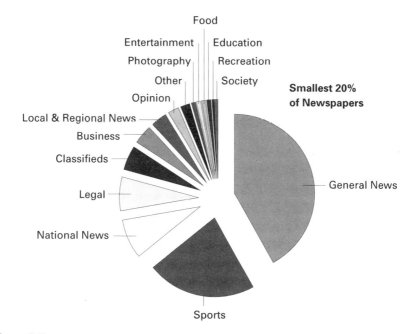

Figure 9.5
Top Beat Shares at Largest and Smallest Papers, 1999
Source: George (2001).

Table 9.1
Summary Statistics

	N	Mean	SD	5%	25%	50%	75%	95%
Newspaper Statistics (1993)								
Consolidated Beats Covered	1602	18.66	13.03	4	9	15	26	45
Newspaper Statistics (1999)								
Consolidated Beats Covered	1554	19.66	27.27	2	7	13	23	46
Market Statistics (1993)								
Consolidated Beats Covered	207	26.36	8.17	11	20	27	34	36
Total Staff	206	82.91	78.86	14	31	60	105	238
Owners	207	6.25	4.99	1	3	5	9	16
Papers	207	7.82	6.97	1	3	6	10	22
Per Capita Newspaper Sales (1995)	199	0.18	0.05	0.09	0.5	0.18	0.21	0.26
Market Statistics (1993)								
Consolidated Beats Covered	207	26.04	9.95	10	18	27	33	43
Total Staff	207	98.88	134.82	12	27	52	110	308
Owners	207	5.84	4.28	1	3	5	8	14
Papers	207	7.54	6.48	1	3	5	10	22
Per Capita Newspaper Sales	199	0.17	0.05	0.09	0.14	0.17	0.20	0.25

Table 9.1 summarizes product-level beat data as well as market-level measures of variety and ownership concentration in 1993 and 1999. The smallest papers cover only about 2–4 beats, while the largest cover about 45. At the market level, the smallest markets cover about 10 beats and the largest about 200. Some changes over time are evident in the data. The total number of papers drops from 1,602 to 1,554 over the time period of the study, although the average number of papers per market drops only slightly, from 7.82 to 7.54. The average number of owners

per market drops from 6.35 in 1993 to 5.84 in 1999, with larger changes in larger markets. The average number of beats covered per paper increases slightly from 18.66 to 19.66 but remains stable at the market level at about 26 beats covered per market.

Analysis and Results

Combining the ownership and beat data from Burrelle's produces a market-level panel that can be used to determine whether ownership concentration leads to greater product variety. Regressing the number of beats covered in a market on the number of owners and a dummy variable for each market shows the effect of changes in the number of owners on changes in beats covered.[10] Table 9.2 presents results. The first column shows the effect of changes in owners, and the second shows the effect of changes in owners controlling for changes in the number of newspapers. Both coefficients on ownership are negative and significant. The magnitude of the estimate indicates that the loss of one owner in a market increases the number of topics covered by about 1 beat. With an average of about 26 beats per market, this represents an increase of about 4 percent. Controlling for changes in the number of papers does not alter the results. It is worth emphasizing that the results in table 9.2 are driven by changes in the number of *owners*, not papers, as the effect of papers is small and insignificant. Ownership concentration appears to increase the amount of variety available in a market.

Table 9.2
Does Ownership Concentration Increase Variety?

	Number of Consolidated Reporting Beats Covered, 1993–1999	
	(1)	(2)
Owners	−1.034	-0.985
	(3.60)***	(3.32)***
Papers	−0.152	
	(0.54)	
Constant	32.390	33.334
	(18.52)***	(14.12)***
Market Fixed Effect	Yes	Yes
DMA's	207	207

Note: T-statistics in parentheses: *** significant at 1% level.

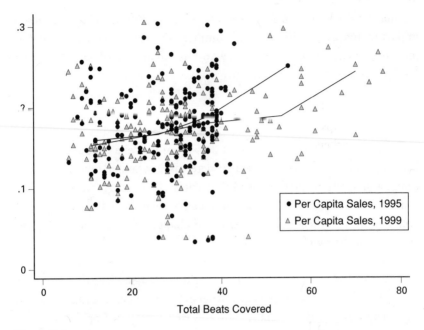

Figure 9.6
Per Capita Newspaper Sales and Number of Beats Covered; 1995, 1999
Source: George (2001).

The fact that fewer owners in a market leads to greater variety suggests that individuals benefit from increased ownership concentration. However it is often argued that the additional variety associated with larger papers is less valuable than duplicative coverage from different sources, which may be a source of viewpoint diversity rather than content diversity.[11] One way of examining the extent to which individuals value the additional content made possible by more concentrated ownership is by studying the effect of ownership concentration on readership. If readers value new variety, readership should increase. If readers value the duplicative content available in less concentrated markets, then readership should decline with concentration.

As a first step in examining the relationship between ownership concentration and readership, it is helpful to look at the relationship between variety and readership graphically. Figure 9.6 shows the relationship between per capita newspaper sales and total content variety for 1995 and 1999 using circulation data from the Audit Bureau of

Circulations' *Circulation Data Bank* (circulation data for 1993 are not available).[12] The relationship appears positive, suggesting that additional content can attract readers to a market.[13]

The relationship between ownership concentration and readership can be studied directly by regressing per capita newspaper sales in each market in 1995 and 1999 on the number of owners and a market fixed effect. Regression results show that losing one owner in a market increases per capita circulation by 0.0028. With average readership at about 0.19, this is an increase of about 1.5 percent. The effect is similar with a control for the number of newspapers in the market, and again it is the number of owners that matters rather than the number of papers. Although the effect of ownership concentration on readership is small, there appears to be no evidence that ownership concentration *reduces* readership. The fact that consolidation increases readership tends to suggest that individuals value the variety that emerges from ownership consolidation.

Conclusion

The results presented in this chapter demonstrate that increases in ownership concentration lead firms to increase content variety available in daily newspapers. Moreover, this additional coverage may extend markets to new readers. Since new readers that enter the market are better off and existing readers benefit from additional choice, consumers do not appear to be harmed by consolidation.

With respect to current policy, results presented here suggest that government intervention to increase the number of media products and media owners within markets may be unnecessary. To the extent that policy is concerned with aspects of diversity other than those associated with content variety, these results identify a benefit of concentration against which other potential costs should be weighed. However, this work challenges the notion that preserving multiple viewpoints necessarily makes consumers better off. If redundant coverage is valuable, then loss of owners in a market should reduce total readership. Since there is no evidence for readership decline, individuals do not appear to be made worse off by consolidation. Arguments that ownership diversity generates external political and social benefits depend ultimately on consumption as well, hence the presence of externalities is not sufficient to justify intervention.

However despite evidence that ownership concentration has not harmed consumers, it is not possible to conclude from this research alone that current policies are misguided. First, this work considers the effect of concentration on consumers only. Nothing can be said about aggregate welfare without taking into account how ownership concentration affects advertising prices, hence policies limiting consolidation may still be warranted when advertiser welfare is taken into account. It also might be the case that increases in ownership concentration and coverage in newspaper markets in the 1990s are related to heightened competition with radio and cable television over this period. Although these results are consistent with findings in the literature that ownership concentration in radio produces greater programming variety, little work has been done to examine competition across media directly and it remains an important area for further research.

In sum, regulation of media markets in the U.S. and antitrust policy in particular presume that more owners and more products lead to greater content variety. However the effect of concentration on variety in differentiated product markets is an empirical question that depends on fixed costs and the value of consumers to advertisers. The analyses summarized here suggest that concentration in newspaper markets does not, in fact, harm consumers. Policies that prevent consolidation in media markets may thus be unwarranted.

Notes

1. The tendency for differentiated product markets to produce too much or too little variety is considered in Spence (1976a, 1976b) and Dixit and Stiglitz (1977).

2. Hotelling (1929) provides a foundation for the literature on product positioning. Spence (1976a, 1976b) and Dixit and Stiglitz (1977) form the basis of the theoretical literature on product variety. For theoretical applications in media markets, see Anderson and Coate (2000). Empirical implications of theoretical work on product positioning and product variety are explored in Waldfogel (1999) and George and Waldfogel (2000).

3. See Compaine (1995) for a useful review of the communications literature on ownership and content.

4. See Compaine (1980) and Neiva (1995) for more comprehensive historical analysis. See Genesove (1999) for further investigation of the effects of technological change on newspaper markets.

5. Data on ownership concentration across media are taken from Dirks, Van

Essen, & Murray, "The More Things Change . . . Top 25 Newspaper Groups 1975 vs. 2001," *Newspaper Acquisitions, 2001.*

6. Consolidation was driven in part by regulatory changes. For example, in 1993 Congress eliminated restrictions on the FCC's ability to amend rules prohibiting newspaper owners from operating broadcast stations in the same market. In the same year, the FCC granted the first permanent waiver of newspaper cross-ownership rules to Fox Television Stations, Inc., allowing cross-ownership of WNYW-TV and the *New York Post.* The Telecommunications Act of 1996 relaxed limits on the number of jointly owned radio stations that could be licensed per market, unleashing a wave of consolidation in radio that further altered incentives for media firms to own newspapers *vis-à-vis* broadcast products across markets.

7. Transaction details are taken from Dirks, Van Essen & Associates, "Near-Record Number of Daily Newspapers Sold in 1996," *Newspaper Acquisitions,* p. 2, 1997 and Dirks, Van Essen & Associates, "Clustering: Growing Regional Groups Retaining Readers as Industry Circulation Slips," Newspaper Acquisitions, p. 2, 1998.

8. Ownership changes are calculated from data published in *Burrelle's Media Directory.* See George (2001).

9. George (2001) reports results for all beats as well as the consolidated categories. Also, note that the market definition used here is the Designated Market Area (DMA), a market measure defined by Nielsen Media Research and commonly used in the media industry. DMA's are similar to metropolitan statistical areas (MSA) in that they include a city and neighboring suburbs. However, unlike MSA's, DMA definitions remain stable over time and encompass rural areas, which makes them more tractable for empirical research.

10. If unobserved preferences for newspaper content across markets remain constant over time, this approach produces unbiased estimates of the effect of changes in the number of owners or owner-equivalents on changes in differentiation or variety. George (2001) treats the case of unobserved determinants of variety that vary over time with instrumental variables regressions. Results are consistent with those shown here.

11. Advocates of strong media regulation often distinguish variety in content or programming from viewpoint diversity. See, for example, the response to FCC's *Notice of Inquiry on the Commission's Newspaper/Radio Cross-Ownership Waiver Policy* by a coalition of minority interest groups, *Comments Of Black Citizens For A Fair Media et al.,* MM Docket no. 96–197 dated February 7, 1997.

12. Readership data from the Audit Bureau of Circulations are not available for 1993 and are incomplete in some markets. Incomplete markets are excluded from the analyses.

13. Regression results in George (2001) confirm that coverage of 10 additional beats in a market appears to increase newspaper sales per capita by only 0.003, a small but positive effect.

References

Anderson, Simon P., and Stephen Coate. 2000. "Market Provision of Public Goods: The Case of Broadcasting." NBER Working Paper 7513.

Audit Bureau of Circulations. 1999. *Circulation Data Bank.* New York: Audit Bureau of Circulations.

Becker, Gary S., and Kevin M. Murphy. 1993. "A Simple Theory of Advertising as a Good or Bad." *Quarterly Journal of Economics* 108:941–64.

Beebe, Jack H. 1977. "Institutional Structure and Program Choices in Television Markets." *Quarterly Journal of Economics* 91:15–37.

Berry, Steven T., and Joel Waldfogel. 2001. "Mergers, Station Entry, and Programming Variety in Radio Broadcasting." *Quarterly Journal of Economics* 116:1009–25.

Burrelle's Information Services. *Burrelle's Media Directory.* Livingston, N.J.: Burrelle's Information Services. 1994, 1996, 2000 editions.

Compaine, Benjamin M. 1980. *The Newspaper Industry in the 1980s: An Assessment of Economics and Technology.* White Plains, N.Y.: Knowledge Industry Publications.

Compaine, Benjamin M. 1982. *Who Owns the Media?: Concentration of Ownership in the Mass Communications Industry.* White Plains, N.Y.: Knowledge Industry Publications.

Compaine, Benjamin M. 1995. "The Impact of Ownership on Content: Does it Matter?" *Cardozo Arts & Entertainment Law Journal* 13:755–75.

Dixit, Avinash K., and Joseph E. Stiglitz. 1977. "Monopolistic Competition and Optimum Product Diversity." *American Economic Review* 67:297–308.

Genesove, David. 1999. "The Adoption of Offset Presses in the Daily Newspaper Industry in the United States." NBER Working Paper 7076.

George, Lisa M. 2001. "What's Fit to Print: The Effect of Ownership Concentration on Product Variety in Daily Newspaper Markets." Michigan State University. Mimeo.

George, Lisa M., and Joel Waldfogel. 2000. "Who Benefits Whom in Daily Newspaper Markets?" NBER Working Paper 7944.

Hicks, Ronald G., and James S. Featherstone. 1978. "Duplication of Newspaper Content in Contrasting Ownership Situations." *Journalism Quarterly* 55:549–69.

Hotelling, Harold. 1929. "Stability in Competition." *Economic Journal* 39:41–57.

Lacy, Stephen. 1987. "The Effect of Intracity Competition on Daily Newspaper Content." *Journalism Quarterly* 64:281–301.

Lacy, Stephen. 1999. "Effects of Group Ownership on Daily Newspaper Content." *Media Economics* 35:35–55.

Spence, Michael. 1976. "Product Selection, Fixed Costs, and Monopolistic Competition." *Review of Economic Studies* 43:217–35.

Spence, Michael. 1976. "Product Differentiation and Welfare." *American Economic Review* 66:407–14.

Spence, Michael, and Bruce Owen. 1977. "Television Programming, Monopolistic Competition, and Welfare." *Quarterly Journal of Economics* 91:103–26.

Steiner, Peter O. 1952 "Program Patterns and the Workability of Competition in Radio Broadcasting." *Quarterly Journal of Economics* 66:194–223.

Waldfogel, Joel. 1999. "Preference Externalities: An Empirical Study of Who Benefits Whom in Differentiated Product Markets." NBER Working Paper 7391.

IV

The Future of Wireless Communications

10

Best Effort versus Spectrum Markets: 802.11 versus 3G?

Lee McKnight, William Lehr, and Raymond Linsenmayer

Introduction

This chapter compares two models for delivering broadband wireless services: best effort vs. QoS (Quality of Service) guaranteed services, such as cellular telephone services. We further focus on the differing "market" versus "engineering" philosophies implicit in alternative wireless service architectures—and visions for the future.

We focus on two particular types of wireless technology: 3G which stands for Third Generation Cellular[1] and Wi-Fi which is the popular name for the wireless local area network technology 802.11b. Interest in these two technologies is warranted because of the substantial global investment in each technology by customers and providers interested in supporting wireless access to data services. To date, most of the investment in 3G has been in acquiring spectrum licenses; while most of the investment in Wi-Fi has been in deploying wireless local area network infrastructure. 3G represents the preferred solution for vertically integrated cellular providers seeking to extend their voice services into the world of integrated voice and data services; Wi-Fi is a popular wireless local area networking technology that has been widely deployed by businesses and more recently by consumers, and even more recently, is being used to offer wireless access to the Internet in a growing number of locations. The success of either of these technologies as the dominant mode for providing wireless Internet could result in quite different industry and market structures for wireless services. Exploring this landscape is one of the goals of this paper.

The question this chapter asks is whether (i) 3rd generation wireless services, as embodied in the planned and soon to be offered services emerging first in Asia and Europe, or (ii) the unlicensed wireless services such as Wi-Fi (as well as other more advanced but still evolving technologies such as Ultrawideband (UWB) which are being experimented with primarily in North America) offer more compelling visions for advanced wireless services. The visions are empirically tested in part through a cost model of a mobile virtual network operator seeking to operate in Europe. For advanced unlicensed wireless services such as wideband, the chapter can only speculate as to the costs at this time. Wideband is still under development through among other things U.S. Defense Advanced Research Project Agency initiatives, and is not yet available for commercial services. Nonetheless, hopefully the speculation and contrast with the (soon-to-be) known realities of 3G services will help highlight emerging cost and policy issues.

First, the chapter reviews the alternative wireless technologies in question. Then a cost model is presented that explores the viability of a Virtual Mobile Network Operator in Europe. The European market was selected for analysis because of the high level of demand for wireless services there, and the relative maturity of its secondary spectrum market mechanisms in specific cases. The chapter then offers conclusions and policy recommendations to accelerate development of new technology to provide viable alternatives for packing more uses and users in the same wireless space, on a "best effort" and/or market basis.

Comparison of 3G versus 802.11

3G ands Wi-Fi technologies have fundamental technical differences, due to the different design objectives of their developers. 3G is a mobile cellular technology that stresses ubiquitous coverage and continuous mobility, which imposes severe restrictions on the available bandwidth. In contrast, Wi-Fi is a local area network technology that offers much higher bandwidth but only over short distances. For example, Wi-Fi supports up to 10Mbps within 300 feet of the base station; and, coverage is typically limited to at most a campus-wide environment (via the linking of multiple base stations). In contrast, 3G systems are expected to offer 100–400 Kbps rates over the serving area of the cellular provider, which may be quite extensive.[2]

Although the two technologies appear to address quite separate market niches—3G for mobile, ubiquitous access and Wi-Fi for wireless local network access—both could provide the basis for competing services that could support quite different industry structures and philosophies for network architectures.

In spite of their obvious differences, there are a number of ways in which the two technologies are similar. First, one could ask about which problem each of these technologies solves, and in what sense these problems are comparable. Both are wireless, which facilitates mobility— broadly construed as the ability to move devices around without having to move cables and furniture. However, 3G is about real mobility (staying connected while traveling in a car across large geographic distances), whereas 802.11b is about local connectivity (conceived as a one-cell technology).

Both are access or edge-network technologies, which means they are alternatives for the last-mile. Beyond the last-mile, both rely on similar network connections. For 3G, this constitutes wireless access to the cell base station, and then a dedicated landline connection to the carrier's router. For 802.11b, this means wireless connectivity to the base station, and then perhaps shared wireline or dedicated wireline service to the ISP hub. Finally, both offer broadband data service, which can be broadly defined as "faster than what we had before" and with potential for "always on." The 3G operator's bandwidth is much more limited than that for an 802.11 operator, except in the unlikely situation where it is used in a fixed wireless mode, which is beyond the scope of this chapter.

How are the two technologies different? This question can be answered most readily by looking at their current business models and deployment strategies. 3G is an extension of the cellular service provider model, which upgrades existing 2G digital mobile voice infrastructure to 3G digital infrastructure and is capable of delivering voice and data services at speeds ranging from 144kbps to 2Mbps (with the latter option only feasibly in fixed mobile applications). 802.11b, by contrast, is an extension of the Ethernet-family of 10Mbps LAN technologies to wireless networks supporting wireless connections at distances up to 300 feet. 3G will require the purchase of additional customer equipment, whereas 802.11b might piggyback on the business deployment of WLANs (Wireless Local Area Networks).

The status of technology development is also quite different. 3G is still projected (the first actual 3G service was started in Japan by DoCoMo in October 2001), while 802.11b is real and emerging. There are lots of business and, increasingly, home wireless LANs currently using the latter technology, with some pay-for-use services (Mobilstar) currently in operation, and roll-outs for more underway (Starbucks). 3G is based on an international standards effort to provide a smooth evolution from existing 2G digital mobile wireless technologies, and includes technologies such as WCDMA, CDMA 2000, and UMTS. The guidelines are specified by the ITU in its IMT–2000 report.

Although the standards picture is clearer in the 3G realm, there is some confusion about which technologies will be adopted in different parts of the world and deployments of 3G networks are only now beginning in Asia and Europe. Chaos is greatest in the United States, where there is less harmony among existing 2G infrastructures. In contrast, Wi-Fi or 802.11b is a specified standard from the IEEE (part of the evolving Ethernet family of standards) and is already incorporated in mass-market products. Although interoperability among 802.11b devices is assured, there are compatibility and co-existence issues associated with 802.11b, which is broadly thought of as one many in the class of WLAN technologies, which includes HomeRF and BlueTooth.

3G is more developed than Wi-Fi with respect to potential business and service models because it represents an extension of existing service provider offerings into new services, but does not represent a radical departure from underlying industry structure. In contrast, there have been only limited experiments with carriers offering wireless LAN services to consumers. The upstream equipment supplier markets, and ultimate consumer demand are undeveloped and unproven with 3G, although the identity of likely equipment manufacturers is well known.

802.11b is more developed from the perspective of upstream supplier markets of equipment for WLANs because of the extensive deployment of this technology and sister-Ethernet technologies in LANs in both home and commercial networking environments. However, the commercialization of 802.11b as a platform for commercial services is largely untried. 3G access devices will include mobile phones, PDAs, and other devices for which power may be more of an issue. However, PCMIA cards will also support wireless PC access. 802.11b was first deployed in PC's but is now also extending to the same types of devices as 3G.

Spectrum policy and management will, of course, be one of the most critical factors in determining the success or failure of the technologies in

Best Effort / Unlicensed Nomadic		Spectrum Market-Based Mobile		
Wide-Area Shared Spectrum	Local Area Shared Spectrum	Licensed/Bought Spectrum	Secondary Spectrum Market	Service Level Agreement/ e-services Trading
(ultra)Wideband	Wi-Fi/802.11	2G (bundled)	3G MVNOs	4G (?)

Figure 10.1
Where Is the Wireless Grid Going to Come From?

question. The contrast here is stark: 3G uses licensed spectrum; 802.11b uses shared spectrum. This has important implications for (i) cost of service, (ii) QoS and congestion management, and (iii) industry structure. These differences are graphically summarized in the figure below.

The spectrum license required for 3G services gives the operator exclusive property rights to the spectrum. This makes it feasible for them to support QoS guarantees that are essential for the commercial viability of services such as telephony and data—although for data, QoS may be more flexibly construed. In essence, the spectrum management paradigm gives the licensee a right not to be interfered with when transmitting in its licensed spectrum allocation. Restrictions on licenses help facilitate the enforcement of these property rights. They define the services to be offered and the types of devices to be used, among other things, which helps assure the licensee that it will be able to operate without molestation in the licensed bandwidth for tasks for which license was granted. Where exclusive ownership exists, it is easy to determine who is at fault when interference is an issue.

In contrast, Wi-Fi—or 802.11b—is a wireless local area network technology that uses shared spectrum in the ISM band. The Ethernet local area network technology that underlies Wi-Fi has been deployed extensively for business networking for many years and is a mature technology. Because Wi-Fi uses shared, unlicensed spectrum, users do not have exclusive property rights and so congestion is a potential problem. The interference paradigm associated with operating on an unlicensed basis, requires all users to tolerate background noise, and limits each user's contribution to this background noise (chiefly via power limits). With more users, more congestion and more interference, this conflicts with a carriers' ability to offer QoS guarantees.

Those who dismiss the potential challenge from shared spectrum services such as 802.11 would do well to keep the advantages of distributed systems such as the Internet in mind. In general, the rapidly falling cost of computation makes it cost-effective to spread intelligence throughout a system. Further, distributed systems can offer increased fault tolerance and need not be restricted to local areas. One example of a wide area technology now under development is Ultra Wideband. Ultrawideband radios, also known as "carrier-free" or "impulse" radios, are characterized by transmission and reception of short bursts of radio frequency (RF) energy (typically on the order of fractions of nanoseconds in duration) and by the resultant broad spectral bandwidth. (DARPA, 2001) Wideband and UWB may offer potential advantages such as: immunity to multi-path cancellation, low probability of detection with low energy density transmissions, enhanced penetration capability with the presence of low frequency spectral content, and minimized hardware complexity. (DARPA, 2001) UWB radios may also take advantage of the capabilities being developed for software radios to create highly resilient and scalable networks. Admittedly, this technology is not yet proven to have commercial advantages and provokes a number of challenges to current spectrum policy in the United States and worldwide, not least because it might introduce noise into radio systems involuntarily sharing their spectrum with wideband users.

In this chapter we can only identify this technology and policy issue as one likely to increase in importance over time, as both local and wide area wireless networks premised on spectrum sharing grow in number and importance in military and consumer markets alike. Can the spectrum market-based alternatives to spectrum sharing systems withstand the challenge? The next section of this chapter reports some preliminary results of the viability of secondary spectrum markets. Our findings are not encouraging.

Case for Secondary Spectrum Markets

The European Community has begun to develop and implement several comprehensive plans for effectively managing spectrum, based on the increased demand for new services. It has recognized that the best way to realize the maximum benefits from radio spectrum is to permit and promote the operation of market forces in determining how spectrum is used. A principal tenet of this market-based approach is that in order for competition to bring to consumers the highest valued services in the most efficient manner, competing users of spectrum need flexibility to respond to market forces and demands.

One suggested method for increasing the efficiency of spectrum use and providing the much-needed flexibility is through the development of secondary markets. With a functioning system of secondary markets, licensees would be able to trade unused spectrum capacity, either by leasing it on a long-term basis (if their own infrastructure is not yet developed) or by selling spare capacity during off-peak periods.

The resulting efficiency gains would effectively increase the amount of spectrum available for users. This would allow for the development of new services and technologies that would otherwise not be available, increasing competition in the marketplace. In addition, as licensees adopt newer digital technologies, they are likely to become more efficient and have additional capacity that can be sold in secondary markets. Facilitating the leasing of spectrum would introduce economic incentives to develop efficient technologies, as licensees will be able to sell spectrum freed by the efficiency gains. The presence of secondary markets makes it more profitable for licensees to be spectrum efficient.

Although there is a general scarcity of spectrum, existing allocations of spectrum are not always used efficiently.[3] There are multiple reasons for this. In some cases, it is the result of legacy technology that reflects the state of the art at the time when the licenses were awarded rather than current technology that is capable of using existing spectrum much more efficiently. Moreover, a licensee's business plan, even when taking future growth into consideration, may not encompass some portion of its assigned frequencies or geographic service area. In establishing a new service, a licensee may not need to use its entire spectrum allocation for a period of several years as it grows its customer and operating base. A licensee may also initially face problems in equipment availability, which will affect its ability to rapidly build out services.

Secondary markets could improve welfare by allowing spectrum to be transferred to its most efficient use. For 3G, secondary markets could

---

The core elements for an efficient spectrum market are:

- A large number of buyers and sellers to create competition necessary for an efficient market
- Clearly defined rights to the spectrum for both buyers and sellers
- Free entry and exit to the secondary markets
- Fungibility of spectrum
- Availability of relevant information to all buyers and sellers
- A mechanism to bring buyers and seller together and facilitate the transaction with reasonable administrative costs and time delay.

Source: FCC, 2000

Figure 10.2
Regulatory Issues in Secondary Spectrum Markets

allow more flexible management of property rights, which could aid in the dynamic reallocation of spectrum rights. For 802.11b, by contrast, secondary markets could help create property rights that are needed to manage QoS. As soon as congestion becomes an issue, the question becomes how to allocate scarce bandwidth and assigning exclusive but transferable property rights may offer one way to address the allocation issue.

Moreover, the technical foment demonstrated by the vibrancy of 802.11b, and the market experiments that may be failing with HomeRF, BlueTooth, LMDS, and other wireless technologies that have seen ups and downs in the marketplace points to the need for the ability to more flexibly reallocate spectrum across technologies, and to be agnostic (as policymakers) about what wireless technology will be best in last mile.

Finally, secondary markets or license flexibility may be useful in developing integrated approaches that might link both technologies (for example, integrated services that uses 3G for control channel and 802.11b for high speed file transfer when available).

Creating viable secondary markets for spectrum will not be easy. Current licensees will be reluctant to participate unless a number of important issues are resolved, including the following: If they lease or resell their unused spectrum, will the government be able to reclaim that spectrum? If they wish to reclaim their spectrum from the buyer but the buyer does not agree, what are the rules? Potential buyers have their own concerns as well. Spectrum can have a major effect on competition. If there were no sellers, would regulators force licensees to offer fallow spectrum for sale? After substantial investment in a network, do buyers have any protection from sellers suddenly reclaiming the spectrum? These are issues that need to be addressed before firms will participate in a secondary spectrum market. An ideal secondary market should be timely, nondiscriminatory, transparent, with carefully crafted rules for license transfers.[4]

To increase the fungibility of spectrum, regulators or businesses may need to standardize spectrum-trading contracts to some extent. Possible attributes include Quality of Service (QOS), bandwidth, frequency bands and time blocks. A new technology that promises to improve the fungibility of spectrum is the "software defined" radio, which would enable devices to use different frequency bands flexibly. Buyers can buy spectrum of any frequency, letting the communications device adjust the frequency used as needed.

To minimize the administrative costs and processing time, modification of certain regulations will be necessary. For one, the requirement for licensees to be responsible for all content on their frequency bands, which would imply even the content of the party they are leasing the bands to, needs to be changed. The requirement for every lease transaction to have the approval of the regulatory body is another impediment to secondary markets. Spectrum has always been a closely regulated resource, and changes are needed to ease some of the regulations.

In Europe, spectrum trading does exist in a limited form. In these transactions, licenses are transferred from one party to another in exchange for some form of consideration as a result of a contract. Spectrum lease or resale contracts are private contracts negotiated by sellers and buyers with very specific agreements on frequency band, time period, and service area. These highly customized contracts have little fungibility and cannot be traded between multiple parties. Buyers and sellers generally contact each other directly, or might use the services of a broker who has the necessary industry knowledge.

Secondary Spectrum Market Pricing Model for Mobile Virtual Network Operators (MVNOs)

License holders, which have historically concentrated on selling a single voice product, will now need to develop, market, and package a much larger range of advanced applications.[5] Offering the full range of mobile commerce, entertainment, banking, shopping, information, and other services from which the majority of 3G revenues will come, will require very different sets of skills and expertise. In order to meet this demand, access these markets, and maximize their 3G revenues, license holders may have a strong incentive to lease parts of their spectrum wholesale to value added resellers called Mobile Virtual Network Operators (MVNOs), which can serve these specific market segments more efficiently and profitably than the license holders themselves.

MVNOs can be defined in a variety of ways based on technical and marketing-based factors. The Yankee Group, for example, classifies MVNOs as service operators that (i) do not own their own spectrum, and (ii) have no radio transport infrastructure. MVNOs do, however, have complete control over (iii) their SIM cards, (iv) branding, (v) marketing and promotion, (vi) billing, and (vii) all customer-facing services.[6] Ovum similarly defines an MVNO as "a network operator in a GSM environment that provides its own SIM card, or, in a non-GSM network, an entity that creates a unique subscriber ID."[7] To date, however, MVNOs have settled for adopting a mere branding approach, just to get into the game. This may continue. The future for MVNOs, according to one analyst, is "brand, service, customer base, (and a) sophisticated billing system."[8]

An important feature of MVNOs is that customers are unable to tell the difference between the virtual operator and the host-network operator in terms of network performance and service. The MVNO adds value by usually having a strong brand name, and understanding its potential customer base better than the host network operator itself. This allows the MVNO to target specific customer segments, and to "repackage" the services of an existing network operator for that segment. The MVNO buys managed network capacity from the host network operator, and presents itself to customers as a fully fledged operator." MVNOs are distinguished from mere service providers as the former typically handle its own billing, while the latter simply resell bulk airtime from the operator."[9]

The original aim of the secondary spectrum market model was to obtain an estimate for the price of 3G spectrum in secondary markets in Europe. Examining a value chain for the provision of mobile services, the firms in the industry can be divided by their functional roles into two categories, bandwidth suppliers and mobile network operators. Bandwidth

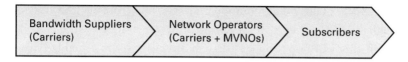

Figure 10.3
The Mobile Service Industry Value Chain

suppliers control the infrastructure of mobile services. They own the licenses to the spectrum and operate the cell sites. Traditional carriers such as AT&T fall under this category. Mobile network operators (MNOs) provide the content and services, both voice and data, to subscribers. Traditional carriers generally provide voice services and they fall into this category. Mobile Virtual Network Operators (MVNOs), such as Virgin Mobile, have neither spectrum nor infrastructure of their own, but provide mobile services through leasing agreements with carriers, and are MNOs as well.

In a secondary spectrum market, bandwidth suppliers would lease the spectrum they own to the MNOs. The price of spectrum would be the price which bandwidth suppliers sell spectrum to MNOs for. Even for traditional carriers (which span both categories), there would presumably be transfer pricing between the infrastructure division and their mobile services division.[10]

We constructed two different models to determine the range for spectrum pricing.[11] For simplicity, we refer to bandwidth suppliers as carriers. In the carrier model, the various costs of carriers are used to find the effective cost of supplying spectrum. The MNO model looks at both revenues and costs, to find the maximum price MNOs can pay for spectrum. These two models provide a lower and higher bound for market prices.

The models focus on the countries in the European Union, in particular those that have already issued 3G licenses.[12] Spectrum licenses can be a major cost component for carriers, and varies widely from country to country. For example, Sweden issued its 3G licenses for only a nominal registration fee, while Germany's 3G auctions raised $46.2 billion. Licensing costs are too large to ignore and too different to predict, hence only countries that have completed their licensing process were considered in the model. The dominant technology in Europe is W-CDMA and almost all carriers will be using this form of 3G technology. Costs used in the model were based upon a W-CDMA architecture.

The models make no assumptions on how spectrum will be traded, although they assume that spectrum can be traded without cost. Although this will not be likely (or will at least require a highly developed secondary market), the nascent secondary spectrum markets in Europe do not allow an accurate estimation of costs. As a simplification, the price of spectrum has been assumed to be constant over time. Dynamic pricing may be more accurate, but it is difficult to take into account the losses firms have to bear in the first few years. Static pricing only holds when the relationship between demand and supply is constant, that is, that carriers are predicting spectrum demand with high accuracy, and are building infrastructure based on these predictions.

Carrier Model Methodology
The aim of the carrier cost model is to determine the cost of supplying spectrum. Specifically, it calculates the minimum cost per Mbyte the carrier has to charge to recoup its investment over a ten-year period,[13] under a specified profit margin. This provides a lower bound for spectrum prices in secondary markets, below which carriers would be operating at a loss. It does not determine an actual market price, since carriers could charge higher prices depending on market demand.

The model starts with the basic profit equation, where

Profits   = Revenues—Costs

Revenues   = Gross Margin* Costs

             = Gross Margin* [Infrastructure Costs + Operating
                   Expenses + Spectrum Licensing Costs]

Since the carriers are defined with spectrum sales as their only source of revenue, the equation can be expressed as

Q* P   = Gross Margin* [Infrastructure Costs + Operating
                   Expenses + Spectrum Licensing Costs]

P   = Gross Margin* [Infrastructure Costs + Operating
                   Expenses + Spectrum Licensing Costs] / Q

Where Q is the quantity of spectrum sold (measured in Mbytes) and P is price per Mbyte (measured in U.S. dollars). Each of the terms is described below.

P This is the price per Mbyte, expressed in U.S. dollars that the carrier has to charge to recoup its costs and meet a specified gross margin target. This value is calculated by the model and is assumed to be constant over time.

Gross Margin This represents the profit target of the carriers, expressed as a percentage. It is a constant specified in the model.

Infrastructure Costs This is the cost of constructing network infrastructure, after amortization. The infrastructure required is based upon projected subscriber numbers[14] and cell buildout. Component costs were assumed to decrease by 10 percent each year. Capital costs are amortized at 6 percent. The cost is expressed in Net Present Value (NPV) form.

Operating Expenses Operating expenses for carriers can be divided into two categories, cell maintenance and general operating expenses. Cell maintenance expenses are based upon the number of cell sites, while general operating expenses were calculated in terms of subscribers. Due to difficulty in obtaining operating expenses for specific items, which generally falls under proprietary information, an aggregate general operating expense per subscriber was used instead. Data was obtained from publicly available industry information. The expense is expressed in NPV form.

Spectrum Licensing Costs This is the price that carriers have paid to obtain 3G licenses in Europe. The information is publicly available from government websites.

Q This is weighted sum of data traffic sold from 2001 to 2010. A weighted sum was used to measure Q in a magnitude equivalent to the other terms of the equation (which are in NPV form).

Subscribers Subscriber projections up to 2004 were obtained from Forrester Research.[15] Detailed projections for individual countries after 2004 were not available, but were instead extrapolated from UMTS-Forum reports.

Cell Buildout   Under the 3G licensing process in Europe, carriers generally had to agree to provide mobile coverage to a prespecified percentage of the population, within a certain period of time. Cell construction was assumed to be linear, reaching the required coverage in the time limit. There was also an assumption that all urban areas would be covered before rural areas. Data was obtained from public sources.

Cost of supplying spectrum

In the interests of space the full mobile network operator model is not presented here, it can be found at <www.murrow.org>. But conclusions from the model, which are relevant to the present chapter, are highlighted here, the cost of supplying spectrum in relation to the amount of spectrum sold was found by varying the number of cell sites built. As cell sites increase, system capacity increases while fixed costs such as spectrum licenses remain unchanged. This is analogous to carriers increasing cell site density to ensure sufficient capacity for users.

Two scenarios were studied. Under the base scenario, carriers would only provide coverage as required by their national regulatory authority, and each carrier would construct their own cell sites. Total system information capacity was assumed to be 668 Mbps / MHz / Cell, which was the maximum data rate of the system.

In the "Most Likely" scenario, where national buildout requirements were low, it was assumed that carriers would nonetheless provide coverage for all urban areas (due to market demand). Carriers were also being allowed to share their cell sites. Total system data capacity was reduced to 450 Mbps / MHz / Cell with the assumption that interference would reduce the maximum throughput.

The differences between the two scenarios are small. Although there are cost savings from cell site sharing, this is balanced by the lower system capacity available per cell site in the "Most Likely" scenario. The average difference in prices between the two curves was $0.02. Subsequent analysis was conducted using the "Most Likely" scenario.

In perspective, the voice traffic component will only amount to 78,000 million Mbytes over the next ten years. Projected subscriber demand for voice and data services will reach a level of 1,500,000 mil Mbytes over the next ten years, which indicates a cost of $0.17 per Mbyte.

Cost Components of Carriers

Examining the costs for the carriers, the cost of spectrum licenses constitutes approximately 35 percent of a carrier's total costs. Infrastructure costs are small (1 percent when amortized, 3.5 percent when not), with operating expenses being the bulk of a carrier's expenses.

Sensitivity Analysis

A Sensitivity Analysis was conducted at the demand level projected by the MNO model.

Operating Expenses

Operating expenses is the largest component of a carrier's cost. Sensitivity analysis was done to identify how spectrum prices change with operating cost per subscriber.

♦ Sensitivity to Cell Sharing

The European Union has issued directives[16] calling for the abolition of restrictions on infrastructure sharing. It is likely that within the next few years, cell sites will be shared between carriers, reducing infrastructure costs and increasing system capacity. Sensitivity analysis was conducted to observe the effects of cell site sharing.

From the combined pricing functions of carriers and MNOs, 3G mobile services will only become profitable if demand rises above 800,000 mil Mbytes within ten years. Since voice traffic will only constitute 78,000 mil Mbytes, there must be significant uptake of mobile data services for the 3G industry to recoup its costs. Fortunately, industry projections place mobile demand at 1,500,000 mil Mbytes. At this point, the price of spectrum will range from $0.17 per Mbyte to $0.39 per Mbyte.

One clear result from the model is that data traffic will be an important component of carriers' revenues. Voice traffic will only constitute 8 percent of total traffic and cannot generate sufficient revenues to cover carriers' costs on its own. This emphasizes the need for MVNOs. In 2G systems, traditional carriers were able to provide voice services, which formed the bulk of wireless traffic. In 3G systems, data services will be the mainstay of mobile traffic. Most carriers are not positioned to provide such services, and furthermore it seems practically impossible for a single firm to provide the plethora of data services needed to sustain a 3G network. MVNOs will be essential to the success of 3G systems.

The models also indicate that the 3G market remains profitable, despite the claims of German carriers that high license fees are driving them into bankruptcy. At the projected demand for data services, subscriber revenues are sufficient to cover the costs of carriers. The German and British auctions were most likely overpriced, but as a whole, European licensing fees are still reasonable. Most of the licenses are owned by a handful of firms or consortiums. For example, Vodafone (either singly or operating within a consortium) has acquired 3G licenses in 6 out of the 10 European auctions / beauty contests. Forrester research predicts that consolidation will leave only five groups serving all mobile users in Europe by 2008. A company such as Vodafone would find the high prices paid in Britain offset by the low licensing fees of Sweden. Aggregated together, revenues are sufficient to cover the licensing fees paid in Europe.

Weakness of the 3G Models

The models only examined the countries that have completed their 3G licensing process. Some of the earlier auctions had licensing fees that would be reached today, and the general trend is toward lower licensing fees. A complete European model (when all national 3G licenses have been issued) should have lower costs than our predictions.

3G markets and regulations are in the midst of a revolution. Many of the 3G systems and services have never been used on a large scale before. Laws are changing as regulators try to facilitate the development of 3G, and market predictions are being modified month to month. Our models are able to accommodate dynamic changes in most variables, but it is difficult to factor in the changes when information about it is constantly changing. The model represents a static prediction, based on best information available at the time of writing. Probable changes to the regulatory environment include a lifting of restrictions on infrastructure sharing and the allocation of further blocks of spectrum by 2005.

Some implications for industry structure and public policy are briefly summarized here. We discuss emerging themes for wireless services and how do these differentially affect two technologies. The implications for the extent of horizontal and vertical integration are significant. 3G is vertically integrated whereas Wi-Fi admits a decentralized approach. But, of course, this does not have to be case. Wi-Fi could be integrated into a 3G model as a local hotspot capability.

Conclusion and Policy Recommendations

In the wired Internet premium services such as for example, content delivery networks offer forms of guaranteed services. On the other hand hundreds of millions of people rely on best effort email and instant messaging services. A similar wireless bifurcation and competition between service offerings relying on guaranteed services, and built therefore at least in part upon spectrum markets, and "best effort" unlicensed services, is beginning to unfold. This competition for spectrum and customers is also a competition of visions, which will intensify in the years to come, as the costs and benefits of wideband services become better understood.

Moving from vision to empirically testable reality, we conclude that secondary spectrum markets are important for the viability of the 3G industry, and not only for reasons of efficiency. One large difference between 2G and 3G networks, observed in our models, was that voice services alone would not generate sufficient revenues for a 3G system. License holders which up to now have concentrated on selling a single product, will need to develop a much larger range of advanced applications, which will have to be marketed and packaged in different ways for different market segments. It will require very different sets of skills and expertise to offer the full range of mobile commerce, entertainment, banking, shopping, information, and other services from which the majority of 3G revenues will come. 3G networks must offer a broad range of data services, which traditional carriers are not positioned to do. Secondary spectrum markets allow carriers to leverage their strengths in network infrastructure while portioning out data services to firms able to serve customers better (and hence increase demand for mobile traffic).

In these secondary markets, our models predict the price of spectrum to be between $0.17 per Mbyte and $0.39 per Mbyte. The actual price will most likely fluctuate with supply and demand, although in the long run, competition should reduce prices toward the lower bound. We recognize that the 3G market in Europe is changing rapidly, and too many variables are uncertain. A rise or fall in auction prices next year, or the implementation of new European directives, could easily change spectrum prices. Our models espouse a methodology for valuing spectrum in secondary markets that needs to be recalibrated as new information becomes available.

The implications for spectrum policy of the wireless technologies addressed in this chapter are potentially the most important issue. Can best effort and guaranteed services coexist in the same bands? What incentives would be needed to induce and enable sharing—presuming as in the wired Internet, technical and operational efficiencies greater than their costs can be obtained through sharing technical resources—not including spectrum? Regulators and policymakers have just begun to consider such issues through for example formal rulemaking procedures of the United States Federal Communication Commission, and technical analyses undertaken by the U.S. Defense Advanced Research Projects Agency and National Telecommunications and Information Administration underway in 2001; below we offer a few suggestions for wireless policymakers, technologists, and business leaders to consider for the future.

Recommendation 1   Demand for mobile services will require new spectrum allocations. Especially where such allocations may be problematic, innovative approaches to spectrum use and sharing such as those described in this chapter should be explored.

Recommendation 2   3G licensing processes should ensure competition in infrastructure provision whenever possible, while permitting in principle infrastructure sharing and enabling roaming between networks. The regulatory framework should not present barriers to infrastructure sharing arrangements if they do not have negative impact on competition between operators. Analogous sharing is a prerequisite for wider-area networks to be built from 802.11local networks.

Recommendation 3   Policies and initiatives should encourage both supply and demand for spectrum usage rights and development of an efficient secondary market in such rights.

Recommendation 4 Large swaths of spectrum for 3G services may be unavailable in, for example, North America due to military needs. If new technology provides a viable alternative for packing more uses and users in the same space, on a "best effort" basis, such a possibility should be explored as a high priority by researchers and policymakers alike.

Notes

1. First generation mobile cellular systems were based on analog technology. Second generation systems based on CDMA and TDMA in the U.S. and GSM in Europe and elsewhere are digital but only support narrowband voice communications. Third generation cellular or "3G" systems will offer enhanced bandwidth to support multimedia digital voice and data services.

2. 3G systems can support up to 2Mbps but this severely limits the number of subscribers that can be served from each cell. Therefore, it is not expected that actual deployments will offer services at this rate, at least initially. Subsequent generations of cellular wireless services are expected to offer higher bandwidth.

3. This chapter draws heavily upon the work done by co-author Raymond Linsenmayer and his colleagues in spring 2001 to develop pricing and cost models of European spectrum markets. In particular, this chapter draws upon the work of co-author Raymond Linsenmayer for his master's thesis. See Raymond Linsenmayer, *Secondary Spectrum Markets in Europe,* MALD thesis, Fletcher School of Law and Diplomacy, Tufts University, 2001 <www.murrow.org>. In addition, the spectrum market model described in this chapter was first developed by Raymond Linsenmayer and his colleagues as a class project in spring 2001 to develop pricing and cost models of European spectrum markets. See Li Jiang, Yong Li, Raymond Linsenmayer, Shushain Colin Ong, *Wireless Spectrum Pricing in Secondary Markets,* Class Project for Professor Lee W. McKnight, ESD.127/DHP 232 *Telecommunications Modeling and Policy Analysis,* Fletcher School/ MIT, Spring 2001 <www.murrow.org>.

4. Policy Statement, FCC, December 1, 2000, P19.

5. As previously noted, much of this section is drawn from Jiang et al., 2001.

6. See *Mobile Virtual Network Operators: Can They Succeed in a Competitive Carrier Market?* The Yankee Group. 2000. p. 1

7. "The Virtual Network Space" by Paul Quigley." *Wireless Week.* September 4, 2000.

8. See By Joanne Taafee. "Mobile Virtual Network Operators—Marking Out Their Territory" *Communications Week International,* March 5, 2001.

9. Jo Shields, "Energis Sees UK as a Test-Bed for Bigger Mobile Ambitions" *Mobile Communications,* March 6, 2001.

10. In competitive markets, the optimal transfer price should be equivalent to the market price.

11. Jiang et al., op cit.

12. At time of writing, they are Austria, Belgium, Finland, Germany, Italy, Netherlands, Portugal, Spain, Sweden and U.K.

13. Most industry analysts use ten years as a benchmark before 3G technology becomes dated and needs to be replaced.

14. Assumption that carriers will purchase equipment (AUCs, Billing Centers, etc.) to ensure that all users can be supported.

15. For more information see Forrester Research, "Europe's Mobile Internet Opens Up."

16. See The 90/388/EEC Service Directive, the 96/2/EC Directive on mobile and personal communications, the 96/19/EC Full Competition Directive, and the European Parliament and Council Directive on Interconnection in Telecommunication with regard to ensuring Universal Service and Interoperability through application of the principles of Open Network Provision.

References

Defense Advanced Research Projects Agency (DARPA), *Networking in the Extreme (NETEX)*, sol BAA 01–46, Defense Advanced Research Projects Agency (DARPA), Information Technology Office, 2001.

The European Parliament and Council, *Directive on Interconnection in Telecommunication with regard to ensuring Universal Service and Interoperability through application of the principles of Open Network Provision.*

Federal Communications Commission, *Public Forum,* FCC, May 31, 2000.

Federal Communications Commission, *Policy Statement,* FCC, December 1, 2000.

Forrester Research, "Europe's Mobile Internet Opens Up," Forrester Research 2001.

Jiang, Li, Yong Li, Raymond Linsenmayer, Shushain Colin Ong, *Wireless Spectrum Pricing in Secondary Markets,* Class Project for Professor Lee W. McKnight, ESD.127/DHP 232 *Telecommunications Modeling and Policy Analysis,* Fletcher School/ MIT, Spring 2001 <www.murrow.org>.

Linsenmayer, Raymond. *Secondary Spectrum Markets in Europe,* MALD thesis, Fletcher School of Law and Diplomacy, Tufts University, 2001 <www.murrow.org>.

Molisch, Andreas F., ed. *Wideband Wireless Digital Communication,* Prentice Hall, 2000.

The 90/388/EC *Service Directive.*

The 96/2/EC *Directive on Mobile and Personal Communications.*

The 96/19/EC *Full Competition Directive.*

Taafee, Joanne. "Mobile Virtual Network Operators—Marking Out Their Territory" *Communications Week International,* March 5, 2001.

Shields, Jo. "Energis Sees UK as a Test-Bed for Bigger Mobile Ambitions." *Mobile Communications,* March 6, 2001.

Quigley, Paul. "The Virtual Network Space" *Wireless Week,* September 4, 2000.

Yankee Group, *Mobile Virtual Network Operators: Can They Succeed in a Competitive Carrier Market?* The Yankee Group, 2000.

11

Property Rights, Flexible Spectrum Use, and Satellite v. Terrestrial Uses and Users

Douglas W. Webbink[1]

Introduction

As far as many consumers and businessmen and women are concerned, increasingly wireline and wireless services, including those provided by terrestrial and satellite systems, are considered to be substitutes and sometimes complements, regardless of the laws and regulations applicable to them. At the same time, many writers and even government agencies (such as the FCC) have suggested that users of the spectrum should be given more property-like rights in the use of the spectrum and at a minimum should be given much more flexibility in how they may use the spectrum. Two recent developments have important implications with respect to "convergence": spectrum property rights and flexible use of the spectrum. The first development involves several proposals to provide terrestrial wireless services within spectrum in use or planned to be used to provide satellite services. The second development is the passage of the 2000 ORBIT Act which specifically forbids the use of license auctions to select among mutually exclusive applicants to provide international or global satellite communications service. The purpose of this paper is to discuss some of the questions raised by these two events, but not necessarily to provide definitive answers or solutions.

Convergence and Spectrum Use

Communications services and technologies appear to be converging faster than laws and regulations can adjust to those changes. Consumers (including businessmen and women) often view various services and products as substitutes or complements, regardless of their regulatory status. For example, many consumers consider services supplied by TV stations, cable TV systems, and DBS operators to be substitutes and sometimes complements. Increasingly consumers see wireless and wireline telephones as substitutes and sometimes as complements. The same consumer reaction likely applies to FM and AM radio signals, audio signals delivered over cable TV and DBS systems, and satellite digital audio radio service (DARS). These examples also suggest that providers of services will increasingly recognize the significance of this substitutability or complementarity and may wish to provide many of these services using the same spectrum as well as wire or fiber optic technology, regardless of the regulations or laws to which they are subject.

Property Rights and Flexible Spectrum Use

Over the last 40 years, a large number of authors have argued that users of the radio frequency spectrum, that is, licensees, should be given property rights or at least more property-like rights in the use of the spectrum.[2] Such rights would include the right to purchase, sell, lease, or give away the resource, the right to combine and subdivide the resource, the right to use it as one wishes, including the right to use as little or as much of it as one wishes, the right to develop or not develop its use at a rate determined by the property right owner and the right to decide who can use the resources and who can be excluded.[3] Generally, these authors argue that only by giving licensees complete or at least more complete property rights, will those licensees face the correct economic incentives to use the spectrum efficiently, that is, to take into account the opportunity cost of the choices they make with respect to spectrum usage, to consider the tradeoffs between expenditures on acquiring hardware, software and additional spectrum, and to make efficient decisions about investment, technological innovation and changes in the services they decide to provide.

In addition, a number of authors and the Federal Communications Commission (FCC) have suggested in rulemaking proceedings that licensees should be given increased flexibility in the ways in which they can use the spectrum to which they are licensed, even if they are not given full property rights in spectrum use.[4] Such flexibility would include the right to decide how much of the spectrum licensed to an individual to use and for what purpose, what technologies to use and what services to provide, etc.

Of course, even if one claims to be in favor of moving toward more property-like rights in spectrum use and increased flexibility in allowable uses of the spectrum, making such general statements does not begin to explain the details of how to implement such concepts. For example, what degree of exclusive property rights should be allowed and with how many restrictions? Similarly, how much flexibility should be allowed and what limits should be placed on that flexibility? What is the government's role in defining the initial bundle of property rights granted, and to what extent should the government be able to modify that bundle of rights for incumbent users? To what extent do increasing flexibility and allowing more property-like rights make resolving inter-ference disputes more complex rather than easier and thus increase trans-actions costs among affected parties? These questions are similar to questions about the extent to which land owners should have rights to use their property as they wish, and the extent to which they should be subject to overall zoning laws and other restrictions on allowable uses. In every case, a key issue is the extent to which private parties acting alone, or a government agency, should attempt to resolve these issues.

Satellite v. Terrestrial Spectrum Use

Recently, the question of whether it is possible and desirable to give more flexibility and more property-like rights to spectrum or radio licensees has come up again in the context of a number of specific proposals and proceedings involving the possible use of the same block or section of spectrum by satellite and by terrestrial wireless systems or by different terrestrial systems. In a number of recent FCC decisions, satellite systems and terrestrial systems have been allocated separate frequency bands or separate sections of a band.[5] When both uses have been allowed to oper-ate in the same band, sometimes one is designated as "primary," (i.e., it has first priority with respect to interference) and the other as "second-ary," (i.e., it has a lower priority with respect to interference).[6] In some bands, however, satellites and terrestrial users are designated as "co-pri-mary," which means they have equal priority, so generally whichever system gets built first is protected against interference from the second system. The usual regulatory process is first to allocate spectrum internationally and then domestically to certain types of uses (mobile terrestrial, mobile satellite, fixed terrestrial, fixed satellite, broadcasting (terrestrial), broadcasting satellite, etc.) and sometimes to two or more of those broad classes of service. After this the service or operating rules are developed and finally entities are allowed to apply to obtain licenses.[7] Satellite systems and terrestrial systems have generally been subject to different interference regulations and build out and other service rules for a variety of historical reasons related to such issues as the potential to cause interference and the cost and speed of building systems.[8]

In the past, writers have argued that government mandated spectrum block allocations often lead to inefficient spectrum uses.[9] Despite increasing amounts of flexibility in allowed spectrum uses, questions are now once again arising about this process of separating spectrum uses and users, because the same block of spectrum, regardless of the purpose for which it is currently allocated and regardless of the current service rules under which licensees may operate, has technical characteristics that make it potentially useful for both satellite and terrestrial use. There are many potential competing demands for the use of any particular block of spectrum. In addition, one aspect of the "convergence" of many different services and technologies offered to consumers and businesses is that there are increasing numbers of situations in which it is likely to be efficient to combine satellite and terrestrial wireless transmission systems in order to deliver particular services to customers, and in some situations it may be efficient to use the same spectrum to operate both satellites and terrestrial facilities.

Some Further Background Thoughts on Spectrum Allocation, Assignment and Use

Traditionally the rules and regulations governing terrestrial services have been quite distinct from the rules governing satellite services. Among other reasons, this was done because for frequencies higher than several hundred megahertz it was assumed that the coverage area for terrestrial signals, even from tall antenna towers, was limited to relatively small areas. This means that many separate terrestrial systems can transmit on the same frequency in different locations throughout the country without causing "harmful" or "unacceptable" interference. In contrast, satellites located in geostationary orbits often use antennas whose signals cover the whole continental U.S. or at least a large portion of it, unless the satellite uses spot beams to cover a smaller regional area. By locating geostationary satellites at least several degrees apart along the geostationary orbital arc, however, it is possible for highly directional antennas located on earth to pick up the signal from one satellite and reject the signal from another satellite, even if both satellites are transmitting on the same frequency.[10] In addition, the costs of building, launching and operating one geostationary orbit (GSO) satellite will be many times the cost of building and operating one terrestrial facility or even a set of terrestrial facilities covering a large metropolitan market.

When, however, individuals talk about "property rights" in spectrum use, they often assume that it is possible (and perhaps even relatively easy) to define the rights of licensees to transmit a certain kind of signal emission with certain power levels, bandwidth and other characteristics or to be protected to a certain level from interference caused by other licensees. In reality, defining such rights may be extraordinarily complex. Moreover, there is no such thing as a transmitter causing *no* interference to a receiver operating on a frequency and at a location close to the transmitter. It is only possible to describe an "acceptable" or an "unacceptable" level of interference, or the existence or lack of "harmful" interference, or even measurable interference, defined by such measures as a desired to undesired signal level, or a specific signal strength level or a power flux density or a signal strength level above a certain so called "noise floor." In addition, the amount of "harmful" interference actually received at any location depends not only on the characteristics of the transmitted signal but also on characteristics of the receiving antenna and radio receiver in terms of sensitivity, selectivity, etc. At present, in the U.S., determinations of acceptable or unacceptable interference levels are made through the rule making process at the FCC. An important issue, therefore, is how and by whom are decisions made concerning defining or determining the existence of "harmful" or "unacceptable" interference. This then also raises the issue of who should determine whether additional licensees could share the same spectrum without causing unacceptable interference, or alternatively whether an incumbent licensee should be allowed to prevent possible interfering operations or to accept interference and share the spectrum, presumably in exchange for some level of compensation.

Two Interrelated Issues

The remainder of this paper primarily focuses on two interrelated issues: the first is the degree to which licensees should be given exclusive property rights that allow them, rather than a government agency, to determine when to allow such sharing and under what conditions to allow that sharing, including what kinds of compensation they might accept for that sharing particularly in situations involving satellites and terrestrial users. In other words, the question to be addressed is to what extent should a government agency, for example, the FCC, make the determination concerning when sharing is or is not feasible or desirable and under what conditions including what kinds of compensation schemes? Related to this is the issue of the extent to which such possible sharing should be analyzed differently depending upon whether the proposed satellite and terrestrial systems are or are not owned and under control of the same party or are owned and under the control of two separate parties. Another way to describe this question is to think of the difference between voluntary sharing by users controlled by the same entity compared to voluntary or involuntary sharing by users controlled by two or more different entities.

The second interrelated issue is a consideration of the impact of one section of the 2000 ORBIT Act, which specified that competing applicants for satellite licenses to provide international or global services may not be selected by auction. In contrast, auctions may be used to select among competing applicants for domestic satellite licenses and many kinds of terrestrial wireless licenses. This antiauction provision of the ORBIT Act may potentially bias political and regulatory decisions concerning allowable uses of the spectrum. For example, it would not be surprising to see future decisions concerning the allocation of unused spectrum or the reallocation of lightly used spectrum facing substantial pressure to be tilted toward terrestrial users and away from international satellite uses because of the money generating advantage of holding terrestrial auctions.

Property Rights: Company Controlled or Government Controlled?

Within the last several years, a number of proposals to the FCC as well as some decisions made by the FCC raise the question of what degree of exclusive property-like rights should be given to licensees and what property rights should be retained or controlled by the government, for example, the FCC, and who should have the authority to change the definitions of those rights. Several of the recent proposals involve the provision of terrestrial based wireless services by the same companies which have been licensed, or who have applied for licenses to operate satellite systems. Other proposals relate to the question of whether to allow an independent company to provide terrestrial services in a band of spectrum that has been assigned to or applied for by a satellite service provider.

For example, satellite digital audio radio service (DARS) licensees Sirius Satellite Radio and XM Satellite Radio have proposed to operate terrestrial repeaters within their own assigned spectrum.[11] Motient Services Inc.[12] and New ICO Global Communications Ltd.[13]i have each requested authority to provide ancillary terrestrial services within their satellite spectrum bands.[14] In contrast, Northpoint and MDS America as well as PDC Broadband Corporation and Satellite Receivers, Ltd. have requested authority to provide a terrestrial service within the 12.2–12.7 GHz direct satellite service (DBS) band in which existing DBS licensees (including DirecTV and EchoStar) are currently operating.[15] SkyBridge has also applied to provide nongeostationary satellite service in that same band.

While these particular examples all involve the question of whether the FCC should allow terrestrial wireless systems to operate in spectrum assigned to or applied for by satellite providers, the reverse situation is also likely to arise in the future, that is, terrestrial licensees or applicants who wish to provide satellite service within their assigned terrestrial bandwidth.

Many of these proceedings are controversial with interested parties presenting quite different and often conflicting points of view. The intent of this paper is not to evaluate the arguments of any particular party in a specific proceeding but rather to consider the underlying policy issues behind the proposals and comments of both supporters and opponents.

The first issue to be discussed concerns who should decide what explicit and what implicit property-like rights are given to licensees to use the spectrum as they see fit. A related issued concerns who should have authority and under what conditions to modify such rules, by, for example, modifying existing allocation rules and then requiring "voluntary" or involuntary relocation of incumbent spectrum users.[For example, satellite space station license authorizations or the specific service rules applicable to those authorizations typically specify various characteristics of space station transmission systems such as the number and location of satellites, operating frequencies, power output or power flux density on the earth, limits on out-of-band emissions and the area of coverage of a particular signal strength, etc. Typically such authorizations are silent concerning whether they include the right to transmit signals on the earth on the same frequencies, even in the areas covered by their signals. Similarly, terrestrial license authorizations or the service rules applicable to those authorizations specify operating frequencies, locations, allowable emission modes and some limit on power levels and out-of-band emissions. Some license authorizations, for example, TV and radio broadcasting licenses, specify the specific location, power output, antenna height and radiation pattern of the transmitting antenna. Others, such as PCS and cellular license authorizations, specify geographic regions in which transmitters may be placed and also specify the frequencies of operation. The authorizations or service rules also specify limits on power levels, out-of-band emissions and maximum antenna heights. Again, however, such authorizations are usually silent on whether the same frequencies may be used by satellites whose signals cover the same geographic regions. Usually, however, the underlying frequency allocations decisions and the resulting allocations table will indicate whether or not spectrum sharing is allowed, and if so, under what conditions, including what are the rules for sharing or coordination of use.

DARS Terrestrial Repeaters or Gap Fillers

The satellite DARS applicants, XM Radio and Sirius, both proposed to use terrestrial repeaters or gap fillers to improve the quality of service in difficult propagation environments, especially urban areas. They proposed to operate them on the same frequencies as their satellite transmissions and only retransmit those signals.[17] While the Commission approved in principle the use of terrestrial repeaters or gap fillers, it issued a Further Notice of Proposed Rule Making asking how it should be done.[18] A related issue in this proceeding involves the extent to which such DARS terrestrial repeaters or gap fillers may cause interference to the Wireless Communications Service (WCS) licensees who are assigned to frequencies immediately adjacent to and in between the frequencies assigned to the two DARS systems.[19]

ICO and Motient Proposals

In a letter to the FCC, New ICO Global Communications Ltd. stated that adding to its 2 GHz mobile satellite system a terrestrial component that would operate on the same frequencies as its satellite transmissions would allow it to extend service to indoor and urban locations that otherwise would be unserved by a satellite only system and thus would increase the commercial viability of the system.[20] Motient Services Inc. has requested authority to operate terrestrial base stations on frequency bands in which it is authorized to provide satellite service, and to provide coverage in areas where the satellite signal is not sufficiently strong because of foliage or terrain as well as to operate within buildings.[21] A variety of questions have been raised concerning whether to allow such terrestrial service within a satellite band at all, and if so whether only those satellite companies that wish to provide service within the bands for which they hold a satellite license should be allowed to do so or whether other entities should also be allowed to operate terrestrial facilities in those bands.[22] A subsidiary issue involves the question of if entities other than the satellite licensees are allowed to operate terrestrial facilities, should any terrestrial facilities that are authorized be granted through a license auction?[23]

Northpoint, SkyBridge etc. DBS Sharing

In the ongoing proceeding concerning possible spectrum sharing in the 12.2–12.7 GHz band between incumbent geostationary DBS licensees, terrestrial applicants such as Northpoint Technology and nongeostationary satellite applicant SkyBridge, there are a variety of issues concerning whether and if so to what extent, the operation of terrestrial service or the operation of nongeostationary satellite service (NGSO) would cause unacceptable or harmful interference to the reception of signals from existing geostationary DBS providers (DirecTV and EchoStar).[24] To the extent that interference may be caused by new users of the spectrum, the overriding policy issue is, once again, whether incumbent licensees or a government agency should decide whether to allow such additional users, and if so, under what conditions.

Who Determines and Who Can Modify Property Rights?

The question to be considered with respect to all of these specific examples and many others likely to arise in the future, is not whether some level of interference might be caused and if so, specifically how it might be mitigated. Nor is the basic issue who should be responsible for what kinds of interference mitigation if such mitigation is necessary. Rather the basic issue is more fundamental than that: it is whether a government agency or actual or potential service providers should decide whether or not they believe there will or will not be harmful interference. In either case, the issue then moves to the question of who has the right to decide whether to allow companies to operate that may or may not cause interference to other companies and how much interference to allow.

One argument that has been made is that in order for the spectrum to be used efficiently, a government agency needs to decide how much interference is significant or harmful and if such interference does exist, who has the responsibility to mitigate it. In essence, according to this view, the government would decide or determine the initial property rights and also have the ability to revise or modify those rights after following the proper administrative procedures.

However, advocates of giving spectrum users more property-like rights argue that companies rather than a government agency should generally make these decisions. In particular, government determined property rights may be either too restrictive or not restrictive enough. That is, the government may restrict the ability of a party to provide services within its authorized band (e.g., by preventing a satellite from providing terrestrial service or a terrestrial licensee from providing satellite service in its band even when it could be done without causing interference to others).

On the other hand, the government may allow independent companies to operate within a band after determining that significant interference will not be caused to incumbents or even after deciding that some significant level of interference will be caused to incumbents, even without the agreement of incumbents.

There is an additional and related policy question. If a new entrant will cause at least noticeable interference (however determined) to incumbent licensees, but will it also increase the level of competition in the provision of some set of services that are provided either by the incumbent spectrum users or by providers of totally different services in different frequency bands or using other media such as wire, coaxial cable or fiber optic cable, to what extent should the government balance the increased level of competition against the increase in the level of interference to incumbents? To the extent that incumbents attempt to prevent new entry and sharing, how does one determine whether such behavior is caused by genuine fear of interference, by a desire to prevent entry of potential competitors even if no interference will be caused, or by both?

An argument against allowing involuntary sharing between satellite and terrestrial users is that companies may have little incentive to resolve real or hypothetical interference problems when such involuntary sharing is mandated by the government. In contrast, when the same party operates both satellite and terrestrial services, it is much more likely to make efficient decisions about dealing with real or hypothetical interference. Or, in the jargon of economists, when two parties are involved they may find it difficult to deal with potential externalities, whereas if the same company provides both services, it may find it much easier to internalize any potential externalities. When one company provides both services either as complements or substitutes, its incentives will be aligned to minimize interference or at least to establish an efficient level of interference.

Spectrum or License Auctions

In the U.S., selecting among mutually exclusive applications for spectrum allocated for terrestrial use may be done by auction (with some restrictions), whereas spectrum used for satellites, if it might be used for international or global use, can not be auctioned. Although the primary policy goal of auctions should not be to raise money for the U.S. treasury, but instead to lead to the best and fastest use of the spectrum, the revenue raising aspects of auctions are a powerful political force.[25] How does one weigh the possible benefits of allowing flexibility in terrestrial operations in the satellite band against the possibility that requests for authorization of terrestrial uses will be used as a way to avoid bidding in an auction?

Many papers have been written concerning the benefits of using auctions to chose among competing spectrum applicants.[26] Proponents of the use of such license auctions assert that auctions lead to faster grant of licenses than any of the regulatory alternatives such as lotteries or comparative hearings or so-called "beauty contests." Because the winner of the auction is the company that bids the most in the auction, auctions generally allow the entities who value the license most to obtain the license. Presumably, therefore, the winner is generally the entity best able efficiently to provide service desired by consumers and businesses. Moreover, auctions provide information which indicates how much bidders believe the spectrum is worth, and therefore provide an indication of the opportunity cost of using or not using the spectrum.[27] Many auction proponents also suggest that the primary goal of such auctions should not be to raise revenue for the government but only to lead to rapid and efficient use of the spectrum.[28] In addition to the U.S., several foreign countries such as Brazil, Mexico and Australia have held auctions or plan to hold auctions for domestic satellite licenses.[29]

At the same time, however, a number of arguments have been raised against using spectrum auctions, especially in the international context.[30] For example, it has been argued that when satellite signals cover multiple countries, if there would be multiple sequential auctions, it would be difficult for an applicant to decide how much to pay for spectrum rights in the first country, assuming that the applicant needed to bid for rights to obtain access to the other countries. Hence there would be substantial uncertainty and it would be difficult to develop rational business plans. In particular, the applicant might fear that there would be a holdout problem, that is, the last country might attempt to extract all remaining economic rents from the applicant or may even, for some political reason, set a minimum price so high that the applicant would be unable or unwilling to pay for it. Indeed, the last country may set the minimum price in order to restrict entry, to protect an incumbent service, or even deny service so that no applicant can provide such service. While these potential problems concerning sequential international auctions are real and should not be ignored, they do not lead to an inevitable conclusion that auctions should be forbidden.[31]

The ORBIT Act's Antiauction Provision

Since 1993 the FCC has had authority to chose among competing license applicants for many services using an auction. Indeed, between 1994 and 2000, the FCC has held at least 37 auctions, awarded at least 23,280 licenses through auction and the net amount bid in those auctions has totaled about $34.6 billion.[32] By statute, certain classes of license applications such as public safety and amateur radio are exempt from auctions. In addition, the Open-market Reorganization for the Betterment of International Telecommunications Act, the ORBIT Act, passed in 2000, states in relevant part:

Not withstanding any other provision of law, the Commission shall not have the authority to assign by competitive bidding orbital locations or spectrum used for the provision of international or global satellite communications services. The President shall oppose in the International Telecommunication Union and in other bilateral and multilateral fora any assignment by competitive bidding of orbital locations or spectrum used for the provision of such services.[33]

It is not entirely clear precisely what is covered by this provision and when it applies and when it does not apply. Most satellite systems proposed recently are designed to provide international or global coverage or usage. Others may be designed only to serve the U.S. market. Apparently the former class of applications would be covered by the ORBIT Act antiauction provisions and the latter would not. However, it is not clear how this law would apply if an applicant changed his or her plans and also how applications should be treated if some applicants apply to provide only domestic service and others apply to provide international service in the same band.

It is also not entirely clear how this provision came to be added to the ORBIT Act, even though the U.S. satellite industry supported its inclusion, because most of the Act's provisions relate specifically to INTELSAT and INMARSAT. What is clear, however, is that many members of the U.S. satellite industry believe that this antiauction provision helps them, because they will not be required to bid in a U.S. license auction to obtain additional satellite orbital positions or spectrum.[34] Unfortunately, the industry members are very likely wrong in this belief about how the ORBIT Act will help them because they have not fully evaluated the possibilities of alternative nonsatellite uses of the same spectrum nor the political importance of the revenue to be obtained for the U.S. Treasury from license auctions. In fact, this provision may lead to strong political pressures to reallocate more spectrum to auctionable terrestrial users and less spectrum to nonauctionable satellite users. Thus, while satellite industry members may believe that they are protected by this statutory provision, it can be argued that they would be far better off without it.

Conclusions

There are two major implications suggested by this paper. First, wherever feasible, it would be desirable to give companies the maximum exclusive property-like rights.[35] In other worlds, it would be desirable to allow them and not a government agency to decide if sharing should be allowed and if so, under what conditions. Ideally, government agencies should only become involved in such decisions if there is a problem concerning monopoly control of the spectrum by incumbents or potential applicants.[36] A corollary to this conclusion is that for companies making business decisions, changing rules such as the property rights implicitly attached to licenses, may impose substantial uncertainty and thus real economic costs on such firms.[37]

Second, with respect to auctions and the ORBIT Act, that particular provision of the law should be repealed. Although there may be situations in which the use of auctions is undesirable, a flat out prohibition on auctions involving international or global services will surely lead to undesirable results. Over the long run that antiauction provision will likely harm satellite companies and their ability to provide service to customers, far more than it will help satellite companies and their customers.[38]

If the antiauction prohibition on satellites remains, public policy decisions on the best uses of the spectrum should not be based upon whether use of the spectrum will generate more or less auction revenue for the U.S. treasury. Auctions can provide important and useful price signals, but only if many competing potential users can bid in an auction. Price signals are likely to be highly misleading if certain classes of users are excluded from bidding. And, in particular, policy decisions concerning the "best" use of the spectrum should not be based on whether or not the licensee bid in an auction, when certain classes are forbidden from bidding.

Notes

1. The views expressed are my own and should not be interpreted to be those of the FCC or any of its Commissioners or staff. I am grateful for useful suggestions from Karl Kensinger and David Sappington. Errors and opinions remain my own. E-mail: <dwebbink@fcc.gov>.

2. See, for example, Thomas W. Hazlett, "The Wireless Craze, The Unlimited Bandwidth Myth, The Spectrum Auction Faux Pas, and the Punchline to Ronald Coase's 'Big Joke': an Essay on Airwave Allocation Policy," AEI-Brookings Joint Center for Regulatory Studies, Working paper 01–02 (January, 2001); Lawrence J. White, "'Propertizing' the Electromagnetic Spectrum: Why It's Important, and How to Begin," *Media Law and Policy* (fall 2000), pp. 51–75; Howard A. Shelanski and Peter W. Huber, "Administrative Creation of Property Rights to Radio Spectrum," *Journal of Law and Economics* 41 (October 1998): 581–607; Glenn O. Robinson, "Spectrum Property Law 101," *Journal of Law and Economics* 41 (October 1998): 609–625; Arthur De Vany, "Implementing a Market-Based Spectrum Policy," *Journal of Law and Economics* 41 (October 1998): 627–646; Douglas W. Webbink, "Radio Licenses and Frequency Spectrum Use Property Rights," *Communications and the Law* 9 (June 1987): 3–29; Milton Mueller, "Property Rights in Radio Communications: The Key to Reform of Telecommunications Regulation," Cato Institute Policy Analysis (June 3, 1982); Louis De Alessi, "The Economics of Property Rights: A Review of the Evidence," in *Research in Law and Economics,* vol. 2, ed. Richard O. Zerbe, Jr. (1980), pp. 1–47; Ronald H. Coase, "The Federal Communications Commission," *Journal of Law and Economics* 2 (1959): 1–40.

For a different view, that suggests that granting exclusive property rights using auctions may impose a variety of costs on society, including creating incentives for oligopoly industry structures, see Eli Noam, "Spectrum Auctions: Yesterday's Heresy, Today's Orthodoxy, Tomorrow's Anachronism. Taking the Next Step to Open Spectrum Access," *The Journal of law and Economics* 41, no. 2 (October 1998): 765–790. For a response to Noam, see: Thomas W. Hazlett, "Spectrum Flash Dance: Eli Noam's Proposal for "Open Access" to Radio Waves," *The Journal of Law and Economics* 41, no. 2 (October 1998): 805–820.

3. According to Shelanski and Huber, "complete" property rights entail the right to hold, transfer, subdivide, or use the property in any way one sees fit and to exclude anyone. Shelanski and Huber, pp. 583–584.

4. See, for example: Gregory L. Rosston and Jeffrey S. Steinberg, "Using Market-Based Spectrum Policy to Promote the Public Interest," *Federal Communications Law Journal,* vol. 50, no. 1 (December 1997), pp. 87–116; Douglas W. Webbink, "Frequency Spectrum Deregulation Alternatives," FCC Office of Plans and Policy Working Paper no. 2, (1980). For a discussion and proposals for ways to increase the efficiency of spectrum use by encouraging secondary markets in the use of the spectrum, see: Principles for Promoting the Efficient Use of Spectrum by Encouraging the Development of Secondary Markets, Policy Statement, 15 FCC Rcd 24,178 (2000). For proposals to develop secondary spectrum markets that mainly emphasize terrestrial wireless use, especially among commercial mobile radio service users, see: Promoting Efficient Use of Spectrum Through Elimination of Barriers to the Development of Secondary Markets, Notice of Proposed Rulemaking in WT Docket no. 00-230, 15 FCC Rcd 24,203 (2000). See also: "Comments of 37 Concerned Economists," in WT Docket no. 00-230, February 7, 2001. For a discussion of how authorization of software defined radios might greatly increase the ease and decrease the costs of implementing more flexible uses of the spectrum, see: Inquiry Regarding Software Defined Radios, Notice of Proposed Rule Making in ET Docket no. 00-47, 15 FCC Rcd 24,442 (2000); and First Report and Order in ET Docket no. 00-47, FCC 01–264 (released September 14, 2001).

5. See, for example: Allocation and Designation of Spectrum for Fixed-Satellite Services in the 37.5–38.5 GHz, 40.5–41.5 GHz, and 48.2–50.2 GHz Frequency Bands, Report and Order, IB Docket no. 97–95, 13 FCC Rcd 24649 (1998). See also Further Notice of Proposed Rule Making, IB Docket no. 97–95, 66 FR 35,399 (2001).

6. See, for example: FWCC Request for Declaratory Ruling on Partial-band Licensing of Earth Stations in the Fixed-Satellite Service That Share Terrestrial Spectrum, Notice of Proposed Rulemaking in IB Docket no. 00-203, 15 FCC Rcd 23,127 (2000) ("FWCC NPRM").

7. In many recent situations involving the provision of new satellite services or services in new or different frequency spectrum bands, companies have actually filed applications to provide satellite service before the allocations or the service rules were finalized.

8. FWCC NPRM, ¶¶ 26–31, 37–44.

9. See, for example: Webbink, "Frequency Spectrum Deregulation Alternatives."

10. In contrast, low earth orbit or medium earth orbit satellites do not remain over one location on the earth to the same extent, which can create much more complicated issues in terms of preventing interference with each other and with other systems, if they are both operating on the same frequencies.

11. Rules and Policies for the Digital Audio Radio Satellite Service in the 2310–2360 MHz Band, Report and Order, Memorandum Opinion and Order and Further Notice of Proposed Rulemaking in IB Docket no. 95–91 and GEN Docket no. 90-357, 12 FCC Rcd 5754 (1997). ("DARS R&O"). See also: Public Notice, Request for Further Comment on Selected Issues Regarding the Authorization of Satellite Digital Audio Radio Service Terrestrial Repeater

Networks, IB Docket no. 95–91, RM no. 8610, DA no. 01–2570, Report no. SPB–176 (released November 1, 2001).

12. Application by Motient Services Inc. and Mobile Satellite Ventures Subsidiary LLC for Assignment of Licenses and For authority to launch and Operate a Next-Generation Mobile Satellite Service System (March 1, 2001). See also: Public Notice, Report no. SAT-00066 (released March 19, 2001).

13. Ex parte letter to Chairman Michael K. Powell in IB Docket no. 98–81 (filed March 8, 2001).

14. Flexibility of Communications by Mobile Satellite Service Providers in the 2 GHz Band, the L-Band and the 1.6/2.4 GHz Band and Amendment of Section 2.106 of the Commission's Rules to Allocate Spectrum at 2 GHz for Use by the Mobile Satellite Service, IB Docket no. 01–185 and ET Docket no. 95–18, FCC 01–225 (released August 17, 2001). ("MSS Flexibility NPRM").

15. Amendment of Parts 2 and 25 of the Commission's Rules to Permit Operation of NGSO FSS Systems Co-Frequency with GSO and Terrestrial Systems in the Ku-Band Frequency Range and Amendment of the Commission's Rules to Authorize Subsidiary Terrestrial us of the 12.2–12.7 GHz Band by Direct Broadcast Satellite Licensees and Their Affiliates, Notice of Proposed Rulemaking In ET Docket no. 98–206, 14 FCC Rcd 1131 (1998). ("DBS NPRM"). See also: First Report and Order and Further Notice of Proposed Rule Making, ET Docket no. 98–206, 16 FCC Rcd 4096 (2000). See also: "MDS America Joins Northpoint in Fight for DBS Spectrum," *Satellite Week,* (May 14, 2001).

16. For a discussion of the issues concerning incentives to cooperate or oppose relocation of incumbent spectrum users, see: Peter Cramton, Evan Kwerel and John Williams, "Efficient Relocation of Spectrum Incumbents," *Journal of Law and Economics,* vol. XLI, no. 2 (October 1998), pp. 647–675.

17. DARS R&O, ¶ 140.

18. DARS R&O ¶ 142.

19. The extent to which the possibility of interference between DARS terrestrial repeaters and WCS is controversial can be seen by the fact that as of December 3, 2001, the FCC Electronic Comment Filing System lists records of over 500 submissions in this docket since 1995.

20. MSS Flexibility NPRM, ¶¶ 10–11.

21. MSS Flexibility NPRM, ¶¶ 15–18.

22. MSS Flexibility NPRM, ¶¶ 23–28.

23. MSS Flexibility NPRM, ¶¶ 37–40.

24. DBS NPRM, ¶¶ 2–8. See also: *Analysis of Potential MVDDS Interference to DBS in the 12.2–12.7 GHz Band,* Mitre Technical Report MTR 01W0000024 (the Mitre Corporation, April, 2001). The level of controversy in this proceeding is indicated by the fact that as of December 3, 2001, the FCC Electronic Comment Filing system lists records of over 900 submissions in this docket since 1998.

25. For an example of a story that suggests the arguments used in favor of auctions and against issuing licenses without using an auction, see: Andrew Backover and Paul Davidson, "8 Companies Get Free Spectrum Licenses: Irked Wireless Firms Say They Would Pay Billions," *USA Today,* (July 17, 2001), p. 57.

26. See, for example, Evan Kwerel and Walter Strack, "Auction Spectrum Rights," U.S. Federal Communications Commission (February 20, 2001); Martin Cave and Tommaso Valletti, "Are Spectrum Auctions Ruining Our Grandchildren's Future," *Info,* vol. 2, no. 4 (August 2000), pp 347–350; Peter Cramton, "The Efficiency of the FCC Spectrum Auctions," *The Journal of Law and Economics,* vol. XLI, no. 2, (October 1998), pp. 727–736; Thomas W. Hazlett, "Assigning Property Rights to Radio Spectrum Users: Why Did FCC Licenses Auctions Take 67 Years?," *The Journal of Law and Economics,* vol. XLI no. 2, (October 1998), pp. 529–575; Evan Kwerel and Alex D. Felker, "Using Auctions to Select FCC Licensees," FCC OPP Working Paper no. 16 (May 1985).

27. Of course, if the class of entities allowed to bid in the auction is restricted, or if the auction winner is already an incumbent monopolist or can use the newly obtained spectrum to become a monopolist, then the amount bid in the auction will not necessarily reflect the competitive market price for using the spectrum or the opportunity cost of its use.

28. Unfortunately, however, as Eli Noam puts it, "Auctions Inevitably Deteriorate into Revenue Tools." Eli Noam, op. cit., pp. 772–775.

29. "Loral Skynet Wins Brazilian Slot Auctions," *Satellite Today* (March 18, 1999); "Mexican Government Poised to Auction Satellite Orbital Location License," *Corporate Mexico: Reforma (Mexico),* (July 12, 2001); "Two Satellite Slots Available for Australian Broadcasters," *Asia Pulse* (May 7, 2001).

30. See, for example, Clayton Mowry, "Auctions? No, no, no." *Satellite Communications* (February 1, 1997); Louis Jacobson, "Lobbying & Law: Washington's Rocket Man," *National Journal* (June 27, 1998); Curt Harler, "Intelsat goes into Orbit," *Communications International* (April 1, 2000); "Regulatory Review: No Satellite Auctions," *Via Satellite* (June 14, 2000); Charles L. Jackson, John Haring, Harry M. Shooshan III, Jeffrey H. Rohlfs, and Kirsten M. Pehrsson, "Policy Harms Unique to Satellite Spectrum Auctions," Strategic Policy Research, Inc., A Study Prepared for the Satellite Industry Association (March 18, 1996). See also: Harold Gruber, "Spectrum Limits and Competition in Mobile Markets: The Role of License Fees," European Investment Bank, (June 2000). See also: Eli Noam, "Spectrum Auctions: Yesterday's Heresy, Today's Orthodoxy, Tomorrow's Anachronism. Taking the Next Step to Open Spectrum Access," *Journal of Law and Economics,* 41 no. 2 (October 1998), pp. 765–790.

31. It is hypothetically possible that absent an agreement to forbid auctions, transactions costs would become so high that no agreement could be reached, but there should be alternatives to deal with potential hold-out problems that do not require forbidding auctions.

32. FCC, "Auction Summary," as of 11/26/01 at <http://wireless.fcc.gov/auctions/summary.html>. Of course, as the ongoing controversy concerning the licenses originally won by NextWave before it went bankrupt demonstrate, the government has not actually collected all of the $34.6 billion.

33. Communications Satellite Act of 1962, Section 647. (Provision added by the ORBIT Act, Public Law 106–180, 114 Stat. 48 (2000)).

34. See, for example: Clayton Mowry, "Auctions? No, no, no." *Satellite Communications* (February 1, 1997); Louis Jacobson, "Lobbying & Law: Washington's Rocket Man," *National Journal* (June 27, 1998); Curt Harler, "Intelsat goes into Orbit," *Communications International* (April 1, 2000); Regulatory Review: No Satellite Auctions," *Via Satellite* (June 14, 2000).

35. An important assumption is that the benefits of added flexibility will exceed any potential transactions costs or externality problems that might arise from that added flexibility.

36. For a similar view, see: "Comments of 37 Concerned Economists" in WT Docket no. 00-230 (February 7, 2001).

37. Of course, if the changes give firms far more flexibility in future activities, even if those changes introduce uncertainty, the benefits of the changes may still outweigh the costs. On the other hand, if changes force incumbent firms to vacate existing spectrum or to adopt new more technically efficient (but not necessarily more economically efficient) spectrum techniques, those changes will almost surely impose costs on those firms even though the changes might also benefit new potential entrants. In addition, it is possible that additional flexibility might make it more difficult for the government or for competitors to monitor the activities of incumbent companies, including determining who is causing interference.

38. Of course, many satellite industry members still believe that auctions for the right to provide international satellite services could lead to higher costs of operations and holdout problems with some countries.

V

Expanding the Understanding of Universal Service

12

Stronger than Barbed Wire: How Geo-Policy Barriers Construct Rural Internet Access

Kyle Nicholas

Introduction: *The Construction of Geo-Policy Barriers*

Perhaps the greatest development in rural communication technology in the middle of the 19th century was an eight foot board tied to the back of a horse. The King Road Drag scraped along country roads leveling humps and filling potholes.[1] The flat roads permitted rural postal deliveries, the development of parcel post and eventually a flood of information from catalog companies and publishers bearing goods and news from the big cities. Postal roads are two-way channels, of course, and although rural people could not take advantage of the commercial potential by mailing their livestock and produce, they could engage friends and relatives through letters as easily as order from Sears & Roebuck. Communication and community were encouraged by a combination of public policy, technology and commercial investment.

Geography influences the ability of today's citizens to access to modern telecommunications networks, and it shapes their opportunities to take advantage of communication technologies as political, economic and cultural resources. In terms of the Internet, geographic factors comprise a kind of "capital." Similar to human capital or social capital, geographic capital can be most easily detected by its absence; the absence of geographic capital leads to an absence of functional Internet access.

The geo-policy barriers referred to in the title are chokepoints, mechanisms of control created through the interaction of geography, market forces and public policies. Together these three not only constrict access but also define the shape of both communication and communities, often in unintended ways. Geographic capital, therefore, can be impinged by three factors: the physical characteristics of places, the actions of telecommunications firms, and the actions of public policymakers.

The idea that infrastructure altered communication potential seemed obvious in the era of the King Road drag, when the words "transportation" and "communication" were virtually synonymous.[2] But what about today, at the dawn of the 21st century? In this era of the Internet, the ability of rural people to communicate, whether for purposes of commerce or community, is still strongly tethered to the capacity of the telecommunications infrastructure in their area. The reach and scope of those wires, poles and switches are shaped by public policy. At the federal level universal service policies have helped extend basic telecommunications to rural areas through a combination of regulatory mandate and wealth transfer. For example, rural telephone companies are crucial enterprises linking rural communities to the broader society and thus have been protected from many of the exigencies of the marketplace.[3] States have also created policies to assist rural citizens in obtaining basic telecommunications. States have used their role as arbiter of telephone tariffs, for instance, to encourage the development of rural connectivity and have protected rural phone companies and cooperatives from regulatory and market challenges through "rural exemptions" to various policies.

Modern telecommunication systems in the U.S. are privately owned and managed, but have traditionally been highly regulated. The breakup of the regulated monopoly (AT&T) in 1984 and efforts to deregulate the telecommunications industry since 1996 have created a situation in which the marketplace plays a bigger role than at anytime in the last century. Telecommunications firms have pledged, even demanded, to compete but little competition has come to residential customers so far. Even in areas where competition is beginning to emerge, the marketplace is

Table 12.1
National Expanded Area Service Policy Variations

Dimension	Eligibility mechanisms	
Community of interest	Statistical	Geographical
Customer scope	Inclusive	Optional
Directionality	Uni-directional	Bi-directional
Pricing mechanism	Flat	Metered
Policy scope	Comprehensive	Case-by-case

highly structured by regulation. But these regulations seek only to mitigate market failure in remote areas, not to ensure adequate connectivity. Furthermore, the creation of telephone exchange areas (those places that generally correlate to the dialing prefix in a telephone number) and Local Access Transport Areas or LATAs (those places that generally separate local from long-distance calling areas) reveals an underlying principle of centralization that corrals geographic capital within geo-policy barriers. This correspondence between market areas and regulatory boundaries has a couple of consequences for rural communities. First, it substitutes markets for communities, and assumes that the need to communicate is a function of dwelling within a contiguous market area. Second, geo-policy barriers can effectively discourage commercial investment in telecommunications infrastructure and impose additional burdens on citizens already struggling to connect to the Internet.

In the post-1996 telecommunications world, states are tasked with providing 75 percent of universal service.[4] Most states have developed a separate class of programs aimed at reducing the costs of long-distance communications for rural citizens. Commonly known as Expanded Area Service (EAS), these programs generally reduce intra-LATA long-distance costs either between specific exchanges or throughout a contiguous geographic area (table 12.1). In the Internet era, the most important of these programs create flat-rate calling zones that allow remote customers to reach an Internet Service Provider (ISP) in a more populous area. By using EAS, remote customers can connect to the Internet from remote areas that do not support an ISP at a flat monthly rate. Conversely, small ISPs can extend their markets in rural areas by using EAS programs to create larger toll-free dial-up areas. But EAS programs do not always help where intended and can exacerbate the isolation and communication difficulties known as the "rural penalty."

The forces that shape basic telecommunications access—geography, commercial investment and public policy—will also determine who will bridge the digital divide in a broadband world. This chapter examines the how interplay of these forces structures communication access in rural Texas. No state has more people living in rural areas than Texas.[5] Perhaps no state so startlingly depicts the notion of a "digital divide." From "telecom alley" north of Dallas to the Silicon Hills of Austin and south to the international port of Houston, Texas is blessed with a robust network of high-speed communications technologies supporting some of the leading lights in telecommunications and computer industries. Away from this sliver of the state, however, the communications picture is less certain. This chapter compares findings from a statewide statistical analysis of rural Internet access with a sample study of seven counties in west Texas, an area about the size of New England. The study examines how the EAS program for rural Texans, known as Expanded Local Calling (ELC), enables access to the Internet. What emerges is a picture of a policy whose quirky contours and irregularities mimic the rugged geography it overlays.

The Study: *Expanded Local Calling in Rural Texas*

This chapter looks at the confluence of policy, geography and telecommunication firm investment in two ways: first, a statistical analysis of telephone exchanges is presented, then, a sample study of seven rural counties illustrates some of the particular challenges facing remote citizens. (See table 12.3 for study selection criteria).

The Texas version of ELC is similar to that of other states, although it varies in some particulars (table 12.2). The distance, in air miles, between central telephone switches determines eligibility for the program. Rural residents can elect ELC if they are 22 or fewer miles from the exchange with which they want to connect.[6] Residents between 22 and 50 miles can also elect ELC, but they must prove a connection with the requested exchange, called "community of interest." Residents whose exchange is more than 50 miles from their nearest neighbor are ineligible, as are customers served by telephone cooperatives and small telephone companies.[7]

There are 1,300 telephone exchanges in Texas of which about 208 serve primarily rural areas. An Urban Influence Code (UIC) determines "remoteness" by measuring county population and proximity to metropolitan areas.[8] This study incorporates UIC 7–9, counties with progressively smaller populations (under 10,000) that are not adjacent to metropolitan counties; in other words, sparsely populated counties some distance from a large town or city. The primary interest of the study is the exchange level characteristics of remoteness, Internet access and public policy. These can be analyzed by the distance from the exchange to the nearest metropolis, the presence or absence of an ISP at the exchange, and the presence or absence of ELC in the exchange area. Remoteness was measured "as the crow flies" using a standard telephone exchange map. A survey of telephone exchanges conducted by the Texas Public Utility

Table 12.2
Extended Local Calling Policy in Texas

Dimension	Mechanisms	Rule
Community of interest	Geographical	CO's 22–50 miles apart
Customer scope	Inclusive	70% of those returning ballots elect for all customers
Directionality	Bi-directional	Only electing exchange customers pay direct fees
Pricing mechanism	Flat	$3.50/month residential $7/month business
Policy scope	Comprehensive	All rural areas subject to PUC regulatory act

Table 12.3
Study Selection Criteria and Data Source

Level of Study	Study Area	Number of Cases	Area Selection	ISP Determination	ELC Determination	Demographic Data Source
Sample Study	5 West Texas and 2 Central Texas counties	25 telephone exchanges	Critical case and comparison group	ISP organization lists, screening phone calls, interviews	ELC petitions, ELC database, interviews	RUPRI exchange data
Statistical Level Study	49 rural counties throughout Texas	208 telephone exchanges	Rural UIC codes (7, 8, 9)	PUC survey of rural telephone exchanges	ELC database	U.S. 1990 Census data

Commission in the spring of 2000 determined the presence or absence of ISPs in exchanges. Data from that survey were paired with data gleaned from an ELC database maintained by the Texas PUC to determine the impact of ELC policy on rural Internet access. Earlier studies, especially the NTIA "Falling Through the Gap" studies, have posited a role for demographic characteristics in shaping the digital divide (NTIA, 2000). Many of those characteristics were collected at the county level for this study, using U.S. Census data to determine education level and Hispanic ethnicity levels.[9] The 1990 Census was also used to assign population and population density. The relative income measure in this study used a state-level index that measures the median income of families within a county as a percentage of median family income across all Texas counties.

Telephone exchanges in Texas have both names, for example, "Six Shooter," and numbers that correspond to the dialing prefix, or nxx code, for that area, for example, "555-." Both names and numbers were used to ascertain the presence or absence of Expanded Local Calling in the 208 remote exchanges under study. When a caller in one exchange connects with another across the invisible exchange boundary, that call becomes subject to applicable nonlocal charges. Sometimes, the call is connected as a "local-long distance" toll call; sometimes it is connected at no additional charge. In the latter case, charges may be reduced as part of a commercial calling arrangement—a flat-rate offer made by the phone company to a group of exchanges—or as the direct result of public policy, such as Expanded Local Calling policies.

As of spring 2000, more than 5,460 petitions for Expanded Local Calling had been filed with the Texas Public Utility Commission. Among those exchanges classified in this study as remote, 104 exchanges representing 49 Texas counties have made 725 ELC petitions, or about 13 percent of all ELC petitions.[10] About 30 percent, or 223, of those petitions were dismissed for some reason. That petition success rate holds for exchanges in each Urban Influence Code (6, 7, or 8), although exchanges with UIC 8—the most remote—made more than half of all petitions. When we examine ELC success from the perspective of geographical areas, however, we can see that exchanges in some area codes are more successful than others. For instance, in our sample study area, exchanges in the 830 area code (Central Texas area) made 23 petitions and were successful about 75 percent of the time. In the West Texas 915 area code, residents made 160 petitions but more than 40 percent failed.

To provide some background for the sample study, I will first discuss findings from the statistical analysis. Exploring these two study components we see that some of the key reasons behind ELC success rates include the role of remoteness, the presence of exempt telephone carriers, and the possible role that social capital plays in advancing through the ELC petition process.

Expanded Local Calling and Internet Access

The legacy of geo-policy barriers, such as exchange areas and LATAs, is mitigated by more recent policies, like ELC, when the policy corresponds to the needs of remote communities. Expanded Local Calling can help communities gain Internet access and expand their range of ISP options. However, ELC does not enhance prospects for connectivity in the most remote, sparsely populated areas. Distance restrictions and carrier exemptions appear to be most directly responsible for policy failure. A statistical analysis clarifies the complex relationship between ELC policy, remoteness and Internet connectivity.

No statistical relationship in this study is as strong or consistent as that between Expanded Local Calling and Internet access (table 12.4). The presence of ELC in an exchange is the key predictor of ISP presence (.507, p<.000). A rural exchange with ELC in place is twice as likely to have an ISP as those without the discount policy. This indicates that ELC can make a tremendous difference in the lives of those residents who can take advantage of it. By extending the reach of rural exchanges, ELC draws them closer into the sphere of advanced telecommunications networks and the benefits of the Internet. But nearly one-third of all ELC petitions are dismissed and we can presume that many other exchanges never attempt to gain the policy relief because they live in exempt areas. As it turns out, ELC is also negatively correlated to distance (–.210, p<.003), and positively correlated to population (.155, p<.026) and population density (.234, p<.001). These relationships allow us to understand Internet access in the context of ELC. Note that the presence of Internet Service Providers is not correlated to population (–.007, p<.919), although it appears weakly correlated with population density (.115, p<.100). Thus, we are not seeing a phenomenon where ISPs simply locate in populated areas and ELC is coincidentally present. Rather, it seems clear that expanded access to more metropolitan exchanges enables residents to take advantage of ISPs that may not necessarily have a direct connection (or "point-of-presence") at their local central telephone office.

ELC and Remoteness

The relationship between distance, ELC and ISP presence is clearly illustrated by clustering the remoteness variable into categories. There appear to be threshold effects for both ELC and ISP presence. Not only are remote exchanges less likely to have either ELC or an ISP[11] but the efficacy of ELC in enabling ISP presence also diminishes with distance because ELC does not apply after the 50-mile cutoff. For instance, 76 percent of all exchanges 50 or fewer miles from a metropolis have ELC and 72 percent have an ISP. Those exchanges in the middle range, between 51 and 76 miles out, 68 percent have ELC and less than half have an ISP. But for those between 75 and 100 miles from a metropolis, ELC rates are 50 percent while ISPs are present in just one third of exchanges. For the six exchanges over 150 miles, just two have ELC or an ISP. These figures suggest a couple of things. First, for exchanges between 50 and 75 miles from a metropolis—the ideal group to be helped by existing ELC policy—about two-thirds can take advantage of the policy and less than half have Internet access. Second, for exchanges more than 75 miles from a metropolis, ELC does not provide much help.

ELC and Demographic Factors

We might expect that ELC would be correlated to socio-economic variables. However, no significant relationship between ELC presence and education or income emerged. Expanded Local Calling policy is most frequently exercised in those exchanges that lie in counties with higher and more concentrated populations, and where Hispanics comprise a relatively small portion of the populace (−.267, p<.000). It is difficult to analyze this relationship, particularly in light of the sample study.[12] Hispanic concentrations are highest in remote counties with low population density, two factors that independently affect ELC presence. The role of ethnicity in adoption of advanced telecommunications has been noted in earlier studies; Hispanics nationally are less likely to own computers or access the Internet than other ethnic groups. But illuminating the precise interaction of ethnicity in ELC adoption will require further study.

Sample Study: *Contrasting Expressions of Geography and Policy*

The concept of geographic capital and the full flavor of geo-policy barriers are revealed in a sample study of rural and remote counties.

Differences within counties—in carriers, in exchange boundaries, and in distance—are revealed with a narrower focus on the exchange, rather than the county, as a unit of analysis. This chapter presents some of the challenges from the legacy of telecommunications policies and commercial investment patterns facing rural residents. Of the 208 rural telephone exchanges in Texas, 25 lie in the general area of the sample

Table 12.4
Variable Correlation

		ISP	ELC	Distance	Density	PCTHISP	Education	Income	PCTunem
ISP	Pearson Correlation	1.000	.507**	-.183**	.115	-.206**	.072	.198**	.085
	Sig. (2-tailed)	—	.000	.009	.100	.003	.304	.004	.224
	N	207	207	204	207	207	207	207	207
ELC	Pearson Correlation–	.507**	1.000	-.210*	.234**	-.267**	-.096	.006	.106
	Sig. (2-tailed)	.000	—	.003	.001	.000	.170	.932	.128
	N	207	207	204	207	207	207	207	207
Distance	Pearson Correlation	-.183**	-.210**	1.000	-.165**	.253**	.280**	-.194**	.132
	Sig. (2-tailed)	.009	.003	—	.018	.000	.000	.006	.060
	N	204	204	204	204	204	204	204	204
Density	Pearson Correlation	.115	.234**	-.165**	1.000	-.416**	-.302**	.070	.316*
	Sig. (2-tailed)	.100	.001	.018	—	.000	.000	.319	.000
	N	207	207	204	207	207	207	207	207
PCThisp	Pearson Correlation	-.206**	-.267**	.253**	-.416**	1.000	-.218**	-.469**	.432*
	Sig. (2-tailed)	.003	.000	.000	.000	—	.002	.000	.000
	N	207	207	204	207	207	207	207	207
Education	Pearson Correlation	.072	-.096	.280**	-.302**	-.218**	1.000	.441**	-.424*
	Sig. (2-tailed)	.304	.170	.000	.000	.002	—	.000	.000
	N	207	207	204	207	207	207	207	207
Income	Pearson Correlation	.198**	.006	-.194**	.070	-.469**	.441**	1.000	-.453*
	Sig. (2-tailed)	.004	.932	.006	.319	.000	.000	—	.000
	N	207	207	204	207	207	207	207	207
PCTunem	Pearson Correlation	.085	.106	.132	.316**	.432**	-.424**	-.453**	1.000
	Sig. (2-tailed)	.224	.128	.060	.000	.000	.000	.000	—
	N	207	207	204	207	207	207	207	207

** Correlation is significant at the 0.01 level (2-tailed).
* Correlation is significant at the 0.01 level (2-tailed).

study.[13] Of these, 19 lie wholly within the seven county study area: nine exchanges are in the five county West area, and ten exchanges in the two county Central area. Because ELC is reciprocal in Texas (petitioned exchanges get the same dialing privileges as those that petition) the surrounding exchanges were examined to see if they had an ELC connection into our study area.

Central Texas Area: *Proximity Aids in Overcoming Geo-Policy Barriers*

In sharp contrast to the West Texas study area, where short trips can take hours, many residents of Llano and Blanco counties drive an hour or less to tap the resources of the Austin and San Antonio metropolitan areas. Exchange areas in this region are smaller, and distances between central switches are generally shorter than their West Texas counterparts. The complicating factor in this area is not so much distance as federal regulatory boundaries that condition both telephone rates and ELC feasibility.

The Kingsland exchange in Llano County is the only successful Expanded Local Calling petitioner in the Central Texas study area. Kingsland customers are connected by ELC to three other exchanges—Marble Falls, Buchanan Dam, and Burnet—all of which lie outside Llano and Blanco counties. Kingsland petitioners overcame an additional hurdle, gaining federal approval to make toll-free inter-LATA connections in each case. Kingsland sits in the San Angelo SMA,[14] whereas Burnet and Buchanan Dam are in the Austin LATA, and Marble Falls is in the San Antonio LATA. Inter-LATA discounts require FCC approval to circumvent the inter-exchange carrier requirement normally applicable in inter-LATA call transfers.

Although there was only a single successful case in the Central Texas area, it points to the role of public information in understanding public policy and to the confusing web of public and commercial responsibilities in telecommunications. Residents of Kingsland had the geographic good fortune and the community wherewithal to get ELC. Expanded Local Calling has also led directly to cheaper Internet access in at least one case in Central Texas. The Marble Falls ISP would incur higher costs without ELC. It operates in all three area LATAs in the area and avoids inter-LATA barriers by employing Remote Call Forwarding (RCF) devices. But RCFs can significantly impact line capacity, quality, and bandwidth reducing both Internet service quality and the serviceable number of Internet customers in a region.

ELC substitutes for remote forwarding devices in the Marble Falls network. For instance, the ISP employed an RCF in Kingsland serving Llano and Tow exchanges. Customers calling in from north and west of Kingsland were transferred via RCF to the Granite Shoals exchange, and then routed through to the ISP's headquarters in Marble Falls. With ELC, the Kingsland calls can be routed directly to Marble Falls, across the LATA, at the flat monthly ELC rate. Many ISPs consider the time and costs associated with maintaining equipment to be a significant growth inhibitor and a drain on cash flow; ELC saves the ISP costs associated with purchasing, operating and maintaining the remote call forwarding devices. Expanded Local Calling also expands the potential market of the Marble Falls ISP by accommodating a greater number of simultaneous connections and increasing line reliability. As broadband considerations come into play, ISPs with landline connections to their customers can employ a greater variety of broadband solutions over greater distances.

West Texas Area: *Small Distances Make the Difference in a Vast Area*

In an area equivalent in size to most of New England, only three of 17 exchanges—Coyanosa, Ft. Stockton, and Imperial—have implemented Expanded Local Calling.[15] Rural exchanges closest to metropolitan areas can use ELC to extend their local calling area, but remote exchanges are held in check by policy exemptions. All of the successful exchanges are located in Pecos County, and all of them are less than 100 miles from Midland.[16] Coyanosa extended its local calling area to Ft. Stockton, Grandfalls, Monahans and Pecos (in Reeves County) exchanges. Imperial elected Crane, Coyanosa, Ft. Stockton, Monahans and Odessa. Grandfalls, an exchange outside the specific study area, elected Imperial, giving Imperial reciprocal discounts. One result of these elections is to interconnect several exchanges in the northern section of the west Texas study area.

In light of these ELC elections, two results stand out related to Internet access. Coyanosa, which is served by two local ISPs, can dial into Ft. Stockton, which has four (the net gain is only two ISPs since the two operating in Coyanosa also operate in Ft. Stockton). Imperial, served by a single local ISP, can dial into Ft. Stockton, the largest town in the study area, with four. Small net gains in total ISPs are not necessarily important; the ISP total in Ft. Stockton is only about half of what is considered a competitive market.[17] But in this case, customers do gain some significant advantages. First, the infrastructure of two Ft. Stockton ISPs can provide higher quality and higher speed service. These ISPs have access to T1 lines from Southwestern Bell and provide ISDN service to their Ft. Stockton customers.[18] Although ISDN is significantly impaired by distance from the central switch, the presence of this advanced service indicates a couple of things for rural customers. Better quality backhaul capacity from Ft. Stockton to Midland improves service reliability and throughput speeds for customers. Extending their reach to Ft. Stockton also puts these small towns within a market sphere that is receiving timelier infrastructure upgrades and has attracted the attention of nearby metropolitan service providers. Second, even the limited competition in the area appears to have an effect on prices. ISPs reported cutting prices to residential customers in light of competitor entry. One ISP cut prices from $30 to $19.95 per month. Third, ISPs operating out of Ft. Stockton are able to take advantage of special features from the dominant carrier, Southwestern Bell. One ISP obtained special prefix feature that allows customers in their service area to dial-up the ISP as a local call. Another ISP uses a "roll-over" feature, in which customers dial a local number that is then automatically forwarded to another number in a distant exchange. These features add incremental costs to ISP's operating expenses, but the customer experiences these features as seamless connections via a local telephone number.

Remote residents gain access in one of two ways. For Imperial, the significant connectivity is gained through a two-step process. In the first step, remote customers, because of their relative proximity to Ft. Stockton, gain access to upgraded services and a relatively competitive market. Ft. Stockton is too far from Odessa or Midland to reach them via ELC. However, because of its relatively large size and its position on a major highway in Southwestern Bell territory, Ft. Stockton it is located on the technological fringe of the Odessa metro area. It can make the second step to upgrades and competition available in a larger Internet market.

Coyanosa residents access the benefits of a metropolitan market in a single step. By extending their local calling range to Odessa, Coyanosa, a high plains ranch town of fewer than 400 people bypassed by the major highways, becomes part of a 250,000 person telecommunications market! In Coyanosa the potential of ELC and of the Internet for rural areas can be fully realized. Telephone companies and other providers are more likely to upgrade infrastructure between Coyanosa and Odessa if customers, either ISPs or residents, demand it. ELC in this sense solves a "chicken and egg" problem relative to infrastructure and demand. It is difficult to assess demand for services in areas without significant exposure to the benefits of those services. ELC allows residents to experience a profusion of Internet provision options and services and provides a better view of the potential market for ISPs. Market cognizance may lead to greater marketing efforts, which in turn heighten awareness of Internet options for Coyanosa customers. Internet Service Providers looking to expand their market territory will look first to capture those customers who can reach them with a local call. ELC in Coyanosa effectively extends the potential reach of ISPs whose primary market is the Midland-Odessa metropolitan area.

When Coyanosa residents access national ISPs that serve Midland, they gain service portability, competitive pricing and new service options. They also gain access to faster backhaul infrastructure eliminating some of the problems that reduce Internet convenience and viability in remote areas. Access to improved, national services—the Internet as it was meant to be—introduces a new sense of connection in Coyanosa both with the Midland-Odessa metro and with the rest of the connected world. Interaction via telecommunications can function to reduce feelings of isolation for remote residents and has important reciprocal effects for businesses and institutions. Connectivity in Coyanosa can shrink the perceived distance between the small town and the metro as well as the actual costs of communication and service delivery. This perceptual shift "moves" Coyanosa closer to the metro or gives them the choice to move closer, extending the reach of small town businesses and consolidating the markets of metropolitan service and information providers.

If Coyanosa demonstrates the positive potential of Expanded Local Calling in West Texas, the Valentine exchange, in Jeff Davis County, demonstrates how the current ELC regulations can work to prevent connectivity. The Texas PUC dismissed all five of Valentine's petitions before election. Valentine failed to articulate a Community of Interest in three cases; one petitioned exchange lay outside the 50-mile limit, and Big Bend Telephone exercised its exemption as a cooperative in the fifth case. As a result, Valentine remains isolated with a single ISP and low-bandwidth service.

Any constituent wishing to petition for ELC receives some specific guidelines on ELC exemptions and community of interest criteria. How then is it that an exchange can petition five exchanges, two of which are exempted by statute and in three cases fail to articulate community of interest? The answer lies in the specific geographic and institutional situation of the town. Valentine is a remote town of 217 people, about half living under the poverty line. Located in Jeff Davis County, it is about 35 miles west of Ft. Davis (pop. 426), the county seat and about 50 miles north of Alpine, the largest town in the area and home of Sul Ross University. Because Valentine relies upon Big Bend Regional Medical Center in Alpine, residents must dial long distance for routine and emergency medical consultation.

Alpine was clearly the primary target of Valentine's ELC petition, but Valentine had what they felt was ample reason to bridge the boundaries of each of the five exchanges. Besides telephone exchange boundaries, another set of invisible lines segregates the people in the Valentine area. School districts do not match up with telephone exchanges or city limits. The Valentine Independent School District is the largest single employer in Valentine, with 18 employees, and some residents naturally work in neighboring districts. People living not far outside of town make long distance calls from home to work and work to home. Similarly, students in VISD turn to area ranches for employment and the district has created some school-to-work programs to help students get jobs nearby. But students who want to call from within the Valentine exchange to ranches as close as nine miles away must place long distance calls. Students commuting to Sul Ross in Alpine are unable to utilize the Internet access they pay for as part of their standard fees without placing a long distance call. Unpredictable and unexpected long distance charges are budget busters for poor American families (Horrigan et al., 1995). In an area like Valentine, long distance charges may dissuade potential callers from checking in with their kids at home, calling their children's teachers, seeking employment, using an otherwise free Internet service, and even asking for routine medical advice.

Valentine made Community of Interest arguments like those above with a focus on Alpine. However, the Texas PUC judged Alpine to be 51.55 air miles from the Valentine exchange and thus beyond the 50 mile limit of ELC. Although Valentine citizens routinely drive to Alpine, it is unlikely any of them had measured the precise air miles between the switches, nor is that information available from phone companies.[19] Similarly, there is no particular reason Valentine residents should know that an independent telephone company serves the Alamito exchange. With those two exchanges ruled out, Valentine needed to make a Community of Interest case for the remaining three in Marfa, Ft. Davis and Van Horn. Their argument for local calling between adjoining school districts was judged insufficient.

A Valentine educator filed the petition, a typical situation in the ELC process. Schools are the hub of rural communities and rural educators are particularly attuned to the costs of parent-teacher communication among other things. Rural schools are generally a significant part of economic development plans, as well. In those areas where long-distance rates discourage communication, the school becomes a hub with no spokes connecting it to the encircling community. Coyanosa, Imperial and Valentine are very similar communities in many respects. Each town has fewer than 800 residents and similar demographics. A key difference between Coyanosa and Imperial—successful ELC petitioners—and Valentine appears to be distance from a metropolitan area. In Valentine, where using ELC to access a metropolitan area is out of the question, even the distance to the nearest large town proved to be unconquerable.

Conclusions: *Geo-Policy Barriers, Communication and Community*

Pathways of wire and glass are the 21st century postal roads and computer algorithms are smoothing the bumps and grooves. The Internet, however, has not yet managed to eliminate the rural penalty. Rather, development patterns are exacerbating the rural disadvantage. The problem is not simply one of infrastructure, but is created through the development of telecommunications markets and the legacy of federal and state communication policies.

The overlapping geographies of the information age constitute some of the greatest challenges to rural connectivity. Exchange areas, LATAs and other geo-policy boundaries arrange citizens into markets, rather than arranging firms to serve communities. Perhaps this should not be surprising since agencies are formed to regulate industries. However, the directive of the FCC is to "serve the *public* interest, convenience and necessity," and similar language can be found in the mission of most public utility agencies. Universal service programs and other regulatory relief, such as ELC, will work best when they place citizens and communities at the "center" and dissolve, rather than erect, barriers to interaction.

It is clear that EAS policies can help rural citizens extend their reach toward Internet access, and that rural Internet Service Providers can utilize the policy to dissolve market and technological barriers; however, the policies discriminate. ELC builds strict, arbitrary boundaries for "community." The most striking example of the Texas PUC's commitment to the firms they regulate is the exemption for rural telephone companies, an exemptions designed to ensure service to rural customers. This exemption creates a feudalistic correspondence between communities and monopoly providers wherein the presence of the small company dictates the fate of the citizen. This logic is extended by the Community of Interest rules that encourage citizens to conceptualize community according to the frequency and intention of telephonic communications with institutions, rather than with each other. Again, the ideology of regulation constructs communities as constituents of commercial and governmental institutions around which they revolve in close geographic patterns.

In terms of Internet access, the "rural penalty" can be usefully reconceptualized as a "remote penalty," with the most remote towns least likely to enjoy the fruits of the communication revolution. Ironically, these policies often exclude the very residents that stand to benefit most from their effective implementation, paring away remote communities through a series of exemptions and requirements that test the abilities of even trained policy experts.

Acknowledgments

The author wishes to thank members of the Telecommunications and Information Policy Institute at the University of Texas at Austin for assistance with data collection for this study.

Notes

1. The importance of the King Road drag is illuminated in Gladwell, Malcolm. (1999, August). Clicks and Mortar, *New Yorker*.

2. See Carey, James. (1989). *Communication as Culture*. Boston: Unwin Hyman.

3. Section 3(37) of the Telecommunications Act of 1996, set forth in FCC Rules Part 51.5 designates rural telephone companies as meeting one of four criteria:

   a. service area includes no incorporated area with more than 10,000 inhabitants or any territory in an urbanized area

   b. the company provides telephone service to less than 50,000 access lines

   c. the company provides telephone exchange service to any LEC with fewer than 100,000 access lines

   d. the company has less than 15% of its access lines in communities of 50,000 or more inhabitants (as of the date of the Act, February 8, 1996.

4. For reviews of the share and administration of universal service programs, see Rosenberg et al., 1998 or the Benton Policy & Practice initiative, "The New Definition of Universal Service," online at:
<http://www.benton.org/Updates/summary.html#admin>.

5. Texas has approximately 20 million residents spread over 261,000 square miles.

6. ELC elections proceed through ballots provided through phone company billing lists. Successful elections require a 70 percent majority of all customers who vote.

7. Small companies in this case provide fewer than 10,000 customer lines. An exemption may also be made for any exchange with fewer than 10,000 access lines.

8. Urban Influence Codes are available from the USDA online at:
<http://www.ers.usda.gov:80/briefing/rural/Data/>.

9. Black and Asian populations were less than 2% in the areas studied. "Hispanic" is a complex identifier, particularly in a state that has been both a Spanish and a Mexican territory, and where Hispanics represent both the earliest and most recent non-indigenous inhabitants. The U.S. Census category "Hispanic" contains "white" and "nonwhite" sub-categories. This study uses the collective Hispanic category and does not distinguish between sub-categories.

10. These figures are accurate as of spring 2000.

11. The exceptions are three remote exchanges clustered along a highway that runs through Alpine, Texas, the seat of a remote state university, served by the dominant carrier, Southwestern Bell.

12. For instance Coyanosa (89% Hispanic) successfully petitioned for ELC and gained Internet access, whereas Valentine (16% Hispanic) failed in its attempt to boost connectivity.

13. One of the key problems in analyzing telephone exchanges at the county level is that exchanges do not map precisely over counties and county level studies tend to mask geo-policy barriers. However, demographic and connectivity data is generally collected at the county level, by both state and federal entities, making broad, generalizable studies at the exchange level difficult.

14. Texas has two designated Service Management Areas, or SMAs, that function as LATAs.

15. Coyanosa and Imperial completed the petition process and conducted successful elections; Ft. Stockton receives ELC dialing discounts via reciprocal privileges as a result of those elections.

16. Ft. Stockton is about 90 miles from Midland; Imperial is 64 miles, and Coyanosa is approximately 77 miles.

17. Greenstein, Shane. (1998). Universal Service in the Digital Age: The commercialization and geography of U.S. Internet access, National Bureau of Economic ResearchWorking Paper 6453, [online] Available at: <www.nber.org.papers/w6453>.

18. A T1 uses two copper pairs to provide 1.54Mbps in optimal range. Integrated Services Digital Network (ISDN) is a series of standards designed to transmit over ordinary telephone copper twisted-pair wiring as well as over more advanced infrastructure. Usually, ISDN offers one voice and two data channels, but can be split into as many as 30 channels. Transmission speeds range up to 128kbps.

19. Point-to-point exchange distances can be obtained from the PUC through a formal Open Records request, but the most likely way to get it is through the ELC petition process.

Sources

Carey, James, 1989. *Communication as Culture*. Boston: Unwin Hyman.

Gladwell, Malcolm, 1999. Clicks and Mortar. *New Yorker,* August.

Greenstein, Shane, 1998. Universal Service in the Digital Age: The commercialization and geography of U.S. Internet access, National Bureau of Economic ResearchWorking Paper 6453, [online] Available at: <www.nber.org.papers/w6453>.

Horrigan, John and Lodis Rhodes, 1995. The Evolution of Universal Service in Texas. Austin, TX: Lyndon Baines Johnson School of Public Affairs.

Benton Policy & Practice initiative, "The New Definition of Universal Service," [online] Available at: <http://www.benton.org/Updates/summary.html#admin>.

Rosenberg, Edwin and John Wilhelm, 1998. State Universal Service Funding and Policy: An overview and survey. Columbus, OH: National Regulatory Research Institute.

13

Telecommunications and Rural Economies: Findings from the Appalachian Region

Sharon Strover, Michael Oden, and Nobuya Inagaki

I Introduction

Many scholars recognize that information and telecommunications industries have become the critical drivers of the U.S. economy. These industries have had a dominant influence on recent growth performance due to their direct contribution to output and employment and through their pervasive impacts on industries and households that use their products and services (U.S. Department of Commerce, 2000). Several studies emphasize the potential benefits that new information technology could bring to rural or distressed areas by reducing the importance of market proximity and transportation costs in business location (Williams, 1991; Parker et al., 1989, 1995). However, like earlier key technologies, the integrated architecture of computing and telecommunications exhibits a clear pattern of uneven distribution. Population density, income, geographic location, and the initial presence of innovative producers are among the main factors that influence production and use of new appliances and software systems and access to high-speed broadband networks (National Telecommunications and Information Administration, 1999; U.S. Department of Agriculture, 2000). These factors, affecting both access and capacity to use advanced telecom technologies, suggest that poorer rural regions actually risk falling further behind as the new information and telecommunications technologies proliferate and become more central to business performance.

Uneven access and capacity underscore the primary challenges rural communities' face in exploiting the new technologies. They must secure cost- and quality-competitive access to advanced telecom services and rapidly build local expertise, training and service capacities to improve local business performance and to attract new firms. The FCC's recent *Report on the Availability of High-Speed and Advanced Telecommunications Services* notes in particular that high-speed telecommunications services are not readily available in rural and low-income areas (FCC, 2000, August).[1]

This research maps current telecom infrastructure and user patterns, information about the effects of access and use barriers on rural businesses, and efforts in Appalachian communities to bridge the digital divide.

II   The Role of Information Technologies in the Economy

It is widely acknowledged that telecommunications industries that produce information and communications products and services have been a crucial factor in the U.S. economy's sustained and rapid growth during the 1990s. There is a common group of Standard Industrial Classification code jobs that, together, represent aggregate employment in the Information/Communication Technology (ICT) sector. These industries accounted for less then 10 percent of U.S. output during 1995–1999, but close to 30 percent of the country's growth (U.S. Dept. of Commerce, 2000). Employment in these industries grew from 3.9 million in 1992 to 5.2 million in 1998, a 33 percent increase. Similarly, an identifiable group of industries can be coded as telecommunications producing and—using industries. Equipment investments alone nearly doubled, from $243 billion in 1995 to $510 billion in 1999 (U.S. Dept. of Commerce, 2000).

Telecommunications infrastructure is a critical component in these indicators. The presence of and ability to use computers, particularly in a networked environment, and access to appropriate software applications, as well as access to fast communications networks for rapid information flow, are critical to effectively extracting the benefits of information technology. Cronin et al. (1993) found, for example, that telecommunications investment rises with economic growth, while economic growth likewise rises with investment in telecommunications. Parker has reported similar results (1995), as have Dholakia and Harlam (1994). Such data suggest that access to broadband communications networks (200 kbps or faster) at affordable rates will be a significant factor in continued economic growth, as will having the education and training institutions available that can convey to workers the appropriate skills to use network capabilities. This process also underscores the importance of having state and local institutions that can improve access and social capacity to use information and communication technologies in firms, in schools, and in residences.

The federal and numerous state governments have recognized the importance of the communications infrastructural elements that enable economic growth, and they have sought to create an environment that encourages wider deployment of advanced communications capabilities. In the current deregulatory era, this has meant a combination of incentives, government-funded programs, and collaborative ventures with the private sector. For example, the 1996 Telecommunication Act's universal service provisions created the E-Rate program to fund Internet connectivity to schools and libraries, and another program to support medical facilities' telecommunications access. The Rural Utility Service currently grants loans for rural broadband improvements.[2] States, having received much more authority over telecommunications inasmuch as they are the first stop in insuring that the Bell Operating Companies are opening their markets,[3] have sought to create terms and conditions that deliberately encourage statewide network capacity and deployment; several have undertaken assessments of their competitiveness and of their broadband assets. For example, North Carolina completed an exhaustive, exchange-by-exchange study for the entire state inventorying service quality and costs (North Carolina Department of Commerce, 2000). Tennessee's Digital Divide Report includes some data addressing telephone penetration on a county-by-county basis (Tennessee TRA, 2000). Some states have leveraged their statewide government communications systems or economic development programs to improve communication services to critical institutions within their boundaries.

A crucial question for more disadvantaged regions is whether the deregulated telecommunications industries can or will provide them with competitive infrastructure opportunities. The number of competing local exchange carriers (CLECs) has escalated generally, many of them providing advanced telecommunications services. However, these new competitors face an environment of large and powerful incumbent companies that have lobbied fiercely for fewer restrictions on their abilities to enter new markets, notably long distance voice service and inter-LATA data transport (or long distance backhaul) services.[4] If telecommunications competition in parts of the country seems more intense, in rural regions such as those characteristic of much of Appalachia it seems nonexistent. The limited data that are publicly available demonstrate that broadband deployment is much more widespread and even competitive in populous metropolitan regions, while it is absent in rural America. The National Exchange Carriers Association estimates that it will cost $10.9 billion to make broadband capabilities available throughout rural America (NECA, 2000).

Skirmishes between telecommunications providers, local populations and their officials, and state and federal regulators have broken out over deploying broadband capabilities to rural areas, or even to secondary or tertiary markets. For example, allowing or encouraging municipally owned utilities to provide telecommunications services has been the subject of litigation as well as opposing state policies around the country (City of Bristol, Virginia, etc., v. Mark L. Earley, 2001; also Strover and Berquist, 2001). The rocky process by which Bell Operating Companies open their networks to competitors has prompted several states to warn or chastise the BOCs for slow or seemingly deliberately obstructionist behavior.[5] Portions of the country that want broadband capabilities but cannot obtain them from their local (and usually de facto monopoly) provider have few alternatives. Satellite broadband systems have been slow to develop; wireless broadband in rural areas has not emerged.

The processes by which high-speed services can be realized in the Appalachian region involve complex interactions among policymakers, telecommunications companies, local communities, and the local economic environment. Understanding the volatile climate of lawsuits, evolving policy, and uncertain competitive terrain is a first step to assessing the prospects for broadband capabilities in the region.

III   Research Plan

In this research we assess broadband deployment and prospects in the Appalachian region. This article reports only a portion of the results of a larger inquiry (Oden and Strover, 2001). Here, we survey secondary data sources and report on the results from phone interviews with federal and state officials responsible for implementing telecom development programs in the Appalachian Region Commission (ARC)region[6] to delineate the size and distribution of federal and state telecommunications programs in the area. We also inventoried the regulations and projects pertinent to telecommunications infrastructure developments in 13 target states with special attention to: (1) deregulation legislation over the past 5 years; (2) access (both telephone and Internet) and universal service programs and provisions; (3) agreements to extend service to communities or state and local governments in exchange for state level approval of telecom company mergers; and (4) special state initiatives that influence the infrastructure (particularly broadband) serving rural areas in particular.

There is no single dataset that compiles a comprehensive and up-to-date listing of state-level telecommunications regulations and related programs. For the current research, we undertook extensive telephone interviews with key informants (generally agency officials) in each state in order to provide the information on the policies and initiatives noted above as well as conducted web-based and literature searches.

We found access to federal level and state data to be problematic in some cases. For example, the FCC's latest dataset on broadband service survey throughout the country has not been released. Consequently, our analyses using that data are based on reports the FCC received in July, 2000, sadly out of date for telecommunications infrastructure assessments.

Our evaluation of "last mile" infrastructure and access in the Appalachian region relied on three data sources. First, statistical data from various federal/state agencies and associations provide a snapshot of relevant capabilities. For example, the FCC maintains a database of central office facilities for the major local exchange companies; the Commission's new Form 477 requires larger providers of local telecommunications and broadband services to report on deployment on a semi-annual basis. The FCC also provides detailed reports on universal service programs. Second, secondary data from several survey results and databases published on the Internet provided valuable up-to-date information for the status of technology deployment in our target areas. Last, we consulted a proprietary database for telephone infrastructure, particularly the distribution of telephone central office facilities across our target states.

IV   Telecommunications Infrastructure in the Appalachian Region

Certain sub-areas within the Appalachian states have particularly poor telecommunications infrastructure, a fate of many rural regions around the United States, while other areas may have excellent capabilities. Table 13.1 illustrates the state-by-state disparities, and the huge growth rates of the past few years.

As table 13.1 illustrates, all the states we scrutinize joined the national trends toward higher computer penetration and rates of Internet access. Virginia and Maryland stand out with the high penetration rates for both, rates that exceed the national average. We suspect this is due primarily to the intense business development in the Washington, D.C./Maryland area.

Table 13.1
Computer, Internet access and telephones

State	Percent of households with computers			Percent of households with Internet access			Percent of households with telephones		
	1998	2000	% Change	1998	2000	% Change	1998	2000	% Change
AL	34.3	44.2	28.9	21.6	35.5	64.4	93.3	91.9	−1.5
GA	35.8	47.1	31.6	23.9	38.3	60.3	91.4	91.1	−0.3
KY	35.9	46.2	28.7	21.1	36.6	73.5	93.3	93.3	0.0
MD	46.3	53.7	16.0	31.0	43.8	41.3	96.5	95.0	−1.6
MS	25.7	37.2	44.7	13.6	26.3	93.4	89.5	89.2	−0.3
NY	37.3	48.7	30.6	23.7	39.8	67.9	94.8	95.1	0.3
NC	35.0	45.3	29.4	19.9	35.3	77.4	93.1	93.9	0.9
OH	40.7	49.5	21.6	24.6	40.7	65.4	95.6	94.8	−0.8
PA	39.3	48.4	23.2	24.9	40.1	61.0	96.8	96.6	−0.2
SC	35.7	43.3	21.3	21.4	32.0	49.5	92.9	93.2	0.3
TN	37.5	45.7	21.9	21.3	36.3	70.4	94.9	95.5	0.6
VA	46.4	53.9	16.2	27.9	44.3	58.8	93.9	95.4	1.6
WV	28.3	42.8	51.2	17.6	34.3	94.9	93.8	94.0	0.2
Nation	42.1	51.0	21.1	26.2	41.5	58.4	94.1	94.4	0.3

Sources: NTIA (1999, July). *Falling through the Net: Defining the digital divide;* NTIA (2000, October). *Falling through the Net: Toward digital inclusion;* Belinfante, A. (1999) *Telephone subscribership in the U.S., February 1999 and March 2001.* Federal Communications Commission; Belinfante, A. (2001, March). Telephone subscribership in the United States (Data through November 2000). Washington, D.C.: Federal Communications Commission.

Note: Bold figures are above national average.

Internet backbone

Backbone providers typically function as the carrier of carriers, transporting other telecommunications service providers' traffic to distant locations. As such, backbone providers play a crucial role in determining the availability and scope of telecommunications services that "last-mile" providers offer to end users. For example, Internet service providers and their customers are likely to suffer from the lack of adequate bandwidth and/or a higher cost/price if fiber backbone facility is lacking in ISPs' immediate local areas.

In addition to their function as the carriers' carrier, some backbone providers also offer services directly to end users. A range of service offering—such as ATM (asynchronous transfer mode), Frame Relay, VPN (virtual private network), and other integrated voice/data services—is available from backbone providers themselves, often in competition with traditional end-user vendors, telephone companies. Backbone providers' end-user offerings are usually geared toward business customers. We expect that backbone providers' presence in a locality stimulates other telecommunications companies' service and technology portfolio in the area.

Fiber optic cables are crisscrossing various areas including densely populated urban areas as well as remote rural regions. However, crossing a region does not guarantee access to fiber throughout entire routes. Just like any other telecommunications network, a backbone network becomes functional only when the user can have access to one of the network's POPs (points of presence). In assessing the access to backbone networks among different communities in the Appalachian region, therefore, we primarily considered the geographic dispersion of backbone POPs.

Figure 13.1 offers a plot of the locations of backbone POPs in the Appalachian region. The pattern of backbone infrastructure development in the Appalachian region is similar to DSL and cable modem environment (see below) in that the majority of counties in the region lacks proximate access to backbone POPs. Among the 407 Appalachian counties, only 56 counties host backbone POPs. In addition, those POP hosting counties are predominantly metropolitan counties. Traffic in Mississippi and Kentucky faces clear disadvantages since there are few POPs local to the Appalachian regions of those states. In Mississippi, for example, data traffic must be hauled either to Tupelo (the location of the

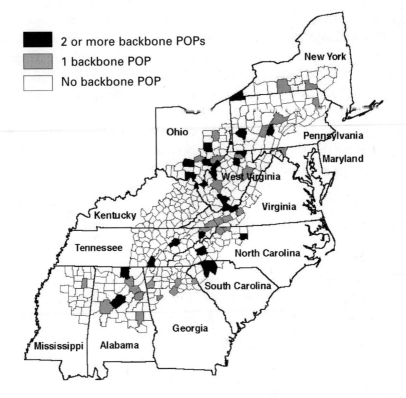

Figure 13.1
Broadband POPs in the Appalachian region (as of July, 2001)

Source: Authors' telephone conversations with backbone network providers; *Boardwatch Magazine's directory of Internet service providers.* (13th Ed.). (2001).

marked POP) or south to Jackson (not in the Appalachian region) or even further north to Tennessee, incurring additional costs. Locations with more POPs correspond to metropolitan areas as well as to counties along major highways (as in the case of Virginia).

"Last Mile" Connectivity

The most common high-speed residential and small business end-user technologies are cable modem and DSL services. When the penetration levels of cable modem and DSL services are examined, we see evidence that these technologies too are underrepresented in the Appalachian Region compared to national averages.

Figure 13.2 illustrates the locations of cable modem service, although the map is misleading in that it displays the counties where there is cable

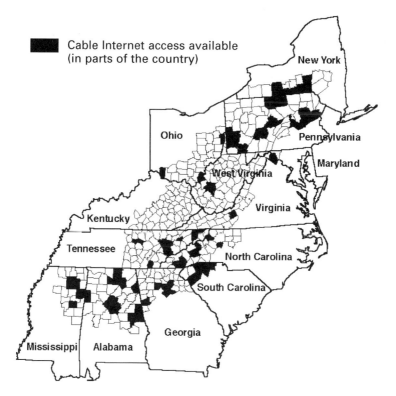

Figure 13.2
Cable modem service in the Appalachian region (as of March, 2001)

Sources: CableDataCom News. (2001, March 7). Commercial Cable Modem Launches in North America. [Online]. Available: <http://www.cabledatacomnews.com/cmic/cmic7.html≥; Cable Modem Deployment Update. (2000, March). Communications, Engineering and Design (CED)Magazine. Cited in National Telecommunications and Information Administration & Rural Utilities Service. (2000, April). Advanced Telecommunications in Rural America: The Challenge of Bringing Broadband Service to All Americans. pp. 46-59. [Online]. Available: <http://www.ntia.doc.gov/reports/ruralbb42600.pdf>.

modem service even though we do not mean to imply that the *entire* county is actually served. Cable modem service typically is available only within towns, not in rural areas. The Appalachian region is sparsely served by this technology, which is confirmed in additional FCC data presented below.

The other major broadband service, DSL, likewise is not broadly available to subscribers in the Appalachian region.[8] Kentucky, Ohio, Virginia, and West Virginia have few DSL-equipped central offices. The other ARC states illustrate much broader penetration of DSL-equipped offices.

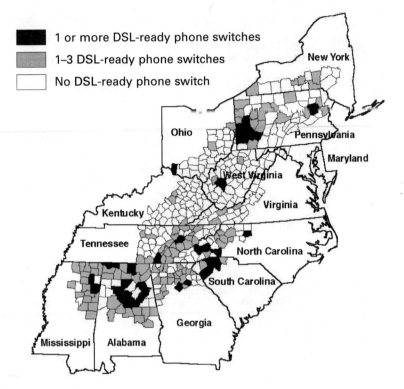

Figure 13.3
DSL equipped offices in the Appalachian region (as of August, 2001)

Sources: Authors' search in the Central Office Finder database at DSL Reports web site.
[Online]. Available: <http://www.dslreports.com/coinfo>; National Telecommunications and
Information Administration & Rural Utilities Service. (2000, April). *Advanced telecommunications in rural America: The challenge of bringing broadband service to all Americans,*
pp. 60–72. [Online]. Available: <http://www.ntia.doc.gov/reports/ruralbb42600.pdf>.

However, our field visits to Mississippi and Virginia demonstrated that
the presence of a DSL-ready office does not necessarily translate into
actual DSL service for the region. For example, the MS counties we visited did not have operational DSL even though Bell South, the dominant
local exchange company, said its offices either were or would shortly be
equipped for the service and even though those equipped offices appear
in public documentation. We find a statistically significant relationship
between the economic vitality of a region (as classified by the Appalachian Regional Commission as either distressed, transitional, competitive, or in attainment) and numbers of DSL-ready central offices: among

the 114 distressed counties, 81 percent have no DSL ready central offices, compared to 63 percent of the transitional counties and 27 percent of the competitive counties.[9]

The FCC's data from Form 477 categorizes high-speed providers as any service providing at least 200 kbps in at least one direction (user to provider or provider to user). Data they collected illustrate that the more populous regions of Appalachia obtained high-speed services, but many other regions have none. The FCC's use of the high-speed designation is problematic because it does not identify whether the service is broadly available, such as DSL, or a single T-1 line, but in the case of the Appalachian region is it easy to see that high-speed services are not pervasive.

In fact, we find that 47 percent of the Appalachian region's zip codes have one or more high-speed service subscribers, compared to the nationwide average of 59 percent of the country's zip codes, a statistically significant difference (table 13.2). That said, however, the availability of high-speed service can be extremely misleading as an indicator of regional connectivity. In our fieldwork we saw that even in economically distressed counties, the largest businesses had T-1 (or better) connectivity, but that fact said nothing about broader connections and capabilities in the county or zip code. It registers simply as a single line to one business.

Telephone Infrastructure
Basic line quality and switching features vary tremendously across the Appalachian region, as in other parts of the country. Competitive pressures are relatively low in the Appalachian sub-regions. For example, most of the states with counties in the Appalachian region have fairly low numbers of competing local exchange companies (CLECs), although in two, New York and Pennsylvania, the Bell Operating Companies have been approved to offer long distance services at this writing.[10] The December 31, 2000, data as illustrated in table 13.3 indicate that New York has the highest CLEC presence—indeed, it is the highest in the country—followed among Appalachian states by Georgia and Pennsylvania, both with 10 percent of their end user lines serviced by CLECs.

One goal of this research is not only to assess competition but also to assess line quality and upgrade activity in the ARC region. The statistics presented above already point to certain deficiencies in the local and

Table 13.2
Percentage of ZIP code areas with high-speed Internet access in 2000

State	ARC region
Kentucky	13%
Mississippi	32%
New York	39%
Ohio	42%
Alabama	45%
Georgia	47%
West Virginia	47%
Pennsylvania	49%
Virginia	51%
North Carolina	53%
Maryland	54%
Tennessee	54%
South Carolina	59%
National %	59%

Source: The Federal Communications Commission. (2000, August). Deployment of advanced telecommunications capability: Second report. [Online]. Available: <http://www.fcc.gov/broadband>.

Table 13.3
End user lines (as of Dec., 2000)

State	ILECs	CLECs	Total lines	% CLEC share
Alabama	2,351,704	191,299	2,543,000	8
Georgia	4,820,788	551,316	5,372,104	10
Kentucky	2,122,021	56,392	2,178,413	3
Maryland	3,802,622	165,502	3,968,124	4
Mississippi	1,304,145	68,891	1,373,036	5
New York	10,962,969	2,769,814	13,732,783	20
North Carolina	5,071,853	286,436	5,358,289	5
Ohio	6,935,139	264,461	7,199,600	4
Pennsylvania	8,017,391	870,618	8,888,009	10
South Carolina	2,260,645	108,233	2,368,878	5
Tennessee	3,291,602	296,281	3,587,883	8
Virginia	4,317,626	414,432	4,732,058	9
West Virginia	927,432	—	—	—

Source: FCC, Common Carrier Bureau statistics, 2001.

Table 13.4
Telephone switches by region and type

State	ARC region			Non-ARC region		
	ILEC switch	CLEC switch	% CLEC switch	ILEC switch	CLEC switch	% CLEC switch
Alabama	218	74	25.3	170	60	26.1
Georgia	107	19	15.1	365	169	31.6
Kentucky	140	4	2.8	268	70	20.7
Maryland	28	6	17.6	218	139	38.9
Mississippi	66	23	25.8	218	128	37.0
New York	195	24	11.0	808	335	29.3
North Carolina	127	27	17.5	412	231	35.9
Ohio	230	6	2.5	711	183	20.5
Pennsylvania	628	134	17.6	267	164	38.1
South Carolina	55	39	41.5	262	70	21.1
Tennessee	192	48	20.0	222	92	29.3
Virginia	115	5	4.2	391	158	28.8
West Virginia	258	32	11.0	NA	NA	NA
Average			16.3			29.8

Source: GDT/Telecommunications Products v. 5.1, CD-ROM. (2001). Geographic Data Technology, Inc.

regional networks. Looking at the telephone infrastructure from a telephone switch standpoint, the Appalachian portions of our 13 target states have low levels of CLEC activities compared to the rest of these states (table 13.4).

The actual cost of providing services in the Appalachian states also is important insofar as longer loop lengths (to serve rural areas, for example) and low population densities mean that those regions should receive more support in order to maintain universal service. Data from the FCC show that eight of the 13 states (Alabama, North Carolina, Tennessee, Kentucky, Georgia, South Carolina, West Virginia and Mississippi) in the Appalachian region have loop costs above the $239 national average for 2001. Maryland's Universal Service Fund (USF) loop costs are lowest, at $193 per loop (its population density is the highest, at 541.0 persons per square mile). Mississippi's loop cost is the highest, at $352.63 per loop (its population density is the lowest of the 13 states, at 60.06 persons per square mile).

The FCC recognizes 1301 rural local exchange companies, which serve approximately 6 percent of U.S. households and cover 35 percent of the country's landmass, excluding Alaska. These companies typically have longer loops and consequently higher loop costs than companies serving metropolitan regions. However, larger companies including the BOCs, not considered primarily rural telcos, also serve numerous rural households. Bell South, for example, serves most of Mississippi's households. Determining the appropriate amount of support companies serving high cost regions should have in order to maintain the goals of universal service has been a topic of considerable study and lobbying. The FCC adopted a formula for universal service support first for non-rural areas in October 1, 1999, and a formula for rural companies in 2001.[11] The impact of that universal service support will be examined below.

V   Universal Service Initiatives in the Appalachian Region

Several federal programs have been initiated to enhance access to basic and advanced telecommunications services, the rationale often being to stimulate information technology capabilities in rural and low-income urban areas. Here we examine one major federal support program under universal service: the high cost support fund. We also examine several state initiatives. State programs are a highly heterogeneous collection of endeavors, ranging from leveraging the states' own telecommunications services for broader purposes to operating statewide E-rate-like programs.

Federal Universal Service
While the concept of universal service dates back to the early 1900s, its meaning and mechanisms have undergone several changes (Mueller, 1997). Today, however, federal universal service refers to a series of FCC rules to make various classes of telecommunications services available at just, reasonable, and affordable rates throughout the county, as mandated by Section 254 of the Telecommunications Act of 1996. The current federal universal service policy can be best described as part evolving process, part formalized and interim regulations, and ongoing proceedings. As such, a thorough description of each component of federal universal service support is beyond the scope of this article. Instead, we

Table 13.5
Distribution of the federal high-cost program in Appalachia in 2000

State	Rural1	Non-rural2	Total
Alabama	$27,833,107	$60,203,436	$88,036,543
Georgia	$73,429,979	$5,919,045	$79,349,024
Kentucky	$18,839,297	$10,608,807	$29,448,104
Maryland	$552,276	$1,852,272	$2,404,548
Mississippi	$23,442,921	$109,658,352	$133,101,273
New York	$43,566,507	$9,015,372	$52,581,879
North Carolina	$24,432,168	$9,638,988	$34,071,156
Ohio	$15,579,591	$3,908,757	$19,488,348
Pennsylvania	$27,296,823	$1,459,563	$28,756,386
South Carolina	$37,895,032	$11,613,882	$49,508,914
Tennessee	$29,524,563	$4,487,319	$34,011,882
Virginia	$10,656,944	$26,516,103	$37,173,047
West Virginia	$25,761,273	$37,249,836	$63,011,109
Total	$358,810,481	$292,131,732	$650,942,213

Note: "Rural" carriers for the purpose of federal universal service are local exchange carriers that either serve study areas with fewer than 100,000 access lines or have less than 15 percent of their access lines in communities of more than 50,000 in 1996. "Non-rural" carriers are local exchange carriers that do not meet the criteria for "rural" carrier designation.

summarize the largest component of federal universal service support—the high-cost program—and discuss its implications for the particular telecommunications needs of the Appalachian region.[12] Although the 1996 Act does not explicitly state it, the high-cost program goes hand in hand with rate reductions in nonbasic services (including long-distance service access charges) so that prices can move toward real costs. Such rate reductions essentially eliminate implicit cross subsidies between nonbasic and basic services, one of the goals in the 1996 Act's reformulation of universal service. Table 13.5 indicates the rural and nonrural high-cost distributions for the ARC states.

In FY2000, the Universal Service Administrative Company distributed $4.4 billion to eligible recipients across the county, and the high-cost and the E-Rate programs account for the bulk of this support ($4.3 billion) (Universal Service Administrative Company, 2001). The high-cost program (with five separate components) has the largest share in the federal Universal Service, with the amount of disbursement reaching $2.2 billion in FY2000. The E-rate program was the next highest share in the

Universal service fund. Of the $2.2 billion high-cost portion of the federal Universal Service Fund (USF), about 30 percent, or $650 million, was distributed to the 13 Appalachian states (table 13.6). We can further disaggregate the federal USF by analyzing the relative importance of the federal high-cost program in each of the 13 states.

It must be noted that a precise measurement of the distribution of the federal USF in Appalachia is virtually impossible because of the way the federal USF is disbursed to eligible companies.[13] This is problematic for our purpose because except for West Virginia, all Appalachian states contain some counties that are not designated as the Appalachia region. For this reason, we will make proxy analyses by focusing on the state-level data.

Table 13.6 compares the amount of per capita federal high-cost support across the 13 Appalachian states and with the national average. The amount of per capita high-cost support roughly represents the relative ease of providing basic telecommunications at an affordable and comparable (to urban areas) rate. There is an inverse relationship between pop-

Table 13.6
Per capita federal high-cost support in Appalachia in 2000

State	2000 Population	Persons per square mile	Total high-cost support	Per capita high-cost support
MS	2,844,658	60.6	$133,101,273	$46.79
WV	1,808,344	75.1	$63,011,109	$34.84
AL	4,447,100	87.6	$88,036,543	$19.80
SC	4,012,012	133.2	$49,508,914	$12.34
GA	8,186,453	141.4	$79,349,024	$9.69
KY	4,041,769	101.7	$29,448,104	$7.29
TN	5,689,283	138.0	$34,011,882	$5.98
VA	7,078,515	178.8	$37,173,047	$5.25
NC	8,049,313	165.2	$34,071,156	$4.23
NY	18,976,457	401.9	$52,581,879	$2.77
PA	12,281,054	274.0	$28,756,386	$2.34
OH	11,353,140	277.3	$19,488,348	$1.72
MD	5,296,486	541.9	$2,404,548	$0.45
Nation	281,421,906	80.0	$2,241,237,733	$7.96

Source: U.S. Census Bureau (2000). *State and County QuickFacts*. [Online]. Available: <http://quickfacts.census.gov/qfd/>; Universal Service Administrative Company. (2001).

ulation density (i.e., persons per square mile) and per capita high-cost support. The amount of per capita high-cost support decreases as the population density increases.

Local service is more costly to provide when there are fewer rate payers and when the rate payers are geographically dispersed. Indeed, this observation corresponds to the universal service policy goal of the Telecommunications Act of 1996. The Act attempted to introduce competition to all aspects of telecommunications services, particularly to the local telephone market without sacrificing the affordability of services. Absent universal service support for carriers that serve high-cost areas, rural telephone markets are not likely to see local telephone competition.

What are the benefits of the federal high-cost program to the 13 Appalachian states? As shown in table 13.7, there are six states—Alabama, Georgia, Kentucky, Mississippi, South Carolina, and West Virginia—whose per capita high-cost support either exceeds or is approximately equal to the national average. These six states are the primary beneficiaries of the federal high-cost program among the 13 Appalachian states.

Large discrepancies exist among different Appalachian states in terms of both the amount of support flowing into these states and the degree to which they rely on the federal support in maintaining affordable and comparable (to urban areas) rates. Indeed, Mississippi is the country's biggest net recipient of the federal high-cost support while New York is the country's third highest contributor to the federal USF. Strictly speaking, those states that make larger contributions than they receive back are not benefiting from the federal high-cost program. On the other hand, however, the federal high-cost support already has generated positive results among net recipient states.[14]

Additionally, state have implemented their own universal service programs to supplement the federal program.

State Universal Service

The Telecommunications Act of 1996 allows individual states to implement appropriate support mechanisms for carriers and telephone subscribers to preserve and advance universal service in states.[15] It must be noted that neither the Act nor any other federal laws and regulations require states to create intrastate universal service funds. Therefore, each

Table 13.7
Flow of USF disbursement and contribution in Appalachia in 2000 (in dollars)

State	USF payments to carriers	Contribution to USF	Net flow of funds
Mississippi	133,052,000	18,872,000	114,180,000
Alabama	87,630,000	30,116,000	57,535,000
W. Virginia	63,061,000	12,557,000	50,503,000
S. Carolina	50,342,000	32,031,000	18,312,000
Georgia	79,527,000	72,344,000	7,184,000
Kentucky	29,606,000	27,969,000	1,637,000
Tennessee	34,352,000	42,882,000	-8,530,000
Virginia	37,126,000	66,613,000	-29,487,000
N. Carolina	34,304,000	65,174,000	-30,870,000
Maryland	2,394,000	48,742,000	-46,348,000
Ohio	19,587,000	76,213,000	-56,626,000
Pennsylvania	28,812,000	92,096,000	-63,285,000
New York	53,021,000	159,102,000	-106,081,000

Source: Cavazos, R. & Eisner, J. (2001, April). State-by-state telephone revenues and universal service data. [Online]. Available: <http://www.fcc.gov/Bureaus/Common_Carrier/Reports/FCC-State_Link/lec.html>.

Note: The figures for the payments from USF to carriers are slightly different from the comparable figures in the total high-cost support column of Table 8 because the figures in Table 9 are rounded up and the two tables are compiled from different source materials. However, the two sets of figures are proximate enough for the purpose of our analysis.

state must make its own decision as to whether it is appropriate to create an intrastate USF and how large it should be. Such discretion given to individual states has resulted in heterogeneous activities among the 13 Appalachian states (and the rest of the country) in devising and implementing intrastate universal service mechanisms. States opted to established USF programs largely to respond to industry claims for recovering revenue lost due to reduced access rates and other deregulation initiatives. In this sense, their USF programs have had little to do with responses to citizen needs although in certain states (e.g., North Carolina) some citizens have tried to persuade legislatures to allow community networks to receive universal service funds.

Implementing complicated regulatory mandates demands a tremendous amount of resources, time, and expertise on the part of state regulators. Formulating a universal service policy exemplifies such a case because of the necessity to assemble a complex regulatory mix that calls for complicated cost calculations, associated changes in intrastate and interstate tariffs, consistency with the federal universal service policy, and the requirement to achieve affordable telecommunications rates and competition at the same time. Quite predictably, there is no uniformity in the commitment to the creation of state USFs among the 13 jurisdictions in Appalachia, as shown in table 13.8.

About half of the 13 states have created or soon will create state USFs in one form or another. Recalling the six states that are net beneficiaries of the federal high-cost universal service program (Alabama, Georgia, Kentucky, Mississippi, South Carolina, and West Virginia), there seems to be no relationship between a state's status in federal funding and its commitment to intrastate support. The universal service policies in four states (Georgia, New York, South Carolina, and Tennessee) were produced through state legislation that defines general policy goals as well as some aspects of implementation procedures for state USFs. In all four states, state PUCs carried out the actual implementation of USFs. In contrast to these four states, Kentucky and Pennsylvania's universal service policies were instituted by PUCs and are not codified into their state statutes.

In addition to these six states, the possibility of creating state USFs has been discussed at one point or another by the PUCs in six more states (Maryland, Mississippi, North Carolina, Ohio, Virginia, and West Virginia), but none has initiated specific proceedings for setting procedures and guidelines.

Table 13.8
Public utilities commission actions for the creation of state USFs in Appalachia (as of August, 2001)

State	USF created planned[1]	Size	State	USF created or planned[1]	Size
Alabama	No		Ohio	No	
Georgia	Yes	$40m	Pennsylvania	Yes	$32m
Kentucky	Yes	NA	S. Carolina	Yes	$41m
Mississippi	No		Tennessee	Yes	NA
New York	Yes	NA	Virginia	No	
N. Carolina	No		W. Virginia	No	

Source: Personal interviews with state public utilities commission staff; the authors' survey of public utilities commissions web sites, the FCC web sites, and general publications.

[1]"Planned" means that the state public utilities commission at least has entered an order defining procedural rules toward the creation of a state USF.

Table 13.9
USF-supported services in Appalachia

State	High-cost	Low-income[1]	Schools/ Libraries	Telephone Relay System[2]
Georgia	*			
Kentucky		*		
New York		*		*
Pennsylvania	*	*		
South Carolina	*	*		
Tennessee	*	*	*	*

Source: Personal interviews with state public utilities commission staff; the authors' survey of public utilities commissions web sites, the FCC web sites, and general publications.

Note: All 13 Appalachian states but Ohio provide low-income support at a state level, but those states that are not listed on the table have not created explicit USFs.

[1]Low-income support includes Lifeline and/or Linkup, and the state low-income support supplements the federal low-income universal service support.

[2]Telephone relay system is a service for people with hearing disability.

The types of universal service support funded by state USFs vary (table 13.9). There is no discernable pattern among the universal service policies among the six states. Each has a unique combination of USF-supported services, but high-cost support and low-income support are the most popular types of intrastate USF support.

A state's decision to create a USF may not be directly contingent on the size of its federal USF distribution. This point may be supported by the fact that Pennsylvania—whose federal high-cost support for nonrural carriers is considerably smaller than the support the state's rural carriers receive (see table 13.5)—excludes Verizon (a nonrural carrier) from the group of USF eligible carriers. That is, Pennsylvania's state USF is not designed to compensate for the shortage of federal support to nonrural carriers; rather, its goal is to further increase the support for rural carriers, which are already receiving a larger federal USF disbursement than nonrural carriers.

VI   State and Local Initiatives

Ever since AT&T's divestiture became effective in 1984, state legislatures and their utilities commissions have had much more responsibility for monitoring and regulating telecommunications activities in their boundaries. Each of the Appalachian states has chosen distinctive paths to handle its regulatory responsibilities. Some appear to have much closer relationships to large, incumbent companies than others; some have considerable staff resources and expertise to help establish policy, while others, such as Mississippi with its two telecommunications staff people, have very limited resources. In this section we investigate the range and depth of various programs and policies states have adopted to enhance the delivery of telecommunications services. Some mechanisms include using state networks to enhance nonstate communications opportunities, using utility commission approval over mergers or 271 proceedings to leverage concessions from carriers, establishing special programs targeting rural digital inequities, and establishing unique joint ventures with carriers in order to achieve improved statewide infrastructure. Certain cities and towns also have initiated telecommunications projects to enhance local connectivity and opportunities for economic development. We discuss a few of these mechanisms below.

Utility Commission Authority

Of all the Appalachian states, New York most aggressively sought an orderly and monitored deregulation program. It began deregulating its local exchange companies in 1985, well before the 1996 Telecommunications Act was passed. In 1995 it opened local exchange markets to competition, and undertook a variety of price controls, gradually lifted, in order to grow competition in the state. Its Public Service Commission required Bell-Atlantic to commit to a one billion dollar infrastructure upgrade program in 1997 as part of its approval of that company's merger with Nynex, and the commission was one of the first to initiate a rigorous review of Verizon as it sought approval under the Section 271 requirements.

Ohio and Pennsylvania also have taken advantage of occasions requiring merger approval to stipulate new or improved services from telephone companies. In approving the Bell-Atlantic-GTE (Verizon) merger in 1999, the Pennsylvania PUC required that the new company provide broadband capability to 50 percent of the state by 2004 and to the rest of the state by 2015, with the proviso that deployment be balanced across urban, suburban and rural areas. In addition to its active role taken in the Bell-Atlantic-GTE merger proceeding, the Pennsylvania PUC stands out by having attempted to restructure its dominant Bell provider. In March 2001, the Pennsylvania PUC entered an order demanding the functional structural separation of Verizon into retail and wholesale units.[16] The goal of the structural separation of Bell companies is to remove barriers for local telephone competition by "structurally" preventing Bell companies from favoring their own local telephone services over those of competing local exchange carriers who lease Bell local facilities. Although the functional separation order was rescinded, this effort indicates Pennsylvania's active commitment to the creation of competitive telecommunications markets. Ohio also required the newly merged Ameritech-SBC to deploy DSL in both rural and urban areas in its 1999 merger approval as well as a $2.25 million fund to assist rural and low-income areas in accessing advanced telecommunications technology. Virginia also extracted several concessions from the merging companies when the state approved the Bell-Atlantic-GTE merger, including infrastructure and service upgrade requirements.

Special Programs
Georgia stands out as a state that enabled municipal governments to be eligible for local exchange carrier licenses as early as 1995. The Governor of Georgia announced a rural broadband initiative in May 2000, which promises to bring broadband infrastructure to rural regions. The network will support download speeds of 1.5Mbps. Another more modest project in collaboration with BellSouth will connect all K–12 school districts to the Internet with a T–1 connection; all Georgia's Appalachian counties are scheduled to receive these connections. As recently as summer, 2001, the state approved a novel nonprofit consortium of 31 towns and cities and one county to offer broadband telecommunications services in a wide variety of locations (GeorgiaPublicWeb, 2001).

Maryland, dominated by Verizon, has several programs to encourage e-commerce and an overall statewide information technology program. In 1998 it instituted a property tax credit (HB 477) that awards commercial and residential tax credits for renovations to accommodate advanced computer and telecommunications systems. Additionally, there are two investment funds to support innovative technology efforts in the state. Its key architecture, however, is its statewide network plan to have a point of presence in all three Appalachian counties and to link communities via high-speed fiber.

Virginia has a unique resource in the form of Virginia Tech University, which has purchased four wireless spectrum licenses in the rural western portion of the state in order to experiment with alternative broadband services. This University also has spearheaded several "electronic village" initiatives. North Carolina and Tennessee are notable for having studied their infrastructure characteristics; in the case of North Carolina, a detailed exchange-by-exchange investigation was undertaken. Ohio also undertook an infrastructure assessment under the auspices of the Econ-Ohio effort centered at Ohio State University's supercomputer center.

Tennessee is one of the seven Appalachian states that approved municipally owned utilities providing telecommunications services (in 1997). The others include Kentucky, North Carolina, Alabama, South Carolina, West Virginia and Georgia. The Electric Power board of Chattanooga was the first municipal utility to be certificated for telecommunications services under that law, and it serves five counties in the Appalachian region.

In addition to sponsoring a statewide network that is available to non-government users, North Carolina also passed a bill in 2000 to create a new state agency charged with overseeing rural economic development and information technology infrastructure in the state. This agency is to serve as a rural Internet access planning body, and has as its goal ensuring that dial-up access is available in every exchange by the end of 2001, and that high-speed Internet access is available by 2003 to all citizens of the state.

West Virginia, Mississippi, South Carolina and Alabama stand out as a handful of states that have sponsored or pursued few initiatives to aggressively enhance their telecommunications infrastructure.

Local Initiatives
Several towns and cities in the Appalachian region have initiated efforts to develop local advanced telecommunications services. They include Calhoun, GA, Abington, VA, Blacksburg, VA, other "electronic villages" in rural western Virginia, as well as the notable challenge by the City of Bristol to Virginia's prohibition on municipally owned telecommunications operations (Neidigh, 2001). Such innovations are notable in that in

most cases (Bristol being the exception), local exchange carriers either aided the towns' efforts or at minimum did not challenge them. They also are notable in that local leaders believed that telecommunications capabilities would substantially enhance their economic base, either by servicing existing businesses or by attracting new businesses.

Bristol's fiber optic network, begun in 1999, allows the utility to manage load requirements and also deliver services for Internet, LAN extensions, telephone and video conferencing, and virtual private networking to schools and government offices. The utility is moving toward an open access network that would allow nonfacilities-based providers access in order to broaden the service base to residential and commercial customers at a competitive price. Its backbone now consists of 125 miles of 144 and 288 count cables, supporting an ATM network operating at 622 Mbps. It is expanding to accommodate gigabit Ethernet, and supports nine points of presence providing collocation facilities. The effort ran afoul of a state law (HB 335) passed in 1998 that prohibited any locality in the state from establishing a "governmental entity" having the authority to provide telecommunications services. Notably, the town of Abingdon was explicitly exempted from this law. Bristol challenged the law and won its case in federal court. However, the case is on appeal at this writing.

In North Carolina, all 29 Appalachian counties had participated in the Connect NC project between 1996 and 1999. Connect NC was an educational campaign targeting the public and private sector leaders in the rural western parts of North Carolina with information regarding the importance of telecommunications connectivity to the economic competitiveness of rural areas. Western North Carolina was divided into six regions and each region developed and pursued various pilot projects with a goal to enhance telecommunications connectivity. A notable effort came from a group composed of Alexander, Burke, and Caldwell counties, which created regional WANs to bring high-speed Internet connection at T-1 speed (1.5 Mbps) to municipal and county facilities including public terminals at libraries.

Another innovative wireless Internet project was implemented in Ohio. Sequelle is a nonprofit corporation created by Washington county Community Improvement Corporation to provide broadband wireless Internet access and support services to Southeastern Ohio and North-western West Virginia at an affordable price. The project is the first in its kind in the nation and aims at promoting economic and community development in rural areas where advanced telecommunication technology is lacking. Sequelle uses the two-way digital FCC-licensed radio frequencies, and it is estimated that Sequelle will have 300 customers by the end of the third year (2002). The projected service cost is about 40 percent of the cost of comparable commercial offerings. The service was initially rolled out in Washington County (OH) and Wood County (WV). The project is estimated to cost $3 million, and is funded by a combination of state and federal funds. The project is designed to become self-sustaining within a few years.

VIII Conclusions

This research has sought to document the status of telecommunications in the Appalachian region with a view to assessing its potential relationship to economic growth and the range of federal and state policies that influence its development. We have found that telecommunications infrastructure in the Appalachian regions is less developed than that in other parts of the country and that it compares poorly to national averages. Broadband technologies such as cable modems, DSL, and even the presence of high-speed services are not as widely distributed in our target region as national statistics would suggest. Statistical analyses show that these distribution patterns are in each case associated with economic activity: more distressed counties have less developed broadband telecommunications infrastructure.

We also find that federal universal service benefits accrue largely to the most rural of the Appalachian states: only Mississippi, Alabama, West Virginia, South Carolina, Georgia and Kentucky have a net positive inflow of funds through the program, although the internal adjustments (from larger, urban-serving companies to smaller, rural companies) among the other states are not to be discounted. These six states are among the most rural of all the Appalachian states, having the lowest population densities among the group we are examining. While state universal service programs have cropped up in part to ameliorate the revenue losses local exchange companies face attributable to deregulation (especially reduced access rates), those programs are not uniform. Most offer some low-income support as well as support to telecommunications companies serving high cost territories. Some states are not allowing that support to flow to the largest, wealthiest companies (e.g., the BOCs or other price-cap companies) and instead favor companies serving exclusively rural regions. In such approaches they hint at the sorts of concerns for balancing costs and supports that will probably become more pervasive in the future.

Several states have proactively initiated programs to enhance telecommunications infrastructure. Seven states also allow municipally owned utilities to offer telecommunications services, expanding the range of choices and the potential for competition in the process. Nearly every state had some special program for enhancing Internet connectivity or broadband access. The least active states appear to be West Virginia, Mississippi, South Carolina, Kentucky, and Alabama, although these too have some state programs to enhance telecommunications access or use.

One factor that appears to enhance state potentials for improved telecommunications is coordination among state agencies within the state. By coordinating network design and use, state-funded infrastructure can be used optimally. When it is absent, programs may be duplicative, underutilized, and more costly.

Most state and federal programs have focused on market-related initiatives to solve their telecommunications problems. We observe, however, that attempting to work with (or against) the market yields only limited returns in the absence of leadership. With more creative collaboration and attention to some of the nonmarket solutions to obtaining and using telecommunications—solutions such as training, education, organizational resource sharing, and developing local leadership—the harnessing of telecommunications capabilities to economic growth can be enhanced.

Notes

1. It concludes that those outside of population centers are particularly likely to "not be served by market forces" alone (p. 83).

2. The Rural Utilities Service (RUS) announced a $100 million loan program in December, 2000, that makes funds available to finance the construction and installation of broadband telecommunications services in rural America, targeting through a one-year pilot program broadband service to rural consumers

where such service does not currently exist. Communities up to 20,000 inhabitants are eligible.

3. Under Section 271 of the 1996 Telecommunications Act, state utility commissions must first rule that Bell Operating Companies have opened their markets to competitors before those companies seek FCC approval to enter long distance markets.

4. Enabling Bell Operating Companies to provide inter-LATA data transport is one of the key points of the hotly debated Tauzin-Dingell bill in 2001 (H.R. 1542).

5. See for example Pennsylvania's Section 271 deliberations at <http://puc.paonline.com/telephone/sec_271.asp≥.

6. The Appalachian Regional Commission region covers portions of Alabama, Georgia, Kentucky, Maryland, Mississippi, New York, North Carolina, Ohio, Pennsylvania, South Carolina, Tennessee, and Virginia, and the entire state of West Virginia.

7. One can have a fiber-optic based link to a digital switch but if one has a very slow computer, that single element will constrain the speed of the last mile. So too, a poor line connection from a central office to a household or business limits even the fastest computer's ability to enjoy something that looks like an advanced service. The last mile, telephone company vernacular for the connection from customer premises equipment (a home, a business) to a central office, is generally the source of limited bandwidth or speed.

8. ADSL is generally not feasible beyond 18,000 feet from a central office. Cable television systems serve towns and cities, not truly rural areas.

9. Distressed counties have a 3-year average unemployment rate that is at least 1.5 times the U.S. average of 4.9 percent; have a per capita market income that is less than two-third (67 percent) of the U.S. average of $21,141 and have a poverty rate that is at least 1.5 times the U.S. average of 13.1 percent OR have two times the poverty rate and qualify on one other indicator. Appalachian Regional Commission, County Economic Status in the Appalachian Region, FY 2001.

10. With FCC approval that a state has met its competitive checklist requirements, the BOCs are allowed to enter into lucrative long distance voice and inter-LATA data transport services.

11. High Cost Methodology Order, FCC 99–306.

12. In addition to the high-cost program, the federal Universal Service Fund supports the E-Rate (schools and libraries), low-income (i.e., Lifeline and Linkup), and the rural health care programs, E-rate being the largest budget component after high-cost support.

13. The federal high-cost program disburses the USF to eligible local exchange carriers, but a large number of these eligible carriers have service territories ("study areas") spanning both Appalachian and non-Appalachian counties. Available data from the FCC do not allow us to identify the proportion of universal service support directed to Appalachian and non Appalachian counties in each state.

14. For example, BellSouth in Mississippi received a USF payment in excess of $100 million in 2000, and the company spent the money not only for rate-reduction purposes but also for various infrastructure upgrade projects. Subsequently, BellSouth's telecommunications infrastructure in Mississippi was enough improved to allow the state government (the Mississippi Department of Information Technology Services) to build a statewide ATM network, which would benefit the state network users (i.e., the state government agencies, local governments, schools, libraries, and universities) by offering greater bandwidth and lower telecommunications costs. Personal interviews with Gary Rawson (Mississippi Department of Information Technology Services), Aug. 3, 2001; Randy Tew (Mississippi Public Utilities Staff), Aug. 3, 2001.

15. 1996 Telecommunications Act § 254(f).

16. The PUC originally sought a full structural separation of Verizon into two independent companies. See, Pennsylvania Public Utility Commission (1999, Sept. 30).

References

Belinfante, A. (1999, Feb.). *Telephone subscribership in the United States (Data through November 1998)*. Washington, D.C.: Federal Communications Commission.

Belinfante, A. (2001, March). *Telephone subscribership in the United States (Data through November 2000)*. Washington, D.C.: Federal Communications Commission.

Boardwatch Magazine's directory of Internet service providers. (13th Ed.). (2001).

CableDataCom News. (2001, March 7). *Commercial Cable Modem Launches in North America*. [Online]. Available:
<http://www.cabledatacomnews.com/cmic/cmic7.html>.

Cavazos, R., and Eisner, J. (2001, April). *State-by-state telephone revenues and universal service data*. [Online]. Available:
<http://www.fcc.gov/Bureaus/Common_Carrier/Reports/FCC-State_Link/lec.html>.

City of Bristol, Virginia, etc., v. Mark L. Earley, Attorney General, ET AL. 2001. 145 F. Supp. 2d 741; 2001 U.S. Dist. LEXIS 6325.

Cronin, F., Colleran, Herbert, E., P., and Lewitzky, S. (1993). Telecommunications and growth: The contribution of telecommunications infrastructure investment to aggregate and sectoral productivity. *Telecommunications Policy, 17*, 677–690.

Dholakia, R. R., and Harlam, B. (1994). Telecommunications and economic development: Econometric analysis of the US Experience. *Telecommunications Policy, 18*, 470–477.

Federal Communications Commission. (2000, June 6). *FCC and states jointly develop a nationwide database of broadband deployment activities*. Press release.

Federal Communications Commission. (2000, August). *Deployment of advanced telecommunications capability: Second report*. Washington, D.C.: Federal Communications Commission.

GeorgiaPublicWeb. (2001, September 4). Georgia public service commission approves high speed connection to rural Georgia. Press release.

Mueller, M. (1997). *Universal service: Interconnection, competition and monopoly in the making of American telecommunications*. Cambridge, MA: MIT Press.

National Exchange Carriers Association. (2000). *NECA rural broadband cost study: Summary of results*. [Online]. Available: <http:// http://www.neca.org/broadban.asp>.

National Exchange Carriers Association. (2000, October 2). *NECA's overview of universal service funds*. [Online]. Available: <http://www.fcc.gov/Bureaus/Common_Carrier/Reports/FCC-State_Link/neca.html>.

National Telecommunications and Information Administration. (1999, July). *Falling through the Net: Defining the digital divide*. Washington, D.C.: National Telecommunications and Information Administration.

National Telecommunications and Information Administration and Rural Utilities Service. (2000, April). *Advanced telecommunications in rural America: The challenge of bringing broadband service to all Americans*. [Online]. Available: <http://www.ntia.doc.gov/reports/ruralbb42600.pdf>.

National Telecommunications and Information Administration. (2000, Oct.). *Falling through the Net: Toward digital inclusion*. Washington, D.C.: National Telecommunications and Information Administration.

Neidigh, B. (n.d.). *What should be the public role in the development of advanced network infrastructure? An analysis of Commonwealth of Virginia restrictions on municipal telecommunications*. E-Corridors Working paper #1. Unpublished paper.

North Carolina Department of Commerce, Telecommunications Services, Office of Information Technology Services. (2000). *Commercially available high speed Internet connectivity in North Carolina: Infrastructure and prices*. Unpublished report.

Oden, M., and Strover, S. (2001). *Telecommunications and information infrastructure and services: Assessing gaps in universal service in the Appalachian region. A report to the Appalachian Regional Commission*. Unpublished report.

Parker, E. B., Hudson, H. E., Dillman, D. A., Strover, S., and Williams, F. (1995). *Electronic Byways*. (2nd ed). Boulder, CO: Westview Press.

Parker, E. B., Hudson, H. E., and Roscoe, A. D. (1989). *Rural America in the information age: Telecommunications policy for rural development*. Lanham, MD: University Press of America.

Pennsylvania Public Utility Commission. (1999, Sept. 30). Global Telephone Order. [Online]. Available <http://puc.paonline.com/Telephone/Global/Global_Telephone_Order.asp>.

Strover, S. (1999). Rural internet connectivity. *Telecommunications Policy,* 25,(5), 291–313.

Strover, S., and Berquist, L. (2001). Developing telecommunications infrastructure: State and Local Policy Collisions. In B. Compaine and S. Greenstein (Eds.), *Communications policy in transition.* Cambridge,, MA: MIT Press.

Tennessee Regulatory Authority. (2000). *Tennessee's digital divide.* [Online]. Available: ‹http://www.state.tn.us/tra›.

Universal Service Administrative Company. (2001). *2000 annual report: Reaching and connecting Americans.* Washington, D.C.: Universal Service Administrative Company.

U.S. Department of Agriculture. 2000. *Advanced Telecommunications in Rural America: The Challenge of Bringing Broadband Service to All Americans.* Washington, D.C.: U.S. Department of Agriculture, April.

U.S. Census Bureau (2000). *State and county QuickFacts.* [Online]. Available: <http://quickfacts.census.gov/qfd/>.

U.S. Department of Commerce. (2000). *Digital economy 2000.* Washington, D.C.

Williams, Fredrick. 1991. *Telecommunications and U.S. Rural Development: An Update.* Aspen, Colorado: The Aspen Institute

14

Universal Service in Times of Reform: Affordability and Accessibility of Telecommunication Services in Latin America

Martha Fuentes-Bautista

Introduction

The term *universal service,* as first used in the AT&T slogan "one system, one policy, universal service," was part of a corporate strategy aimed at undermining the position of multiple rival networks that served the United States in 1907. The AT&T strategy was to peddle the idea of consolidating independent telephone exchanges into local monopolies that could interconnect as many users as possible (Mueller, 1997). The benefits of a pervasive network that overcame the rather fragmented and disconnected scenario of previous years was an excellent showcase for this model. One result was that the achievement of universal service was subordinated to the existence of a monopoly for basic telephony for decades. The social dimension of the concept grew up along with spawning public telephone and telegraph monopolies (PTTs) that served countries in Europe, Africa, Asia and Latin America for more than 80 years. However, with the exception of the wealthiest nations, the rate of investment of PTTs was insufficient to meet the demand of telecommunication services in most nations.

Since the mid 1980s liberalization policies seeking to achieve industry efficiencies have emerged as an alternative path to attain the goal of universal service. These waves of liberalization struck Latin America with particular energy. The International Telecommunication Union (ITU) (2000) estimates that, between 1988 and 1998, more than two thirds of the Latin American PTTs were partially or fully privatized. Animated by capital that by and large came from wealthier nations, basic telephone networks in the region have grown twice as fast as the telephone systems of developed countries. Despite this burst of capital and services, not much more than one-third of the region's households have a fixed phone (ITU, 2000:3). Achieving 100 percent service penetration is still a pending goal in developing nations that have pursued liberalization policies. The issue becomes even more urgent to address in light of the rapid growth of the Internet or computer-mediated communications (CMC) in developed nations, a situation that threatens to widen the gap between the First and the Third world.

By reviewing the cases of Argentina, Brazil, Chile, Mexico, Peru and Venezuela, this study traces the evolution of the universal service policies designed and pursued during the first decade of liberal reforms. This study addresses broader questions of how different approaches to telecommunication reform are fostering higher levels of service penetration in developing countries, and what types of governance they have brought about. The goal is to identify particular trends of telecommunication services penetration, and to draw lessons that help to improve the strategy of network development of these nations, most of which are currently engaged in a second round of legislative reforms.

Theoretical Framework

Universal Service: A Concept in Transformation

The basic conceptualization of universal service in the telecom business is commonly associated with the availability of telephone lines accessible to the public, in both economic and geographical terms. As Mueller puts it, it is "a telephone network that covers all of a country, is technologically integrated, and connects as many citizens as possible" (1997, p. 1). This ambitious parameter calls for no distinctions between rural and urban areas, economic strata or social categories.

Universal service is pursued through diverse means that usually focus on the supply side of telecommunication services. Universal Service Obligations' (USO) strategies include:

1. Extending the service to unserved populations in inner city and rural areas.

2. Meeting unsatisfied demand for access lines targeting customers on waiting lists.

3. Making telecommunication services affordable for low-income citizens, commonly known as the 'unphoned'. Strategies aiming at this goal go from the expansion of pay phone networks (public telephony) to tariff systems that benefit the poorest households. (Tyler, Letwin and Roe, 1995).

Focusing on infrastructure accessibility, or service affordability and reliability, universal service policies are key to assure network expansion beyond the limits established by free market dynamics. Despite the apparently clear definition and policy objectives, a technical description of what is "essential" in telecommunications has proven to be a complex and controversial topic. Technological convergence and blurring market barriers have altered the structure of the telecommunication business as well as traditional definitions of *basic service*. Teledensity or the number of fixed phone lines per hundred inhabitants, the index traditionally used to weigh the concept, is nowadays considered an "imperfect measure of universal service" (ITU, 1998b, p. 20). Some have proposed instead to use household service penetration as an indicator to gauge universal service (Mueller, 1996; ITU, 1998b),[1] since it indicates residential use. However, neither of these indices reflects the direction and segmentation of a network's expansion, nor do they account for other access methods such as mobile telephony, satellite and digital channels, which are currently used by citizens of developing and developed countries to access national and global networks.

The rapid pace of technological developments, and economic constraints still faced by developing markets are also inducing administrators to review the notion of *universality* in two directions. The first, concerned with new telecommunication services *availability*, suggests an enhanced version of the network that encompasses main telephone lines, mobile cellular subscribers and digital access. The second focuses on *accessibility* to the network and stresses the existence of an access point (e.g., a telephone) within reasonable distance for everyone. Table 14.1 summarizes some indicators related to each concept.

Some authors argue that these concepts address different problems and are not mutually exclusive. Service availability and accessibility can complement each other to the degree to which new technologies capable of supporting information services (wireless, satellite) increase the means

Table 14.1
Universal Service and Universal Access Indicators

Universal service (availability)	Universal access (accessibility)
% of households with a telephone	Access to a telephone established in terms of:
Mobidensity (Number of fixed lines plus mobile cellular lines per hundred inhabitants)	• time or distance from a telephone • minimum population units per phone
Digital access (ISDN channels)	Payphones per 1000 inhabitants or per main lines

of interconnection to national networks, making them more affordable to the public. Hudson (2000) considers that the economic and demographic diversity of developing countries demand a *"multi-leveled"* definition of access identifying expansion targets within communities, institutions and households. Minges (1999a, 1999b) advocates for a similar model that places *universal access* as a step toward *universal service*. He illustrates the situation through the example of the recent evolution of the Swiss telephone system. Between 1995 and 1998, the teledensity in Switzerland decreased from 60.6 to 56 main lines/100 people, as a result of residential and commercial customers migrating to mobile cellular services and ISDN networks. However, the author argues, the network as an aggregate—including all three services—actually grew more than 20 percent, adding up to a million subscribers over the same period.

Responding to completely different realities and needs, the mobile cellular networks of countries such as in Lesotho, Cote d'Ivoire, Paraguay, and Venezuela have reached penetrations equivalent to half of the national teledensity (ITU 1999, 2000). Wireless communications are used to overcome geographic and financial barriers commonly encountered in the deployment of services in developing nations. Although the experience there is not new, it does indicate how technologies that act as product substitutes for the fixed telephone can enhance our definition of basic services.[2]

Attending to the changing meaning of *basic service* and *universality*, Hudson proposes that developing countries should understand universal access as a "dynamic concept with a set of moving targets." It should not tie goals to specific technology or service provider (e.g., wired or wireless service), but rather state them in terms of "functions and capabilities, such as ability to transmit voice and data" (2000:3). This view can open to administrators new alternatives for policy design through a *"multi-network"* perspective, one that considers the total sum of capabilities enabling a citizen's access to a national telecommunication network. Criticism of the *"multi-network"* perspective arises from the difficulties in accounting for penetration of new services (e.g., mobile telephony) by social strata and geographical area. The ITU considers that broadening the definition to these services "may lead to telecommunications investment becoming narrowly focused upon those who can afford to pay for the new services thereby increasing regional disparities and exacerbating information poverty" (1998b, p. 85).

In its latest review of the concept, and despite important transformations in technology and the structure of markets, the ITU has assumed a fairly traditional definition of universal service, avoiding major discussions about possible redistribution mechanisms for telecommunications investment, and new statistical mechanisms allowing higher accountability. In the 1998 World Telecommunication Development Report, the organization concludes that there is "no compelling reason, at present, to expand the definition of universal service to include individual access to information services" (85). The report advocates for a "practical definition of universal access" that targets "increased levels of household telephone penetration" in developed countries, and "community access through the provision of public telephones" in developing nations (p. 90).

This conceptual divergence is interpreted as the result of the growing gap between the poorest nations that are struggling to build a basic telephone network, and the wealthiest countries already engaged in the creation of the information superhighway. As Gil-Egui and Steward assert, the consequence of such a dichotomy is a "dual rhetoric that speaks of universality of plain old telephone for the Third World and broadband for the First World" disregarding the higher upgrading cost that the poorest nations will have to face in the future (Gil-Egui and Steward, 1999, p. 2).

However, this paper argues that the inherent contradictions of such distinctions can be overcome through a multi-network approach that extends USO to all technological solutions existing in the market and takes into account user' preferences and active role in defining different levels to gain access to the national network. This would require further development of competition as well as more effective and flexible regulation to target market imbalances in dynamic technological scenarios. In the dawn of a second generation of telecommunication reforms in developing countries, an assessment of universal service policies played out in these nations during a period better characterized as the transition to total competition can shed light on available paths to attain universal service.

Risks and Opportunities of Liberalization

Since the onset of liberalization, a considerable amount of research has tried to test the implications of telecommunication reform attending to economic and technological criteria. As Mosco (1988) warns, few of these efforts have gone beyond dichotomist discussions that oppose public to private, and government control to free market. Although this research has produced detailed descriptions of the new industry structure, pricing strategies and regulations, most of the time it misses the opportunity to assess the way in which market constraints have been rebuilt, and the implications of such changes for diverse social groups. Different approaches to liberalization have included a diverse mix of ownership strategies (privatization, corporatization, strategic partnership, leasing of basic infrastructure), and levels of market competition (private monopoly, duopolies, competing product substitute markets). This diversity of strategies makes it virtually impossible to talk about a typology of approaches to telecommunication reform. However, efforts should be made to assess the social implications of the different market structures and practices brought about by liberalization.

Here, I shall suggest that one way to discuss the different approaches to reform can be related to the reconceptualization of USO and other conditions for network expansion, which have particularly important repercussions for developing countries embarked on those reforms. Through USO, the State reformulates the relationship between operators, the public and the regulator. USO also targets market inefficiencies, setting some conditions for operation without hampering the economics of the business. They should be designed to meet the needs of particular populations with problems of access attending to claims of the public.

Comparative studies of telecommunications reform in developing countries have mainly focused on the dichotomy of controlled versus free markets. Typically, these analyses contrast the outcomes of liberalized versus regulated scenarios in an attempt to identify the benefits or setbacks of liberalization. A number of different studies have found in common an immediate "efficiency effect" after reform, with a tendency for slow-down overtime (Grande, 1994; Petrazzini, 1995; Straubhaar et al., 1995). General assessments on the impact of liberalization policies on developing countries lend weight to a positive view that shows increasing penetration at the household and small firm levels (Petrazzini, 1996).

Other studies have explored the impact of privatization on network growth. In their account of teledensity evolution in Asian and Latin American countries that underwent liberalization policies in the first half of the 1990s, Petrazzini and Clark (1996) found that "in countries with privatized telecommunication (penetration) grew twice as fast compared with countries that did not privatize" (p. 37). The authors also examine the effect of competition on the rollout of new services such as cellular phones. Testing variables possibly affecting cellular density growth such as GDP levels, researchers found that none of them was as important as competition.

More recently, Jayakar (September, 2000) empirically tests changes in residential teledensity in 30 countries as a function of economic growth, diffusion effects and three policy variables: ownership, industry structure and regulatory independence. The research identified diffusion effects and policy variables as significant predictors of telephone penetration at the household level. The author tests the model accounting for possible differences between rich and poorer countries. Interestingly, variables such as privatization or de-monopolization were found not significant as explanatory variables of growth in household service penetration. Gutierrez and Berg (2000) examine institutional, regulatory and economic determinants of telephone penetration in Latin America through a longitudinal study of 19 countries (1985–1995). A multiple regression analysis identifies income, political democracy, changes in the regulatory environment (including privatization) and the growth of cellular phones as the most relevant factors accounting for the expansion of fixed telephone networks. These findings agree with previous assessments (Mody and Tsui, 1995) that support the idea that competition and the presence of an independent regulator, rather than a simple shift from public to private ownership, are key to network expansion.

For countries with populations historically deprived of telecommunication services, the idea of overall network expansion seems to fulfill the promises brought about by liberalization. However, after more than a decade of liberal policies, almost two thirds of Latin American households do not have fixed telephones yet, and the penetration of mobile and fixed phones combined only covered 50 percent of the population (ITU, 2000). The region has become a major puzzle. It has hardly any unmet demand of telecommunication services,[3] and yet, there are low rates of service penetration. A considerable 'depressed' demand seems to be one of the unwanted consequences of liberalization in the region (ITU, 2000:3). Rising local access prices, fostered in the context of tariff rebalancing, threaten to exclude a good part of the population.

As Milne notes (2000), tariff rebalancing is a necessary condition for an industry undergoing severe changes in its market structure. On the one hand, in competitive markets prices must reflect underlying costs, and basic services should operate without cross-subsidies received in the past from long distance or other services. On the other hand, technological innovations have affected the cost structure of the business, and incumbent companies need to adjust their tariffs to patterns that made them competitive. Even in those countries with closed markets for basic services, monopolies face competitive pressures of call back services, mobile cellular phones and IP telephony that become substitutes of fixed telephony.

Price rebalancing has tended to raise residential rentals facing operators and regulators with the dilemma of balancing sustainability and affordability of the service.[4] The tensions between the two conflicting goals are higher in low and middle-income countries where scarce economic sources limit the ability of maneuver of market agents. Testing a model that relates telephone service affordability to income distribution, Milne found that in low and middle-income nations price restructuring leading to significant increase in residential charges, "risks driving some subscribers off the network, and can slow down the rate of network expansion" (2000:919). It is important to assess how issues of pricing relate to service penetration. Do they support or hinder universal service goals? What alternative solutions are giving regulator of less developed countries to the tensions between liberalization and service affordability?

By comparing trends of telephone cost and telephone service penetration in Argentina, Brazil, Chile, Mexico, Peru, and Venezuela during the last decade, this paper discusses how different approaches to telecommunication reform have fostered higher levels of access in developing countries during the transition from state monopolies to total liberalization. The discussion is framed by a survey of the universal service policies put in place by the six countries, and an analysis of their performance indicators. The goal is to draw lessons that would help to improve the regulatory strategies of telecommunication administrators, and to discuss the implications for new forms of governance defined in more liberalized scenarios. The key question is, have these changes contributed, and if so, in what ways, to more balanced and fairer systems of communication in developing countries?

Methodology

Design of the Study

The analysis focuses on the elaboration of country profiles that identify the nation's universal service policy as defined in contracts and bylaws designed by telecommunication administrators. This study follows Hudson's (2000) proposed model for evaluation of universal access in developing nations presenting the evolution of different performance indicators over an eleven-year period. Finally, a comparative assessment discusses the ways in which universal service regulations have unfolded in the studied countries relating them to new forms of governance brought by liberal reforms.

Data

In 1997, the International Telecommunication Union started to keep track and report trends in telecommunication reform worldwide through the Sector Reform Unit (SRU), an arm of the Telecommunication Development Bureau (BDT). The work generated by the SRU included country profiles available on the World Wide Web. These data as well as the latest assessment of the Inter-American Telecommunication Commission (CITEL, 2000) on universal service are used as primary data sources. An evaluation of service penetration by country is supported with indicators gathered from the ITU's Stars database (2000) and ITU's Americas Telecommunication Indicators (2000).

Operational Definitions

Universal Service and Universal Access   In line with the redefinition of universal service to include more than the wired telephone, this study looks at advances in *universal service* goals through two different indicators: (1) the percentage of households with a telephone line;[5] and (2) telephone penetration defined as the sum of dedicated lines plus wireless lines (mobile cellular) per 100 inhabitants. Both indexes combined are considered as a unique indicator of telephone penetration.

Progress in *universal access* is measured as the number of payphones per 1000 inhabitants. Although the indicator does not account for rural versus urban penetration, it serves as a reference of the number of people that may have access to a neighboring telephone. Public telephony as a percentage of the overall fixed-line network can be used as a parameter to measure commitment that administrators and operators may have to spread the service.

Liberalization   This concept is operationalized as the year in which the supply of basic telephone service is liberalized through the introduction of competition in local or long distance services, or through the introduction of competition in products which substitute for the local service, such as mobile cellular services.

Service Affordability   The major components of pricing of the fixed telephony are installation charge, a one-time charge for new user, and the monthly subscription charge, applicable to all users. This study includes data on price of line installation as percentage of annual average per capita income, and monthly connection charge as percentage of monthly average per capita income. Same indicators are presented for mobile cellular telephony as a way to observe the competitive pressures played out in the process of tariff rebalancing. Data for this exercise is gathered from the ITU Start database. Some limitations for comparison arise from the lack of available information for all the eleven points in times.

Countries Overview

Argentina

In 1990 the Empresa Nacional de Telecomunicaciones (ENTEL), a state owned monopoly, was privatized and split into two separate regional companies that enjoyed a seven-year monopoly on basic services with a possible extension for 10 years based on satisfying contract requirements.[6] These requirements were laid out in 1991 in terms of the amount of investment to be made in the whole network, without specifying areas or services to be included in USO. The target was to achieve an average annual growth rate of 6 percent for the next five years. Government oversight was limited to determining the quality of operation. A newly created regulatory agency was mandated to guarantee, among other things, universal service. Operators assumed the expressed commitment to serve 400 areas in the northern region, and 280 in the southern region through public and semipublic service plans, and licenses were granted to independent operators who had been handling areas not covered by the public enterprise (CITEL, 2000). In spite of the mostly competitive environment, lack of interconnection regulations retarded the full operation of these licensed carriers during these first years (Straubhaar et al., 1995).

From the outset of the reform, competition was allowed in value-added services, private networks, satellite transmissions and mobile cellular services. Cellular operators were organized into regional duopoly markets. The main two competing companies were Movicom and Movistar. The first began operations in the country in 1989 when a consortium led by BellSouth was awarded a license to introduce the service in the Buenos Aires metropolitan area. In line with the 1990 privatization plan, Telefónica and Telecom were subsidized to compete in this market. However, in 1993 both companies became partners in the creation of Movistar and its service: the Miniphone. This association lasted until October 1999 when the joint venture was closed due to differences between the partners. Subscribers were then distributed between two companies: TCP and Telecom Personal. Table 14.2 presents the evolution of telephone penetration in Argentina. In this liberalized environment, fixed lines kept growing over the last decade. This growth has slowed down while mobile telephony reached record rates of expansion.

Table 14.2
Argentina—Telephone Penetration

Argentina				Reform			
	1988	1990	1992	1994	1996	1998	2000
Phonelines per 100 inh.	10.0	9.3	10.8	13.7	17.4	19.7	21.5
Mobile pho. per 100 inh.	0.0	0.0	0.1	0.7	1.6	7.0	12.2
Telephone Penetration	10.0	9.3	10.9	14.4	19.0	26.7	33.7

Table 14.3
Argentina—Accessibility and Availability

Argentina			Reform			
	1988	1990	1992	1994	1996	1998
% of Residential lines	74.9	76.0	80.0	81.0	82.3	83.8
Residential phones/ 100 households	28.7	27.1	32.7	41.8	53.6	61.0
% Payphones/ main lines	0.8	0.8	1.0	1.2	1.3	1.5
Payphones per 1000 inh.	0.8	0.7	1.1	1.7	2.3	3.0

One of the major achievements in Argentina has been a consistent increase of accessibility and availability of telephone services (table 14.3). Household penetration grew at average annual rates of 10 percent with a marked deceleration of this tendency after the target year of 1996, when the process became markedly more competitive. Expansion of public telephony indicates a compromise to serve social needs.

However, the major change experienced at the end of the first phase of liberalization was the tremendous growth of mobile telephony. The major factor accounting for this growth was the introduction of the Calling Party Pays (CPP), a system whereby the caller is charged for making the call. This tariff scheme, along with the steady decrease of relative cost in subscription costs (table 14.4), boosted mobile telephony increasing the penetration of the service 180 percent during two consecutive years (1997–1998).

The restructuring stage, which guaranteed exclusivity to regional monopolies, was extended until 1999. In this period conceptualized as a transition toward total competition, licenses for basic service operators

Table 14.4
Argentina—Telephone Service Affordability

Argentina	Reform					
	1988	1990	1992	1994	1996	1998
Fixed phone connection/ income per capita	74.9	76.0	80.0	81.0	82.3	83.8
Mobile phone connection/ income per capita	28.7	27.1	32.7	41.8	53.6	61.0
Res. mon. phone subc./ monthly per capita income	0.8	0.8	1.0	1.2	1.3	1.5
Res. mon. mobile subc./ monthly per capita income	0.8	0.7	1.1	1.7	2.3	3.0

contained a detailed list of USO, which included: installation of semi-public long distance service in every community of 80 to 500 people; installation of wirelines in communities where at least 30 customers request the service; and new targets to enhance the public telephone network. In addition to these requirements in infrastructure development, in July 1999, the government passed General Regulations on Universal Services, which extended infrastructure commitments, and created three universal service categories: high-cost areas, specific customers and specific services. The actual plans recently designed to match these concepts aim at providing service to retirees, pensioners, low consumption customers, users with physical limitations, and educational and health institutions. The Regulations established that providers of telecommunication services must contribute to the Universal Service Fund with a percentage of total income earned from operations. The new legislation adopted a dynamic concept of universal service with periodic review.

Brazil

By the beginning of the 1990s, Telebrás was a holding company with 28 subsidiaries representing 27 local operators and a long distance carrier, Embratel. The holding served 91 percent of Brazilian fixed telephone subscribers. The remaining 9 percent was in the hands of four independent operators. Uneven development was the main characteristic of the Brazilian corporation by the late 1980s. Seventy-three percent of Telebrás'

Table 14.5
Brazil—Telephone Penetration

Brazil		Reform					
	1990	1992	1994	1995	1996	1998	2000
Phonelines per 100 inh.	6.2	7.3	8.0	8.5	9.6	12.1	14.9
Mobile pho. per 100 inh.	0.0	0.0	0.4	0.8	1.6	4.7	13.6
Telephone Penetration	6.2	7.3	8.4	9.3	11.1	16.7	28.5

revenue came from Embratel and Telesp, the local operator of wealthy Sao Paulo state. Although the transition to a democratic regime reaffirmed the public monopoly in telecommunications in the new constitution of 1988, the new political scenario brought about changes to the state run corporation. Telebrás started to trade its shares in the stock market in 1989, creating a system in which the state sold its stock in the company, while retaining managerial control. By the mid-1990s, it was estimated that foreign investor held 36.7 percent of the equity (Worhlers de Almeida, 1998).

The Brazilian approach to reform was not privatization but the maintenance of state control over a corporation funded with public capital that faced competition in different markets. In August 1995 the Cardoso government launched the reform of public institutions including the telecom reform that began with the removal of the constitutional monopoly reserved to Telebrás. Priority was given to promote competition in the cellular telephone market, satellite telecommunication, data transmission, and other added-value services. Other important steps of the reform included tariff rebalancing, the merger of operators into regional groups, and the implementation of autonomous management structures. In 1997 the government awarded 10 licenses for mobile telephony, thus introducing competition into this market. Table 14.5 clearly shows that the State-run holding attained considerable improvements in telephone penetration before privatization.

In 1998 Telebras was divided and sold in a public bid establishing a duopoly system, which will operate until 2002. The government used privatization to attract foreign capital to finance the external deficit of the balance of payments, and to obtain fresh sources for the Treasury. Telebrás was broken up vertically and regionally into -12 sub holding

Table 14.6
Brazil—Accessibility and Availability

Brazil	Reform					
	1990	1992	1994	1995	1996	1998
% of Residential lines	69.5	70.0	67.9	67.6	68.1	N/A
Residential phones/ 100 households	17.8	19.8	21.1	22.4	25.3	28.6
% Payphones/main lines	2.4	2.4	2.6	2.6	2.7	2.8
Payphones per 1000 inh.	1.6	1.7	2.1	2.2	2.6	3.0

companies and sold separately. Three regional operators offered a mix of wired telephony for local services and internal region long distance (the *Baby Braz:* T1/Telco North-Northeast/ T2, T2/Telco Center-South, and T3/Telesp); one operator for national and international long distance (Embratel); an eight spin-off creators supplying mobile telephony. The most profitable is Telesp, which serves Sao Paulo (ITU, 2000). The same year as privatization a new Decree on the General Plan of Universal Goals set USO binding license holders for the fixed telephone service. The plan sets goals of individual and collective access, and pays special attention to educational and health institutions with demands for advanced services and to individuals with special needs. Under this environment, telephone accessibility and availability continued to advance at a good pace (table 14.6).

One of the major achievements of the Brazilian strategy was the tariff rebalancing process. The Cardoso government radically adjusted the structure of the price system. The result was a cut in installation charges from a peak of 1,500 U.S. dollars in 1992 to 50 U.S. dollar in 1998 (ITU, 2000). The adjustment combined with the adjustment of the Brazilian currency and a better overall economic performance drove the relative costs of the service down (table 14.7).

Chile

For most of the 20th century the Chilean telecommunication system evolved as a private enterprise.[7] During the period of state control (1973–1986), the national system was reorganized into two regional monopolies for local services, CTC and ENTEL. Competition in long

Table 14.7
Brazil—Telephone Service Affordability

Brazil	Reform				
	1994	1995	1996	1997	1998
Fixed phone connection/ income per capita	49.2	26.9	22.7	1.5	0.9
Mobile phone connection/ income per capita	8.6	8.0	6.7	6.1	N/A
Res. mon. phone subc./ monthly per capita income	0.2	0.8	0.7	1.7	1.0
Res. mon. mobile subc./ monthly per capita income	12.5	7.9	6.6	6.0	N/A

Table 14.8
Chile—Telephone Penetration

Chile	Reform							
	1986	1988	1990	1992	1994	1996	1998	2000
Phonelines per 100 inh.	4.5	4.9	6.6	9.5	11.3	14.9	18.6	22.1
Mobile pho. per 100 inh.	0.0	0.0	0.1	0.5	0.7	2.2	6.5	22.4
Telephone Penetration	4.5	4.9	6.7	9.9	12.1	17.1	25.1	44.5

distance was introduced in 1986, the same year that key components of CTC and ENTEL were privatized. During the first period of liberalization (1986–1993) the government set no USO. This left the pace of network expansion to market forces. In this environment, telephone density grew at a healthy annual average rate of 16 percent. In spite of the strong growth of mobile and fixed telephony (table 14.8), by the early 1990s the network was showing two major flaws: a virtual halt of service growth in rural areas, and the decrease of payphone penetration (SUBTEL, 2000). Figures in table 14.10 clearly depict the problem. The situation also revealed the flaw in having a weak regulatory agency with few legal tools at its disposal to deal with the problem.

In 1994, an amendment to the law established a Development Fund with contributions from long distance service providers. This was aimed at subsidizing the expansion of public telephones in marginal, low-income and rural areas. The reform privileged universal access goals over

Table 14.9
Chile—Accessibility and Availability

Chile	Reform						
	1986	1988	1990	1992	1994	1996	1998
% of Residential lines	70.4	72.0	75.5	76.9	77.0	77.0	77.0
Residential phones/ 100 households	14.5	16.1	22.4	33.4	40.1	52.6	66.2
% Payphones/main lines	1.8	1.9	2.0	1.5	0.6	0.5	0.5
Payphones per 1000 inh.	0.8	0.9	1.3	1.4	0.7	0.8	0.9

universal service provision. The standard for universal access formulated by law mandated at least one payphone in any community with more than 60 inhabitants, located at least half an hour's driving from the next nearest telephone. Preliminary estimates indicate that at the current rate of expansion, 80 percent of the rural population will be covered by the year 2002 (SUBTEL, 2000). In 1999 an important amendment to the law changed the original goal of "payphone" to "telecommunication services." Although the ramifications of the shift are as yet unclear, it may suggest a move away from universal access to universal service definition. The Chilean Secretariat of Telecommunications has acknowledged the need for adding rules that boost access to telecommunication services, mainly in the case of lower income groups of the population.

Over the 1990s, the affordability of the telephone service in Chile was guaranteed by the sustained improvement of the economy as a whole. Chile has one of the world's cheapest tariffs systems for long distance service but the installation costs and rates for local calls (11 U.S. cents per minute) are above the regional average (ITU 2000). The consistent increase of the overall income level keep the relative cost of the service down making it affordable to the population (table 14.10).

Mexico
In 1990 a consortium led by Grupo Carso from Mexico, in partnership with BellSouth and France Telecom, bought 20 percent of Teléfonos de México (TELMEX) stock, thus acquiring rights to operate a monopoly of basic services until 1996.[8] Once laws removing caps on foreign investment were lifted, the government then also sold its holding to

Table 14.10
Chile—Telephone Service Affordability

Chile	Reform					
	1993	1994	1995	1996	1997	1998
Fixed phone connection/ income per capita	8.0	N/A	4.0	3.7	3.4	3.2
Res. mon. phone subc./ monthly per capita income	5.7	N/A	5.2	4.5	4.2	3.9

international investors. Regional duopolies were established for mobile cellular services. TELMEX was able to participate in all these markets through its subsidiary TELCEL (Straubhaar at al., 1995). During this period, TELMEX was required: a) to achieve an average annual growth of 12 percent in main lines through 1994, b) by 1994, to install payphones in each town with a population greater than 500, and c) to raise the payphone penetration up to 2 per 1,000 inhabitants in 1994, and 5 per 1,000 in 1998. The Telecommunication Act of 1995 laid out social coverage as an objective for public networks. The mandate was formulated through new plans for rural and public telephony, providing cellular facilities to grocery stores, health centers and mobile satellite connection to medical services (ITU 2000).

In 1996, the long distance market was opened to competition while the basic service continued to be developed under regional duopolies through the entrance of other providers that competed with TELMEX. Expansion of fixed lines has kept conservative rates while mobile telephony has double after the end of the exclusivity period.

By that year the company had only partially fulfilled USO established by the concession. The annual growth target was attained during the first four years of privatization, but network expansion dropped to 4 percent in 1994 and 5 percent in 1995. In 1996, it experienced zero-growth. At the same time, the increase in overall telephone penetration was not comparable to the growth in household penetration suggesting that the expansion was driven by commercial demand. TELMEX met the 1994 target in payphones. But the number of public phones declined in 1996. And TELMEX fell far short of fulfilling its 1998 requirement (see table 14.12).

Table 14.11
Mexico—Telephone Penetration

Mexico	Reform						
	1988	1990	1992	1994	1996	1998	2000
Phonelines per 100 inh.	5.3	6.5	7.5	9.2	9.3	10.4	12.5
Mobile pho. per 100 inh.	0.0	0.1	0.3	0.6	1.1	3.5	14.2
Telephone Penetration	5.3	6.6	7.9	9.8	10.4	13.8	26.7

Table 14.12
Mexico—Accessibility and availability

Mexico	Reform					
	1988	1990	1992	1994	1996	1998
% of Residential lines	70.0	71.0	71.1	71.0	74.6	N/A
Residential phones/ 100 households	20.3	23.7	28.2	33.2	33.9	34.5
% Payphones/main lines	1.2	1.6	1.9	2.6	2.7	3.2
Payphones per 1000 inh.	0.6	1.0	1.4	2.3	2.5	3.3

An important flaw in the Mexican strategy stemmed from the lack of population data needed to estimate the coverage of the payphone network. By 1998, TELMEX had provided the service to 16,000 localities with more than 500 inhabitants. However, most rural towns have less than 500 inhabitants leaving almost 10 million people (10 percent of the population) out of expansion plans for public telephony (ITU, 1998b).

Facing economic pressures during the peso crisis, TELMEX held expansion plans back. However, over the same period, mobile cellular service penetration was growing by rates between 20 percent and 90 percent per year. The growth of mobile telephony was based on two pricing strategies: CPP and prepaid plans. Although the tariff rebalancing process situated fixed phone in a competitive position (table 14.13), by the end of 1999 85 percent of TELMEX cellular subscribers were using the prepaid plan "Amigo" (ITU, 2000). Cofetel, the Mexican regulator, currently reviews the CPP system to determine if revenue split (20/5 U.S. cents) between mobile and fixed operators reflects the costs of both operators. The underlying question is if a system that sets advantages to

Table 14.13
Mexico—Telephone Service Affordability

Mexico		Reform				
	1989	1990	1992	1994	1996	1998
Fixed phone connection/ income per capita	9.9	15.5	11.9	11,7	6,8	? 5
Mobile phone connection/ income per capita	N/A	16.3	3.5	0.6	0.4	N/A
Res. mon. phone subc./ monthly per capita income	1.1	1.8	2.7	3.2	3.3	3.9
Res. mon. mobile subc./ monthly per capita income	N/A	13.4	13.2	12.1	10.0	7.2

mobile users is in fact discriminating against subscribers of fixed-lines. As the price of mobile services continues falling the disadvantage for fixed-phone users will become more evident.

Recent accounts of the post-liberalization period have shown that USO constituted a major point of contention between TELMEX and competitors in disputes over interconnection and regulatory transparency (Burkart, 2000; Gómez-Mont 2000). By 1999, the regulatory authority had not identified a universal service program that balanced the interests of all providers in the market. TELMEX wanted to have USO reduced, eased or shared with competitors. However it was also ready to use USO as an argument to justify high interconnection charges. As Burkart notes, "with so little put into expanding the [network], either through interconnection or through and aggressive universal service plan, the development of markets of basic services cannot proceed." (2000:235)

Peru
Peru privatized and merged Entel and CPT, the state-owned telecommunication enterprises, in 1993. Telefónica of Spain won the auction of Telefónica del Peru (TP), a newly created consortium that consolidated local and long distance operators into one national company. The transaction ranked TP as the company with the highest cost per line in the region. The outcome surprised observers who considered that the four-year exclusivity period awarded to the company was particularly short

Table 14.14
Peru—Telephone Penetration

Peru	Reform						
	1990	1992	1993	1994	1996	1998	2000
Phonelines per 100 inh.	2.6	2.7	3.0	3.3	6.0	6.3	6.4
Mobile pho. per 100 inh.	0.0	0.1	0.2	0.2	0.8	3.0	4.0
Telephone Penetration	2.6	2.8	3.1	3.5	6.8	9.3	10.4

in comparison with previous privatizations (e.g., Mexico, Venezuela). The high value of TP stemmed from market power guaranteed in the monopoly franchise—including mobile telephony-, which in fact promoted the vertical integration of the holding and reducing competitive pressures of product substitute (mobile telephony, see table 14.11) during the first years of the privatization (Briceño, 1999).

The monopoly franchise established goals of network expansion (250,000 new lines by the year 1999), and provisions for the installation of at least one telephone in 1,540 rural settlements with population over 500 inhabitants. Under the framework of the franchise commitments, TP agreed with the regulatory agency, Osiptel, on a program of telecenters developed in partnership with small entrepreneurs aimed at providing public telephony to low-income areas. In 1995 the plan was enhanced through the program of *Cabinas Públicas,* telecenters that offer Internet access. The Scientific Peruvian Network (Red Científica Peruana) opened the first of these centers in 1995. Since that year, the telecenter network has continuously grown becoming a prosperous network of 1,000 sites. The demand is driving prices down and the cost of one hour of computer/Internet connection currently varies between 0.7 and 0.85 U.S. dollar (Proenza et al., 2000).

At the end of the monopoly (1999), the major success of the reform in Peru was the strong growth of public access (see table 14.15). Household penetration and fixed phone expansion has stagnated since 1996. A somehow repressed demand seemed to have jumped on the bandwagon of mobile telephone expansion. As with the case of Argentina, the introduction of CPP systems in 1996, combined with prepaid plans, triggered demand for cellular phones, which already enjoyed a more competitive price structure (table 14.16). The reform fulfilled the goal of tariff

Table 14.15
Peru—Accessibility and Availability

Peru	Reform					
	1991	1992	1993	1995	1997	1999
% of Residential lines	70.0	70.6	N/A	N/A	82,0	N/A
Residential phones/ 100 households	9.0	10.1	N/A	N/A	28.1	N/A
% Payphones/main lines	1.5	1.5	1.1	2.5	2.4	3.6
Payphones per 1000 inh.	0.4	0.4	0.3	1.2	1.6	2.4

Table 14.16
Peru—Telephone Service Affordability

Peru	Reform						
	1992	1993	1994	1995	1996	1997	1998
Fixed phone connection/ income per capita	17.3	32.2	25.2	20.0	17.1	13.1	5.9
Mobile phone connection/ income per capita	N/A	N/A	N/A	N/A	N/A	N/A	N/A
Res. mon. phone subc./ monthly per capita income	0.9	2.0	3.6	4.3	5.7	7.3	7.0
Res. mon. mobile subc./ monthly per capita income	N/A	N/A	26.8	22.9	11.6	12.2	N/A

rebalancing of fixed telephony, but during the period of adjustment, the demand moved to the cheaper option available in the market. By the end of 1998 TP introduced the "Popular Telephone," a prepaid plan for fixed subscribers that a year later accounted for 14 percent of all TP's customers (ITU, 2000). The experience speaks of the need and opportunities for options that reach a demand restricted by economic difficulties.

Venezuela

The privatization of the C.A. Teléfonos de Venezuela (CANTV) was part of the reorganization of state enterprises, a plan inscribed into major economic reforms undertaken by Venezuela in 1989.[9] A consortium led by GTE won the auction of 40 percent of the shares by the end of 1991.

Eleven percent of the stock was allocated to company workers. The remaining 49 percent of stock originally in the hands of the State, has been partially sold in national and international stock markets. Today 89 percent of CANTV's equity is privately held.

CANTV monopolized local and long distance services for 10 years, with the exception of public telephony, a business which the government allowed new entrants into to supply service in areas not covered by CANTV. Five years after privatization, the government had licensed 30 firms in public telephony and 3 for rural areas. But long discussions over interconnection fees and what constituted "not attended" areas delayed the growth of competition in these segments. Since 1990, the mobile cellular market has operated as a duopoly, in which CANTV competes through a subsidiary (TELCEL). Full competition prevails in private networks and value-added services.

The concession for the basic service monopoly committed CANTV to meet goals of quality and service expansion specified by regions. The requirements included the addition of 355,000 new lines per year between 1992 and 2000, with fixed caps for new public telephones. After 1995, making use of contractual provisions, CANTV renegotiated these requirements arguing that the recession in the Venezuelan economy since 1993 has drastically altered the scenarios for demand originally envisaged in the concession. Conatel, a sector regulator that has been shaken by constant changes in its administration, has led the renegotiation of terms of the concession. As in Mexico, economic recession impacted heavily on targets for telephone service penetration, an indicator that has experienced negative growth in recent years (table 14.17).

However, unlike the Mexican case, household service penetration in Venezuela has increased at a faster pace (table 14.18). Waiting lists,

Table 14.17
Venezuela—Telephone service penetration

Venezuela	Reform						
	1990	1991	1992	1994	1996	1998	2000
Phonelines per 100 inh.	8.2	8.1	9.0	10.9	11.7	11.7	10.9
Mobile pho. per 100 inh.	0.0	0.1	0.4	1.5	2.6	8.7	14.4
Telephone Penetration	8.3	8.2	9.4	12.4	14.3	20.3	25.3

Table 14.18
Venezuela—Accessibility and Availability

Venezuela		Reform				
	1990	1991	1992	1994	1996	1998
% of Residential lines	68.3	69.0	68.0	67.6	68.6	71.1
Residential phones/ 100 households	26.3	30.7	33.5	40.5	44.7	45.9
% Payphones/main lines	2.1	2.0	2.5	2.4	2.1	2.8
Payphones per 1000 inh.	1.7	1.6	2.2	2.6	2.5	3.2

Table 14.19
Venezuela—Telephone Service Affordability

Venezuela		Reform				
	1990	1991	1993	1995	1997	1998
Fixed phone connection/ income per capita	1.2	1.5	1.5	0.8	1.9	2.4
Mobile phone connection/ income per capita	N/A	N/A	N/A	N/A	N/A	0.3
Res. mon. phone subc./ monthly per capita income	0.4	0.4	1.1	1.1	2.1	2.4
Res. mon. mobile subc./ monthly per capita income	N/A	N/A	16.1	15.6	9.2	9.9

which were mainly composed by residential customers, has disappeared. This trend, in the context of decreasing fixed phone penetration was accompanied by a very strong expansion of mobile cellular services, a phenomenon that indicates the migration of the demand for basic services from wired networks to wireless services.

Today, Venezuela is one of twelve telecom systems worldwide where there are more mobile subscribers than fixed lines in use. Various factors account for the phenomenon. First, the political tension and turmoil that characterized Venezuela during the past decade frustrated efforts by the regulator at different times to rebalance tariffs. Second, the economic performance of the country never kept up with the process of devaluation of the Venezuelan currency. As a result, fixed telephone charges have become more expensive in relative terms (table 14.19). Third, aggressive competition in the market of mobile telephony was based on the implementation of prepaid plans accounting for the 73 percent of the subscriber base (ITU, 2000).

In 2000 the government and Congress cooperated on setting up a new regulatory framework to open the market of basic services. A new Telecommunication Act was recently approved including the creation of a Universal Service Fund with contributions of for-profit telecommunication service operators of 1 percent of their annual gross income. The Act assumed an active concept of universal service, encompassing all available services in the market (including Internet access), and the government launched an e-government initiative, which required all regional and national authorities to offer electronic services by the year 2002.

Comparative Analysis of Trends

Has liberalization delivered the promises set forth a decade ago? In some terms, it has exceeded them but in others it has fallen behind. Consistent with past studies (Mody and Tsui, 1995; Straubhaar et al., 1995; Petrazzini and Clark, 1996) this review shows that liberalization, and more importantly competition, resulted in significant increases in availability and accessibility of telecommunication services diversifying access points and increasing options. Regardless of the approach embraced by telecommunication administrators, liberalization has served the goals of accelerating overall basic service penetration. However, countries are facing problems in maintaining or increasing network access at the same pace after the first phase of reform, typically about four years after competition is introduced. After the fifth year of liberalization, network growth levels off resulting in a plateau in household and payphone penetration. This trend is present regardless of the USO strategy embraced by the country. Curiously, countries with no USO (Chile) or with flexible USO (Argentina) exhibit a better performance of household penetration (figure 14.1).

In spite of the evidence, developing countries have bet more on privatization than on competition when coming to redefine their supply strategies. In their attempt to make the sale more attractive to buyers, less developed nations have awarded monopoly conditions to private

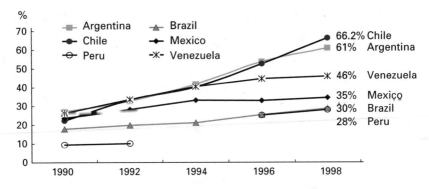

Figure 14.1
Availability Household telephone penetration (Phones/100 households)
Source: ITU

operators while reducing regulatory oversight. Later, in the transition from monopoly conditions to market structures, administrators find themselves lacking the tools to align telecommunication policies with social and economic needs (Melody, 1999).

The main achievement of managed liberalization schemes, those that imposed USO on private monopolies (Brazil, Mexico, Peru, Venezuela), seems to be related to stronger rates of public telephone penetration (figure 14.2). It may indicate a higher commitment for assuring service accessibility and meeting social goals. However, some of these cases also present a common problem: Mexico and Venezuela renegotiated and restated USO by lowering caps for expansion of the overall network, while focusing on plans of public telephony. One of the major obstacles to evaluating the real benefits of this strategy is the lack of data on rural versus urban penetration. Plans to expand private or public telephony as expressed in licenses, contracts and bylaws did not relate service targets to specific populations (low-income groups, disabled people). Operators do not report data on penetration in rural areas either to ITU databases or to CITEL records, limiting their plans for rural areas to public telephony.

In trying to balance the contradictory interests of operators and the public, administrators have had to agree on more conservative scenarios for network expansion. The situation could certainly point out a tendency to wrongly estimate the parameters set forth in reform scenarios.

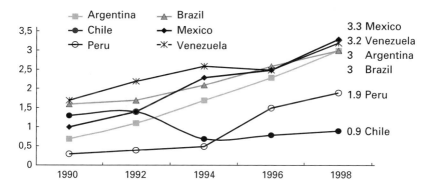

Figure 14.2
Accessibility Payphones per 1,000 inhabitants
Source: ITU

It could also be evidence of the lack of an assertive administration in a more deregulated environment. In either case, it represents the need for flexible regulatory mechanisms that target specific groups in greater need.

Saturation of demand cannot be argued as a reason for the deceleration of growth. In countries with overall telephone penetration between 61 percent and 10.4 percent, universal service is still a pending goal. One reason for this could be a failure to deal effectively with issues of affordability and tariffs as the network progresses from one stage of development to another. Tariff rebalancing has reduced connection charges while driving monthly charge up (figure 14.3). Venezuela, in particular, has been affected by increasing telephone charges, a factor that may explain the migration of users to mobile telephone services. In countries with severe problems of income distribution, and that have continuously faced economic difficulties, there is still a tremendous need for more socially desirable pricing schemes.

Experience with the massive use by mobile service providers of prepaid plans as part of their marketing strategies shows the advantages and strong potential response to repressed demand. Fixed telephone providers in Peru (1998) and Venezuela (2000) have implemented similar plans discovering that low-income groups have more purchasing power than expected. The alternative emerged as a marketing strategy of the incumbents to cope with the competitive pressures of mobile telephone operators, but regulators remain inactive about this important issue.

Phone connection/Income per capita   Monthly charge/Monthly income

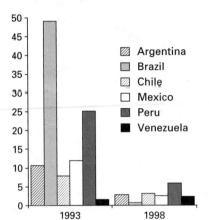
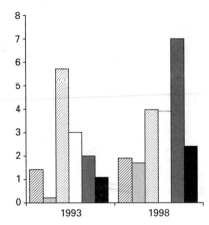

Figure 14.3
Affordability Tariff and income
Source: ITU Start database

The virtual stoppage in fixed-line network expansion should be directly related to the tremendous growth in mobile cellular services. In theory, mobile telephony should enhance the options for increasing service availability and accessibility. But in the case of some of these nations, cellular phones may not just become a supplement to a fixed phone but a substitute for it.

Although the ITU considers this scenario as a favorable one, from the industry point of view, the period of exclusivity represented higher economic pressures for the expansion of fixed-line networks. The majority of the reforms have set free cellular markets while keeping monopolies for basic services, as a way to assure to fixed phone operators revenues that guarantee profitability and network expansion. However, in countries with low telephone penetration and a high demand for service, monopolies moved slower than mobile cellular services in responding to demand.

Mobile cellular altered the equation by becoming a shortcut to meet people's needs. In countries with higher fixed-phone penetration, cellular operators seek subscribers more aggressively, offering lower prices, hence making the service more accessible to people. However, in countries with low telephone penetration the high demand is usually translated into higher prices for mobile services, setting them off as the preserve of

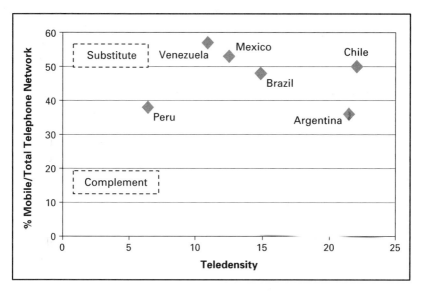

Figure 14.4
Fixed/Cellular Substitution
Source: ITU

higher income groups. In these nations the cellular market captures a highly profitable segment of the population. However, options of access are not enhanced for lower income groups.

The relevant indicator to observe the phenomenon is not teledensity, but substitution rates—the ratio of mobile cellular subscribers to total telephone subscribers, which indicates "the degree to which mobile cellular is used as an alternative rather than a supplement to fixed-line networks" (ITU, 1998b, p. 49). A high ratio suggests that many cellular subscribers have no alternative for telephone service. Substitution rates are higher in Mexico, Brazil and Venezuela, that is countries with lower per capita income, whose fixed telephony had lower penetration rates at the moment of introduction of mobile services (see figure 14.4).

Venezuela is a good example of the trend being examined here. Since 1998 the number of subscribers to cellular phone services has exceeded subscribers of fixed telephones. Teledensity statistics register a negative growth of –4 percent , but the combined indicator of *telephone penetration* increased 21 percent. What type of challenge then does this phenomenon pose to regulators?

The need for a redistribution of resources in freer markets has led to a second round of legislative reforms. The first generation of USO, highly focused on general target of service accessibility, is being replaced by a second generation of USO. Chile (1994), Peru (1995), and Mexico (1997) and more recently Argentina (1999), Brazil (2000), and Venezuela (2000) have started to explore this path through new legislation and the creation of Universal Service Funds. The establishment of public funds with contributions from competiting telecommunication providers is a starting point to solve the Gordian knot of financing the incorporation of citizens deprived from the service. However, it is important to move beyond the supply-side discussion to consider the demand-side of who is effectively receiving the service and what means are more appropriate to enforce USO. The Mexican and Venezuelan cases suggest that more attention should be paid to alternatives that increase individual access, in particular taking advantage of the rapid growth of mobile cellular networks. Community solutions, such as telecenters, have also not been completely developed in governmental policy. With the exception of Peru and Chile, no other analyzed countries implemented public policies to bring communities into the effort of enhancing access. Venezuela and Brazil have recently launched national policies on public Internet access through telecenters.

Policy Implications

Mosco remind us that telecommunication reforms redefine the role of the state as settler of social claims. Drawing on political and social theory, he identifies four modes of state intervention relevant to telecommunication. They are representation, expertise, social control and market control. 'Representation' marks the degree of incorporation of the social in the decision making process from the point of view of a more deliberative formulation of regulations. 'Expertise' suggests an extremely narrowed procedure in regulation formulation carried out by boards of experts. 'Social control' and 'market control' are set off by the degree of direct or indirect control exerted upon the operations not only by the state but also by labor unions, other business sectors, and the public. Social control relies on corporatism while market control sees competition as the major form of governance. Based on this model, this study tries to identify shifts of modes of governance brought about by telecommunication reforms in five Latin American countries.

The shift from state corporatism to market competition models in the six studied countries has not gone beyond the *'expertise'* form of governance outlined by Mosco (1988), in which the power of newly created regulatory agencies remains captive to technical debates that represent the interest of a narrow group of providers with little concern for social claims. In this context, the 'hybrid' regulatory system of the transitions has hampered USO in countries that try to apply strict rules to monopolies of basic services, and a set of more flexible commitments to substitute services, such as mobile cellular, that operate in competition. The virtual failure of USO policies in Venezuela and Mexico should be interpreted in light of these contradictions.

Mansell and Wehn's (1998) international assessment of the progress of the information society suggests that in the deployment of 'the network of networks' that substitutes for the homogeneous network of PTTs, developing countries should combine three major strategies: (1) the increase of competitive pressures, (2) the use of all technologies available in the market for enhancing means of interconnection, and (3) the enforcement of USO. These authors argue that in this process led by technological convergence, regulation is "necessary to provide a foundation upon which markets can function more effectively than they could otherwise" (p. 16). The *multi network* perspective should be enhanced through a *multi-leveled* approach, a set of moving targets addressing the needs of access at the public, institutional and individual level (Hudson, 2000). All these elements demand a better and more active regulator, one capable of articulating innovative USO targeting users with special needs.

An alternative to moving away from the *expertise* model toward the path of *market control* is more and more effective competition in a diversified market. Multiplicity of providers increases the negotiation power of the regulator as settler of social claims. A good example of the step that should be taken in this direction is the strategy displayed by the Chilean and Brazilian authorities in dividing up the market and introducing competition along with privatization.

Once the network increases its points of access through different services, policy makers should take advantage of the reconfiguration fostered by competitive markets to meet social goals. Regulators need to develop a single definition of universal service that extends social commitments to all operators of the telecommunication market. This definition should cut across services without being bundled into technological specificity. It ought to incorporate factors from the consumer-demand perspective accounting for the urban-rural continuum, and social and economic strata. Peru, Chile, Argentina, and Venezuela have adopted steps in this direction. But it is not yet clear how this new conceptualization of *basic telecommunication service* will get enacted through concrete plans.

Technological convergence is reshaping the market. Regulation is key to set in motion the process that uses the sum total of capabilities available in the market to meet the needs of specific segments of the population still deprived from telecommunication services. As Melody (1999) has argued, universal service regulations can provide an answer that bridges divergent interests and captures network externality benefits that competitive markets cannot achieve. This is possible through the incorporation of "unphoned" users who still may have resources to pay for the basic service, thus enhancing network externalities. However, this would demand a market-regulated system that attends to a wider range of social claims than is currently the case, by setting fair rules for all participants in the market, including consumers and newcomers.

Acknowledgments

I am grateful to Sharon Strover and Joseph Straubhaar for their wise and helpful comments on earlier drafts. I take full responsibility for limitations and defects of this work.

Notes

1. The strength of this indicator is based on three aspects: a) a phone at home is considered the closest connection of citizens in times of emergency or distress; b) it captures countries' specificities such as different household sizes; c) and it is related to income level. The ITU (1998b) considers that countries with household penetration of 90% or above to have reached universal service.

2. In fact, the WTO Secretariat recognizes the multi-access notion through the inclusion of mobile services and circuit-switched data transmissions, along with voice telephone services, in the list of services ruled by the 1997 GATS commitments or limitations on market access and national treatment for basic telecommunications.

3. Conventional statistics of telephone demand, as revealed in waiting lists reported by operators, estimate 92% of demand in Latin America has been satisfied (ITU, 2000:89).

4. Reviewing preview studies on effects of tariff rebalancing, Milne (2000) concludes that rebalancing inevitably favors some customer groups over others, in particular heavy users (typically business and high income groups). However, outcomes of the evaluations differ from country to country, or between social groups. The author hypothesizes that income levels of the nation or community make a difference.

5. This indicator is estimated using a proxy based on number of residential lines as a percentage of households. Data was gathered from the ITU Start database.

6. The majority of the shares in Telecom Argentina belonged to a joint venture between France Telecom and STET from Italy while Telefónica from Spain controlled Telefónica Argentina. Foreign private investors bought 60% of company shares while the remaining 40% were sold to employees (10%) and the public (30%). Imprecise regulations and delays in the organization of the regulatory agency triggered severe criticism of the process and led to the renegotiation of the concessions for both companies a year after the privatization took place. Therefore, it is considered that the reform was not fully in place until 1991 (Francés, 1993).

7. In its early years of development the Chilean national network consisted of several small local service providers interconnected through the Compañía de Teléfonos de Chile (CTC), owned by the ITT. In 1964 the state stepped into the business opening the Empresa Nacional de Telecomunicaciones (ENTEL-Chile), which coexisted with CTC as a second player in the market. In 1971, during the government of Salvador Allende, CTC was taken over by the government, which attempted to consolidate all companies into a public holding. However, after the 1973 coup, the military government launched a program of liberalization in the industry that allowed the resale of telephone lines and competition in terminal equipment. In 1982 the state began to sell its share in small local companies. And in 1986, it made public offers of its shares in CTC and ENTEL, with Telefónica of Spain emerging as the largest buyer. The changes were accompanied with a reform of the telecom law that freed tariffs in those areas of the country where market conditions were sufficient.

8. TELMEX was developed as a private monopoly until 1971, when the Mexican government bought the majority of the stock owned by ITT and Ericsson. Keeping a minor participation of national private investors, the company grew as a public corporation with subsidiaries in the most diverse businesses (satellite and telegraph, real estate, advertising, and construction) (Francés, 1993). However, a growing technological gap and the deviation of funds to subsidiaries hindered network expansion, and by the end of the 1980s, the underdevelopment of the basic network had become a stumbling block for plans of economic modernization. The government of Carlos Salinas de Gortari justified the privatization of TELMEX as a solution to major bottlenecks in the provision of telecommunication services.

9. The strategy originally set a step-by-step liberalization of the market through the separation of operative and regulatory functions, the corporatization of CANTV, and the liberalization of mobile cellular markets and value-added services. However, the need for multilateral funds to keep macroeconomic balance, and the lack of sources to pay back the considerable foreign debt of the company meant the corporatization strategy was turned into a plan for full privatization in 1990.

References

Briceño, A. (1999) Regulating anticompetitive behavior in the Internet market: An applied imputation model for Peru. In S.E. Gillet and I. Vogelsang. *Competition, regulation and convergence: Current trends in telecommunications policy research.* 27–49. London: Lawrence Erlbaum.

Burkart, P. C. (2000) *The network* hacendados: *TELMEX in Mexico's Political Economy of Communications.* Unpublished dissertation. The University of Texas at Austin.

Compaine, B., and Weinraub, M. (1997) Universal access to online services: an examination of the issue. *Telecommunications Policy, 21* (1), 15–33.

CITEL (2000) *Universal Service in the Americas.* Organization of American States.

Gil-Egui, G., and Steward, C. M. (June, 1999) *Local needs vs. multinational interests: The role of the ITU in the Development of the universal access policies in the era of the global information infrastructure.* Paper presented at the Annual Conference of the International Association for Media and Communication Research, Leipzig, Germany.

Gómez-Mont, C. (2000) *Opening telecommunications in Mexico under NAFTA.* Paper presented at the Annual Conference of the International Communication Association, Acapulco, Mexico.

Grande, E. (1994). The new role of the state in Telecommunications: An international comparison. *West European Politics 17* (3), 138–158.

Gutierrez, L.H., and Berg, S. (2000) Telecommunications liberalization and regulatory governance: lessons from Latin America. *Telecommunication Policy 24,* 865–884.

Hudson, H. (2000) *Access to the digital economy: Issues in rural and developing countries.* Available at <http://mitpress.mit.edu/UDE/hudson.rtf>.

International Telecommunication Union (2000) *Americas Telecommunication Indicators 2000.* Geneva: ITU

International Telecommunication Union (1999) *Yearbook of statistics: Telecommunication services,chronological time series 1988–1997.* Geneva: ITU.

International Telecommunication Union (1998a) *Trends in telecommunication reform.* Geneva: ITU.

International Telecommunication Union (1998b) *World telecommunication development report:Universal access and world telecommunication indicators.* Geneva: ITU.

Jayakar, K. (September, 2000) *The impact of telecommunications reforms on residential teledensity: Analysis of a cross-country panel data.* Paper presented at the Research Conference on Information, Communications, and Internet Policy. Alexandria, VA.

Mansell, R., and When, U. (Eds) (1998) *Knowledge Societies: Information technology for sustainable development.* United Nations: Oxford University Press.

Melody, W. (1999) Telecom reform: Progress and prospects. *Telecommunications Policy 23,* 7–34

Milne, C. (2000) Affordability of basic telephone service: an income distribution approach. *Telecommunication Policy 24,* 907–927.

Minges, M. (1999a) *Developing Policies for Universal Service,* Paper presented at the ITU/BDT Workshop on Telecommunication Reform, Botswana, May 1999. Available at: <http://www.itu.int/treg/RelatedLinks/LinksAndDocs/uso.asp>.

Minges, M. (1999b) *Indicators for Universal Access.* Paper presented at the ITU/BDT Workshop on Telecommunication Reform, Botswana, May 1999. Available at: <http://www.itu.int/treg/RelatedLinks/LinksAndDocs/uso.asp>.

Mody, B., and Tsui, LS. (1995) The changing role of the state. In Mody, B., Bauer, J and Straubhaar, J. (1995) *Telecommunications politics: Ownership and control of the information highway in developing countries.* 179–198. New Jersey: Lawrence Erlbaum Associates.

Mosco, V. (1988) Toward a theory of the state and telecommunication policy. *Journal of Communication 38* (1), 107–124.

Muller, M. (1997) *Universal service: Competition, interconnection, and monopoly in the making of the American telephone system.* Washington, D.C.: The MIT Press and The AEI Press.

Petrazzini, B. (1996) *Global telecom talks: A trillion-dollar deal.* Washington, D.C.: Institute for International Economics.

Petrazzini, B. (1995). *The political economy of telecommunications reform in developing countries: Privatization and liberalization in comparative perspective.* Westport, CN: Praeger.

Petrazzini, B., and Guerrero, A. (2000). Promoting Internet Development: The case of Argentina, a case study. *Telecommunication Policy 24,* 89–112.

Petrazzini, B., and Clark, T. (1996) *Costs and benefits of telecommunications liberalization in developing countries.* Paper presented at the Institute for International Economics Conference on Liberalizing Telecommunications, 29 January, Washington.

Proenza, F., Bastidas-Buch, R., and Montero, G. (2000) *Telecentros para el desarrollo socioeconómico y rural.* Washington, D.C.: Inter American Development Bank (IADB). Available at <http://www.iadb.org/regions/ITDEV/TELECENTROS/Telecentros.pdf>.

Straubhaar, J., McCormick, P., Bauer, J., and Campbell, C. (1995) Telecommunication restructuring: The experience of eight countries. In Mody, B., Bauer, J and Straubhaar, J. (1995) *Telecommunications politics: Ownership and control of the information highway in developing countries.* 225–244. New Jersey: Lawrence Erlbaum Associates.

SUBTEL (2000) *Acceso Universal: Una política de acción.* Report of Subsecretaría de Telecomunicaciones de Chile and Departamento de Ingeniería Industrial de la Universidad de Chile. Santiago, Chile.

Tyler, M., Letwin, W., and Roe, C. (1995) Universal Service and innovation in telecommunication services: fostering linked goals through regulatory policy. *Telecommunications Policy 19* (1), 3–20.

15
Bringing the Internet to Schools: The U.S. and E.U. Policies

Michelle S. Kosmidis

1 Introduction

The Internet has changed the way people communicate, learn, and work. Efforts have been made to integrate information technology and Internet into the educational systems for a number of compelling reasons. The new technology is considered as an important pedagogic tool, which complements rather than replaces traditional teaching at schools. It prepares the young workforce to be more employable in the new economy, which is more information-based. Furthermore, such integration could help to eliminate the 'digital divide' through providing unequivocally access to all students to new technologies regardless of social or economic background.

Measures have been taken to promote Internet access and usage in elementary and secondary schools in both the United States (U.S.) and European Union (E.U.).[1] At a first stage public policy appears to support Internet access to schools, while at a second stage it may concentrate on Internet access specifically to classrooms. This distinction is significant as the latter policy choice (Internet access to each classroom) involves huge costs.

It is beyond the scope of this paper to discuss the precise effects of information technology on students' learning, which is analyzed in other research studies.[2] Instead it focuses on regulatory and economic issues related to the costs of effective Internet access to schools: communications costs (telephone and Internet Service Provider (ISP) charges); and noncommunications costs, such as costs for hardware (computers) and internal connections (such as network wiring, modems, routers, network file services, wireless local area networks (LANs)), maintenance and technical support, teachers' training, and specialized software.

The question this paper addresses is who should pay for any of the aforementioned costs. To tackle this question, available data on costs of Internet access to schools will be analyzed in order to identify the type of costs related to such access, the magnitude of communications costs, and the proportion of these costs in relation to the total information communication technology (ICT)[3] school expenditures. The key principles for covering such costs should be operator neutrality, technological neutrality, and should not distort competition.

This paper shows that communications costs comprise only a small proportion of ICT school expenditures. Empirical evidence in both the E.U. and U.S. suggests that competition gives incentives for operators to provide discounted tariffs for Internet access to schools. The issue is whether there should be any additional support, and how it should be funded.

This paper finds that noncommunications costs are significantly higher than the cost of communications services. The E.U. Member States finance the additional costs through general national budgets or joint public/private partnerships, while the U.S. imposes a "tax" specifically on telecommunications operators providing interstate and international services. It concludes that telecommunications operators should not be obliged to pay for these noncommunications costs. As we will see later, such taxation on the telecommunications industry is costly, inefficient, and not necessarily equitable.

The paper also examines the difficult question of the effectiveness of each policy approach by analyzing the penetration rates of Internet access to schools in the United States and the 15 E.U. Member States. Indicators like number of pupils per computer (with Internet access), and number of instructional rooms with computers (with Internet access) demonstrate the use of Internet as a learning tool. Furthermore, the type of connection and speed is crucial for the use of Internet in schools. Data show that the United States is ahead of the E.U. average—although some Member States (early liberalizers like Sweden and Denmark) are doing better than the European average and have comparable results with the United States.

This paper will describe the U.S. policy where the universal service fund supports Internet access to eligible schools (section 2). It will present the E.U. policy of encouraging operators to provide special (flat rate) tariffs (at the dial-up layer) to schools and/or funding through a general government budget (section 3). Section 4 compares policy outcomes showing the penetration of Internet access to schools in the U.S. and E.U. In conclusion, this paper compares the two policy lines for Internet access to schools.

2 Internet Access to Schools in the United States

Introduction

Prior to 1984, the availability of affordable telephone access to all American households was achieved through AT&T's internal pricing structure. After the 1984 AT&T break-up, and as competition was being introduced into the long-distance market, an explicit Universal Service Fund was established in order to sustain affordable access for high cost rural areas and low income users.

In 1994, the Clinton-Gore National Information Infrastructure (NII) initiative announced its commitment to develop a seamless national network of information and telecommunications services. One goal was to connect all K-12 schools and instructional rooms (e.g., every classroom, computer labs, and library/media centers) to the Internet by the year 2000.

Consistent with this initiative, the Telecommunications Act of 1996 expanded the concept of universal service obligations to include support for schools, libraries and rural health providers in the 1996 Telecommunications Act. The federal government's choice of supporting Internet access to schools through telecommunications and not educational policy may be a result of its limited policy instruments and budgetary resources in the latter area, which is largely dominated by the state level.

In implementing the 1996 Act, the FCC, in May 1997, outlined a plan in its Universal Service Order to guarantee affordable access to telecommunications services for all eligible schools (and libraries).[4] The federal universal service costs for Internet access to schools and libraries (the so-called E-Rate program) was capped at $2.25 billion per year (matched with equivalent state funding) out of the total annual explicit universal service costs of $4.65 billion. Funding from the E-Rate program was available starting from January 1, 1998.

The following sections describe the selection criteria for schools receiving discounts, and evaluate the actual allocation of funding of the E-Rate program.

Administrative Process for Allocating Funds

This section describes the administrative structure for allocating funds, which is quite complex and leads to burdensome and inefficient processes in receiving funds. The School and Libraries Division (SLD) of the Universal Service Administrative Company (USAC), a nonprofit entity established by the FCC, allocated universal service support for schools and libraries.

The criteria for determining eligible schools, level of discounts, and eligible services are as follows. Eligible schools are those (public or non-public) elementary and secondary schools that do not operate as a for-profit business, and do not have an endowment exceeding $50 million. Eligible schools must develop a state-approved educational technology plan in order to show how they intend to integrate the use of technologies into their curricula, and to show that there is sufficient budget to acquire nondiscounted elements of the plan (i.e., hardware, software).

The level of discounts (ranging from 20 to 90 percent) received by eligible schools (and libraries) depends on the poverty level measured as the percentage of students eligible for the subsidized National School Lunch Program,[5] and the rural location of the school. A matrix has been established for the link between school's eligibility and the level of discount. For instance, schools or consortiums that have more than 75 percent of their students receiving subsidized school lunches receive a 90 percent discount on eligible services.

Services eligible for discount include specified telecommunications services,[6] Internet access services (email service), and internal connections.[7] The fund will not finance customer premises equipment (CPE) or hardware, such as personal computers.[8] Where requests exceed available funds, telecommunications and Internet services have priority over internal connections. Schools and libraries have the maximum flexibility to purchase the services and technologies to suit their needs (wireline, wireless or cable technology), making it technology neutral.

Once the application for discount has been approved, the school will receive the applicable discount on its telecommunications services, Internet access and/or internal connections, and pay the remaining portion of the costs to the vendor or service providers. The vendor or service providers present the discounted bills, and get reimbursed by the Fund Administrator (USAC).

In order to fund the various universal service programs, all telecommunications carriers providing end-user interstate and international telecommunications services are obliged to contribute a fee to the fund based on their interstate and international end-user telecommunications revenues.[9]

Policy Debates and Evaluation of Actual Allocation of Funding

During the introduction of the E-Rate program there was much debate concerning the scope and fairness of the program. This section focuses on the main concerns over the new funding scheme, and evaluates the actual allocation of funding.

One concern was over the extension of the scope of universal service to finance Internet access to schools by taxing the telecommunications industry. Indeed, in 1997 three companies (GTE, BellSouth, and SBC Communications) appealed the FCC's Universal Service Order claiming that the E-Rate was an illegal tax.[10] They argued that a federal agency such as the FCC did not have the authority to impose a tax on them— only Congress did. Furthermore, they argued that it was unfair to burden the telecommunications industry with network infrastructure costs of schools.

Indeed when looking at the allocation of the total funding in terms of type of services during January 1998–June 2001, the highest proportion of the funding is allocated to internal connections. More specifically, on average during this period 57.5 percent of the E-Rate funds financed the acquisition of equipment and services for internal building connections, 34.1 percent telecommunications services (which also includes dedicated lines), and 8.4 percent Internet access costs.

Another concern was the lack of operator neutrality in the FCC's choice of who should contribute to the E-Rate fund. Only interstate telecommunications carriers, and not Internet Service Providers (ISPs),

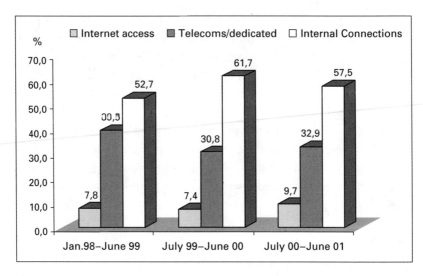

Figure 15.1
Schools and Libraries funding commitments by type of services
(Jan. 1998–June 2001)
Source: FCC, Universal Service Monitoring Report (October 2001)

had to contribute to the fund. There appears to be a policy inconsistency in the E-Rate program where ISPs are exempt from contributing to a service that is entirely Internet-related.

In July 1998, the three largest long-distance telecommunications companies (AT&T, MCI, and Sprint) started expressly passing on the cost to customers with a 'universal service' line item on their phone bills. This started a debate over the impact of the E-Rate program on consumers, as a response, the FCC scaled back its annual finance from $2.25 to $1.9 billion to cover a longer period of 18 months (from January 1, 1998–June 30, 1999) instead of the initially planned 12 months.[11]

Recent studies (Prieger 1998; WIK 2000) show that the federal universal service obligations (USO) tax on the telecommunications industry is actually quite costly and inefficient. Prieger (1998) estimated a deadweight loss or "inefficiency" of end-user revenue taxation ranging between $1.2 and 4 billion per year. This revenue taxation has a negative impact on consumer behavior as it is directly passed on to them causing a reduction of services consumed, and consequently a reduction of industry revenues.

Since one of the goals of the E-Rate program was to reduce the digital divide in the United States, it is important to evaluate the funding allocation to the poorest school districts. According to a report by the U.S. Department of Education (2000b) only 14 percent of total E-Rate funds went to the highest poverty public school districts (with more than 75 percent of their students eligible for reduced price lunches) during the period of January 1998–June 2000. Application rates are lower in poorest school districts because they do not have the human and financial resources to apply for funds; they cannot afford the remaining 10 percent of charges after the E-Rate discount; or lack basic infrastructure (like electrical outlets) and computers to incorporate the new technology. E-Rate funding per student in particular for internal connections was especially high in these higher poverty districts.

In evaluating the procedures of allocating E-Rate funding, the General Accounting Office issued a report in 2001, which showed that about 24 percent of the total funds ($3.7 billion) committed for years 1998–1999 remained unspent. Slow bureaucratic application and invoice procedures have been blamed for this failure.

There is an ongoing debate on whether to transfer the federal E-Rate program to the states to be distributed through a block grant program rather than the current burdensome application process.[12]

3   Internet Access to Schools in the E.U.

In Europe there is a growing consensus that its citizens will have to learn to use the new information and communications tools from an early age if they want to succeed in a knowledge-based society and labor market. Internet access to European schools is becoming more common although there is a wide variation of such access among E.U. Member States with Denmark and Sweden being the most advanced.

The E.U. Action Plan *Learning in the Information Society (1996–1998)* was launched in 1996 to encourage various activities to connect schools to communications networks. It was only three years later in December 1999 that the European Commission launched the *eEurope* Initiative with the goal of bringing Europe on-line.[13] At the Lisbon Summit in March 2000, the Heads of State and Government committed themselves to a number of measures, including target dates, to bring *eEurope* forward. One of *eEurope* targets is to connect all schools to the Internet by the end of 2001, and all classrooms to high-speed Internet and multimedia resources by the end of 2002—two years later than the U.S. 2000 target. Some Member States already had action plans, projects, and goals to connect schools earlier.

In contrast with the U.S. regime, the current (and recently proposed) E.U. legislative framework does not allow any subsidy associated to Internet access to schools and usage to be included in the universal service obligations[14] funding schemes. Instead the E.U. policy choice is to connect schools to the Internet either by encouraging competition among operators to provide 'special tariffs' or service packages to schools and/or through joint public/private initiatives.

Competition with Special Tariff Packages

The European Commission encourages National Regulatory Authorities (NRAs) to allow incumbent and new operators to offer 'special tariffs' to schools (at the dial-up layer) for Internet access and usage.[15] These special tariffs should not distort competition and incumbent operators should not abuse their dominant position, for instance, through predatory pricing. Operators will be willing to compete for the provision of such service to schools as it is hoped that it will get students hooked up to Internet, which will have a spillover effect on usage at homes.

In Europe telecommunications charges are typically usage dependent (contrary to the United States) and therefore unpredictable and difficult to handle in annual school budgets. The benefits of 'special packages or tariffs' offered to schools are that they are by far a *less expensive and more predictable cost* compared to estimated 'standard' rates.[16] At times special flat rate prices for schools are one fifth of estimated 'standard' prices. For instance, British Telecom offers annual access to schools with unlimited usage for $590 (euro 631) with a Public Services Telephone Network (PSTN) connection, and for $1047 (euro 1,120) with an Integrated Services Digital Network (ISDN) connection. This would compare to the estimated U.K. standard rate of $7760 with PSTN, and $4030 with ISDN access in year 2000. In France, Wanadoo provides unlimited Internet access to schools for a flat annual charge of $70 (euro 75), but telephone usage charges are billed separately.

Table 15.1
Estimated EU average "standard" price for Internet access to schools (Jan. 2000)

	Per school	Per pupil	Comments
PSTN	$3902	$3902	One user per time
ISDN (Basic)	$4020	$2010	Assumes two simultaneous users
ISDN (Primary)	$7327	$229	32 simultaneous users
Leased Line 2 MBIT	$11275	$352	32 simultaneous users

Notes:
1. All estimated 'standard' calculations include an annual PSTN rental cost, a usage cost (based on an assumed use of 200 hour per month for each school), and annual ISP charges. Tariffs from Teligen (2000).

2. PSTN allows for one connection; Basic ISDN (bandwidth of 128 kbit/s) allows for two simultaneous connections and Primary ISDN for 32 simultaneous connections.

3. There are considerable differences between Member States with estimated 'standard' prices for Internet access to schools varying between $3263–$15,058 for ISDN-Primary connection, and $6075–$20,530 for leased line (2 Mbit) connection.

Table 15.1 presents the estimated E.U. average "standard" price for Internet access to schools, which is considerably higher than "special" tariffs. Such standard prices vary widely according to each Member State.

Competition issues in relation to abuse of dominant position and distortion of competition have been raised through the provision of 'special' or free Internet access to schools. In accordance with Article 82 (ex Article 86) of the Treaty a dominant operator cannot "directly or indirectly impose unfair purchase or selling prices or other unfair trading conditions." In the United Kingdom[17] and France[18] the incumbent operators provided very low price Internet access to schools. Competitors complained that they could not compete with the incumbent's offer since they had to pay a high interconnection rate.[19] In both countries these cases were resolved by enforcing lower interconnection rates allowing the new entrants to compete and in some cases even provide cheaper rates to schools (such as the case of cable operators in the United Kingdom).

Joint Public/Private Initiatives for Bringing Internet to Schools

E.U. Member States are free to finance ICT expenses from general budgets. These initiatives can be supported either by public (national, regional and local level) sector alone, or by joint public/private partnerships. The

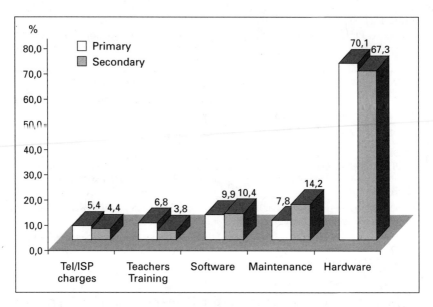

Figure 15.2
ICT school expenditures in England (2000).
Source: DfEE (2000) Statistics of Education

choice of private industry participation must be in accordance to E.U. transparency and nondiscrimination principles. Government initiatives are invariably focused on Internet access, hardware, network infrastructure, and/or teacher training.

An example of public/private partnership is Germany's 'Schulen ans Netz' (Schools Online). The German Federal Ministry of Education and Research (BMBF) and Deutsche Telekom (DT) jointly launched a federal initiative with the goal to connect 10,000 schools to Internet between 1996 and mid-1999 ($33 million). The two partners strengthened their commitment with a further $55 million to connect all 36,000 schools to Internet by the end of 2001 (therefore a total of around $88 million). The federal states are providing additional funding, while there are numerous other sponsors from industry.

Data on the progress of U.K. governmental initiative (National Grid for Learning (NGfL)) show that communications costs are very low in relation to the total ICT school expenditures. A recent survey shows the total annual ICT expenditures for teaching and learning in primary and secondary schools was around $440 million in 2000 (DfEE 2000).[20]

Hardware accounted for the highest cost of around 70 percent of the total ICT expenditures.[21] Communications costs (telecommunications and ISP) accounted only for 4–5 percent or around $20 million of the total ICT expenditures.[22] These communications charges are estimated at $599 (£370) per primary school and $2965 (£1830) per secondary school.

After analyzing the different policy choices in financing Internet access to schools in the United States and the E.U., the following section will analyze and compare the outcome of each policy choice.

4 Comparing Policy Outcomes in the U.S. and E.U. Member States

A recent U.S. survey shows that public schools in the United States have nearly reached the goal of connecting every school to the Internet (NCES, 2001). The percentage of public schools connected to the Internet has increased from 35 percent in 1994 to 98 percent in 2000. The successful policy outcome in the United States may not necessarily be a result of effective policy choice of funding Internet access to schools through the E-Rate program in the United States. First, one must note that there was significant (and even higher) annual growth of penetration before the disbursal of the E-Rate program in November 1998. Second, Internet access to all schools was already at 89 percent in 1998 (Crandall and Waverman, 2000). Furthermore, the aforementioned GAO findings in section 2 (which show that 24 percent of the 1998–1999 E-Rate funds still remain unused) put into question the actual impact of the E-Rate program.

The E.U. average of schools connected to the Internet was lower than the United States at 89 percent at the beginning of 2001. One must note,

Table 15.2
Percentage of schools with Internet access in the USA (1994–2000)

School characteristics	1994	1995	1996	1997	1998	1999	2000
Elementary	30	46	61	75	88	94	97
Secondary	49	65	77	89	94	98	100
All public schools	35	50	65	78	89	95	98
All instructional rooms	3	8	14	27	51	64	77

Source: National Center for Education Statistics (2001).

however, the wide disparities between E.U. Member States. The Nordic European countries like Sweden and Denmark, which financed earlier in the mid-1990s Internet connection to schools through their state educational budget, have comparable results with the United States.[23] In these countries the liberalization of the telecommunications market began back in the mid-1980s (like in the United States), much earlier than in most other E.U. countries.

The southern European countries like Greece and Portugal lag behind in terms of Internet access to schools. Statistics on Greece show that only 22 percent of primary schools and 58 percent of secondary schools are connected to the Internet, while results in Portugal are 56 percent and 91 percent, respectively (CEC 2001). Low Internet access to schools may be a consequence of the less developed telecommunications infrastructure and late liberalization in the two countries.[24] Both Greece and Portugal were granted 2–3 year transitional periods on the formal E.U. liberalization date (1 January 1998) in order to ensure universal service before the opening of their markets. Moreover, in March 2001 the European Commission approved Greece's proposal to use E.U. Structural Funds in order to fulfill the goals of the eEurope initiative, including connection of all schools to the Internet.

Internet connection to classrooms reveals the policy aim to use the new technology as a pedagogical tool. In the United States, the percentage of public school instructional rooms with Internet access increased dramatically from 3 percent in 1994 to 77 percent in 2000. However, only 60 percent of classrooms in schools with the highest penetration of students in poverty (75 percent or more students eligible for the free lunch program) are connected to the Internet. In Europe there are no solid data on this aspect reflecting for the moment its current priority to connect to schools rather than classrooms.

The earlier figures do not tell us the full story on Internet access to schools, since many schools are connected to the Internet but with a low number of available PCs. Therefore, other important indicators are the ratio of students per PC, and students per PC with Internet access. In the United States in 2000, the ratio of students per instructional computer in public schools was 5 to 1 and per instructional computer with Internet access was 7 to 1 (NCES 2001). The average E.U. ratio of students per PC was 12 to 1, and per Internet PC was 24 to 1 in early 2001 (CEC

Table 15.3
Internet connection to schools in the EU (and USA) (2000-01)

	Number of pupils per computer		% of schools connected to Internet	
	Primary	Secondary	Primary	Secondary
Belgium	11	8	90	96
Denmark	4	1	98	99
Germany	23	14	90	98
Greece	67	17	22	58
Spain	14	14	91	95
France	16	10	63	97
Ireland	12	8	96	99
Italy	22	9	87	98
Luxembourg	2	6	86	100
The Netherlands	8	9	91	100
Austria	11	9	53	95
Portugal	26	18	56	91
Finland	7	7	99	99
Sweden	10	4	100	100
The United Kingdom	12	6	93	98
EU average*		12		89
The United States **		5		98

Source: CEC–SEC (2001) 1583; Eurobarometer surveys 101, February–May 2001.
* EU average includes all schools (primary, secondary and professional schools).
**NCES, 2001: US data from 2000.

2001). Again, when looking at the ratio of pupils per PC in secondary schools in particular Member States, Denmark, Sweden, and Finland are as advanced as the United States compared to the rest of the E.U. countries surveyed. On the contrary, in Portugal and in Greece the ratio of pupils per computer is rather high: 18 to 1, and 17 to 1, respectively. This high ratio is an indication that in these countries Internet is not yet used in classrooms for educational purposes.

The type of network connection and speed determines the ability of the school to connect to the Internet. In the United States, 77 percent of schools used dedicated leased lines, 11 percent dial-up connections, and 24 percent other types of connections (including ISDN) in 2000. But even before the introduction of the E-Rate program there were some evident improvements in network connections to public schools.

In Europe, in February 2001, Internet connection to schools was dominated by narrowband technologies (such as dial-up connections, and ISDN). Around 72 percent of schools use ISDN connections, 33 percent standard dial-up connections, while only 5 percent use ADSL, and 6 percent use cable modems (multiple connections are possible) (CEC 2001). The high proportion of narrowband connectivity suggests that the use of Internet in schools is less developed in Europe compared to the United States. Furthermore, the limited use of leased lines in Europe may be a result of the existing expensive tariffs.

5   Conclusions

Governments in the U.S. and E.U. Member States seem to agree that Internet access to schools (and classrooms) is important for the twenty-first century. The issue of controversy is who should pay for the costs of Internet access to schools. An important issue emerges on a "digital divide" among schools.

This paper shows that communications usage costs do not serve as the most important barrier to the development of Internet access to schools in the United States and the E.U. Empirical evidence in the U.S. and U.K. show that communications costs (telecommunications and Internet access) account for a small portion of the total school ICT expenditure. Available data also show that the primary factor affecting ICT school costs is the purchase and installation of computers and other hardware. Secondary costs relate to maintenance, teachers' training, and software.

Telecommunications operators should not be obliged to pay for costs related to infrastructure and educational purposes. Imposing extra financial obligations on telecommunications operators may undermine the development of competition (infrastructure and services) for telecommunications, and does not necessarily reach equity objectives.

Looking at a different question of the effectiveness of policy outcome, the United States is well ahead of the E.U. average in bringing Internet to schools. High penetration rates may simply be a result of early market liberalization and Internet take-off in the United States. Progress may also be related to the fact that Internet usage in the United States is not linked to per minute usage, as in Europe. Notably the more liberalized countries like Sweden and Denmark have similar results with the United States. Furthermore, it is not clear whether the E-Rate program (which was disbursed in November 1998) had a major impact on Internet access to schools. Considering that Europe started much later than the United States, the penetration rate is increasing rapidly through special usage tariffs and government educational initiatives. One must be cautious when comparing U.S. and E.U. statistics as there is a wide performance variation between E.U. Member States. While the Nordic European countries have comparable results with the United States, the southern European countries like Greece and Portugal are lagging behind in all areas. The limited connectivity and usage rate is related to the late liberalization in these countries, and their less developed infrastructure.

At times the comparison of policy outcomes between the U.S. and E.U. was difficult owing to the lack of data in the E.U. Member States. The *e-Europe Initiative* and its related "benchmarking" exercise should be more rigorous and systematic in gathering more relevant data on Internet access to classrooms, and general ICT school expenditures. Collection of other socio-economic data of schools would also be useful to evaluate the policy outcome, most notably to assess the possibility of a "digital divide" between European schools.

In developing policy to address Internet access and usage at schools, policy should be technology and operator neutral and it should not distort competition. Both the U.S. and E.U. policies are technology neutral, while there are some concerns over operator neutrality. Overall, specific noncommunications expenditures related to assisting schools should come from education or national budgets and not by introducing additional distortions to the telecommunications sector.

Acknowledgments

I would like to thank Mr. M. Scanlan, Dr. D. Stockdale, and Prof. H. Williams for their comments. I would also like to thank Dr. R. Pepper for hosting me at the FCC at the beginning of 2001, which allowed me to finalize this research. The author takes full responsibility for any errors. The views expressed are strictly personal and are not necessarily shared by the Organization to which the author belongs.

Notes

1. The development of Internet in schools can vary from an information awareness tool for students (a few PCs for each school); learning computer applications as a subject in a single laboratory with approximately 30 PCs; and as a platform for teaching with a number of PCs in each classroom.

2. A number of studies show the positive effects of technology in schools and classrooms on student achievement, motivation level, and speed of learning. See USDE (2000a), pp.22–23; also PIC (1997), pp.34–40.

3. ICT school expenditures include communications and noncommunications costs as defined earlier.

4. For consistent comparison with the E.U. this paper does not discuss in detail Internet access to libraries. For the record, however, libraries received 4percent of total E-Rate funding during the first two years of the program.

5. This program is administered by the U.S. Department of Agriculture and state agencies that supply free or inexpensive lunches to economically disadvantaged students.

6. Local, long-distance and toll charges, dedicated lines, leased DS-1, T-1, ISDN, xDSL, Directory assistance charges.

7. Telecommunications wiring, routers, hubs, network file servers, switches, hinds, network servers, certain networking software, wireless LANs, Private Branch Exchange (PBX), installation and basic maintenance of internal connections.

8. The fund will not finance CPE and hardware, such as personal computers (with the exception of network file servers), telephone handsets, fax machines, modems, nor will it finance asbestos removal, the costs of tearing down walls to install wiring, repairing carpets, repainting, learning software, or teacher/librarian training.

9. Interstate telecommunications includes, but is not limited to: 'cellular telephone and paging services; mobile radio services; operator services; PCS; access to inter-exchange service; special access; wide area telephone services (WATS); toll-free services; 900 services; MTS; private line; telex; telegraph; video services; satellite services; and resale services.' See FCC (1997).

10. Eventually BellSouth and SBC withdrew their appeal, and only GTE remained as a litigant. In July 1999 the Court of Appeals rejected GTE's complaint, and in May 2000, the US Supreme Court refused to hear the litigants' appeal, therefore terminating E-Rate opposition. See USDE (2000b), pp. 19-21.

11. The FCC also wanted to prevent the E-Rate charges from rising faster than access charge reductions (in July 1997 the FCC reduced access charges by the amount of $1.9 billion).

12. The current Bush Administration discussed the possibility of removing the administration and oversight of the E-Rate program from the FCC to the Department of Education.

13. See
<http://europa.eu.int/information_society/eeurope/action_plan/index_en.htm>.

14. The scope of universal service obligations includes the provision of voice telephony, fax and dial up internet connection, as well as public pay phones, emergency call access, operator and directory services. During the adoption of the new EU regulatory framework there was discussion to include Internet access to schools in the scope.

15. In the current regulatory framework, the Voice Telephony Directive (98/10/EC) allows for the provision of special tariff schemes, and requires transparency and cost orientation for tariffs of carriers possessing Significant Market Power (SMP).

16. All estimated 'standard' calculations in this section include an annual PSTN rental cost, a usage cost (based on an assumed use of 200 hour per month for each school), and annual ISP charges. Tariffs from Teligen (2000).

17. In May 1997 British Telecom (BT) was the first operator in Europe, which proposed to offer flat rate PSTN and Basic ISDN tariffs for Internet access to schools. Following a public consultation, in October 1997, OFTEL established the cost floors for the prices that BT could charge schools in order to make sure that other operators could compete for this service. For more details see OFTEL (1997a & b).

18. In 1998 a group of new operators (Cegetel, Bouygues, and Colt Telecom) filed a complaint against France Telecom (FT) for providing discounted fees for Internet access to schools. FT planned to fix prices at $950 a year for Internet access for 10 hours a day for 10 PCs. New operators could not compete with this offer because they had to pay high interconnection charges to FT on top of their costs. After negotiations, FT agreed to lower its interconnection rates.

19. In Europe, competitive operators that serve ISPs have to pay an interconnection fee to incumbent operators. On the contrary, in the United States, under the reciprocal compensation scheme set forth in the 1996 Act, CLECs that serve ISPs actually receive termination fees from the ILEC.

20. The average expenditure per school was $11016 (£6800) for primary schools, and $67716 (£41,800) for secondary schools. The average expenditure per pupil was $49 (£30) in primary schools and $76 (£47) in secondary schools. (DfEE, 2000).

21. Hardware includes computers, peripheral equipment, upgrades and replacements. The amount spent on internal wiring, which is the biggest expense in the United States, is not clearly specified in this survey.

22. A US study also supports that telecommunications costs account for 4–11 percent of total expenditures. PIC (1997).

23. Although one must note that the EU data are from early 2001.

24. More precisely, the European Commission granted a transitional period for public voice telephony and infrastructure liberalization to Spain until 30 November 1998; Portugal and Ireland until 1 January 2000 (although Ireland renounced its derogation on December 1, 1998); Greece until 1 January 2001; and Luxembourg until 1 July 1998.

References

Crandall, R. W., and Leonard Waverman (2000). *Who pays for universal service? When telephone subsidies become transparent.* The Brookings Institution: Washington, D.C.

DfEE (2000). *Statistics of Education: Survey of Information and Communications Technology in School, Issue No. 07/00, October 2000.*

Eurobarometer (2001). Flash 101: Headteachers February–May 2001.

European Commission (2001). *eEurope 2002 Benchmarking: European youth into the digital age.* Commission Staff Working Paper, SEC (2001) 1583 (9 November 2001).

European Commission (2001a). *Benchmarking Report following-up the "Strategies for jobs in the Information Society."* ESDIS/Ministries of Education, Commission Staff Working Paper, SEC (2001) 222 (7 February 2001).

Federal Communications Commission (FCC) (2001). *Universal Service Monitoring Report, October 2001,* CC Docket No. 98–202.

Federal Communications Commission (FCC) (1997). *Universal Service Order,* FCC 97–157, Docket 96–45.

GAO (2001). *Schools and Libraries Program: Update on E-Rate Funding.* GAO-01-672, Washington, D.C.

National Center for Education Statistics (NCES) (2001). *Internet Access in US Public Schools and Classrooms: 1994–2000.* Washington, D.C. May.

OFTEL (1997a). *Access to the Internet for Schools. Consultation on BT's proposal.* July 1997.

OFTEL (1997b). *Access to the Superhighway for Schools: A statement following consultation on the regulatory framework for BT's prices for schools.* October 1997.

Policy Information Center (PIC) (1997). *Computers and Classrooms: The Status of Technology in U.S. Schools.* Policy Information Report. Princeton, NJ.

Prieger, J. (1998). Universal Service and the Telecommunications Act of 1996: The fact after the Act. *Telecommunications Policy,* 22,1.

Teligen (2000). *Report on Telecommunications Tariff Data.* Brussels: EC, DG INFSO.

U.S. Department of Education (USDE) (2000a). *E-Learning: Putting a world-class education at the fingertips of all children.* Washington, D.C.

U.S. Department of Education (USDE) (2000b). *E-Rate and the Digital Divide: A Preliminary Analysis from the Integrated Studies of Educational Technology.* Doc. # 00-17, prepared by Michael J. Puma, Duncan D Chaplin, and Andreas D. Pape, The Urban Institute, Washington, D.C., 2000.

WIK (2000). *Study on the re-examination of the scope of universal service in the telecommunications sector of the EU, in the context of the 1999 Review.* Bad Honnef.

Index